The Music of Elliott Carter

The Music of Elliott Carter David Schiff

SECOND EDITION

Cornell University Press

Ithaca, New York

First published in 1983 by Ernst Eulenburg Ltd
This second edition first published in 1998
by Cornell University Press
Ithaca, NY 14850

Photoset by RefineCatch Ltd, Bungay
Printed in England by Clays Ltd, St Ives plc

A CIP record for this book is
available from the Library of Congress

ISBN 0–8014–3612–5

The permission of various publishers to reproduce poems and extracts as itemized below is
gratefully acknowledged:

Farrar, Straus and Giroux Inc., and Faber and Faber Ltd
   Robert Lowell: extracts from 'Myopia: A Night' from *For the Union Dead*. Copyright © 1956,
   1960, 1961, 1962, 1963, 1964 by Robert Lowell
   'Words for Hart Crane' from *Life Studies* (Selected Poems). Copyright © 1956, 1959 by Robert
   Lowell.

Alfred A. Knopf Inc., and Faber and Faber Ltd
   Wallace Stevens: extracts from 'Notes Toward A Supreme Fiction' and 'The Poems of our
   Climate' from *The Collected Poems of Wallace Stevens*. Copyright © 1954 by Wallace Stevens.

Liveright Publishing Corporation
   Hart Crane: extracts from 'The Bridge', 'The Broken Tower', and 'The Return' from *The
   Complete Poems and Selected Letters and Prose of Hart Crane*, edited by Brom Weber. Copyright ©
   1933, 1958 and 1966 by Liveright Publishing Corporation, New York.

Princeton University Press
   St John Perse: extracts from *Winds*, trans. Hugh Chisholm, Jr, Bollingen Series 34. Copyright
   © 1953 by Princeton University Press.

The New York Review of Books
   Charles Rosen: extract from an essay in *The New York Review of Books*. Copyright © 1973
   Nyrev Inc.

Viking Penguin Inc.
   John Ashbery: 'Syringa' from *Houseboat Days*. Copyright © 1977 by John Ashbery.

The author gratefully acknowledges the permission of the Trust Under the Will of Igor Stravinsky
and of Robert Craft to reprint the conversations between Igor Stravinsky and Robert Craft about
Elliott Carter, on pages 252–3, from *Dialogues and a Diary* by Igor Stravinsky and Robert Craft.
Copyright © 1963 Igor Stravinsky, Robert Craft.

For permission to reproduce music examples as indicated below, the author is grateful to Boosey &
Hawkes Music Publishers Ltd and G. Schirmer Inc.
Boosey & Hawkes: 4, 11, 23, 24, 25, 38, 39, 40, 41, 45, 49, 50, 61, 62, 69, 70, 71, 72
G. Schirmer Inc: 1, 2, 5, 7, 8, 9, 10, 12, 13, 14, 15, 16, 17, 18, 19, 20, 21, 22, 26, 29, 30, 31, 32,
33, 34, 35, 36, 37, 42, 44, 46, 47, 48, 56, 57, 58, 59, 60, 63, 64, 65, 66, 67, 68

10 9 8 7 6 5 4 3 2 1

Contents

Words from the Composer

In the late 1970s, Sir William Glock, former Controller of Music for the BBC and at that time editor of Eulenburg Books, asked me to find someone to write about my music, and I discussed the matter with David Schiff, my composition student at the Juilliard School. After completing studies in English literature at Columbia University under Lionel Trilling, David had gone on to devote himself to musical criticism and composition, and he immediately offered to write the book. Under the editorship of Sir William, who encouraged him to avoid excessive musical analyses in order to reach the general musical public, he produced the first version in 1983.

In this second version, much rewritten, David has admirably kept pace with my wayward course as I approach ninety. Needless to say, I am most grateful for his remarkable efforts.

Elliott Carter

Preface to the Second Edition

Elliott Carter was seventy-five when the first edition of this book appeared. Few would have predicted then that he was beginning a significant new phase of his composing career, or that this 'late period' would be so productive and last so long. The sheer size of Carter's late oeuvre would have demanded a significant extension of the first edition, but the importance of these new works and the unexpected ways in which they develop Carter's style made a radical surgery of the old edition necessary. And in addition to Carter's ever-expanding body of works, the critical and scholarly literature on his music has grown significantly since the first edition.

For the author, these changes have been blessings in disguise; by demanding a greater economy in my discussion of the music, they helped me to deal with the humbling task of revising an earlier work. Listening to all the music again has been a pleasure; rereading the prose of my younger self has been sobering. Readers, if there are any, who admired my rhetorical excesses should hold on to their first editions; I hope I have removed all traces from the new version.

In this revision I have altered the structure of the book. The first edition was divided into a biographical sketch, a discussion of musical techniques and a chronological account of the music. In the new edition I have written a completely new introduction and have arranged the discussion of the music by genres rather than chronology. To save space and avoid redundancy I have replaced the long chapters on musical time and space with a technical glossary. The narrative aspect of the book is thus all contained in the opening essay. Most of the discussion of individual pieces that appeared in the first edition has been tightened up; in a few cases, these analyses are substantially new.

One aspect of the first edition that has not changed is its intended audience. I have been gratified to find that the book has been helpful for performers, listeners, composers and critics – that was my original intention and that of my editor Sir William Glock and of Elliott Carter as well. In the United States, however, it is assumed that a book like this is aimed primarily at graduate students of music theory. This premise creates a problem, for the kind of detailed analysis performed by theorists is usually incomprehensible for non-theorists. Thanks to many conversations with the composer and my study of his sketches at the New York Public Library,

Library of Congress and the Paul Sacher Stiftung, I have tried to include as many of his own ideas about how he has composed the music as possible. Fortunately there is now a considerable body of theoretical and musicological writing about Carter; I hope the information in this book can serve as a resource for such analysis.

Foreword to the First Edition

This book is a study of Elliott Carter's music from his earliest surviving student efforts to his latest work. It is intended as a guide for listeners, performers and composers. Although the book is not a biography – that would have demanded a different scope and emphasis – I have tried as much as possible to view the music from the perspective of the composer's development and also to relate Carter's compositional techniques to those non-musical arts with which he has been deeply involved.

I wrote the book during a period when I was also studying composition with Elliott Carter at the Juilliard School. For the better part of three years I met him at least once a week to discuss my music, his music, the music we were both hearing and thinking about; I remember in particular his detailed, penetrating reactions to the first performance of *Lulu* by the Met that occurred during this time. I have been privileged therefore not only to be able to get to know his music and writings, but also to know the man, and to be in close contact with the on-the-spot workings of his musical mind – for Carter is as intensely and spontaneously critical of his students' music as he is of his own. I was also able to study the letters and sketches in the Special Collections of the Research Library of the Performing Arts at Lincoln Center, and have spoken to performers of Carter's music and to many of his friends.

Nevertheless, this book is neither an oral history nor a collection of documents. It is *my* perspective on Carter's music. Where the composer and I have occasionally differed I have indicated his viewpoint, but this account should be read as an outsider's interpretation of the music and the composer is in no way responsible for any errors of judgment or fact that may appear.

A monograph can easily begin to appear monomaniacal, and the reader will often react by demanding more balance. Arthur Berger in his fine book on Aaron Copland anticipated this problem with words that I would apply to my book as well:

> It is generally considered a virtue in a book on a creative personality to balance favourable comment against unfavourable. This is thought to make for an honest report, while anything approaching eulogy is suspiciously viewed as the expression of a fanatic or as a form of paid publicity. It should therefore be said that the effort spent

in analysing ... scores so closely would seem hardly worthwhile were it not for a conviction of their very great quality. The still greater effort to put these analyses into words would be pointless were it not a matter of primary concern to acquaint others with music that has aroused in me such strong feelings.[1]

I would augment this statement only by explaining the absence of any attempt by me to 'place' Carter among contemporary composers. I have avoided this primarily because it tends to treat other composers superficially. Little is gained by facile comparisons based on chronology or national character, and very often those artists who in retrospect seem to have had the most in common have been viewed as diametric opposites during their lifetimes. If Carter is to be compared with other composers of his generation, I think the most enlightening contrasts might be drawn with Wolpe, Gerhard or Lutosławski, all of whose careers resemble his to a certain extent. But if Carter's development is some day to be placed in relation to that of other artists of our time it would seem more interesting to cross artistic barriers and link his work to that of Louis Kahn, Willem de Kooning, or Robert Lowell.

Notes

1 Arthur Berger, *Aaron Copland* (New York: Oxford University Press, 1953), p. v.

Acknowledgements

In writing the original version of this book I was indebted to the pioneering articles by Richard Franko Goldman, William Glock and Abraham Skulsky; to Wilfred Mellers's *Music in a New Found Land*, and to the writings of Bayan Northcott, Kurt Stone, Robert P. Morgan, and Charles Rosen. Three books proved indispensable aids to my study of the music: Allen Edwards's book of stimulating conversations with Carter, *Flawed Words and Stubborn Sounds; The Writings of Elliott Carter*, meticulously selected and edited by Else Stone and Kurt Stone; and the catalogue of the exhibition honouring the composer on his sixty-fifth birthday by the Music Division of the New York Public Library, *Elliott Carter, Sketches and Scores in Manuscript*, which was prepared by Richard Jackson, Head of the Americana Collection of the Music Division of the New York Public Library, assisted by Pamela S. Berlin and John Shepard.

Many people helped and guided me in writing the first edition. Helen and Elliott Carter were unstinting in their time, assistance, advice and encouragement. Charles Rosen not only offered me what seems in retrospect to have been a crucial bit of editorial advice but also gave me a place to work, without which the book would not have been possible. Paul Jacobs, Richard Hennessy and Allen Edwards kindly read parts of the book in draft and offered many helpful suggestions. Minna Lederman Daniel provided me with vivid accounts of the composer's early career, and was an enormous help in putting my large task in perspective. John Shepard of the Music Division of the New York Public Library was a great help in tracking down Carteriana at the library, and for preparing the bibliography.

Many performers shared their knowledge of the music with me and helped me to see it from a performer's point of view. Among them were Ursula Oppens, Robert Mann, John Graham, Barbara Martin, Karen Lindquist and Marvin Wolfthal. Yehudi Wyner lent me tapes of performances by himself and his wife Susan Davenny Wyner, and of an extended and probing interview he had done with Carter for Canadian radio.

I also received help, advice and encouragement from Phyllis Birnbaum, Richard Goodman, Simon Emmerson, Bayan Northcott, Brigitte Schiffer, Tim Souster, Maureen Beedle and Julian Mitchell Dawson. I was particularly indebted to Sir Peter Maxwell Davies for letting me attend his classes at Dartington Summer School of Music.

I was most fortunate to have Sir William Glock as my original editor. Not only has he been a long-time champion of the cause of contemporary music, but as an editor he was both patient and precise. Knowing that my writings would be closely and sensitively read made my job immeasurably easier.

I would like to add some important acknowledgements and thanks for this new edition. Felix Meyer, curator of the Carter collection at the Paul Sacher Stiftung did everything possible to make my work there productive and enjoyable. My travel to Basel was made possible by Reed College, for which I am most appreciative. Elizabeth Woerner, media librarian at Reed College, was a great help in tracking down articles. Anne Shreffler and John Link have shared many of their insights into Carter's music with me. I have benefitted greatly from hearing Carter's recent music performed by Heinz Holliger, Oliver Knussen, Lucy Shelton, Fred Sherry and Ursula Oppens, all of whom have also discussed the music with me. I'm particularly grateful that the Third Angle Ensemble of Portland gave me the opportunity to conduct *Triple Duo* on two occasions with an outstanding group of players. And, of course, I am greatly thankful for the continuing friendship of Helen and Elliott Carter. Finally, I could not have written either version of the book without the love, support and patience of my family.

David Schiff

Reference Abbreviations

CEL   *Elliott Carter: Collected Essays and Lectures, 1937-1995*, edited by Jonathan Bernard (Rochester, 1997)

FW   *Flawed Words and Stubborn Sounds*, a conversation with Elliott Carter by Allen Edwards (New York, 1971)

MNFL *Music in a New Found Land* by Wilfred Mellers (New York, 1964)

MQ   *The Musical Quarterly*

PNM   *Perspectives of New Music*

RFG   *Richard Franko Goldman, Selected Essays and Reviews*, edited by Dorothy Klotzman (Brooklyn, 1980)

WEC   *The Writings of Elliott Carter*, edited by Else Stone and Kurt Stone (Bloomington, 1977)

INTRODUCTION: The International Theme

'It is by carrying on the European tradition and by following the methods of some of its experiments in the context of his own experiences that our composer affirms his own identity and the identity of American music.'[1]

1 Overture

A string quartet sits on stage – oddly. To the left, a violin and cello; to the right, a violin and viola. Between the two pairs a small, but unexpected space, perhaps six feet wide. The players eye each other nervously across this divide. The left-hand violinist gives a beat with his head; the right-hand violinist gives a beat with his head – a different beat. Suddenly all four begin scraping at their instruments furiously. After a few seconds you begin to notice that they are not following the same path – and that their toes are tapping at different speeds. One pair becomes more spasmodic, their sounds come in erratic bursts; the other proceeds dogmatically in even notes – and then fades away, exposing the ornate filigree of the other duo to the harsh, judgmental glare of silence. For the next twenty minutes this strange game of parallel play proceeds. Each 'team' jumps, at its own rate and with its own logic, from one idea to another and then back so that you hear a play of contrasts, fast against slow, mechanical playing against expressive playing, arco against pizzicato – but also expressive strumming against mechanical plucking, slithering lines against sporadic bursts of rapid motion, anguished adagios against serene lentos. Through all its changes the music never loses its rhythmic energy, a driving force that reminds a certain kind of listener of feverish mid-sixties jazz. But the music doesn't sound like jazz (or like most classical music for that matter) and it doesn't have themes you can hang on to; it is nothing but color, gesture and motion – with so many notes flying around that it is hard to discern any tonal order. The music sounds overloaded and disorienting, but you may begin to notice that it is neither crazed nor relentless. It changes, moving from one mood to the next with peaks of intensity and carefully placed moments of (relative) relaxation. It changes but it also returns to previous ideas, or at least hints at them so that, like a Beethoven quartet (another kind of listener begins to think), it seems to construct a sense of its own past, but without ever returning to the same place twice. The music sounds avant-garde in its frenzied motion but it doesn't feel avant-garde; there's no attempt at shock or *épater* – it feels, you may find yourself thinking, like a classic. After this double helix of episodes the duos converge in dense chords of ever greater dissonance. Their clangor suddenly abates and the cello steps forward with an impassioned phrase: is it the answer to that mad chordal question? You are embarrassed to have even had that thought – and the music seems equally ashamed of its momentary loss of ambiguity. The cello phrase vanishes after just two bars. The other instruments begin again with fragments of their ideas, regressing in fractiles back to the opening birth-cry. With the same screech that launched it, the music ends. It has been a wild ride for the players and for you. Some listeners are baffled, others elated. After one such performance Aaron Copland walked out on stage and told the audience, 'If that's music, then I don't know what music is any more.' After another, the quartet returned to the stage to play Ravel. Between movements my father turned to me and said, 'Ravel is pretty boring after Carter.'

2 James, Stevens, Carter

The Third Quartet, described above, was written at the very center of Carter's composing career (he was sixty-three); it can stand, at least provisionally, for the whole of his works. Its central fact is the empty space between the duos, an abyss which the players can look across but never traverse. The gap defines Carter's music the way the net defines a tennis game; it divides the music into two sides which are never allowed to move in unison or at the same speed, a harsh restriction which imposes on the music a double voice. The music constantly and unresolvably speaks in the plural – and yet its doubleness is also its identity.

The plural voice – two voices here and in *Syringa*, among many other works; three in *Triple Duo*; four in the Second and Fourth Quartets; five in *Penthode* – is the premise of all of Carter's mature music, written from 1948 to the present. It would not play such a persistent role if it were merely a technical device; its source lies deep in Carter's character and development. To approach an understanding of it, we can call the gap between the two duos the Atlantic Ocean.

From earliest childhood, the Atlantic was a central fact of Carter's life. He was born in New York, into a prosperous family whose business, founded by his grandfather, was importing 'finery' or lace. Because it was expected that he would carry on in the trade, Carter spent half his youth in Europe and was taught French, Flemish and even Romansch; he spoke

French before he could read English. After his education at Harvard, he spent three years in Paris studying, like so many other Americans, with Nadia Boulanger. He returned to Europe after the war for many short visits and extended residences. He composed the Variations for Orchestra, the Concerto for Orchestra and *Night Fantasies* in Rome, and the Piano Concerto in Berlin. But he never became an expatriate. Home was in New York, in an old apartment building in Greenwich Village (not far from the residences of John Cage, Edgard Varèse, and Stefan Wolpe) with windows facing south to the towers of Wall Street and the World Trade Center, or (from 1952 to 1990) in a modest rebuilt farmhouse in Waccabuc, forty miles north of the city, a wooded bedroom community of immodest estates belonging to bankers and the horsey set. Waccabuc is also just a short drive from the country home of Charles Ives, Carter's early mentor, in West Redding, Connecticut.

For American artists, the Atlantic is a physical fact, or a metaphysical fact, or an irrelevance. Whistler, James and Eliot crossed eastward for good. Pound, Stein, Thomson, Fitzgerald, Hemingway, Wright, and Baldwin lived parts of their lives as Americans in exile. Others, like Whitman and Stevens, stayed home, or looked to the west and across the Pacific. For some, living abroad was merely a matter of comfort and convenience, of living where the food was better, as Virgil Thomson put it. For others, notably James and Eliot, expatriation was a statement of protest against the conditions of American life, against democracy, or Unitarianism, or capitalism, or liberalism, or the absence of 'history' or tradition.

In his midatlantic perspective on Europe and America, Carter continues the line of Henry James and Wallace Stevens. Like these two predecessors, Carter conceives the Atlantic more as an idea than as a physical obstacle. Henry James turned the transatlantic crossing into a cultural myth, the 'international theme.' The symbolically named Christopher Newman of *The American* is a self-made millionaire without any sense of the past, and, as his first name implies, an ironic rediscoverer of Europe, where, despite all his good intentions, he will get everything wrong – as will most of James's long list of American naïfs and naïves, Daisy Miller, Isabel Archer, Lambert Strether, Milly Theale. They come to Europe with the uncountable wealth of post-Civil-War America at their disposal yet they remain outsiders or are undone by their own innocence. At times James's theme verges on fairy-tale: the snow-white Isabel Archer against the black-hearted Gilbert Osmond. In the late novels, however, where

James enters the world of modernity, both the theme and his treatment change. The stereotypes of Europe and America demystify each other – without, however, disappearing. The action of the novels becomes almost completely subjective. Instead of the social objects and relations that we expect in novels, James gives us a world of perceptions, where the points of view seem more important than what is actually seen – *seem*, because despite James's oblique and cryptic style, weighty moral issues, grounded in material wealth and sexual desire, are always at stake. In emphasizing mind over matter, James created novels which were both un-European and un-American. Unlike European novels – those of Proust, Mann or Joyce, for example – James's novels appear to take place in an abstract world, cut off from history and politics. Compared to American writing – Twain or Howells or Sinclair Lewis – they also lack a sense of everyday life. No one ever seems to have a job or go the bathroom, as American undergraduates and critics often point out.

Wallace Stevens, who never physically traveled to Europe, was the spiritual heir to the later James in his insistence that the subject of poetry was the imagination. The outer trappings of the international theme appeared in Stevens through his use of the French language, which he considered cognate with English and employed as an indication of an aesthetic distance or playfulness; his Frenchified vocabulary gave Stevens the misleading reputation of being a dandy, but he was really a philosopher–comedian. A radical subjectivity, placing mind over matter as James did, forms the core of all of Stevens's work; the 'real' world seems even more distant in Stevens than it does in James, for in his poetry the imagination constantly reinvents the real. Stevens's insistence that the world consists of ideas, not objects, which in its gross outlines resembles the ideas of Christian Science, remains provocative because it is ironic – Stevens knows that the jar he placed (poetically) in Tennessee, an image of the power of art to order nature, is an insignificant bit of litter in the great sea of American junk. The idea that the jar can reshape the wilderness is one of Stevens's many elegant jokes.

As Carter's spiritual forbears, James and Stevens are poets of an ironic subjectivity that places them between European notions of historical objectivity and unironic, ahistoric American materialism. This position made them suspect from both sides of the ocean, but most intensely from the American side. The repeated charge is élitism; their art is often branded as anti-democratic. As the critic Granville Hicks put it:

... for the most part James's novels and tales seem completely remote from the lives of the vast majority of men. And why should one read a novel if it does not give him a sense that he is moving with enhanced powers of perception and a greater certainty as to direction, through the strange world of which he is a part?[2]

The accusation of élitism often merges with one of anti-Americanism, and not necessarily from the political right; in American cultural debates, any side can claim the flag. In his early essay 'Parable of American Painting,' Harold Rosenberg, the champion of 'action painting,' contrasted European-derived art, 'redcoatism,' with authentic American art, 'coonskinism.' Rosenberg here creates, or at least reinforces the myth of American mindlessness:

[The coonskinners] have studied the manoeuvers among squirrels and grizzly bears and they trust their knowledge against the tradition of Caesar and Frederick. Their principle is simple – if it's red, shoot![3]

Rosenberg summoned up another reductive (and seductive) contrast in his essay 'French Silence and American Poetry':

The silence of the French poet arises on the opposite side of the globe from the silence of the Kansas farmhand.

With the latter, silence just is; an emptiness coming from American space and time . . .

When [the Frenchman] succeeds he is in the same position as the Kansas farmhand: sitting on a rail and waiting for something to show up. Whatever it is, it will be something totally real.[4]

This may be a New York intellectual's (tongue-in-cheek?) fantasy of Kansas, but its ideal of an art in which the real is not mediated by thought is a credo of much American art, the poetry of Williams which demands 'no ideas but in things,' the pop art of Warhol, the works of John Cage which assume that sounds are 'things' without meaning. Set against the awestruck materialism of these artists, the haughty idealism of James, Stevens and Carter becomes less 'abstract' than it first appears; it is an expression of dissent from the dominant strain in American culture. The debate between these two traditions (and between both of them and the 'normal' quotidian world of advertising, best-sellers, movies, television and popular music) is an ongoing argument about the place of art in American society.

The debate over the place of *music* in American society has usually been framed in terms of European and native traditions; American composers have found different ways to connect the two. For Leonard Bernstein, for instance, Europe represented the glories of the high cultural past; America, the pop cultural present. He served the first as a conductor of the classics, the second as a composer for Broadway. Other American composers have synthesized the old and new worlds by applying the genres and compositional techniques of Europe to the vernacular materials of America: hymn tunes, spirituals, jazz or popular song. This recipe for American music goes back at least as far as Dvořák, but it has always seemed, even to many of its practitioners, like a superficial solution. Charles Ives abandoned this approach after his Second Symphony and sought to develop forms and techniques that were as American as his materials. But Ives's image of America remained its vernacular music, at least the vernacular music of his childhood: marches, ragtime, parlor songs and hymns. His works lent authority to the idea that democracy was best represented by incorporating the 'music of the people' into an artistic design.

Carter's music and writings show little engagement with American popular culture, except his output during the Second World War when patriotism required it. But they also show scant evidence of interest in the standard European repertory of the concert hall; Carter says he used to walk out of concerts of Beethoven and Brahms when he was young and he can still be scandalously impious about the classics. Carter has listened to a lot of jazz and knows the concert repertory inside out; his stance is a matter of conscious refusal, to use a Boulangerism, not ignorance. Like James and Stevens, Carter chose to create an art of ideas and perception. His music would not portray the American scene, but represent the workings of a mind engaged in the possibilities and perplexities of American life.

In his teenage years, Carter discovered the American ultramodernists or experimentalists: Ives, Ruggles, Varèse, Cowell, Rudhyar, Crawford and Nancarrow. Later he found European roots in the modernist school; Debussy, Stravinsky, Bartók, Schoenberg and Berg. American ultramodernists and European modernists shared a desire to reconstruct music from basic principles of rhythm and sound. The Americans, however, believed that a new music could be formed without reference to the

European past, a path that would ultimately lead to John Cage's dismissal of all willed forms of musical choice. Many of the Europeans were hyper-conscious of the relation between their music and the past and, after the First World War, restored traditional elements of rhythm and form even when they meshed uneasily with their new tonal language; by the 1930s both Schoenberg and Stravinsky denied that they were modern at all. Taken to extremes, the American position was philistine; the European, ultramontane. The ultramodernists opposed 'art,' while high modernists used the devices of neo-Classicism to draw a line between itself and the modern world. Carter later likened neo-Classicism to a masquerade in a bomb shelter.[5]

Carter's mature style dares to bring together these seemingly irreconcilable musical sources, fusing the experimental techniques of the ultramodernists with the lofty artistic ambitions of European modernists; but it took many years to achieve, and was often misunderstood as an unfocussed eclecticism (a charge implied by Aaron Copland: 'Elliott Carter ... has shaped a music of his own out of a wide knowledge of the music of our time ...'[6]). Over the years, the rich yield of Carter's oeuvre has shown that what people criticized as eclecticism was a gift for synthesis. Carter's creation of a style from contradictory elements gives musical form to a passage from Stevens's *Notes Toward a Supreme Fiction*:

> He had to choose. But it was not a choice
> Between excluding things. It was not a choice
> Between, but of. He chose to include the things
> That in each other are included, the whole,
> The complicate, the amassing harmony.[7]

It would be hard to say to what extent James, Stevens and Carter chose their midatlantic perspective and to what extent the facts of their lives, similar in some respects but quite different in others, placed them outside both American and European mainstreams. Their perspectives give their work certain shared qualities which are both strengths and limitations. Harold Bloom has identified these aspects suggestively when he says that the 'best poets of that climate [Whitman, Dickinson, Crane, Stevens] are hermetic precisely when they profess to be vatic democrats, and they are curiously extemporaneous when they attempt to be most élitist .... A deep uncertainty concerning the American reader combines with ambitious designs upon that reader, and the result is a poetic stance more self-contradictory than that of most modern British poets.'[8] Substitute

'American audience' for 'American reader' and 'modern European composers' for 'modern British poets' and Bloom's insight places Carter in this same poetic 'climate' which Bloom calls the 'central vehemence of American poetry.' How central this climate is to American music is an open question. In the history of American music 'vehemence' can be found in Ives's 'Emerson,' Ruggles's 'Sun Treader,' Varèse's *Arcana* and Copland's Piano Variations, but Carter's interweaving of the hermetic and the spontaneous, of the democratic and the élite, of uncertainty and ambition is unique.

3 Mr. Ives and Mlle Boulanger

For Carter, the conflict between Europe and America coalesced around his formative relationships with Charles Ives and Nadia Boulanger; given the indifference of Carter's father and mother to his musical interests, Ives and Boulanger took on the roles of surrogate parents. Carter's complex relationship with Ives and his music, which began when Clifton Furness, his music teacher at the Horace Mann School, introduced them in 1924, is revealed in articles Carter wrote between 1939 and 1975[9] as well as in the conversation books with Allan Edwards and Enzo Restagno. Ives took Carter to hear the Boston Symphony Orchestra at Carnegie Hall (where the Iveses had a box) and to concerts at the loft of the pianist Katharine Ruth Heyman, who specialized in modern music. Carter recalls that they would then return to Ives's house near Gramercy Park where Ives would critique the music at the keyboard:

> He invariably felt that new pieces like, I think, Ravel's *Daphnis et Chloe* or Stravinsky's *Le sacre* (although I am not sure about the latter) revealed extremely simple-minded ways of dealing with new harmonies and rhythms. I remember vividly his 'take-off' at the piano of the Ravel chord and of the repetitiousness of Stravinsky. Ives was very literate and sharp about this – he seemed to remember quite clearly bits of what he had heard and could parody them surprisingly well. His point was that almost all contemporary composers of the time had chosen the easy way out.[10]

Ives also performed his own music for Carter:

> . . . the respectable, quiet, Puritan atmosphere was oddly disturbed, a gleam would come into his eyes as fiery excitement seized him, and he would smash out a fragment of 'Emerson', singing loudly, and

exclaiming with burning enthusiasm. Once the captain of the football team at Yale, he put the same punch into his music. It was a dynamic, staggering experience, which is hard even now [1939] to think of clearly. He hated composers who played their works objectively, 'as if they didn't like them.' This strong wiry Yankee vitality, humor and transcendental seriousness were very much to our taste and we always came away from Ives full of life's glad new wine and a thousand projects for the future.[11]

Although Ives preferred Beethoven and Brahms to Debussy and Stravinsky, he did not dismiss all contemporary music as simpleminded. He allied himself with the American ultramodernists through his financial support for the journal *New Music*.[12] Among the composers of this group[13] were Ives's friends Carl Ruggles and Henry Cowell, as well as Ruth Crawford, Carlos Salzedo and Edgard Varèse.[14] So in addition to his enthusiasm for Ives's music, Carter came to admire the ultramodernist school (though he seems to have been put off by the 'Blavatskian' ideas that some of them espoused) and studied Cowells's *New Musical Resources*.[15] For Carter, though, this new American music was not a rebuke to European modernism, but part of his broad exploration of modern music, literature, film and philosophy.[16] Carter has described the parallels between European and American modernism in his essay 'Expressionism and American Music' while noting that the Americans were only dimly aware of European developments; many of the pre-war monuments of European modernism, such as *Pierrot lunaire* and *Le sacre* were not played in New York until the early twenties. But Ives and the ultramodernists made a lasting impression on Carter, particularly in his thinking about rhythm. Carter illustrated his 1955 essay 'The Rhythmic Basis of American Music' with musical examples from Ives's Fourth Symphony and *Calcium Light* and from Nancarrow.[17] He notes in particular Ives's use of polyrhythms, of simultaneous streams of music at different tempi, as in *Central Park in the Dark* and *Three Places in New England* and of notated rubato. These are all techniques that Carter would use for his own purposes in later composition, along with ideas suggested by Crawford, Cowell, Nancarrow and Salzedo.

Beyond questions of technique, Ives and the ultramodernists bequeathed Carter a rich legacy of ideas and musical concepts. We can crassly reduce Ives's teachings to one crucial belief; that music should not

be 'simple-minded' – an idea that would stay central to Carter's composing and teaching and which would separate him from the politically
motivated program of musical simplicity later advocated by Aaron
Copland. For Ives, complexity was not just a matter of technical
experimentation; music had a larger spiritual function which required
complex means of expression, as he demonstrated most successfully in
Three Places in New England and the Fourth Symphony. In Ives's music,
complexity served the poetic purpose of evoking, in both realistic and
ideological terms, a notion of democracy based on his idealization of
New England town meetings, prayer services and the events of the
Revolutionary and Civil Wars. Carter was well aware of the meanings
Ives attached to these devices, but like many of his contemporaries, he
found Ives's political views and the programatic aspect of his music
old-fashioned.

Balancing Ives's demand for complexity were the radically reductive
ideas of Cowell's writings, which suggested ways of writing music without
regard to older ideas of tonality and meter. As Carter would note later on,
Cowell anticipated the 'association of pitch-interval ratios with speed
ratios after the manner "discovered" later by certain Europeans.'[18] –
indeed rediscovered by Carter himself in the Double Concerto. Cowell and
Ives were proposing a music that had little connection with the European
past. European composers, too, had approached this position before 1914;
but in the 1920s they would rebuild their connection to the past through
neo-Classicism.

Ives wrote Carter a charming letter of recommendation for Harvard,
which, however, gave no indication that Carter might be a composer:

> Carter strikes me as rather an exceptional boy. He has an instinctive
> interest in literature and especially music that is somewhat unusual.
> He writes well – an essay in his school paper –'Symbolism in Art' –
> shows an interesting mind. I don't know him intimately, but his
> teacher in Horace Mann School, Mr Clifton J. Furness, and a friend
> of mine, always speaks well of him – that he's a boy of good
> character and does well in his studies. I am sure his reliability, indus-
> try, and sense of honour are what they should be – also his sense of
> humour which you do not ask me about. [19]

Other letters indicate that Carter remained in touch with Ives during his
Harvard years, but a different kind of evidence points to a strain in the

relationship. Intellectually, Harvard was pushing Carter in the direction of anti-romanticism:

> I was greatly affected by the reigning philosophies of the period. At one end of the spectrum was Irving Babbitt, who in his classes and his widely read *Rousseau and Romanticism* inveighed against romanticism and the modern. Coming from a very different point of view was the wonderful Alfred North Whitehad, whose philosophy of organicism and progression made a deep impression . . . .the prevailing atmosphere of anti-romanticism . . . led many of us at the time to take an interest in plainsong and in medieval, Renaissance and baroque music.[20]

At Harvard, Carter remained an enthusiast for ultramodern music but he did not compose any music he thought worth saving. By 1928 he was advanced enough as a pianist to propose the following program[21] (though he does not recall what was actually played apart from the Schoenberg pieces):

Program

Wednesday Evening, December Twelfth, at Eight-thirty o-clock
At the Home of
Mr. and Mrs. Charles A. Goodwin, 84 Scarborough Street
played by
Clifton Joseph Furness and Elliott C. Carter

Part I

Sacre du Printemps	Stravinski
Concerto (mechanical piano roll)	Stravinski
Le Boeuf sur le Toit	Milhaud
Six Piano Pieces	Schoenberg
Sonate a Quatre Mains	Poulenc

Part II

Puppezetti (mechanical piano)	Casella
Impressioni dal Vero	Malipiero
American Dance	Henry F. Gilbert
'Thoreau', from Sonata 'Concord, 1840–1860'	Charles E. Ives

Part III

Parades	Satie
Larghissimo, from Piano Concerto	Stravinski
Nusch-Nuschi Dances	Hindemith
Ballet Mechanique (mechanical piano)	George Antheil

Though Carter refers to composing songs and a quartet in a letter to Ives, he was not studying composition at Harvard. The music department there struck him as hopelessly conservative, with the exception of Walter Piston, who had recently returned from studies with Boulanger and whose Three Pieces for Flute, Clarinet and Bassoon were Carter's first exposure to neo-Classicism.[22] Carter chose to study literature, Greek, mathematics and philosophy at Harvard; he pursued the oboe and solfeggio at the Longy School. His one surviving composition from this period, a short Joyce song which Carter submitted to *New Music* and which was only rediscovered there many years later, is not the work of a compositional prodigy.

Carter stayed on at Harvard to get an MA in music; Holst was a visiting professor at the time. But the music written at this stage that remains, a quasi-Arabian score for oboe and drums which Carter wrote for a performance of *Philoctetes*, gives little indication of his talent. (Carter had spent time in Tunisia in 1927 transcribing local music for Baron d'Erlanger.) This score contained one fertile seed: Carter used a melodic fragment from ancient Greek music, known as the Seikilos Song. Its opening motif returns in *The Minotaur* and 'Anaphora.' Carter was a young man full of impressions and ideas; but in his own judgment he lacked the technique needed to give his ideas a form. Harvard taught music in a conservative, academic way that seemed to have no bearing on Carter's interests. Piston suggested that he could correct this situation through study with Boulanger. Well-mannered, fluent in French and Harvard-educated, Carter may have given a few signs to his new mentor of the Christopher Newman within himself.

At Harvard, Carter had faced an unproductive choice between traditional technique and modern composition; Nadia Boulanger promised to bridge this gap. Her pedagogy linked the music of Machaut and Monteverdi to that of Fauré and Stravinsky. Students performed Monteverdi madrigals and Bach cantatas, and they were also able to hear Stravinsky himself perform his latest works: the *Duo Concertante*, *Persephone* and the Concerto for Two Solo Pianos. What bound all this music together for Boulanger was technique or 'métier,' which was to be acquired through the study of strict counterpoint, score-reading and harmony. The lessons of technique were applied to composition through the idea of the grand line which tied all the events of a piece together seamlessly and inevitably – a view of composition consistent with Boulanger's view of musical history. A passionate and powerfully opinionated teacher, Boulanger gave students the impression that she had all of European music under her command; some were aware, as Carter was, of her limitations, for she had no sympathy for the Schoenberg school or Bartok.[23] But these were minor problems more than offset by Boulanger's prodigious knowledge and charismatic manner.[24]

Other Americans, notably Piston and Copland, emerged from Boulanger's teaching as fully-formed composers; Carter did not. He wrote many years later that he continued to compose 'discouraging pieces that seemed never to approach the quality that I wanted . . . I came back to America feeling that I hadn't yet learned how to compose as I wanted to.'[25] Instead of composing, he devoted himself to the study of counterpoint and sang in an early music chorus conducted by Henri Expert. Carter was also distracted from composition by the mounting political tensions of the time; he was in Paris during the Stavisky affair when Fascists and Communists clashed in the streets, and he met many people who were fleeing from Germany.

Like the influence of Ives, Boulanger's impact on Carter was delayed but potent. Carter's most obviously Boulanger-style works, _The Minotaur_ and the Woodwind Quintet, did not appear until the late forties. But their neo-Classical style was of only passing interest to Carter; a deeper Boulanger influence can be felt in many of his other works. The study of strict counterpoint forced Carter into the habit of thinking of music as a problem with multiple solutions, all of which needed to be explored before the best could be discovered. It also taught him the benefit of generating music from strict principles, and of thinking of melody, harmony and rhythm in systematically related ways. He has often said that his study of Bach cantatas with Boulanger was a defining experience; in the short run, their example inspired his early compositions for chorus, but in the longer run the concentrated texture and intense expression of many of the cantatas would serve as an ideal for Carter's instrumental works, as well as such later vocal works as _A Mirror on Which to Dwell_ and _Syringa_.

Despite the impact of Boulanger's teachings, however, Carter, like a

Jamesian naïf, somehow missed the main point of her teaching – the launching of a career as a composer. Boulanger was a pedagogue but not an academic; as an essential adjunct to her teaching she was a kingmaker who actively promoted her favored protegés in the concert world; Carter was not among their number. Unlike Copland, he could not quickly translate Boulanger's lessons into an American idiom; her teachings seemed to deny the validity of the American music to which he was most closely connected. (Many years later, when Boulanger heard the String Quartet No. 1, she told Carter that she never thought he would write a piece like that.) As he had at Harvard, Carter destroyed almost all the compositional work of this time.

4 Carter as Pocahontas

Carter's inner struggle began to find expression only after he returned to the States in 1936. He first settled in Boston where he tried to find work as a choral conductor. He received a commission from the Harvard Classics Club to write music for a performance of Plautus's *Mostellaria* and composed two witty neo-Classical arias that demonstrated the skill he had attained in Paris, as well as a *Tarantella* for chorus based on a text from Ovid which became a favorite of the Harvard Glee Club and which is his earliest published work. But he soon moved to New York, where he wrote criticism for the journal *Modern Music* and became music director of Ballet Caravan. Carter's life for the next five years would be divided between New York and Cambridge, but also between two rather different personae. Most of his compositions from this period were written for university choruses. He set sophisticated secular texts (he has never composed religious music) in a style which reflects his training in early music but lacks any hint of jazz or popular melody or Americanism – all elements that would have given the music a broader appeal. He seemed to be heading for a career, if that is what it can be called, as a composer of well-made pieces for the Harvard Glee Club. By contrast, in New York he was known in musical circles as 'Fighting Kid Carter,' pugnacious and independent-minded, as evidenced by his positive reviews of Bartók and Berg at the time. He was active in advanced political and artistic circles; his friends included Copland, Varèse, and Duchamp. These contradictory aspects of Carter's personality puzzled many of his contemporaries. They found the ballet *Pocahontas* equally perplexing.

Ballet Caravan was a touring company created by Carter's Harvard contemporary Lincoln Kirstein to bring ballet on American subjects to high-school auditoriums around the country. Kirstein commissioned Carter to write a score for a ballet based on the story of Pocahontas. Although Ballet Caravan was a populist experiment typical of the New Deal era, *Pocahontas* had obscure and 'arty' sources. Kirstein was fascinated by Theodore de Bry's seventeenth-century engravings of idealized Indians costumed as Greek gods – these Indians already looked like ballet dancers. Kirstein's scenario quoted Hart Crane's poem *The Bridge*:

> There was a bed of leaves and broken play;
> There was a veil upon you, Pocahontas, bride, –
> O Princess whose brown lap was virgin May;
> And bridal flanks and eyes hid tawny pride.

Although Carter would later base *A Symphony of Three Orchestras* on Crane's poem, he thought at the time that Kirstein's citation was merely an attempt to give the ballet some literary prestige. Carter's approach to the story was different from Kirstein's, a confusion of purpose that may have contributed to the ballet's failure. For Carter, the story of Pocahontas was a cultural allegory about the European conquest of America. He used stylistic contrast to portray his own identification with the Indian princess who was abducted from her homeland and brought to England in the interest of civilization. The ballet begins with a musical evocation of the Virginian forest. Instead of pastoral forest murmurs, however, Carter used dissonant chords and pounding off-beats which recall *The Rite of Spring*; the work, Carter wrote later, that made him decide to become a composer. When the Englishmen John Smith and John Rolfe enter, the music suddenly shifts to a Hindemith-inspired neo-Classicism. Pocahontas's own music sounds like an American pop tune, surrounded by proto-jazz cadenzas. The scene of John Smith's torture by the Indians reverts to the primitivism of the opening, building to a climax of Ivesian chaos; it breaks off suddenly when Pocahontas intercedes to save Smith. The ballet ends with a pavane danced by Pocahantas and Rolfe in England. Carter modeled his pavane on Elizabethan keyboard music, but gave it a dirge-like quality without any feeling of celebration; Pocahontas is trapped in the unyielding rhythms of the European dance.

Like an early James novel, *Pocahontas* contrasts the American innocence of a native princess with European malevolence; but it is also an expression of Carter's creative dilemma. The stylistic 'code' of the music sets American energy against European elegance without being able to imagine an outcome other than repression and defeat. Pocahontas, neither primitive nor civilized, saves Smith's life by silencing the most Ivesian moment of the music, but her reward for heroism is a marriage whose music would sound more fitting at a funeral.

The personal revelations of the ballet were invisible to its audiences and remain obscure today, but a few years later Carter acted out Pocahontas's tragedy overtly in a piece of journalism. Ives's *Concord Sonata*, which Carter had known in the twenties, had its first public performance in New York in 1939 by John Kirkpatrick. The *New York Herald Tribune* critic Lawrence Gilman proclaimed that the sonata was 'the greatest music composed by an American, and the most deeply and essentially American in impulse and implication.'[26]

Carter wrote a review for *Modern Music*, a journal that represented the views of the Boulanger-trained American composers. Aaron Copland had written a mixed review of Ives's *114 Songs* for the journal in 1934 which makes clear the distance that separated Ives from the younger generation.[27] Carter, however, had placed himself in a perilous position. He knew the music and its composer intimately, yet his knowledge of both was that of a boy fifteen years younger than his present self. As a critic, he had too much personally at stake; reviewing Ives, Carter was also taking the measure of his younger self, and he found much lacking. He unleashed his Boulanger-honed acumen on Ives's music:

> In form and aesthetic it is basically conventional, not unlike the Liszt Sonata, full of the paraphernalia of the overdressy sonata school, cyclical themes, contrapuntal development sections that lead nowhere, constant harmonic movement which does not clarify the form, and dramatic rather than rhythmical effects. Because of the impressionistic intent of most of the music, the conventional form seemed to hamper rather than aid, resulting in unnecessary, redundant repetitions of themes, mechanical transitions uncertain in their direction; unconvincing entrances of material; dynamics which have no relation to the progress of the piece. Behind all this confused texture there is a lack of logic which repeated hearing can never clarify, as they do for instance in the works of Bartók and Berg. The rhythms are vague and give no relief to the more expressive sections, and the much touted dissonant harmonies are helter-skelter, without great musical sense of definite progression. The aesthetic is naïve, often too naïve to express serious thoughts, frequently

depending on quotation of well-known American tunes, with little comment, possibly charming, but certainly trivial. As a whole, the work cannot be said to fill out the broad, elevated design forecast in the composer's prefaces.[28]

Though this passage is surrounded by praise for Ives, Carter had subjected his old mentor and spiritual father to a merciless composition lesson, in which Ives's most extended essay in complexity of expression is shown in fact to be simple-minded – the *coup de grâce*. As he had done at the most dramatic point in the ballet score, Carter cut down Ives's music at the height of its power, an act of critical parricide – yet at the same time an act of critical honesty (Carter never recanted on his critique).

In criticizing Ives, however, Carter articulated for the first time his own compositional goals, though they would not be attained for a decade, by which time he would finally get up the courage to free himself of Boulanger's grip as well. Just how constricting that grip was can be gleaned by a reading of Carter's homage to Fauré, Boulanger's master, written in 1945. Carter writes that Fauré 'was not interested in attracting the listener by large dramatic effects or sumptuous orchestration.' Neither did he believe in the exploitation of any other of 'those extremes of music- al language which overcome the listener by their violence and strangeness and all too quickly lose their effect.'[29] Carter's article is clear and intelli- gent but also dutiful and lifeless; unintentionally, perhaps, he shows that Fauré's music exemplifies a European classicism refined to the point of enervation.

5 Getting around Copland

Pocahontas premièred the same evening as Copland's *Billy the Kid*. Copland, building on the works of Roy Harris and Virgil Thomson, shed his angular New York manner and began, with a stunning success, to write a new kind of American music, far from Ives, far from ultramodern- ism and equally far from Europe in its content, if not its musical tech- niques. The mounting horrors in Europe, and the continuing economic crisis at home led America to turn inward. Copland's cowboy ballets, like Harris's cowboy symphonies, were the musical equivalent of American isolationism.

The contrast between the two new ballet scores was fatal for Carter. *Pocahontas*, Carter later wrote, was 'dismissed as cacophonous, as belong- ing to a dated, outworn style whose only purpose was to be unintelligible, while Copland's ballet was (quite rightly) hailed as ushering in a new, more transparent and understandable style.'[30] Carter's *Modern Music* reviews show that he was impressed by the new simplicity of Copland and Harris, and his next large works, the Symphony No. 1 of 1942 and the *Holiday Overture*, written to celebrate the liberation of Paris in 1944, followed the lead of the new Americanism, but without much success. (Carter recalls that the simpler style of the Symphony only led to many bad performances by doctors' orchestras.) The *Holiday Overture*, which starts out like Piston and ends like Ives, won a prize, but Koussevitsky refused to perform it. Copland, who would conduct the Overture frequently in later years, told Carter that it was 'another complicated Carter piece.' Copland may have taken Carter's mild manners as a sign of gentility; at this time it was still easy to pigeon-hole Carter as a 'Harvard composer.' Richard Franko Goldman wrote in 1951 that '[Carter] has had the reputation of being an intellectual composer with a gift for calculated complexity applied to a background of Boulanger and Piston, a composer of music never lacking in skill but sometimes ingeniously uninteresting.'[31] Copland, who advanced the careers of Paul Bowles, Leonard Bernstein, Lukas Foss and Harold Shapero, did not mention Carter in his surveys of up-and-coming composers in 1939 or even in 1949. Copland also omitted any discussion of Carter (and Britten as well) from his book *The New Music 1900–1960*, published in 1968. (Carter 'thanked' Copland for these omissions in a letter, 'since it is by this it is made more clear than ever that my music has taken an opposite direction.')[32]

After his marriage in 1939 to the sculptor and art critic Helen Frost-Jones, Carter temporarily retreated to academia, taking a job in St. John's College in Annapolis, Maryland. Helen Carter once told me that she had encouraged her husband to take the job because he was getting nowhere in New York due to Copland's negative influence. Copland offers unintended evidence in his book *Copland 1900–1942* which quotes a letter from Copland to Koussevitsky about the Suite from *Pocahontas*: 'I need not tell you about the quality of the piece as you can see that for yourself.'[33] St. John's is a small, liberal arts college in which all students and faculty devote themselves to the study of Great Books.[34] Carter's teaching, however, was soon interrupted by the war, during which he worked for the Office of War Information. New York, which was hailing the new compositions of Samuel Barber, Leonard Bernstein and William Schuman, may have thought that Carter was now out of the running, but he was just playing possum; the most significant outcome of his years in

Maryland was the support of two musicians, the composer Nicholas Nabokov and the conductor and critic Richard Franko Goldman, who would play crucial roles as advocates for Carter's music in the years to come.

After the war, Carter proved that he was very much a contender with the Piano Sonata of 1946, although it would be some years before the sonata, which was considered virtually unplayable at the time it appeared, revealed its full stature. No previous work by Carter was so ambitious in scale, virtuosity and expressive range, or so daring in its rhythmic language and harmonic sophistication. The sonata contains elements of Americanism that place it close in style to Copland's Sonata of 1943 and Barber's Sonata of 1949 – though critics tended to hear it as an imitation of the Copland (with typical Carter complexities) or less successful than the Barber (which was premièred by Vladimir Horowitz) as a virtuosic vehicle. Copland's Sonata, built entirely out of short, reiterated ideas, pushes simplicity to the point of mystical stillness; it is the musical equivalent of Rosenberg's Kansas farmhand sitting on the fence waiting for something to happen. Carter's Sonata, which alludes to Copland's Piano Variations as well as his Sonata, moves in the opposite direction; its materials are dramatic and charged with energy; both of its movements connect slow and fast tempi in complex ways. The hymn-like chords that open the Sonata suggest Copland, but the mercurial changes of mood and speed and the un-Copland-like convolutions of the form point to the influence of Ives.

Despite the Copland echoes, therefore, Carter's Sonata may be understood more clearly in terms of his evolving and primal relationship to Ives and his music. Carter had followed his traumatic review of the *Concord Sonata* with two reconciliatory essays published in 1944 and 1946. In light of the *Concord* review it might be tempting to say that Carter's Sonata, with its sophisticated deployment of all the devices of sonata and fugue, is the *Concord* rewritten by Boulanger – but the music shows instead that Carter was exploiting many of the devices that he had once criticized in Ives. Like the *Concord*, Carter's sonata is haunted by Beethoven – the Hammerklavier Sonata rather than the Fifth Symphony. Like the *Concord*, it uses cyclic devices derived from Liszt; Charles Rosen has pointed out many parallels between the Carter and Liszt Sonatas. Again like the *Concord*, it pursues a style of simulated improvisation and concludes with a quiet, Thoreau-esque meditation.

Carter's Piano Sonata, although it has attained a solid place in the repertory, has a surprisingly isolated position in his oeuvre; in his later music Carter abandoned all of its Coplandesque trappings, its pandiatonic harmonies and metric shifts, while he retained its Ivesian dramatic scale. The sonata is at once a homage to Copland and a critique of Copland's stylized Americanism. Setting Copland against Ives, Carter was here for the first time revealing his grand ambition – to surpass both of them. But he hid his ambitions behind the mask of Copland's style; he had yet to find his own idiom. Two years after the Piano Sonata, that idiom suddenly emerged in the Cello Sonata where, for the first time, the stylistic contrasts and contradictions that had marked Carter's music from the beginning turned into a new kind of counterpoint; style became structure.

6 Fusion

The move from the Piano Sonata to the Cello Sonata was not direct. In between, Carter wrote *The Minotaur*, a large ballet score intended for choreography by Balanchine, in a neo-Classical style that owes nothing to America and everything to Paris. It is Carter's most Stravinskian score, but it also contains, in its *pas de deux*, a lovely homage to Chabrier. Stylistically, *The Minotaur*, like the Sonata, seems to be a dead end; but it indicates that Carter constructed his breakthrough style of 1948–55 out of a fusion of American and European elements. Just as the Piano Sonata augments Copland's version of the American with that of Ives, Carter would now confront a larger version of Europe than the one he had learned from Boulanger. The late works of Debussy which Carter was studying in the late forties led to his re-examination of European modernism. *The Minotaur* was the last piece Carter wrote that suggests Stravinsky; he would now take on Bartók, Berg and Schoenberg.

With the Cello Sonata, Carter set out on a course of exploration which would synthesize the ideas of European modernism with those of the American ultramodernists. Carter, who spent much time after the war editing Ives's music with Henry Cowell, returned to the music of his boyhood enthusiasm for inspiration. He has said that at this time, in response to the experience of the war, he felt the need to re-examine every aspect of music; this pursuit led him to a reconsideration of both European and American forms of expressionism and to a systematic study of rhythm:

> . . . I was preoccupied with the time-memory patterns of music, with rethinking the rhythmic means of what had begun to seem a very limited routine used in most contemporary and older Western

music. I had taken up again an interest in Indian *talas*, the 'tempi' of Balinese gamelans (especially the accelerating *Gangsar* and *Rangkep*), and studied the newer recordings of African music, that of the Watusi in particular. At the same time, the music of the *quattrocento*, of Scriabin, Ives and the techniques described in Henry Cowell's *New Musical Resources* also furnished me with many ideas. The result was a way of evolving rhythms and rhythmic continuities sometimes called 'metric modulation', worked out during the composition of the Cello Sonata (1948).[35]

Although Carter's description of this period may give the impression of a carefully planned change of style, the sketches point to a more complex situation in which Carter was actually considering two very different paths of development. Preliminary sketches for the First String Quartet show none of the rhythmic innovations of the final score, but seem to extend the style of *The Minotaur* in the more chromatic direction of the music of Roger Sessions. (Carter had praised the 'intransigent rigor' of Sessions's music as early as 1940;[36] Sessions's dense and chromatic Symphony No. 2 was premièred in 1948 and was one of the first works by an American to show the influence of Schoenberg.) Preliminary ideas for the Variations for Orchestra are labeled 'Symphony #2' and similarly lack any dimension of rhythmic research. Carter once wrote that every piece represented a crisis in his life. In the late forties he seems to have been torn between two identities, one conservative and neo-Classical in taste, as indicated by the choice of text for 'Emblems' and the style of *The Minotaur*; the other radical. The triumph of the radical side may have surprised the composer himself as much as it surprised many of the people closest to him.

Carter began the composition of the Cello Sonata with a jazzy scherzo clearly indebted to Debussy's Sonata, but not significantly different in style from the works that preceded it; in the next movement, though, he introduced proportional tempo changes and polyrhythms that stem from Cowell and Nancarrow. After pursuing these devices further in a finale, Carter appended a new opening movement, which alludes to Ives's *Concord Sonata*; here, the two instruments often seem rhythmically independent, not only in meter, but in implied tempo and in rhythmic style as well, for the piano plays metronomically while the cello plays in an expressive rubato fashion. The unanticipated first movement created a new circular formal plan for the sonata as a whole, with a 'beginning' at the center and the ending leading back to the opening, as in Joyce's *Finnegans Wake*.

What listeners first noted in Carter's new style was its use of melodic lines built out of notes of similar rhythmic value, often moving in small melodic intervals. This made the music sound different from the Second Viennese style of expressive, recitative-like melody stretched out to large intervals; Carter's melodic lines were often expressively neutral but rhythmically potent, characteristics of American speech and music. In his essay 'The Rhythmic Basis of American Music' Carter cites the precedents of jazz and Roy Harris:

> In jazz . . . . the melodic line frequently has an independent rhythmic life; the metrical units are grouped into irregular (or regular) patterns, in melodic motives whose rhythm runs against the underlying 1, 2, 3, 4 of the dance rhythm. Roy Harris carried this technique further by writing long, continuously developing melodies in which groups of two, three, four, or five units (such as eighth notes) are joined together to produce irregular stresses, but with the underlying regular beat of jazz omitted.[37]

Carter's lines are Harris-like in this respect, but because Carter augmented Harris's technique with the complex polyrhythms of Ives and Nancarrow, they achieve a heightened intensity as elements in a polyphony which combined such lines moving at different speeds.

Carter's new rhythmic polyphony seems to wed the abstract rhythmic rules of species counterpoint with the rhythmic impetus of jazz. If Harris left the implied jazz beat unstated, Carter now omitted the usual harmonic basis of counterpoint; the lines were not connected by the rules of tonal harmony, although, because of their small intervals, they often had a tonal feeling when heard in isolation. The new rhythms freed pulse from the constraints of meter, and the new harmonies defied the limitations of tonal voice-leading without quite crossing into the amorphous world of Schoenbergian atonality. The expanded harmonic idiom of the new style seems more a response to the rhythmic innovations than to the pressures of chromaticism. At points in the First Quartet, for instance, the instrumental lines are so independent that they seem to share no harmonic framework; the music struck listeners as aharmonic rather than atonal. Carter had now created a forceful personal style; but, inspired by modernist literature and film, he turned his interest from rhythm and harmony to the larger questions of continuity and form: 'Musical discourse needed as thorough a rethinking as harmony had had at the beginning of the century.'[38]

Following the Cello Sonata with a series of studies for winds and timpani, Carter achieved his synthesis of European modernism and American ultramodernism (and some aspects of the American symphonic mainstream as well) in the String Quartet No. 1, an epic work written in 1951 during a year spent living in the Arizona desert. As he had done in *Pocahontas*, Carter subliminally identified his transatlantic theme with stylistic allusions: the Quartet echoes Bartók's Fourth String Quartet, Berg's Lyric Suite and Debussy's Violin Sonata (as well as Beethoven's *Kreutzer* Sonata), and quotes ideas from Ives and Nancarrow. (While living in Arizona, the Carters visited Nancarrow in Mexico.) But where Carter had once used such allusions narratively, here he subsumed them into innovative musical processes; the music has its own logic and its own form of narrative.

Carter had found an idea which would take his music beyond the classical structures of European high modernism and the experiments of the American ultramodernists; that idea was change. The First Quartet evokes a state of flux. Carter built change into the musical structure through two procedures: metrical modulation and polyrhythmic form. The term metrical modulation was used by Richard Franko Goldman in a review of the Cello Sonata written in 1951.[39] Carter has come to prefer the term tempo modulation, since it is the tempo that changes, not the meter; but the changes in tempo themselves spring from a novel polyphony built out of lines of music moving at complex ratios of five against three or seven against four. In the First Quartet's opening movement these lines are frequently renotated so that a metronomic speed that has been written in quarter notes continues as, say, quintuplet quarters. This change usually happens with no break in the music, but it makes possible new cross-rhythmic relationships which can give rise to other seamless tempo changes. By these means, the tempo of the music becomes its most dynamic element. Carter achieved a rhythmic flexibility that contrasted sharply with the unvarying tempi of neo-Classical Stravinsky, though it had precedents in Ives and Berg.

Carter emphasized the idea of change on the formal level by a strikingly simple device. The quartet has four movements; Carter interrupts the music not three times but twice, in the middle of movements rather than at their beginnings and endings. Each of the four movements thus flows into the next. The interruptions have the dramatic effect of lifting the needle off a record; after each break the music seems to continue exactly at the point at which it had stopped. The quartet, divided into two different, formal schemes of three and four movements, was polyrhythmic in its macrostructure as it was in its smallest details.

Four years after the Quartet, Carter transposed his new synthesis to the orchestra in his Variations. The new work was commissioned by the Louisville Orchestra but Carter composed it in Rome. Several important events occurred as it was being written: the Rome première of the First Quartet, Furtwängler's performance of the complete *Ring* cycle in Rome, and, in America, the deaths of Carter's father and of Charles Ives.[40] In the Variations Carter once again configured European and American elements in a brazenly agonistic design. The Variations follows the outlines of Schoenberg's op. 31 and is the only work by Carter to show traces of twelve-tone technique; at its climax, though, it recalls the high point of Debussy's *Jeux*. The seventh variation is a homage to Ives; Carter divides the orchestra into string, brass and woodwind groups, each pursuing its own ideas, as in *The Unanswered Question*. Here, too, Carter uses rhythm and form to bring the European and American elements together. Besides the main theme, there are two other themes which Carter calls, a bit confusingly, 'ritornelli'; they return but always in changed form. One gets faster on each appearance; the other slows down. Carter made this process most audible in the fourth and sixth variations where the tempi are, respectively, a continual slowing and continual accelerating. Although there are breaks between most of the variations, these boundaries are porous; the first variation begins during the theme itself.

For some critics, the First Quartet and the Variations are the greatest American music of the 1950s, but in America they were little played, despite appreciative reviews and excellent recordings by the Walden Quartet and the Louisville Orchestra. (The New York Philharmonic did not perform the Variations until 1972.) The most successful American classical works of the fifties – Menotti's *Amahl and the Night Visitors*, Barber's *Knoxville Summer of 1915* and Douglas Moore's *The Ballad of Baby Doe* – continued the more conservative styles of the previous decades. The Quartet and Variations, however, received important performances in Europe and established Carter's reputation there among contemporaries like Dallapiccola and Petrassi, and among the younger generation. Ironically, while some Americans were put off by the 'European' qualities of these works, Europeans were attracted to their distinctively American flavor (as is clear from the descriptions of Wilfred Mellers, who was also the first critic to link Carter with Stevens).[41]

The contrast in reception on the two sides of the Atlantic drew Carter to Europe for much of the decade; there he made contact with the emerging avant-garde whose ultramodernism went far beyond the older American variety. From Europe, Carter sent back reports on Nono's *Il canto sospeso*, Boulez's *Le marteau sans maître* and *Improvisations sur Mallarmé* and Stockhausen's Klavierstück XI; the provocative cast of the new music filled him with a mixture of admiration and *déjà vu*. He found the nihilism of some of the avant-garde music reminiscent of the Greenwich Village of his youth, but the major revelation was the fact that these pieces, of surpassing difficulty, were being played at all. Carter has written that after hearing a rehearsal of *Le Marteau* he went to the director of the Südwestfunk, Dr Heinrich Strobel and told him: 'You know there's a wonderful work of Ives, the Fourth Symphony, that the SWF Orchestra should play –' – a suggestion that, Carter feels, eventually led to the long-postponed première of Ives's Symphony in 1964 under Stokowski.[42] The fact that a performance of Ives's most difficult score was now a real possibility freed Carter of all the inhibitions ground into American composers by American conservatories and orchestras. Carter abandoned the style of the Quartet and Variations and took off in yet another new direction. In later years Carter stated that his truly representative works only began with the Second Quartet, written when he was fifty.

7 Polyvocality

The most obvious change in Carter's new style is its disjunctive syntax; the long lines which had given the First Quartet its powerful rhythmic impetus seem to have disappeared, phrases are more fragmented, and the harmonic idiom is decisively atonal. These changes disturbed some of Carter's previously sympathetic critics. Wilfrid Mellers, the first writer to place Carter between Copland and Ives in the American pantheon, found that in the Double Concerto 'the virtual disappearance of lyricism means that the "life-process" of the musical characters seems decidedly less human.'[43] Mellers's judgment may have been premature, for with greater familiarity Carter's new style reveals an even greater emotional intensity than was present in his work of the fifties.

In moving his style forward, Carter once more extended his range of European and American influences. Parts of the Second Quartet, for instance, are probably the closest Carter ever came to the disjunct motion of the 'post-Webern' style that dominated European music; yet at the same time the Quartet refers to Ives's Second Quartet, where the four instruments are distinct characters whose conversation gives way to arguments. In Carter's Quartet the four characters seem to be playing not just different lines but different pieces simultaneously, though their parallel monologues eventually converge. Similarly, the Double Concerto at first appeared to be a response to the spatial compositions of Boulez, Stockhausen and Berio, but it opens with a device suggested in Cowell's *New Musical Resources*, the association of harmonic and temporal intervals. The brittle sonorities of the piano and harpsichord, and the complex ratios of their rhythms, recall Nancarrow's player piano studies and its percussion writing bespeaks the influence of Varèse. Despite Carter's ever-widening range of sources, however, these new works unveil the defining device of Carter's mature style – the divided ensemble. Carter imposed the condition of absolute polyvocalism on his music, splitting the musical materials between instruments so that they can never speak in the same harmonic and gestural language. Contrary to Mellers's fears, the new style was not dehumanized, but rather 'humanized'; more than ever, the music seems to speak, but in at least two voices. Carter now conceived his music in explicitly dramatic terms:

> ... I regard my scores as scenarios, auditory scenarios, for performers to act out with their instruments, dramatizing the players as individuals and participants in the ensemble.[44]

In the Second Quartet, Carter was inspired by Beckett's *Waiting for Godot* and *Endgame* – he asked that the players sit as far apart as possible, like Beckett's characters who seem only to speak to themselves. The four instruments have different harmonies, different tempi and different styles of playing; only in the last movement do they attempt to find a common ground, which they never reach. In the Double Concerto each solo instrument has its own orchestra, and each orchestra has its own repertory of harmonies, tempos and gestures.

The transatlantic conflict that had haunted Carter's work now assumed a fundamental structural role; out of the argument within himself, to paraphrase Yeats, Carter created a music of argument. By giving the clash of styles and character a structural role, Carter had found a way to make his music European and American at the same time. The division of characters in these works, however, does not oppose obvious European and American archetypes. The music is American in its conflicting voices, an Ivesian metaphor for democracy which Carter strips of nostalgia and presents either as irony or tragedy – or both. The music is European in the way it gives its argument a complex and tightly woven form, far from the populism of the American mainstream or the anti-art stance of the experimentalists. Using a European high art notion to subvert American 'populism,' Carter insisted on his right to produce masterpieces.[45] The polemical subtext of Carter's new style discovery fueled the powerful and varied series of works that he composed after the Double Concerto, the two turbulent orchestral concertos of the sixties, the collage-form chamber works of the early seventies, the visionary *Symphony of Three Orchestras* and, as a culmination of this style, his two greatest works of polyvocality: *Syringa* and *Night Fantasies*.

8 Turning Eastward

The twenty years from the Second Quartet to *Night Fantasies* could be termed Carter's American period, even if he spent much of the sixties living in Europe. In this time he finally won the highest critical recognition and honors, including two Pulitzer Prizes. All the works of this period were commissioned by American ensembles and performers.[46] During this period Carter also taught at the Juilliard School. Among his students there were Ellen Taaffe Zwilich, Tod Machover and Tobias Picker. Many of his works from this time also have American themes. The Concerto for Orchestra, which reflects the political unrest of the late sixties, was based on a Whitmanesque poem (by the Frenchman St. John Perse) about winds blowing over America; *A Symphony of Three Orchestras* sprang from Hart Crane's poem *The Bridge* and opens with a magical evocation of New York's harbor. With *A Mirror on Which to Dwell*, a setting of six poems by Elizabeth Bishop, Carter began a trilogy of works based on American poetry; *Syringa*, on a John Ashbery text, and *In Sleep, In Thunder*, to poems of Robert Lowell, soon followed.

Carter's mature vision of America was far from the willed simplicity of Copland or the idealized nostalgia of Ives. These works mirror, instead, the energy, violence and instability of contemporary American life, sometimes finding pathos in this situation, sometimes elation, and at other times tragedy. But Carter, resolutely 'élite,' and true to the tradition of James and Stevens, viewed the American scene subjectively, abstractly and iron-ically. In the course of the seventies critics, especially the influential John

Rockwell of the *New York Times*, attacked Carter's music for its distance
from the American mainstream of popular culture: 'Among our aca-
demics and lovers of Europe, among those who worry that American
culture is but a poor transplant of the European original, there is an
instinctive veneration of tradition and busy ingenuity, and a concomitant
distrust of the simple.'[47] A reaction against Carter's music, however came
from 'élite' elements as well. Samuel Lipman, pianist and the publisher of
the neo-conservative journal *The New Criterion*, had performed Carter's
Piano Concerto in 1973; in the November 1987 issue of his magazine he
recanted: 'For me the Piano Concerto of Elliott Carter, in its level of complexity and dissonance, in its rapidity of movement and change, in the
demands it makes on both performers and audience, securely occupies the
line separating viable from non-viable music . . . I have no doubt at all that
whatever the fate of Carter's mature work may be, composition cannot go
further in the direction he has adumbrated and remain what can be recognized as music.'[48] With the rise of minimalism and neo-Romanticism,
American music was returning to the models of Copland and Barber;
Carter, for all his honors, became an increasingly isolated figure.

In 1981 Carter changed publishers, moving from New York's Associated Music Publishers to London-based Boosey & Hawkes. His first work
for Booseys was a song cycle commissioned by the London Sinfonietta, for
which Carter chose poems by an American poet and friend, Robert Lowell,
who had taken up residency in England in the last years of his life,
divorcing his second wife Elizabeth Hardwick and marrying his third,
Caroline Blackwood. The six poems Carter selected for *In Sleep, In Thunder*
depict a poet torn between two families, an old one in New York and a new
one in London. The texts were emblematic of the composer's own creative
(though not marital) condition as well. Though he would continue to live
in New York, Carter's creative spirit once again turned toward Europe;
during these years he would speak with renewed admiration of 'my dear
old Nadia Boulanger.' Out of this new intercontinental orientation, Carter
began to construct a long and fecund 'late period.'

In the years since 1980, the overwhelming majority of Carter's works
have been European commissions, a measure both of his ascending reputation to the east of the Atlantic and the reaction against modernist
music in general that was taking hold to the west. As the activities and
resources of new music groups in America were on the decline, Carter
received, for the first time, the encouragement of orchestral conductors, in
particular Oliver Knussen in England, Pierre Boulez in France, Michael

Gielen in Germany, and Heinz Holliger in Switzerland; David Robertson and Daniel Barenboim also became important proponents for Carter in this period.[49] European recognition brought with it many festivals of his music (few of which were covered in the American press) and a stream of commissions for occasional pieces. With *Riconoscenza*, written in honor of Goffredo Petrassi, Carter initiated a series of short works, which soon became as important a genre for him as the *Sequenze* are for Berio. Capping the European connection was the acquisition of Carter's papers and sketches, many of which had been on deposit in the Library of Congress and the Library of the Performing Arts at Lincoln Center, by the Paul Sacher Stiftung in Basel. In a move that some American musicians found almost treasonous, Carter placed his sketches near to those musical cultures which now showed the most interest in his work.

Carter's late phase has lasted long enough for it, too, to be broken down into phases; but the general tendency of this period has been toward an ever-greater lucidity. Carter has reconfigured the gapped counterpoint that defined his music. In *Triple Duo*, three pairs of instruments go their separate ways, but the spirit of the music is playful rather than contentious, and in the last part of the music the six players take turns in articulating a continuous melodic line; Carter's revival of Schoenberg's 'obbligato recitative' technique is even more extensive in *Penthode*, where five quartets of instruments spin out a single, wide-ranging melody – an effect Carter says was inspired by performances he heard in Berlin by the North Indian Dagar Brothers. Despite its habitual divided syntax, *Penthode* is a music of connection, not opposition, and its form replaces the complex assemblages of episodes that Carter had used in the seventies with an elegant three-part da capo aria form, replete with a parody cadenza which passes from the contrabass clarinet up to the piccolo; polyvocality here merges into a single super-voice. In this radiant work, written expressly for Boulez, Carter seemed to be making his peace with music itself under the sign of a new or 'second' classicism – though Carter has rejected any suggestion that he was being, once again, 'neo-Classical.'[50]

In the late period, Carter has been drawn to the idea of lightness, as found in a phrase of Italo Calvino which Carter used as the title of his short piece *Con leggerezza pensosa*: 'Above all I hope to have shown that there is such a thing as a lightness of thoughtfulness, just as we all know that there is a lightness of frivolity. In fact, thoughtful lightness can make frivolity seem dull and heavy.'[51] In the Oboe Concerto, written for Heinz Holliger, the soloist embodies the idea of lightness; at its opening the oboe's line descends from an altissimo A against a dirge-like music in the orchestra; in the course of the work, the oboe seems to teach the orchestra how to 'lighten up,' though not without some resistance on the orchestra's part, as embodied in oppositional ideas given to a solo trombone. The Violin Concerto takes the ideal of thoughtful lightness even further, achieving in its sparse scoring and simply drawn contrasts a Mendelssohnian lucidity, even though it retains, in its schism of orchestra and soloist, the Carterian pathos of isolation.

Carter's alienation from the American musical scene has been most evident in his strained relationship with American orchestras and conductors. In the Concerto for Orchestra and *A Symphony of Three Orchestras* Carter defiantly dissected the orchestral body; an implied expression of anger that became overt in March 1984 when Carter walked out of Orchestra Hall in Chicago during introductory comments by Maestro Leonard Slatkin that Carter found insulting. In 1996 the Maestro Kurt Masur cancelled a commission (for the third movement of *Symphonia: Sum Fluxae Pretiam Spei*) that the New York Philharmonic had previously secured. Such experiences led Carter to postpone the completion of several American commissions ('Why do they commission a new piece when they don't play my old ones?' he frequently asked.) Due to the considerable efforts of Oliver Knussen, however, Carter returned to the orchestra with *Three Occasions* and finally with his magnum opus, *Symphonia: Sum Fluxae Pretiam Spei*.

While these two orchestral triptychs are built on polyrhythmic structures, Carter does not divide the orchestra into smaller groups associated with these structural levels. For 'Anniversary,' the third of the *Occasions*, dedicated to his wife on their fiftieth wedding anniversary, Carter composed a terse, abstract Symphonia Domestica; the work begins by superimposing two contrapuntal lines and midway through the piece an offspring third line enriches the polyphony. Like the common-thread melodies of the late chamber works, however, the three lines migrate across the orchestra in changing colors, doublings and densities; Carter treats the orchestra as a single instrument of infinite resources. He carries his new bravura orchestral style even further in *Symphonia* which was inspired by a Latin poem, 'Bulla' (Bubble), by the seventeenth-century English metaphysical poet Richard Crashaw. Despite its obscure literary basis, *Symphonia* is not antiquarian; Carter has said that he wanted to give music the feeling of high-speed air travel; the first movement, Partita, has the propulsive thrust of an SST (from this perspective, we might say that the Atlantic barely exists). The second movement, Adagio tenebroso, is also contemporary but in a completely different way; it sounds like a dirge for all the tragedies of the twentieth century. It is typical of Carter's late concern for lightness, however, and his enduring concern to deal with the fleeting nature of musical time, that he concludes the *Symphonia* with an Allegro scorrevole, a 'Queen Mab scherzo' as he has described it, rather than a finale.

The movements of Carter's 'Bubble' symphony, as *Symphonia* has been dubbed, premièred in Chicago, London and Cleveland under Argentinian/ Israeli, British and Hungarian conductors: the ultimate statement of the international theme. The figure of the bubble, moreover, once again affirms Carter's links to James and Stevens, for the bubble is an emblem of the imagination: immaterial, irrelevant, perishable, free.

> And yet nothing has been changed except what is
> Unreal, as if nothing had been changed at all.

Notes

1 CEL, p. 71.
2 *The Grand Tradition*, (New York, 1933), p. 121.
3 *Tradition of the New*, p. 18.
4 Ibid., p. 89.
5 FW, p. 60.
6 *Copland on Music*, p. 177.
7 *It Must Give Pleasure*, VI.
8 *Agon* (Oxford, 1982), p. 330.
9 See CEL, pp. 87–118.
10 CEL, p. 100.
11 CEL, p. 88.
12 Carter was an editor at *New Music* for several years after World War II.
13 The 'ultramodernists' are now usually called 'experimentalists.' See Nicholls, *American Experimental Music* (Cambridge, 1990).
14 Conlon Nancarrow is often associated with this group, but Carter did not meet him until 1939; Carter published Nancarrow's Rhythm Study No. 1 in *New Music* in 1951.
15 See Shreffler, 'Elliott Carter and His America' in *Sonus* 14, No. 2 (Spring 1994), pp. 38–66.
16 See Bernard, *MQ*.
17 CEL, pp. 57–62.
18 CEL, p. 79.
19 CEL, p. 108.
20 Carter, 'My Neo-Classicism'.

21 From the archives of the Wadsworth Atheneum, Hartford, Connecticut, provided by Donald Harris.

22 See Howard Pollack, *Harvard Composers*.

23 Carter recalls finding her at a rehearsal of Berg's Three Pieces for Orchestra in the early sixties. She had studied the score closely, but told Carter: 'This is terrible – just like the music my students used to write in the twenties!'

24 See Carter's portrait of his Boulanger years in CEL, pp. 281–292.

25 CEL, p. 191.

26 Burkholder, ed., *Charles Ives and His World* (Princeton, 1996), p. 320.

27 Aaron Copland, 'One Hundred and Fourteen Songs' in *Modern Music* XI, 2 (January–February 1934), pp. 59–64.

28 CEL, p. 89. Carter has been taken to task by many writers on Ives. Burkholder states that Carter's criticism 'shows no grasp of how Ives conveys his experiences of music through the way he reworks it and the forms he uses.' J. Peter Burkholder, *All Made of Tunes: Charles Ives and the Uses of Musical Borrowing* (New Haven, 1995), p. 469, n. 69.

29 CEL, p. 119.

30 CEL, p. 205.

31 RFG, p. 68.

32 *Copland Since 1943*, p. 296.

33 *Copland 1900–1942*, p. 283.

34 Carter described the program in an essay, 'Music as a Liberal Art,' CEL, pp. 309–313.

35 CEL, pp. 228–229.

36 CEL, p. 50.

37 CEL, p. 58.

38 CEL, p. 229.

39 'Current Chronicle,' MQ 37, No. 1 (January 1951), pp. 83–89.

40 These events affected Carter strongly; he also gave up smoking at this time, and his handwriting changed as well.

41 MNFL, pp. 102–121.

42 CEL, p. 105.

43 MNFL, p. 120.

44 CEL, p. 221.

45 Virgil Thomson, who often taunted Carter for his pursuit of the 'genre chef-d'oeuvre', wrote in 1972 that Carter was an 'élite' composer, 'a conservative composer, in the sense that his aim is to say modern things to the classical educated.' *Virgil Thomson Reader*, p. 496. Appearing in the pages of the *New York Review of Books*, Thomson's words have a certain irony of their own.

46 Carter wrote the Piano Concerto for the Boston Symphony, the Concerto for Orchestra and *A Symphony of Three Orchestras* for the New York Philharmonic and Third Quartet for the Juilliard String Quartet. For the New York ensemble Speculum Musicae he composed *A Mirror on Which to Dwell* and *Syringa*; and he composed *Night Fantasies* for four pianists who were particularly devoted to his music: Paul Jacobs, Gilbert Kalish, Ursula Oppens and Charles Rosen.

47 *All American Music*, p. 443. Rockwell's chapter on Carter, a tour-de-force of damning with faint praise, accuses Carter of 'careerism.'

48 *New Criterion*, vi, 3 p. 11.

49 For Knussen, Carter composed *Remembrance, Anniversary*, Adagio Tenebroso and *Of Challenge and Of Love*; for Boulez, *Penthode* and *esprit rude/esprit doux I* and *II*; for Holliger, the Oboe Concerto, Quintet, *Trilogy* and *A Letter in 6 Letters* as well as the orchestrated version of the early *Pastoral*.

50 Restagno, p. 90

51 Italo Calvino, *Six Memos for the Next Millennium* (Cambridge, Mass., 1988), p. 10.

Technical Glossary

accelerando:/ritardando: *rhythmic characters* where the pulse speed seems to quicken or slow. Carter either notates this in terms of a constant tempo (Ex. 1) or by notating a changing tempo (Ex. 2).

Ex. 1 Notated acceleration

all-interval hexachord: (0, 1, 2, 4, 7, 8) the unique six-note collection that contains all twelve three-note *chords* (Chart 1).

Chart 1 The all-triad hexachord (0, 1, 2, 4, 7, 8)

all-interval tetrachords (0, 1, 4, 6) and (0, 1, 3, 7), the two four-note collection that contain all six *interval-classes*[1] (Chart 2).

Chart 2 All-interval tetrachords

all-interval twelve-tone chords: twelve-note *spatial set* made up of the

* Violin II: in measures 568 and 569, the five accented C-sharps should be played as regular beats (*non accel.*).

Ex. 2 Tempo acceleration

eleven *intervals*. Although Alban Berg made use of an all-interval set in his Lyric Suite, Carter has based his use of such chords on the list generated by Stefan Bauer-Mengelberg and Melvin Ferentz.[2] These chords often function as a 'tonic' sonority (Ex. 3).

Ex. 3 All-interval twelve-tone chords

character-patterns: association of *intervals*, *metronomic speeds*, *polyrhythms* and *rhythmic characters* used to dramatize the musical personalities of instruments or instrumental groups and to make clear the *stratification* of texture. Beginning with the Second Quartet, character patterns take the place of thematic structures in Carter's music. Chart 3 indicates the deployment of character patterns in the Second Quartet.

Instrument	Intervals	Rhythmic type	Expressive character
Violin I	m3, p5, M9, M10	free	bravura
Violin II	M3, M6, M7	pulse	laconic
Viola	aug4, m7, m9	rubato	espressivo
Cello	p4, m6, m10	accel.-ritard.	impetuous

Chart 3 Character patterns in the 2nd String Quartet

chords: Carter uses the word 'chord' to mean any collection of three or more pitches. This is similar to Allen Forte's term 'pitch class set,' with similar notions of equivalency. According to both Carter and Forte there are twelve three-note chords, twenty-eight four-note chords, thirty-eight five-note chords and fifty six-note chords. (See Appendix A.)

circular form: a connection between the ending of a work and its beginning that suggests that the work could be imagined as a continuous loop. Carter first used this device in the Cello Sonata, where, in fact, the first movement was composed after the last. He has cited *Finnegans Wake* as his inspiration for this device, as well as Cocteau's film *The Blood of a Poet*.[3]

collage: in art, the pasting together of disparate materials; by analogy, construction of music through the juxtaposition and superimposition of contrasting materials. Carter's sketches show that he often composes in a non-linear fashion, assembling a work out of small episodes which are not composed in the order they may take in the final work; he often encouraged his students to work this way as well. Carter has pointed to the example of Stravinsky's music as an encouragement to thinking of form in this way:

> Through these recent years, when I saw him now and then, certain things that I wanted to make clearer, at least to myself, have nagged at me, but I was never able to formulate them into questions that would bring the answer I wanted. The possibility of such questions came to me first during a time when Robert Craft was conducting my Double Concerto in Los Angeles, and Mr and Mrs Stravinsky invited me to their house on North Wetherly Drive. A little discouraged and shy in the midst of such August figures as Spender, Isherwood and Huxley, who were also there, I went off into a corner soon to be joined by Stravinsky himself, and we began musicians' talk until I got up the courage to ask him how he composed. At which he took me to his workroom, and showed me a large book of blank pages into which short fragments of musical sketches, roughly torn out of larger sketch-pages, had been pasted. Since the original sketch pages had been papers of different qualities and colors and the musical fragments (sometimes only two or three notes) had been written on staves that were hand-drawn, often in quite fanciful curves, the scrapbook itself gave a very arresting visual appearance. This was the workbook for *The Flood*, which I don't think had yet been performed. He proceeded to explain how he chose fragments from his sketches, tore them out, reshuffled them in different orders until he found one that satisfied him, and then pasted them down. I was genuinely surprised to learn of such an unexpected way of composing, of which, if I had not known whose music it was, I might have had doubts as to the results . . . Some time later I began to realize that what I saw corresponded to glimpses I had had of this technique in his music elsewhere. The description and quotation of Stravinsky telling how he cut up the final fugue in *Orpheus*, given in Nicholas Nabokov's *Old Friends and New Music*, as well as in a brilliant lecture by Edward Cone on the *Symphonies of Wind Instruments*, recalled to

me how pervasive cross cutting was in the music. I had not expected to see it so graphically demonstrated.[4]

compound form: presentation of two or more different formal models. Such formal polyphony appears in the First Quartet which is written in four movements which, however, are interrupted twice to produce a three-part design. Carter explains that design as follows:

Note that while there are really four movements in this piece, only three are marked in the score as separate movements, and these three do not correspond to the four 'real' movements. The four 'real' movements are Fantasia, Allegro scorrevole, Adagio and Variations. But the movements are all played *attacca*, with the pauses coming in the middle of the Allegro scorrevole and near the beginning of the Variations. Thus there are only two pauses, dividing the piece into three sections. The reason for this unusual division of movements is that the tempo and character change, which occurs between what are usually called movements, is the goal, the climax of the techniques of metrical modulation which have been used. It would destroy the effect to break off the logical plan of the movement just at its high-point. Thus pauses can only come between sections using

Riconoscenza per Goffredo Petrassi
© 1985 Hendon Music Inc.

Ex. 4 Cross-cutting

the same basic material. This is most obvious in the case of the pause before the movement marked Variations. In reality, at that point the Variations have already been going on for some time. [5]

cross-cutting: in movies, jumping back and forth between shots (as opposed to panning or tracking); by analogy, jumping from one musical idea to another without transition. *Riconoscenza*, for solo violin, is a simple example of this technique; it cross-cuts three types of material, each of which develops independently of the others (Ex. 4).

cross-pulses: simultaneous statement of different regular metronomic speeds.

epiphanic form: form where the relations between musical ideas are revealed non-linearly across a piece rather than in the form of theme and variation or development. The term 'epiphany' was adopted by James Joyce to mean the sudden revelation of meaning; in Joyce's work it evolves from the singular revelations in the stories of *Dubliners* to the continuous shining forth of symbolic meanings in *Ulysses*. Carter points to Schoenberg's *Erwartung* and Debussy's *Jeux* as musical precedents for this technique, and has also cited the inspiration of Balanchine's choreography

String Quartet No. 2
© 1961 Associated Music Publishers, Inc. Used by permission

Ex. 5 'Fantastico' character

where 'every individual momentary tableau ... is something that the viewer has seen interestingly evolve, yet is also only a stage of a process that is going on to another point; and while every moment is a fascinating and beautiful thing in itself still what's much more fascinating is the continuity, the way each moment is being led up to and away from ...'[6]

fantasia: In Carter this term usually implies a free-associational continuity with many jumps and transformations of material.

fantastico: a rhythmic character in which the playing appears to be free of any regularity (Ex. 5, see previous page).

Harmony Book: Carter's personal catalogue of chordal analysis and synthesis, developed since the time of the Piano Concerto.

interval-class: an interval (I) and its inversion (12–I) such as the minor third (3) and major sixth (9). In serial and set theory intervals and their inversions are considered equivalent. Therefore there are six interval-classes.

intervals: the eleven possible distances (twelve minus one through eleven) between two different pitches within one octave of the chromatic scale.

Ex. 6 'Link' chords

inverted arch form: a formal scheme which places the greatest contrast at the beginning and end of a work and the least at its center. This is the inverse of the arch form employed by Wagner, Strauss and Bartok, in which the climax is the central event of a work. In Carter's Variations for Orchestra the opposition of ideas is presented most dramatically at the extremes of the work while the central variation reduces contrast to a minimum. Carter often uses *Klangfarbenmelodie* at central moments of 'neutralization.'

Klangfarbenmelodie: from Schoenberg, melody of tone color. Carter first used this idea in the *Eight Etudes and a Fantasy*. In Etude 3 a D major triad is sustained with changing instrumentation. In Etude 7 the technique is applied to the single pitch G.

'Link' chords: *all-interval twelve-tone chords* found by theorist John F. Link that contain adjacent statements of the *all-triad hexachord*. Carter employed these chords in *Symphonia: Sum Fluxae Pretiam Spei* (Ex. 6).

metrical modulation: a proportional change in tempo effected by the reno-tation of a *metronomic speed* as in the instruction 'new half note equal previous dotted quarter.' Although this term was first used by Richard Franko Goldman in 1951 to describe the Cello Sonata, Carter had employed proportional tempo relations as early as the Symphony No. 1 of 1942; and he was influenced by Rudolph Kolisch's 1943 article, 'Tempo and Character in Beethoven's Music'[7] to think of tempo in structural terms. In Carter's music tempo modulation takes various forms. In the first movement of the Symphony No. 1, for instance, the two main con-trasting thematic ideas are in the tempo relation of 2:3. This technique recalls the method of the first scene of Stravinsky's *Les Noces* where there are three tempi in a ratio of 1:2:3; but Carter, even as early as the Symphony, makes things more complex by making gradual changes in the overall tempo while preserving the tempo ratio between the two ideas. In the second, third and fourth movements of the Cello Sonata, Carter simi-larly contrasts material through proportionally related tempi, but he also co-ordinates the tempo relations between movements, so that material from one movement reappears in the next with the same metronomic speed although with different notated values. In the first movement of the First Quartet musical ideas moving at contrasting metronomic speeds appear simultaneously; the texture is polyrhythmic throughout. Here tempo modulations are often used to continue one strand of the poly-phony while enabling its combination with ideas at different speeds. Most of the tempo modulations in this movement are therefore inaudible, unlike

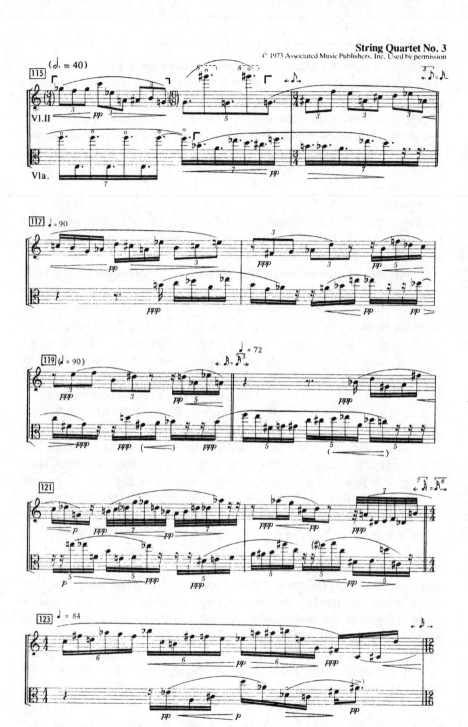

Ex. 7 Metrical modulations

the sudden jumps in tempo employed by Stravinsky. A passage from the Third Quartet illustrates the seamless modulation of tempos with changing polyrhythms (Ex. 7). In later works Carter has often based the field of possible tempos, and therefore the possibilities of tempo-modulation on a constant pulse. A good example is the oboe solo in 'Sandpiper.' The oboe plays rapid notes at a metronomic speed of MM 525 which is notated in several different values. The oboe's speed remains the same while the tempo of the music changes.[8]

constant speed in oboe: M. 525
Tempo 1: 525/5 = 105
Tempo 2: 525/7 = 75
Tempo 3: 525/4 = 131+

Chart 4 'Sandpiper': tempo relations

metronomic speed: the speed of any notated duration figured in terms of beats per minute as shown on a metronome. For instance if the tempo of the music indicates that the quarter note is MM 120, the metronomic speed of quintuplet sixteenth notes will be 5 x 120=600 (Chart 4).

mosaic texture: construction of a musical texture out of one or two short musical ideas. Carter first employed this technique in Etudes II, IV and VIII of the *Eight Etudes and a Fantasy*. Carter once pointed out to an audience that the structure of Etude IV was 'very similar to that of the parquet floor on which we are standing. You see it is made of small blocks of wood – all of the same dimension'[9] (Ex. 8).

Ex. 8 Mosaic texture

musical space: the registral range of sounds used in a work.[10] Carter has written of an 'emancipated' musical space, freed of the gravitational division between soprano, alto, tenor and bass voices that are taught in traditional music theory. The First Etude of the *Eight Etudes and A Fantasy* emancipates musical space by frequently crossing the instrumental lines (Ex. 9).

musical time: Carter describes musical time as a special temporal condition which brings together the properties of objectively measured time and subjectively experienced time.[11]

polyrhythm: simultaneous statement of different divisions of a beat, or of a larger temporal duration. With simple polyrhythms, such as three against two, the pulses coincide often. Carter, however, often makes use of slow polyrhythms that rarely coincide. *esprit rude/esprit doux*, for instance is based on a pattern of 21:25 stretched over the entire work. See *structural polyrhythm*.

Ex. 9 Musical space 'emancipated'

rhythmic characters: different styles of rhythmic performance which vary in their relation to strict metronomic time. See *fantastico, rubato, accelerando, tempo giusto*.

rubato: a *rhythmic character*; indicates that notated durations are to be stretched or compressed (Ex. 10).

Ex. 10 'Rubato' character

spatial set: a group of pitches whose relation is primarily understood in terms of *musical space* rather than linearly; a spatial set is thus different from the usual sequential notion of a series.) In Carter's music the spatial set usually takes the form of a *twelve-tone tonic chord*.

stratification: division of the musical texture into separate layers with contrasting harmonies, tone-colors, rhythms and expressive characters. Counterpoint based on stratification rather than imitation is fundamental to Carter's music from the Second Quartet onward. An elegant example of stratification is the duet *esprit rude/esprit doux* for flute and clarinet. Each instrument has its own intervallic vocabulary. The flute plays minor thirds, major thirds, perfect fourths, minor sevenths and major sevenths; the clarinet, minor seconds, major seconds, perfect fifths, minor sixths and major sixths. Each instrument plays rhythms derived from the slow pulses of a 25:21 *structural polyrhythm* which begins in both parts on the downbeat of bar 6 and does not coincide again until the down beat of the last bar. The slow pulses of this polyrhythm are exposed in bars 51 to 61 where the flute plays durations of 42 triplet eighths and the clarinet, durations of 56 quintuplet sixteenths (Ex. 11).

structural polyrhythm: a slow *polyrhythm* used as the background rhythmic structure of a piece. Carter first employed this idea in the Introduction and Coda to the Double Concerto; in his later music the calculation of a structural polyrhythm on graph paper is usually the first step in composition, a clear indication, if one were needed, that for Carter rhythm always comes first, albeit in a highly abstract form. In explaining a

esprit rude/esprit doux

Ex. 11 Stratified texture

technique which may appear arcane, and which is rarely audible to the listener, Carter has said that he wanted to develop a more systematic way of approaching all the tempo relations in a piece, and also wanted to develop the structural equivalent of the slow phrase rhythms of tonal music. In practice Carter feels free to make the structural polyrhythm explicit at some points in a piece while not articulating it at others and he has also felt free to omit parts of the polyrhythm, as he did in the last section of the *Triple Duo*.[12]

tempo giusto: a *rhythmic character*; indication that rhythmic values are to be strictly observed. Carter often uses the term *meccanico* to indicate this style of playing.

tempo modulation: see *metrical modulation*.

2nd violin pulse	Tempo	Ratio
♩.=70	♪=105	2:3
♩=70	♪=140	1:2
(5-tuplet) ♪⸝=70	♪=112	5:8
♩=70	♫.=112	5:8
	♪=186.7	3:8
♩..=70	♪.=163.3	3:7
(3-tuplet) ♪♪⸝⸝=70	♪=93.3	3:4
♩ ♪=70	♪=175	2:5
(5-tuplet) ♩ ♪⸝⸝=70	♩=84	5:6
(7-tuplet) ♫♫♫♫⸝=70	♩.=60	7:6

Chart 5 Tempo relations in the 2nd String Quartet

time screen: Carter uses this term to picture the way *musical time* is projected on real time; his sketches indicate that he thinks of the time screen as a construction of a field of related *metronomic speeds*.[13] The tempo field for the Second Quartet, based on a fundamental pulse of MM 70 is typical (Chart 5).

twelve-tone tonic chords: recurring twelve-note harmonies or *spatial sets* that define the harmonic identity of a work. Carter has pointed to the precedents of Scriabin, Strauss and Stravinsky for his use of a distinctive harmony in each work. Such a 'tonic' chord first appears in the Double Concerto where it is made up of sixteen pitches. The Piano Concerto used two contrasting 'tonic' chords while *A Symphony of Three Orchestras* employs four. In *Night Fantasies* Carter first used a large family of twelve-tone chords related by a similar symmetrical structure (Chart 6).

Chart 6 Twelve-note chords in the: (a) Concerto for Orchestra, (b) Third Quartet, (c) *A Symphony of Three Orchestras*

Addendum: terminology

American	British
whole note	semibreve
half note	minim
quarter note	crotchet
eighth note	quaver
sixteenth note	semiquaver
thirty-second note	demisemiquaver
sixty-fourth note	hemidemisemiquaver
measure (or bar)	bar
half-step	semitone
English horn	cor anglais

Notes

1 See James Boros, 'Some Properties of the all-interval hexachord', *In Theory Only* 11, 6, pp. 19–41.
2 Mengelberg and Ferentz, 'On Eleven-interval Twelve-tone Rows', *PNM* 3, 2 (Spring–Summer 1965), pp. 93–103.
3 CEL, p. 233.
4 CEL, p. 142.
5 CEL, p. 227.
6 FW, p. 99.
7 *MQ* XXIX, 2 (April 1943), pp. 169–87.
8 For a detailed discussion of the evolution of Carter's rhythmic language, see Bernard, *PNM*.
9 CEL, p. 226.

10 See the discussion of musical space in Robert Cogan and Pozzi Escot, *Sonic Design* (Englewood Cliffs, N. J.: Prentice Hall, 1976), pp. 12–85.

11 See Carter's essays on musical time in CEL, pp. 224–228, 262–281, 313–319 and Jonathan Bernard's discussion of these essays in Bernard, *MQ*.

12 See John F. Link, 'Long-Range Polyrhythms in Elliott Carter's Recent Music.'

13 See 'Music and the Time Screen,' CEL, pp. 262–281.

1 Chamber Music

1 String Quartets

Carter's five quartets are the spinal column of his body of works. Written between 1950 and 1996, they take up the genre of the modernist string quartet where Bartók had left off. Like the Bartók quartets, Carter's are virtuosic and meditative, emotionally intense yet structurally rigorous. Like Beethoven's and Bartók's, they may be seen to form a spiritual autobiography.

The first four quartets have been recorded, at the time of writing, by the Composers, Juilliard and Arditti Quartets; the last group has also recorded the Fifth. Of all Carter's works the quartets have had the most benefit of interpretive attention by players and an evolving critical reception. Like all performed art works, they have 'grown up,' and in unexpected ways. The Third Quartet, which at the time of its première seemed the *ne plus ultra* of musical difficulty, has turned into something of a crowd pleaser. It is the most extroverted and colorful of the quartets, and listeners find it easy to follow in live performance where the contrasts between the duos are visible as well as audible. The Second Quartet, which also gained an early reputation as a challenging work for players and listeners, now sounds like the most classical of the four because of its concision, formal clarity and relative lightness of texture. The audience may read about Samuel Beckett and Charles Ives in the program notes (or in this book), but what they hear has the elegance and emotional warmth of a Mozart quartet. The Fourth Quartet, by contrast, elicits perplexed reactions from listeners. Some have compared it to Beethoven in its eloquent dramatic conflicts, or Schubert in the lyrical outbursts of its last movement, but others find its dense argument difficult to untangle; the scherzando movement, in particular, seems to pose problems for performers who have not yet found out how to project its comic inversion of ideas heard in more serious terms in the opening section.

The First Quartet, the work that put Carter on the musical map, now sounds isolated from the others, almost the work of a different composer (even though its echoes can be heard in the Fourth). In the note to the revised edition of 1994 Carter says that the First Quartet 'is primarily a linear, melodic work like many of my earlier ones, and differs from my later work, which deals with other concerns.' On all-Carter programs, the First inevitably is played last, not necessarily because it is most accessible, but because it remains the grandest of the quartets in conception, the one that stands closest, for all the innovations of its syntax, to Beethovenian models. Where the other quartets demand concentrated listening, the first calls for an expansive, imaginative response; the listener has to create a mental movie for which the quartet, so rich in its evocative powers and broad in its vision, is the soundtrack. The Fifth Quartet came as a delightful surprise to those who heard its New York première. Although full of Carterian materials, it views them from a new vantage point, surrounding them with a contemplative, other-worldly silence. The music, which alternates movements and the sound of 'practicing,' felt lace-like (Carter would know all about lace) because its tenuous continuity contains so many holes. Once more Carter had redefined the medium.

Quartet No. 1

Carter has written the following about the origins of the First Quartet:

> The First Quartet was 'written largely for my own satisfaction and grew out of an effort to understand myself', as the late Joseph Wood Krutch (a neighbor during the 1950–51 year of this quartet) wrote of his book *The Modern Temper*. For there were so many emotional and expressive experiences that I kept having, and so many notions of processes and continuities, especially musical ones – fragments I could find no ways to use in my compositions – that I decided to leave my usual New York activities to seek the undisturbed quiet to work these out. The decision to stay in a place in the lower Sonora Desert near Tucson, Arizona, brought me by chance into contact with that superb naturalist Joe Krutch who was then writing *The Desert Year*. Our almost daily meetings led to fascinating talks about the ecology of the region – how birds, animals, insects, and plants had adapted to the heat and the limited water supply, which consists of infrequent, spectacular, but brief cloudbursts that for an hour seem about to wash everything away, and then very long droughts. There were trips to remote places such as Carr Canyon, the wild-bird paradise, but mainly it was right around the house that exotica (for an Easterner) could be seen – comic road runners, giant suguaros, flowering octillos, all sharing this special dry world. It was indeed a kind of 'magic mountain' and its specialness (for me) certainly encouraged the specialness (for me at that time) of the Quartet as I worked on it during the fall and winter of '50 and the spring of '51.[1]

By going to the desert, Carter left his routine patterns of living in order to discover a new kind of time. Friends refer to this time in the desert as a 'conversion,' for a new composer emerged with the First Quartet, uncompromising and visionary:

> I decided for once to write a work very interesting to myself, and so say to hell with the public and with the performers too. I wanted to write a work that carried out completely the various ideas I had at that time about the form of music, about texture and harmony – about everything.[2]

The First Quartet was not commissioned but it was composed while Carter had a Guggenheim fellowship. Carter doubted if it would ever be performed. He submitted it, however, to the Concours à Quattuor de Liège. Although he felt that sending the score to Belgium (in the *nom de concours* of 'Chronometros') was like dropping a message-filled bottle off a boat in mid-ocean, he was later surprised to read that the Quartet had been awarded first prize. The Liège competition was supposed to give the première of its winning composition, but in fact the work was first played in New York before the prize was awarded, by the Walden Quartet on 26 February 1953 at McMillan Theater, Columbia University. (Carter notes that this performance forced him to renounce the Liège prize). An important European performance was given by the Parrenin Quartet in Rome in April 1954 at a festival sponsored by the Congress for Cultural Freedom. This performance, attended by Luigi Dallapiccola, Goffredo Petrassi, Roman Vlad and William Glock, among others, immediately established Carter's European reputation.[3]

The First Quartet approaches the scale of Beethoven's op. 127 or Schoenberg's op. 7. It owes little to the classical tradition, though it is clearly indebted to the examples of Berg's *Lyric Suite*, Bartók's Fourth Quartet and, in particular, Ruth Crawford's String Quartet. As Carter has often stated, the wealth of relationships and dreamlike continuity of the quartet were meant to translate the formal devices of Eliot, Joyce, Proust or Eisenstein into musical terms.

The Quartet is divided into four movements – Fantasia, Allegro scorrevole, Adagio, Variations – which flow into one another. The stream of music, however, is broken twice, dividing the music into three parts; the breaks do not correspond to the divisions between movements and are heard as arbitrary interruptions of the musical flow. This startling formal gesture underscores the poetic role of change in the music. The climactic moments of the work transform one movement into the next; to break between movements would have meant leaving out the crucial musical events of the work. The breaks during movements dramatize the contrast between the special time world of the Quartet and the general, everyday time that surrounds it.

The fundamental harmonic matter of the First Quartet, the all-interval four-note chord (0, 1, 4, 6), appears at the opening in several forms, most clearly as a harmony in bar 5 and as a melodic motive in bars 11 and 12 (Ex. 12). This chord occurs in various spacings, inversions and transposi-

String Quartet No. 1
© 1956 Associated Music Publishers, Inc. Used by permission

Ex. 12 Statements of all-interval tetrachord

tions throughout the piece, more as a primal sonority like the 'Elektra chord' than as the systematic fusion of intervallic harmonies that Carter would use it in later works. The music, though far more chromatic than any of Carter's previous music, is full of triads, though these, too, are treated as sonorities, not functional harmonies; the bass is nowhere given the structural function it plays in tonal music. Though much of the piece sounds atonal, it begins and ends with important emphases on the pitch E and gives much evidence of careful attention to the linear motion of pitch. The opening, for instance, emphasizes the chromatic neighbors of E, and an audible chromatic progression is heard from the first E to the F in bar 12, and to the G in bar 20 which leads, linearly, to the G sharp in the second violin in bar 22. Although various kinds of post-tonal thinking are evident in the quartet, harmonic analysis should also consider these linear and pitch-centric aspects of its language.

In one respect the First Quartet remains unique in Carter's oeuvre – its cinematic continuity. Because the music unfolds in a more sustained way than is the case in most of Carter's later works, the transition of one idea to the next plays a more important role. In this work Carter set himself the challenge of writing music without traditional phrase structures such as antecedent-consequent phrase pairs, sequences or ostinati, without imitative counterpoint and also without motivic development – all traditional ways of sustaining the musical argument. He developed a repertory of transitional devices in this work that have few precedents in earlier music. Consider, for example, the entrance of the second violin after the opening cello solo. It begins its pizzicato line in bar 12, drops out after four bars, and then begins again at 22 – the first time, to my knowledge, that a composer has written a mistaken entrance into a piece. There are many other similar surprises in the first movement: the unprepared irruption of fast music in the first violin at 103 that disappears five bars later as mysteriously as it began; or the appearance at 46 and 206 of passages where two instruments seem to violate the contrapuntal premise of the music by doubling a line in octaves, a deviation which has its 'pay off' after 296 where a three-octave doubling opposes the rising line of the viola. All these surprises work against the more apparent organicism of the piece in which ideas seem to emerge from others in a flowing manner. In general, the continuity devices that Carter employs create a syntax of fluid free-association. Ideas appear without motivation or preparation; they are not answers to questions. Most frequently Carter overlaps ideas so that the listener may not notice where a particular idea begins or ends, like a thought that becomes conscious only after we have been mulling on it for some time.

Fantasia The title implies a musical/psychological double meaning, bringing together Henry Purcell and William James. The music is a contrapuntal study and also an evocation of the stream of consciousness. The counterpoint is not fugal, but it does employ devices of invertible counterpoint. Instead of imitating each other, the instruments superimpose different ideas (Ex. 13). Five main themes (and many subsidiary ones) are presented in changing combinations. Theme 4 begins with a quotation from the opening of Charles Ives's First Violin Sonata, a score Ives had given Carter. The tempo of the music changes frequently as different speeds are superimposed, but there is rarely a sense of a simple tempo. The listener hears cross-tempi which rapidly change in character as faster or slower strands come to prominence or fade into the background.

Ex. 13 Superimposed themes

Some of the main themes are shown in Chart 7 (see over page).

Each theme has an identifying intervallic shape, gesture and absolute speed. As the tempo changes, the notation of the themes will also change. This process can be seen by comparing violin I at bar 22 with violin II at bar 58; both are playing theme 2 which has an absolute speed of MM 36. In the first violin this speed is notated in durations of ten triplet eighths at a tempo of quarter=120; in the second violin it is notated as five quarter-note beats at a tempo of quarter = 180 (Ex. 14).

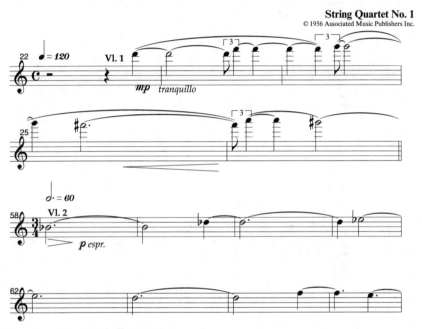

String Quartet No. 1
© 1956 Associated Music Publishers Inc.

Ex. 14 Renotation of rhythmic values

Like the first movement of the Cello Sonata, the Fantasia is in three large sections. These, however, are prefaced by an opening cello solo (bars 1–22) which returns an octave higher in the viola (with new counter-point) in bars 138–165 to mark the beginning of the middle section of the movement. The cello solo, besides making several statements of the all-interval tetrachord, also forecasts some of the most important thematic material of the entire work. Bars 3 and 4 suggest the upper duo of the Adagio, bars 5 and 6 the lower duo, while bars 7 and 8 anticipate one of the motifs from the Variations. What is not anticipated in the cadenza is the dynamic rhythmic character of the work. Carter has written that the

Chart 7 String Quartet No. 1: Fantasia, main themes

relation of the cadenza to the rest of the work was inspired by Jean Cocteau's film *Le Sang d'un Poete* 'in which the entire dreamlike action is framed by an interrupted slow-motion shot of a tall brick chimney in an empty lot being dynamited. Just as the chimney begins to fall apart, the shot is broken off and the entire movie follows, after which the shot of the chimney is resumed at the point it left off, showing its disintegration in mid-air, and closing the film with its collapse on the ground . . . I interpret Cocteau's idea (and my own) as establishing the difference between external time (measured by the falling chimney or cadenza) and internal dream time (the main body of the work) – the dream lasting but a moment of external time but from the dreamer's point of view a long stretch.'[4] The cadenza frames the dream-world of the Quartet, but lies outside it. The unexpected reprise of the cadenza in the viola at the start of the development section feels like a passing moment of insomnia. Carter makes a rhythmic transition out of both passages by changing the lengths of bars from 10/16 to 9/16 so that the pulse accelerates – passages that gave rise to the term metrical modulation.

The 'exposition,' bars 22–138 explores the combinational possibilities of the main themes. In bars 22–24 themes 2, 1 and 7 are superimposed; theme 3 enters the texture in bar 25 and theme 4 comes in at 27. Theme 5 enters in bar 41 and theme 6 first appears in bar 50. Theme 8 appears first in the viola in bar 70; because it has the most lyrical character of all the themes it takes on something of the structural role of a traditional second subject, a function strengthened by the restatement of this theme in the first violin at 112, transposed an octave and a half-step higher. The middle section, launched after the viola's unexpected restatement of the opening cello cadenza, at bar 138, develops the rhythmic processes of the first section. Instead of the harmonic regions that would appear in a tonal development section, Carter uses new regions of tempo in the middle section. The themes are distorted and transmuted under the influence of large polyrhythmic events such as the remarkable prolation at 198 where each line as it enters moves at a speed one and a half times faster than the previous line. The 'development' might be divided into two contrasting sections. From 180 to the climax at bar 204 Carter explores changing polyrhythmic ratios in two accelerating phrases. From 182 to 192 the first violin anchors this process by stating a constant pulse of MM 60; in bars 190–203 the cello takes over this function with a constant pulse of MM 56. The second half of the development begins at 206 with a mutated version of theme 2 stated in octaves in the second violin and violas

String Quartet No. 1
© 1956 Associated Music Publishers Inc.

(1) (♩. = 60)

(2)

Ex. 15 Climax and transition

surrounded by rapid lines in the other instruments; the theme 2 variant
ends at 227 with a cadence of three repeated chords that anticipates an
important figure from the last movement (and was anticipated in bars 5
and 6). At 228 the texture once again superimposes four different ideas,
though none of them is a strict restatement of one of the themes; this
passage could be termed a false recapitulation. It leads to a dramatic
restatement of the theme 2 variant at 255. This statement begins with
a stronger appearance of the three-chord cadence, which develops to a
climax at 295 but is interrupted by reappearances of the original themes
beginning at 275. The 'development' and 'recapitulation' thus overlap;
but the recapitulation itself appears in highly varied form with new textures and a reordering of themes. Theme 7 appears as a quasi-unison at
275; theme 5 comes back at 280. Against the dramatic extension of the
three-chord theme and themes 5 and 7 in violin I, violin II and the cello,

the viola enters unobtrusively with theme 4, the Ives theme in augmentation. At 311 the texture once again changes, producing the effect of a recapitulation/coda. Now the four themes are superimposed: theme 5 in violin I; theme 8 in violin II; theme 4 continuing in the viola and theme 3 in the cello (Ex. 15 – see pages 62–3). Because of the prominence of the lyrical theme 8, this passage has the effect of a return of the 'second group,' but the texture gradually changes. The first violin moves ever upward in register, until it intertwines with the high violin II line at 345. The Ives theme in the viola gradually accelerates until it approaches the speeds of the other themes. A dynamic and registral peak is reached at 347 over a high pedal in the cello. Against this pedal, violin II begins to play rapid notes; as they continue and the pedal drops out we suddenly find ourselves in the new texture of the Allegro scorrevole.

Allegro scorrevole The Fantasia's contrast of speeds gives way to a uniform motion of sixteenth notes at MM 540 – a tempo associated with theme 6 in the Fantasia. Thematic contrast similarly is replaced by the mosaic development of a seven-note figure containing the four-note all-interval chords (Ex. 16). This figure is inverted, played backwards, transposed, fragmented, permuted. The form of this movement suggests an alternation between scherzo and trio; the second statement of the scherzo, however, is interrupted by the break between movements I and II. The scherzo begins again after this break and the trio returns but only for its opening section. Instead of a third return of the scherzo, which we might expect on the model of Beethoven, the second appearance of the trio leads directly to the Adagio. The 'scherzo' sections are reminiscent of the Allegro misterioso of Berg's *Lyric Suite* while the 'trio' sections suggest, in passing, the 'Tenebroso' passages of that work. The first scherzo runs from bar 356 to 378. The trio enters with sustained notes at 379; this dramatic contrast in mood is not treated as simply as in the Berg model, for the slow music evolves to a more dramatic section which is built around a passionate cello solo in bars 394–426. The sustained passage return at 427, so that it functions as a frame for the more agitated passage, but the long notes now begin with a pizzicato attack. At 442 the scorrevole music begins again, but is now developed at greater length.

Though he avoids imitative counterpoint, Carter employs traditional contrapuntal devices such as pedal and stretto, but also some novel inventions. At 513 each instrument states a different fragment of the theme.

Violin I plays a two-note figure in an implied metre of 5/16 (the passage is notated in 6/16); violin II plays a four-note figure in 8/16; the viola plays a five-note figure in 7/16 and the cello plays a three-note figure in 6/16. Beginning at 501, Carter launches a new counterpoint of widely spaced

Ex. 16 Mosaic development

held notes so that the texture becomes a double mosaic, particularly after 525. The appearance of held notes relates the scorrevole to the 'trio'; but it also sets up a subliminal cadence on the final note before the interruption. The four final sustained notes, C in the cello, B in violin II, G in the viola and G sharp in violin I, state the all-interval tetrachord.

Adagio   The alternating fast and slow sections of the Allegro scorrevole polarized musical time; the Adagio polarizes musical space. Though the

Ex. 17 High point and transition

music often sounds Ivesian, the model for its dialogue is the Andante con moto of Beethoven's Fourth Piano Concerto, which also inspired the second movement of Carter's Sonata for Flute, Oboe, Cello and Harpsichord. The quartet divides into two duos playing apparently unrelated music. Viola and cello sound a passionate recitative. The violins, beginning almost inaudibly in their highest register, state the tranquil idea first heard in bars 3 and 4 of the quartet. The duos are first heard separately, then are superimposed. The lower duo gradually ascends while the violins move slowly downwards, so that by bar 110 their opening vertical relationship is reversed. At bar 130 the instruments seem to meet in a unified, expressive 'slow movement' – but their communion is fleeting; the two pairs restate their oppositions briefly, but with climactic finality from bars 150 to 155. Once more the texture changes dramatically at a registrally high point: beginning with the pianissimo sustained minor third in the violins all four instruments join in a rapid unbroken stream of sixteenths (Ex. 17 – see pages 66–7).

Against the flowing scales, angular motifs erupt as triple-stopped chords or in pizzicato. These motifs, beginning with the final viola and cello statement of the Adagio, are the themes of the Variation movement. They are subjected to the variation process as soon as they appear, spinning faster and faster until they vanish, exposing new slower motifs to the cyclonic process of the music. When the first group of themes have spun beyond the vanishing-point, the music suddenly breaks off.

Variations   Although Part III is entitled Variations, variations have been in progress since bar 167 of Part II. Those before the break will reappear at bar 334 of Part III, marking the completion of a cycle. The themes are not large phrase structures, but melodic or rhythmic ideas. Carter has said: 'I wanted the wind to blow through the music.' He alters the traditional variation form which consists of a series of discreet episodes. Here the themes are melodic, motivic or rhythmic ideas, not large phrase structures. Instead of varying one idea after another Carter has, as it were, shuffled variational fragments on several themes so that they appear, vanish and reappear unpredictably; the Variations are as 'fantastic' in continuity as was the opening Fantasia. To ensure some unity to this complex arrangement, Carter used a single variational device: acceleration. He employs the familiar idea of 'divisions,' but here the different themes accelerate in differing ways. There are seven main themes, here shown in their slowest form.

Chart 8 String Quartet No. 1: Variations, main themes

Several of the themes are polyrhythmic; at the beginning of the Variations Carter quotes a passage from Conlon Nancarrow's Study No. 1 as a homage to his polyrhythmic experiments. As these themes accelerate, their component pulses are split between different instruments as at bars 209 and 294 (Ex. 18). As the themes become faster, their character changes as well. The passacaglia-like minor thirds of the opening eventually turn into a tremolando, while the slow chorale-like chords gradually evolve back into the slashing polyrhythmic triple-stops first heard in the coda of II. The recurrence of the coda of II at bar 334 of III serves as an important landmark. The listener now becomes aware that the themes

String Quartet No. 1

Ex. 18 Polyrhythmic theme

have evolved into the motifs heard during the fade-out of II. The variational process does not stop here, however. The themes continue to
accelerate into new forms, which begin to connect the Variations to the
Fantasia. The slowest and last theme to appear (in the first violin at bar
281) evolves very gradually while the other material speeds off into the
distance. Its intervals gradually expand as it accelerates, until it is finally
transformed into the motif of the opening cello cadenza, now grandly
expounded by the first violin (Ex. 19). With the most stunning gesture of
all, the first violin competes the motion of the work in solitude, slowing
the music to stillness on a celestial high E.

Ex. 19 Concluding violin solo

Quartet No. 2

*Commissioned by the Stanley String Quartet; completed Waccubuc, N.Y., 19
March 1959. Awarded the Pulitzer Prize 1960, The New York Music Critics
Circle Award, 1960 and The UNESCO First Prize, 1961. First performance: The
Juilliard Quartet (Robert Mann, Isidore Cohen, Raphael Hillyer, Claus Adam),
Juilliard School, N.Y., 25 March 1960.*

Hearing them (the First and Second Quartets) now, I get the impression of their living in different time worlds, the First in an expanded one, the Second in a condensed and concentrated one although this was hardly a conscious opposition at the times of their composition. Each presents as different a version of the humanly experienced time as the two imagined by Thomas Mann in 'By the Ocean of Time,' a chapter in *The Magic Mountain*, where he writes: 'It would not be hard to imagine the existence of creatures perhaps upon smaller planets than our own, practising a miniature time economy . . . And, contrariwise, one can conceive of a world so spacious that its time system too has a majestic stride . . .'

Although both quartets are concerned with motion, change, progression in which literal or mechanical repetition finds little place, yet the development of musical expression and thought during the eight years that separates them seems to me far-reaching. The difference, aside from that of timescales, might be compared to the types of continuities found in Mann's own writings, where in the earlier ones, characters maintain their characterized identities with some revelatory changes throughout a work, while in the Joseph novels, each character is an exemplification of an archetype whose various other incarnations are constantly referred to (as Joyce does in another way in *Finnegans Wake*). Recurrence of ideas in the First Quartet is, then, more nearly literal than in the Second where recall brings back only certain traits of expression – 'behavior patterns', speeds and interval-sounds – that form the basis of an ever-changing series of incarnations but link these together as a group. The musical language of the Second Quartet emerged almost unconsciously through working during the fifties with ideas the First gave rise to.[5]

The Second Quartet, as its long list of prizes indicates, marked Carter's belated arrival in American musical life. Owing to lucid technique it has probably been more analysed than any of his other works. Its stratified intervallic and rhythmic designs seemed close to the serialism emerging on American campuses in the late fifties, though the distance in temperament separating Carter from the academic serialists is obvious in the 'Shop Talk' interview given at Princeton in 1960,[6] and in the 'conversation' with Ben Boretz published in *Perspectives of New Music* in 1971. Carter's own discussion of the Second Quartet makes it clear that the novel techniques of the piece stemmed from poetic considerations which were themselves intensifications of the expressive researches of the First

Quartet. Parts of the earlier Quartet sounded like four independent pieces being played simultaneously. This conceit subverts the social contract of ensemble playing and became the essence of the Second, which might have been entitled 'Four Players in Search of a Quartet.' Indeed, Carter originally wanted the four instruments to sit as far apart as possible 'like characters in a Beckett play' – though this has not proved possible in live performance.

The technical rigor of the Second Quartet served a dramatic end. Carter simplified the game-rules of his music in order to create a complex, compact totality. The musical elements are rigorously partitioned among the four instruments. Intervals, speeds, colours and gestures are divided up to create four 'character-continuities.' (See Chart 3, page 36.)

The first violin is 'fantastic, ornate, mercurial,' the second violin 'has a laconic, orderly character which is sometimes humorous.' The viola is 'expressive,' the cello 'impetuous.' The resulting texture has little in common with that found in other quartets, though the contrast of characters may have been suggested by the second movement, 'Arguments,' of Ives's Second Quartet – Ives's conservative, square, second fiddle, Rollo, shares some traits with the second violin here. Unlike the textures of a Haydn or Beethoven quartet, the four instruments do not share material – not until the fourth movement – nor do they play accompaniment, background figuration. Instead of sharing the burden of musical exposition, as in the obligato counterpoint of the classical quartet, here each instrument is like a character in an opera made up primarily of quartets. (Carter had in mind particularly the quartets from *Aida* and *Otello*.) As in opera, the dramatic interest stems from the changing relations between characters. Carter cites three kinds of relations in the Quartet: discipleship, companionship and confrontation. The instruments either imitate each other, co-operate to create overall effects, or oppose one another. The form of the work expresses these relations in terms of two interlaced processes. Within the frame of the introduction and coda, the four movements move towards greater co-operation, while the three cadenzas dramatize increasing opposition – the form is a double curve, played without interruption (Chart 9, page 74).

As Carter points out, the four characters are archetypical musicians – the first violin is a virtuoso, interested mainly in showing off, the viola is a bit too-consistently doleful, the cello self-indulgently romantic; the second violin, like a composer, tries to create order among its narcissistic neighbors. Psychologically the four could be termed manic, compulsive,

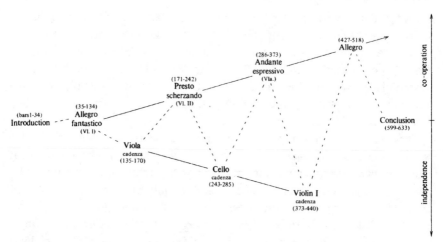

Chart 9 Formal plan

depressive, hysterical. But perhaps more relevantly to the specific forms the characters take on in the music, the four instruments exist in independent time-worlds – like the mysterious figures in Kafka's parables. The first violin plays in a fragmented way, making sharp contrasts between fast and slow motion; it seems to be unaware of time. The second violin recalls Carter's description of the French organist's improvisations, 'ticking away like a complicated clock, insensitive to the human meaning of its minutes and hours.' The viola, playing with a constant expressive rubato, stretches and bends clock-time to match its moods, while the cello accelerates and ritards in great sweeping arcs, imposing its own subjective time-experience on the others, until it finally draws them all into a speeding whirlpool (bars 563–90).

The sharply opposed worlds of the four instruments create a nervous, alienated mood, familiar from the experiences of urban life where many psychological types co-exist. The music is fragile, punctured with silences and shadows. The characters could be drawn by Giacometti – they are always on the edge of a threatening emptiness. They express themselves in contrasting aphorisms of despair; even the opening cello phrase seems a contraction of the heroic cello cadenza that introduced the First Quartet – not a 'novel in a sigh,' but a neurotic tic.

The Second Quartet synthesizes the formal patterns of the First Quartet and Variations for Orchestra. There are nine sections, played without a break: Introduction, Allegro fantastico, Cadenza for Viola, Presto scherzando, Cadenza for Cello, Andante espressivo, Cadenza for Violin I, Allegro, Conclusion.

These sections form an interwoven double-series, framed by the Introduction and Conclusion. The four 'movements' resemble, in their sequence of tempi, those of the First Quartet. The first three are dominated by one of the instruments: the Allegro fantastico by violin I; the Presto scherzando by violin II; the Andante espressivo by the viola. In the four movements there is a progression from opposition to co-operation between the instruments. In the Allegro fantastico the florid character of the first violin contrasts with the fragmented statements by the other instruments, who gradually begin to assert themselves. In the Presto scherzando the second violin maintains a steady pulse of MM 140 in pizzicato against the fragmented, filigree-like commentary of the other instruments, whose tempo is MM 175. With the Andante espressivo the instruments begin to imitate each other. The movement is a four-part distorted canon. Each phrase in the viola is imitated by the other instruments, in answers distorted by their own intervals and expressive habits. In the final Allegro the instruments exchange characters and begin to build common structures. The connective function of the two all-interval tetrachords becomes increasingly clear, and a new rhythmic figure, containing all the polyrhythmic relations of the work, dominates the rhythm – see bars 458–69 and Chart 10. Beginning at bar 549, the pulse rhythm

Chart 10 2nd String Quartet: 'Fusion' motif

String Quartet No. 2
© 1961 Associated Music Publishers, Inc. Used by permission

of the second violin and the florid outbursts of the first are taken up by all
the instruments in a large polyrhythmic design which leads to a group
acceleration, an extension of a gesture previously used only by the cello.
Precisely where all four instruments should fuse, however, at bar 588,

* Throughout the "Conclusion", all the notes of Violin II (usually pizzicato) end motives whose other note or notes are heard in another part.

Ex. 20 Climax

there is a furious explosion of sound whose fragments float slowly away during the conclusion (Ex. 20).

The cadenzas form a contravening series, moving from co-operation to conflict. The viola's solo seems to be greeted by polite laughter, but the cello's large accelerating and retarding phrases are set against a relentless clockwork in the violins. Finally the first violin's cadenza is confronted by the indifference of the other instruments; a palpable silence interrupts the violin's music for four bars at bar 405.

The double series of movements thus creates a twofold progression towards order and unity, and at the same time towards disorder and non-cooperation. The double sequence also allows much of the material of the Quartet to be heard twice, in changed circumstances. The brash fioratura of the first violin in the opening movement becomes alienated and desperate in its cadenza. The viola's warmly expressive music sounds a bit preposterous during its cadenza, but returns to inspire the most emotionally intense music of the Quartet in the Andante espressivo. The cello does not dominate a movement; its cadenza however is the keystone of the work's arch, and its rhythmic contrast of free and mechanical shapes serves as the central image of the Quartet's polarities. Similarly the second violin does not have a cadenza, because its relentless MM 70 pulse is the architectural basis of the Quartet's entire time-world. It alone seems to survive the concluding explosion; in the last pages of the Quartet the second violin completes the fragmented phrases of the other instruments, and it ends the work with a soft statement of one of the all-interval chords plucked quietly at its heart-rate tempo (Ex. 21). Although some listeners have compared the second violin's character to 'Rollo,' the Philistine fiddler in Ives's Second Quartet, he may also represent an aspect of 'Chronometros,' the time-measuring composer, E.C.

Quartet No. 3

The Third Quartet was commissioned by the Juilliard School for the Juilliard Quartet, to whom it is dedicated. It was premièred by the Juilliard Quartet – Robert Mann, Earl Carlyss, Samuel Rhodes and Claus Adam – at Alice Tully Hall, Lincoln Center on 23 January 1973. The Quartet was awarded the Pulitzer Prize for Music in 1973, thirteen years after the Second Quartet was similarly honored.

The Third Quartet is even more unusual than its two predecessors in its textures, form and sonority. It is also far more difficult to perform. Tempo modulations occur so frequently, and the relationships of cross-pulses are so complex that the Composers Quartet employed a tape-recorded click-track to give each player the tempo. (The Juilliard Quartet, though, performed the quartet without such assistance.) Beyond its rhythmic

String Quartet No. 2
© 1961 Associated Music Publishers, Inc. Used by permission

Ex. 21 Conclusion

difficulties, however, the work calls attention to instrumental virtuosity. Triple and quadruple stops abound and pizzicato passages demand a Segovian technique.

The sound, texture, and form of the Third Quartet are inextricable. The

Chart 11 3rd String Quartet: reproduction of Carter's handwritten chart

texture is dense and mysterious. The musical materials are forcefully characterized, not in the psychological manner of the Second Quartet, but in terms of sonority. The listener feels the impact of each highly-colored event: slashing chords, delicate filigree, clockwork pizzicato pulses, flamenco strumming, insect-like buzzing and scurrying, arching expressive lines, motionless, wide-spaced intervals. There is only one phrase in the entire work where the gesture of a single instrument emerges from the dense, overgrown contrapuntal fabric (see the cello, bars 462–3.) Although the instruments are never called upon to produce untraditional sounds, the overall sonority is novel.

The design of the Quartet grows from its fundamental dualism. Sensitive rubato and espressivo gestures are set against mechanical, strict, impersonal ones. The opposition of gestures reflects the opposition of formal strategies. Carter was particularly interested here in developing a form that would be simultaneously organic and fragmented. Events in the work are sometimes gratuitous acts, seemingly without motivation; yet the overall form implies an unbroken circle. The music is at once a series of contrasted episodes and a continuous process.

The scheme of the work extrapolates that of the Adagio of the First Quartet: the four instruments are rigorously divided into two duos playing unrelated music. Where the divided ensemble was but one aspect of the First Quartet's variable contrapuntal texture, in the Third Quartet it is a constant. Violin II and the viola form Duo II; violin I and cello, Duo I. The two duos pursue separate ways, never exchanging material. They are fundamentally opposed in rhythmic style: Duo II plays in strict tempo throughout; all of its material derives from complex cross-pulses. Duo I plays in a rubato style. The listener may invoke a number of analogies as suggested by this pairing of opposites – mechanism against living forms, the right hemisphere of the brain against the left, Apollo against Dionysus.

Duo II plays six different types of music-movements – each associated with an interval:

1. Maestoso – perfect fifth
2. Grazioso – minor seventh
3. Scorrevole – minor second
4. Pizzicato giusto, meccanico – diminished fifth
5. Large tranquillo – major third
6. Appassionato – major sixth

Duo I plays four movements:

1. Furioso – major seventh
2. Leggerissimo – perfect fourth
3. Andante espressivo – minor sixth
4. Pizzicato giocoso – minor third

Duo I uses the major second in all its movements, so that the eleven intervals are partitioned between the two duos. Although the material of each movement is dominated by the sound of a single interval, Carter extends the harmonic partitioning to include all the three- and four-note chords. These are divided into three groups, one for each duo and a third for the harmony between duos. The overall harmony of the Quartet is controlled by a recurring all-interval twelve-note chord first heard in bar 15. The pitch location of each interval in this chord is stressed in each of the individual movements.

The Third Quartet is Carter's most rigorously contrapuntal work. Its technique may be traced to the renaissance counterpoint Carter mastered in Paris. The pulse rhythms of Duo II suggest cantus firmus; but the traditional species of academic counterpoint never extended to rhythmic proportions as complex as 63:64 and 20:21, both of which appear here. Similarly the flamboyant, free textures of Duo I can be seen as an extension of florid counterpoint. As in Renaissance polyphony, the linear motion of each part and the harmonic relation between lines are governed by intervals; but rather than the traditional use of 'consonances,' the controlling elements are the dominant intervals of each movement and the three- and four-note chords associated with them. Thus the polyphony has the rigor of older counterpoint but a much greater range of harmonic possibilities, and a far greater freedom of part-writing.

The contrapuntal technique of each duo appears most clearly in isolation. At bars 67 to 72 Duo II plays its pizzicato meccanico material in changing ratios of cross-pulse (8:15; 9:10). The interval of the diminished fifth appears both linearly and contrapuntally between the two parts, as indicated by the dotted lines. At bars 96–105 the pizzicato giocoso of Duo I is heard alone. It stresses the interval of the minor third linearly and harmonically within each pan; the overall harmony is governed by four-note chords 3, 9, 13 and 14, all of which combine two minor thirds. The rhythm style of both lines is rubato; the changing subdivisions of the beat indicate small ritardandi and accelerandi within each phrase.

The dense counterpoint between duos – as when the two pizzicato episodes are combined at bars 90 to 96 – may remind the listener of the 'textural' music of Ligeti or Xenakis or of Ornette Coleman's 'Free Jazz,' but it is perhaps closer to medieval music. Each duo is complete in itself, the superimposition of contrasted layers reveals a higher unity as intervals, chords and rhythmic styles interact. The play of intervals is particularly striking throughout. At bars 254–62 the major thirds of Duo II's Largo tranquillo are heard against the minor sixths of Duo I's Andante espressivo. The slow gliding motion of each duo contrasts the colours of two intervals. Unlike the textural music it superficially resembles, the Third Quartet is everywhere imbued with the spirit of polyphony. Every note is part of a linear design, so that there is an uninterrupted sense of motion. Listeners returning to the Quartet are often surprised by its sudden transformation before their ears from apparent chaos to clarity.

The movements of each duo are cross-cut in the following order:

Duo II 1, 2, 3, 4, 3, 2, 1, 5, 6, 5, 4, 6
Duo I 1, 2, 3, 4, 2, 1, 4, 3, 2, 4, 1, 3

These sequences are interspersed with silences so that all the movements of both duos are heard in isolation somewhere in the work. The ordering of movements ensures that no two of them in a duo are ever heard in the same succession. The superimposition of movements is planned so that every combination of movements between the two duos is heard. For the overall pattern see Chart 12.

While Duo I has introduced all its material in the first third of the Quartet, Duo II does not reveal its Largo tranquillo and Appassionato material until the second half. Changes from movement to movement in each duo are usually sudden, but are always covered by continuing music in the other duo. The music is thus fragmented and continuous at the same time, combining the arbitrary, 'unmotivated' juxtapositions of collage with the 'motivated' continuity of organic development. Each movement, moreover, though broken up, has one climactic point, as well as more subdued passages, so that there is a continuous give-and-take between the duos in terms of relative importance. Given the mathematical severity of its design, the Quartet is surprisingly dramatic. Because the ten movements are cross-cut there is a great deal of non-literal recapitulation that serves to guide the listener through its tangles of sound. Moreover the sequence of movements emphasizes the superimposition of similar materials: Pizzicato giusto with Pizzicato giocoso from 90–6; Scorrevole and Leggerissimo from 136–51; Largo tranquillo and Andante espressivo from 253–65; Furioso and Appassionato, 410–39. The sequence also

Duo I (played continuously)	Duo II (played continuously)
Furioso	⎰ Maestoso
(pause)	⎱ Maestoso
Leggerissimo ⎤	Maestoso
Leggerissimo ⎬	(pause)
Leggerissimo ⎦	⎰ Grazioso
Andante espressivo ⎤	⎱ Grazioso
Andante espressivo ⎦	⎰ Pizzicato giusto, meccanico
(pause)	⎬ Pizzicato giusto, meccanico
Pizzicato giocoso ⎤	⎱ Pizzicato giusto, meccanico
Pizzicato giocoso ⎬	(pause)
Pizzicato to giocoso ⎦	⎰ Scorrevole
(pause)	⎬ Scorrevole
Leggerissimo ⎤	⎱ Scorrevole
Leggerissimo ⎦	⎰ Pizzicato giusto, meccanico
Furioso ⎤	⎱ Pizzicato giusto, meccanico
Furioso ⎦	⎰ Grazioso
(pause)	⎬ Grazioso
Pizzicato giocoso ⎤	⎱ Grazioso
Pizzicato giocoso ⎦	⎰ Maestoso
Andante espressivo ⎤	⎱ Maestoso
Andante espressivo ⎬	(pause)
Andante espressivo ⎦	⎰ Largo tranquillo
(pause)	⎬ Largo tranquillo
Leggerissimo ⎤	⎱ Largo tranquillo
Leggerissimo ⎦	⎰ Appassionato
Pizzicato giocoso ⎤	⎱ Appassionato
Pizzicato giocoso ⎦	⎰ Largo tranquillo
Furioso ⎤	⎱ Largo tranquillo
Furioso ⎬	(pause)
Furioso ⎦	⎰ Scorrevole
Andante espressivo ⎤	⎱ Scorrevole
Andante espressivo ⎦	⎡ Appassionato
(short pause)	Appassionato
Furioso	⎬ Appassionato
Coda: Furioso; Andante; Leggerissimo;	
Pizzicato giocoso	⎣ Appassionato

Chart 12 Formal plan

brings the most extremely contrasted movements together near the end of the piece: Furioso against Largo tranquillo from 338–52 and Scorrevole against Andante espressivo, 381–95.

The Third Quartet's design is reminiscent of literary works such as

Faulkner's *As I Lay Dying* or Virginia Woolf's *The Waves* in which fractured episodes describe a continuous action from different points of view. Every episode differs in its way of emerging, developing and fading out; each superimposed combination has its own poetry. Compare, for example, the frenzied collision of Leggerissimo and Scorrevole movements with the very different interplay of Leggerissimo and Andante espressivo. The movements are changed by their context so that the focus of the work gradually becomes the connections between the two duos. Beginning at bar 396 these linkages are made explicit as the Appassionato of duo II and the Furioso of duo I are cross-cut at an increasingly rapid pace until they merge in the twelve-note tonic at 429. The harmonic arsenals of each duo are then unleashed in a crossfire of held triple stops beginning at 443 (Ex. 22). This remarkable passage, the Quartet's climax, compresses the material of all the movements. Significantly the work does not end with this gesture. The solo cello at bar 462 – with the one and only individual melodic statement of the Quartet – briefly clears the air: but then fragments of all the movements build to a furious ending – which flows right into the Quartet's opening.

Quartet No. 4

String Quartet No. 4. Dedicated 'To the Composers String Quartet' composed in 1985–6 in New York and Rome. Completed in June 1986. Premièred by the Composers Quartet at Festival Miami, 17 September, 1986. Recorded by the Arditti, Juilliard and Composers Quartets.

The String Quartet No. 4 is a synthesis of the previous three quartets, combining the Beethovenian [or Ivesian] prophetic stance of the First, the instrumental drama of the Second and the complex textures of the Third. It is even less traditional in its syntax, springing as it does from Carter's 'late' technique of polyrhythmic and harmonic organization, and yet closer to the classical quartet in its formal outlines. There are four movements: Appassionato; Scherzando; Lento; Presto. Although they are played without breaks and show no connection with the formal strategies of the sonata, their characters adhere to the classical archetypes. The sound world of the quartet, however, is gritty and acerbic. The emotional tone of the work's opening links it to the tense mood of *In Sleep, In Thunder*; in the course of the work, however, the initial anxieties are challenged and gradually transformed so that in the last movement the music achieves an ecstatic lyric intensity.

String Quartet No. 3
© 1973 Associated Music Publishers, Inc. Used by permission

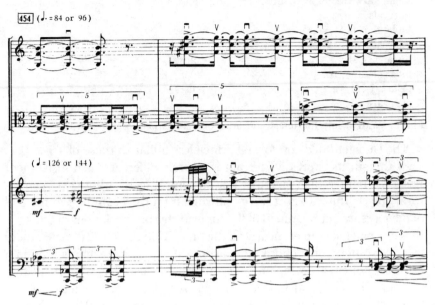

Ex. 22 Triple stops

Speeds calculated on basis of ♩ = 63
Violin I 4/98 M 36/7 = 5.1428. . . .   120 pulses
intervals: 2, 6, 9
Violin II 3/35 M = 5.4   126 pulses
intervals: 3, 6, 11
Viola 5/42 M = 7.5   175 pulses
intervals: 4, 7, 10
Cello 1/15 M = 4.2   98 pulses
intervals: 1, 5, 8

Chart 13 4th String Quartet: stratification of speeds and intervals

The Quartet builds on formal principles similar to those of *Triple Duo*, even though its expressive terrain is entirely different. Each instrument has its own intervallic repertory and structural speed (Chart 13). A structural polyrhythm of 120:126:175:98 runs from the beginning to the end of the piece, resulting, much of the time, in rhythmic relations of 8:6:5:7 – the cello plays septuplets nearly all the time. As in the Third Quartet, there is a twelve-note tonic chord, here arranged as two hexachords around a central tritone with complimentary intervals in parallel order: [8, 2, 1, 5, 3] 6 [4, 10, 11, 7, 9] Carter has analyzed this chord in terms of the intervallic distribution of the instruments (Chart 14). These abstract considerations are made flesh through the characters of the four instrumental protagonists. These characters bear a certain resemblance to those of the Second Quartet – the Fourth can be heard as a twenty-fifth year reunion. The characters have become more complex with age. The first violin is still aggressively flamboyant, dominating the early parts of the work, but its harmonic materials are more consonant than in the Second Quartet, giving its utterances a greater warmth. The second

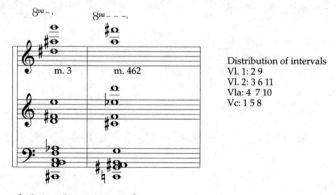

Distribution of intervals
Vl. 1: 2 9
Vl. 2: 3 6 11
Vla: 4 7 10
Vc: 1 5 8

Chart 14 4th String Quartet: tonic harmony

violin, marked 'giocoso, leggero sempre,' formerly an objective time keep-
er, displays a dry wit that turns to anger. The viola, 'cantabile sempre,' is
blithely, persistently, lyrical. The cello, 'capriccioso sempre,' seems mysteriously thoughtful, its utterances sometimes marked (like the composer's) by a hesitant stammer.

The Quartet can be heard as an intensifying dispute, accompanied by a
rising sense of intoxication. The four movements show the characters in
different kinds of conversations, or confrontations. The first violin dominates the opening movement like an irrepressible raconteur, with the other
instruments murmuring submissively. For much of the movement the first
violin is marked dynamically louder than the other instruments, so as to
put it in the spotlight. Surprisingly, though, its line is full of interruptions
and widely spaced notes. Its phrases are often long, irregular accelerandos
or ritardandos, stretching and squeezing the sense of time. The other
instruments occasionally take advantage of the hesitations and pregnant
pauses to assert their own identities. The unpredictable pacing of the first
violin's oration gives the movement an unsettled quality.

The second movement, which seems to begin over the first violin's
repeated objections, is a more even-handed conversation, as the instruments toss phrase fragments back and forth. Again, though, Carter,
invokes classical precedent only to undermine it. The conversation often
sounds less like an ordered debate than like the jabber of monkeys, as the
protagonists interrupt each other, step on each other's lines, or pursue
their own ideas. The second violin and viola, for example, both seem to
get momentarily stuck in their thoughts: see bars 129–132 and 167–173
(Ex. 23). The movement should sound like a parody of the first movement
(much in the way that the Scherzo of the *Hammerklavier* Sonata is a
parody of the Allegro, as Charles Rosen suggests.)

String Quartet No. 4
© 1986 Hendon Music Inc.

Ex. 23

The Lento, almost a chorale, reduces the characters to their harmonic
essence, and forges harmonic connections between them. It is also rent by
silences, which either confirm the possibility of communion, or deny it.

The meditative mood of this movement recalls the Adagio of the First Quartet, but its texture is more flexible. Instead of the rigid separation of tranquility and agitation found in the earlier quartet, here the instruments continually change roles in an evolving dialogue between a slow harmonic progression and expanding lyric utterances. After 294, just as the four instruments seem to be approaching unanimity the second violin nervously breaks the mood. The instruments now force their intervals into a dense cluster.

The Presto sets off from this harmonic black hole with an explosion of lyricism. Carter employs the three-element 'unifying' texture of the last sections of *Triple Duo* and *Penthode*. Expressive lines, pulse lines and filigree move through the Quartet in changing configurations. Individual instruments, however, resist the rush toward an emotional climax. The viola breaks in with its anodyne lyricism at 342, and the second violin registers its displeasure with a 'ruvido' recitative on the G string beginning at 359. The Presto seems to reach its emotional goal in a passionate duet for the first violin and cello from 407 to 430 which suddenly breaks off in silence. In the remarkable coda that follows the unifying and stratifying elements of the piece oppose each other starkly, separated by lengthening silences. The quartet progresses from eloquence, to wit, to communion, to passion, with each of these moods subject to a musical conversation which Andrew Porter has likened to a philosophical colloquy at All Souls'.

Carter had brought together the forces of a rigorously abstract musical language and a high rhetorical drama in many previous works, but in the Fourth Quartet the line between abstract materials and rhetorical gesture is hard to draw, due, perhaps, to the fact that a single system underlies the entire piece. Thus even though the different movements have clearly contrasting characters, they contain similar materials and events, so that there are many echoes and cross-references between them. For example, each movement contains an episode where the instruments form eight-note harmonies out of their constituent intervals (as at bars 65–66; 159–165; 244–246 and 288–295) (Ex. 24). These episodes interrupt the dramatic situation of each movement with an abstract statement of the basic harmonic materials of the piece. They also show that the piece is built not classically but cinematically, like *Triple Duo*, out of many short episodes in changing textures and in unpredictable sequences, with many sudden changes of focus. These relationships confirm the composer's note that the four movements, and their classical associations, are really a

Ex. 24 Harmonic episode

background to the unbroken continuity of the work, the stage on which it is played, so to speak.

At the time of its première, some critics likened the questioning gestures of the coda to late Beethoven. The quartet as a whole has the gravity of, say, op. 127, but Carter still approaches Beethoven through Ives, particularly Ives's Second Quartet. As in the Ives, though in abstract terms, discussion gives way to argument, which in turn gives way to the possibility of a transcendent vision. As in Ives, also, the European ideal of the string quartet as conversation (whether at All Souls' or not) seems both intensified and comically undermined – the four protagonists find it much easier to talk than to listen. Carter has written that the Quartet expresses the relation between individuality and co-operation in a common effort. The clash between these two forces, the sense that one principle will only survive at the expense of the other, is an American conflict, and the pathos of the end of the quartet has strong Ivesian resonances. (I hear this element most clearly in the recording by the Juilliard Quartet.)

Quartet No. 5

The Fifth Quartet was commissioned for the Arditti Quartet (to whom it is dedicated) by Antwerp, City of Culture 1993; Wittener Tage für Neue Musik; Festival d'Automne à Paris; and Lincoln Center, New York. It was composed from January to July 1995 and premièred in Antwerp on 19 September 1995 by the Arditti Quartet.

The Fifth Quartet may be said to mark the beginning of Carter's late late style. Here he strips his music down to its essentials. Carter explained the novel form of the quartet in his program note:

> One of the fascinations of attending rehearsals of chamber music, when excellent players try out fragments of what they later will play in the ensemble then play it and then stop abruptly to discuss how to improve it, is that this pattern is so similar to our inner experience of forming, ordering, focusing and bringing to fruition our feelings and ideas. These patterns of human behavior form the basis of the fifth string quartet.

The music dramatizes two kinds of creative processes simultaneously. The musicians appear to be rehearsing the music and then playing it; the pattern of the music itself, however, suggests the process of composition, where ideas appear as fragments, sometimes to be rejected, at other times coming together to form larger shapes. The sketches show that the compositional process acted out in the music mirrors Carter's own work on the piece; he wrote it in small sections not proceeding linearly from the beginning to the end but gradually putting small phrases together and polishing them.

For its harmonies Carter returned to the tetrachordal system he had used in the second Quartet and Double Concerto. As in the second and fourth quartets each instrument has a vocabulary of intervals, but here they all share intervals with each other:

Violin I		2	3	5		8		
Violin II	1		3			7		10
Viola	1			4	5		9	
Cello		2				6	7	11

The harmonies of the quartet are based on the eight-note chords which contain two all-interval tetrachords (see interval chart for the Double Concerto, Chart 38, page 241).

As in the Second Quartet there are also two different kinds of music in the work. There are six movements, in three pairs: two fast (Giocoso, Allegro energico), two slow (Lento espressivo, Adagio sereno) and two scherzos (Presto scorrevole and Capriccioso). They are heard in the sequence Giocoso, Lento espressivo, Presto scorrevole, Allegro energico, Adagio sereno, Capriccioso. The paired movements are contrasted in mood and tone color. The Giocoso is a light-hearted, fragmented piece dominated by the first violin (the only instrument that does not play pizzicato in this movement); the Allegro energico is more violent and centers around the viola. (Carter's sketches use the term 'viola arrabiata' to describe the instrument's angry gestures.) The Lento espressivo is a Carterian chorale with changing four-to-eight note harmonies; the adagio sereno is played entirely in harmonics, so it sounds like a transposition of the Lento to a higher register. The Presto scorrevole is played in a rapid legato; the Capriccioso is all pizzicato. These movements feel like bagatelles; their styles review all of Carter's string quartet archetypes, as if he were putting his own words in quotation marks. Before and between these movements are an introduction and five interludes of varying length. Here the music is deliberately shapeless and without sustained intention. It floats in a different time world from the purposive focus of the movements. Carter makes the two worlds sound different by thinning the texture drastically. Often one instrument plays at a time and the music is punctured (more than it is punctuated) by rests (Ex. 25).

The relation between movements and interludes also varies in the course of the piece. Movements often begin tentatively during an interlude, though the listener cannot predict which ideas will lead to a fuller statement and which will be left as unexplored experiments. The Giocoso movement officially begins at bar 25, but the first violin has been playing it since bar 21. On the other hand, before the Lento, the instruments seem to be preparing to play the Adagio. Just before the Presto the second violin plays a dramatic phrase, which it takes up again after the Presto. The

Ex. 25 Silence-punctured texture

Allegro energico emerges fragmentarily in the viola during interlude III, beginning at bar 175. In interlude IV the cello puts ideas together to form a passionate solo and in interlude V the first violin continues this gesture but with greater impetuosity. The Adagio sereno attempt to enter during interlude IV, but is interrupted by loud recalls of the Allegro energico. In interlude VI each instrument plays an expressive melody based on its own intervals, but this lyric impulse is undercut by pizzicati beginning in the cello in bar 301 that gradually turn into the Capriccioso.

The effect of the contrast of movements and interludes is paradoxical; the most intense and original parts of the piece are the interludes. Instead of coming together in the 'movements,' the interludes deconstruct the movements, liberating them from their own obsessions, as if Carter was setting himself free of his own clichés. If the work places us inside the mind of the composer, it also allows him to play the role of Prospero dismissing the toys that he has invented. The contrast between interludes and movements is not absolute or static, however. The interludes become more purposive, or perhaps retrospective, as the piece progresses; the movements reach a peak of emotional intensity in the Allegro energico, then move beyond passion and conflict to good-humored acceptance. The piece ends with a smile.

Notes

1 CEL, p. 232.
2 FW, p. 35.
3 See William Glock's review in *Encounter* 2, 6, June 1954.
4 CEL, p. 233.
5 CEL, pp. 231–232.
6 CEL, pp. 214–224.

2 Chamber Music for Wind Instruments

Woodwind Quintet

The Woodwind Quintet was written in 1948 and dedicated to Nadia Boulanger. Its idiom is close to the second movement of the Cello Sonata, which was written at the same time, but it does not pursue the rhythmic experiments of that work. Critics have seen it as a farewell to Carter's Parisian style and Carter has encouraged this view by saying that he wrote it deliberately to be the kind of music Nadia Boulanger always wanted him to compose. His view, though, is anachronistic. At the time it was written Carter was close to Arthur Berger, Harold Shapero and Irving Fine, and his quintet reflects the aesthetic of the 'Boston neo-Classicists' as they were called. Moreover, sketches from this period show that Carter was continuing to draft music in a far more conservative style than the one indicated by the Cello Sonata, and had not yet made a decisive break with the past. The divertimento style of the Quintet does not necessarily relegate it to the category of neo-Classicism, for Carter would continue to write works of this character in between weightier compositions, as evidenced by the Sonata for Flute, Oboe, Cello and Harpsichord, the Brass Quintet and even *Triple Duo*.

The Woodwind Quintet displays a Haydnesque inventiveness in instrumental counterpoint and a concise formal design. The work is in two movements, contrasting B minor and B flat major in a way familiar from the Piano Sonata and *Emblems*. The opening texture, however, is prophetic. Each instrument plays individually characterized material: the flute, a lyrical theme; the oboe, a staccato, mechanical pulse; the clarinet, dramatically flamboyant runs; the horn, sustained notes; the bassoon, light, irregular staccato phrase groups. In the course of the movement these personality traits are contrasted in various ways and migrate from instrument to instrument, so that at the recapitulation only the horn, the outsider of the ensemble, retains its original role. The contrast of instruments recalls places in Milhaud's six little symphonies; but it is not pursued here with far-reaching effect, for there is also much traditional thematic thinking.

The second movement is a jazz-inspired rondo. The bouncy opening material returns in ever-intensified variations. Beginning with breathy fragments, the movement builds in energy, sending up loudly syncopated bursts of sound like a miniature fireworks display. The pop sounding materials evolve toward combustion in a way similar to the *Holiday Overture*.

Eight Etudes and a Fantasy
for Woodwind Quartet (flute, oboe, clarinet and bassoon), 1950

The *Eight Etudes* began as blackboard exercises. Carter taught a class in orchestration at Columbia University in 1949. The class had the services of a few excellent players trained by Richard Franko Goldman and the students were expected to compose works for that ensemble. Disappointed in his students' efforts, Carter began to sketch small woodwind pieces on the blackboard, each one exploiting a different aspect of the ensemble. The Etudes became studies for Carter as well as his students. By isolating specific compositional problems he discovered many of the techniques that would become the basis of his mature style.

Etude I   A study of the musical space defined by the four woodwinds. Besides defining the limits of the available range, it compresses a large variety of textures – unisons, doublings, canonic imitation, free counterpoint of contrasting materials – within twenty-four bars. Carter was particularly interested in the varied spacing and doubling of chords. The instrumental lines constantly cross so that the sonority changes from chord to chord (see Ex. 9, pages 44–5).

Etude II   A twenty-eight-note figure in flowing sixteenth notes is stated by each instrument at different transpositions. The statements are repeated exactly, but in changing temporal relation between instruments. While the melodic content of each line is fixed, the resulting harmony and texture are variable, as is the placement of entrances. Each instrument sustains the last note of the figure, which creates a changing harmonic pattern of its own. The four sustained pitches – F, F sharp, A flat and C sharp – contain five of the six possible interval classes, so that the intervallic harmony also varies while the pitches stay fixed. For players, the challenge of this Etude lies in matching the articulation of the four instruments – the fast figure is easy for the flute, tricky for the bassoon. The flautist Samuel Baron suggested that Etude II sounds like musicians warming up backstage before a concert. Carter says that it 'sounds like four birds that sing as birds do, sporadically, the same song over and over.'

Etude III A D major triad is sustained throughout, its color changing through the 'sneaked' entrances and smooth articulation of the instruments. Besides being a study in color (like Schoenberg's famous Chord-Colors piece which is its model), the Etude, marked Adagio possibile, is also a study in breathing for the players, and its dynamic arch suggests one very long breath.

Etude IV The only material is a rising half-step always heard in a rhythm of two adjacent eighths followed by a rest. The strict rules of the game produce a variety of configurations, as different doublings, spacings, and contrapuntal relations appear. The players must respond to their changing role in the texture: sometimes they are contributing to a chromatic line, sometimes they link other instruments; elsewhere, as at the cross-rhythm ostinato at bar 78, each is an independent element (Ex. 26).

Ex. 26 Mosaic cross-rhythms

Etude V Like the first Etude, this is a study in musical space, articulated in independent step-wise lines in order to explore the colors of different instrumental registers. The opening is nearly identical with one of Walter Piston's *Three Pieces* for flute, clarinet and bassoon.[1] The instruments are in an unusual configuration, with oboe and bassoon in their high register and flute and clarinet in their low range. At bar 16 the space is turned upside-down as a high A in the bassoon is taken over by the flute, which then moves down through its lowest register, pushing the other instruments deep into the bass. The cadence inverts the sonority heard at the close of Etude I.

Etude VI A study in (relatively) unusual effects for individual instruments and ensemble. Double-, triple- and flutter-tonguing, as well as trills and harmonic fingering, are combined to create changing textures. The crossing of lines and echoing of pitches between instruments produce new varieties of the *Klangfarbenmelodie* effect heard in Etude III: the rapidly articulated four-note chord at bar 33 is particularly striking. The extravagance of color leads to extravagant formal gestures – the fast motion of the piece suddenly breaks into a slow flutter-tongued canon (reminiscent of *Pierrot lunaire*) and a high trill in three instruments sets up a portentous (and comic) statement in the very low bassoon that will later reappear in the Fantasy.

Etude VII A study on one note. The absence of any variation in pitch puts the emphasis on ensemble, color and dynamic shapes. A three-part form is articulated by variations in attack and dynamics. Unlike the long, calm breath of Etude III, the dynamic envelope of this Etude is wide and unstable, suggesting fast motion, even though no entrances can be heard and the tone is sustained without interruption. Note the two ensemble fortissimos at bars 19 and 21; the second is a dynamic retrograde of the first, and together they form a point of focus that gives the Etude a clear shape despite the absence of pitch variation or clear rhythmic motifs (Ex. 27). The Dorian Quintet played this piece in Warsaw in 1958; it may have influenced the course of modern Polish music. Many versions of the one-note piece have followed its example.

Etude VIII This double mosaic is perhaps the most difficult of all the Etudes to play. An uninterrupted stream of rapid sixteenth notes doubled

Ex. 27 Study on one-note

in octaves passes from instrument to instrument in changing phrase-lengths and instrumental combinations. Against it, widely spaced single notes, mostly sforzando and short, also pass across the instrumental space. The superimposed extremes in tempo and the constant traversal of the extreme ranges of the instruments suggest a synthesis of the techniques of all the Etudes that will be made explicit in the Fantasy.

Fantasy Written after the Etudes, the Fantasy combines them all, giving the illusion that the Etudes are warm-up exercises for the episodes of an elaborate fugue. The Fantasy is both strict and innovative; it is Carter's farewell to traditional contrapuntal procedures and at the same time a preparatory sketch for the Fantasia of the First Quartet with its novel textures and continuity. The fugal subject is eight bars long and derived from three of the Etudes (Ex. 28). The opening motif stems from the bassoon in bar 52 of Etude VI. The septuplet sixteenths come from Etude VIII and move at the same speed as the sixteenths in that Etude. The

Eight Etudes and a Fantasy
© 1959 Associated Music Publishers, Inc. Used by permission

Ex. 28 Fugue subject

cadential motif comes from bars 4–6 of the first Etude. The subject thus suggests two developmental paths, both of which are pursued. There is traditional imitative development of the subject including stretti, double counterpoint and prolation canons, but this development is at the same time deflected and distorted by the appearance of the materials of the Etudes. Most importantly, the tempi of the Etudes transform the fugal development. The Fantasy begins at the tempo of Etude I. At bar 17 the tempo modulates to MM 126, the speed of Etude VII. At bar 35 the tempo of Etude II appears; at bar 48, the tempo of Etude VI; at bar 99 Etude IV rises to the surface. As the tempo modulates, reminiscences of the Etudes are heard as episodes in the fugue; the fugal subject continues on its way, undeterred by the interruptions but at new speeds. The subject is heard at tempi of MM 84, 126 and 90; at bar 108 it appears at two tempi simultaneously, in the ratio of 4:7. The end of the Fantasy brings its two processes together. In a series of stretti, the subject accelerates, until it turns into a trill. Superimposed on the accelerating design is a statement of the subject in long-held notes, passing from instrument to instrument in *Klangfarbenmelodie* related to Etudes III and VII.

Because of the length and difficulty of the Eight Etudes Carter has suggested several arrangements for performing excerpts from the work. He asks that Etudes III or VII should not be played unless they are included in a group of at least five other Etudes. Similarly the Fantasy is not to be played unless preceded by at least Etudes I, IV, VII, VI, or VIII – its allusions to the Etudes make no sense unless they have already been heard. This last stipulation underscores the new formal concept of the Fantasy. If it were just a fugue it could stand on its own. The Fantasy, however, is not a fugue, but an imagined action around a fugue. By analogy with Carter's description of the Brass Quintet, the scenario of the Fantasy might be described as follows. Four players begin to play a fugue on a subject related to the Etudes. As they hear other possible connections, they pursue them, rather than the fugue, so that at several places reminiscences or extensions of the Etudes obliterate the fugal texture. More connections between the Etudes appear, until the associative process itself whirls past the vanishing point, leaving only the fugue subject, which now seems part of a much slower time-world.

Brass Quintet

Commissioned by and dedicated to the American Brass Quintet, the work was written between 15 May and 29 August 1974 and received its first performance in a Charles Ives Festival Broadcast of the BBC (see WEC, 322–5). Much of the Quintet was composed in Aspen where both Carter and the American Brass Quintet were in residence; Carter was able to try out many passages of the work as it was being composed.

Although the Brass Quintet was written quickly, its form and textures seem nearly as complex as those of the Third Quartet – as if in composing the Quartet Carter had done enough contrapuntal research for two works.

A brass quintet is an awkward ensemble to balance and sustain. Trumpets and trombones, although related in timbre, do not overlap in range as the violin and cello do, and are limited in tone-colors. The pairs of trumpets and trombones tend to pull apart in sonority. The horn, which should link the other instruments, is so different from them in sound that it only further splinters the ensemble. The solution many composers have tried – that of using a variety of mutes – only compounds the problem; the mutes create the illusion of hearing not five unrelated instruments but ten or fifteen.

Carter's strategy for solving the problem of disunity was typically structural. In order to link all the members of the ensemble and also to produce great variety of tone color, he built the work out of a series of duos and trios, using all the instrumental combinations possible. The Quintet is collaged out of these smaller ensembles (which always overlap) and also out of 'quodlibets' in which all five instruments display their individual characters, in the following sequence:

Q 1. Trio 1, Duo 1, Q 2, Duo2, Trio 2, Q 3, Trio 3, Duo 3, Q 4, Trio 4, Horn Cadenza, Q 5, Duo 4, Trio 5, Slow movement, Duo 5, Coda.

Each trio and duo is based on a single interval, as is the horn cadenza:

trio 1 – two trumpets and first trombone – minor sixth – 'lightly'
duo 1 – horn and second trombone – perfect fourth – 'vigorously'
duo 2 – second trumpet and horn – minor third – 'humorously'
trio 2 – first trumpet, horn, second trombone – perfect fifth – 'majestically'
trio 3 – trumpets and horn – major second – 'smoothly flowing'
duo 3 – two trombones – major third – 'extravagant'
trio 4 – first trumpet, trombones – major sixth – 'lyrically'
horn cadenza – augmented fourth – 'menacingly'
duo 4 – trumpets – major seventh – 'furious'
trio 5 – horn and trombones – minor second – 'angry'
duo 5 – second trumpet, first trombone – minor seventh – 'dramatic'

These different episodes and their intervals give each instrument a unique intervallic and gestural vocabulary which comes to the fore during the quodlibets:

	m2	M2	m3	M3	p4	A4	p5	m6	M6	m7	M7
Tpt 1		M2					p5	m6	M6		M7
Tpt 2		M2	m3					m6		m7	M7
Hn	m2	M2	m3		p4	A4	p5				
Tb. 1	m2			M3				m6	M6	m7	
Tb. 2	m2			M3	p4		p5		M6		

The slow movement, first heard at the opening of the piece and anticipated during the quodlibets, brings all the harmonies of the work together.

As in the Second Quartet, there is a double structure, one emphasizing the total ensemble, the other its smaller components. The horn solo at the work's center, with its menacing tritones and romantic echo effects, represents the extreme in individualism, while the slow movement, given a climactic position unique in Carter's work, celebrates the pleasures of communal music-making. The expressive weight and surprising placement of the slow section may have been a reaction to the predominantly fast music of the Third Quartet, though all the works of the seventies use dramatic, asymmetrical forms different from the more balanced designs of

Carter's earlier music. The conflict in tendencies here is treated with much humor.

Typical of Carter's playfulness is the ensemble's harmonic response to the horn. The horn's tritones – traditionally the most dissonant intervals – here sound romantically nostalgic. The other instruments counter them with cruel octaves – traditionally the most consonant intervals, but in the context of non-tonal music, shocking and disruptive. Consonance becomes the devil in music.

The short episodes from which the Quintet is built are more sharply and variously characterized than those of the Third Quartet. 'Pop' elements are heard in the jazzy music of duo 1 and in the concert-in-the-park 'cornet' solo of the first trumpet in trio 4 (201–32). The brilliant fanfare for two trumpets in duo 4 could stand on its own, as could the clownish acrobatics of the two trombones in duo 2 (bars 150–68), with their 'rips.' The superimposition of the trombones' glissandi on the cascading music of trio 2 is perhaps the most spectacular textural event of the work, though the menacing eruption of the solo horn at the height of the first trumpet's soaring lyrical song is the most dramatic intersection of events.

Despite the brilliance of the duos and trios, however, the slow movement stands out as the climax of the work. Here finally the potentials of the total ensemble produce a sustained harmonic meditation. Based on a fixed-pitch design, the music slowly changes in color, density and

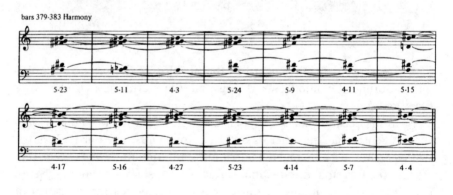

Chart 15 Brass Quintet: harmonic scheme

harmony. In the course of the movement every interval, three-, four- and five-note chord appears in an unbroken progression whose highpoint is the magical, radiant appearance of chord 7 – the pentatonic scale at bar 383 (Chart 15 – see previous page). Just as the episodes of the Quintet demonstrated the expressive possibilities of each interval, so the slow movement reveals their luminous connections.

Notes

1 Pollock, *Harvard Composers*, p. 117.

3 Chamber Music for Piano and other Mixed Ensembles

Sonata for Cello and Piano

The Sonata was written for the cellist Bernard Greenhouse, who gave it its first performance with the pianist Anthony Makas at Town Hall, New York on 27 February 1950. The score is dated 'December 11, 1948. Dorset Vermont – New York'. The first edition was published by the Society for the Publication of American Music. A corrected edition, dated 1966, is published by AMP.

The idiom and form of the Cello Sonata grew out of an attempt to write a work that would exploit the differences between the two instruments rather than trying to disguise them. The implications of this strategy became increasingly apparent in the course of composition. The movement that is most severe in its articulation of instrumental contrast, the first movement, was composed last. The opening bars of the work state the basic harmonic material for all four movements (Chart 16).

Chart 16 Cello Sonata six-note set

The first bar contains a six-note set (0, 1, 2, 5, 7, 8) that is immediately repeated in transposed form; the set is not given consistent serial treatment, however. The opening chord, articulated as a minor third plus a perfect fifth, recurs throughout the work, as do other four-note chords combining these two intervals, or those of major sixths and perfect fourths. If the pitches of the original four-note chord are reordered they appear as two major thirds connected by a minor second. Three related four-note chords made of two major thirds and a minor second are heard melodically and harmonically throughout the work. An important motive first heard at bar 20 in the piano outlines the relationships of major thirds that are everywhere prominent (Ex. 29).

The opening bar of the Sonata also emphasizes the pitches A sharp and B, which assume an important polar function as they do in many of Carter's earlier works. However, the harmonic ambience of the Cello

Ex. 29 Harmonic theme

Sonata is significantly more chromatic than that of any of Carter's previous music, so that while the polar function of the pitch remains important it is no longer associated with diatonic scale patterns and chords. The
half-step relationship between C and C sharp heard in bar 7 and between C
sharp and D heard at the cello's entrance in bar 6 also plays a significant
role in the work.

The harmonic materials presented at the beginning are neither thematic – the opening shape is not developed – nor serial in implication or
treatment. The opening serves instead as a sonority whose characteristics
define the nature of the musical exploration that follows. Many aspects of
the initial sound – intervallic content, absolute pitch, spacing, rhythm,
color and character – take part in the evolving discourse of the piece.
The opening presents the work's genetic matter. In the Cello Sonata, for
the first time in Carter's music, such genetic structure decisively replaces
thematic exposition, and transformation now takes the place of development and recapitulation.

The Cello Sonata is in four movements whose beginnings and endings
are linked to suggest a circular design. Each movement begins with the
transformation of material from the end of the previous movement.

As the connection between the end of the fourth movement and the
beginning of the first is stronger than that between the first and second,
the second movement functions as the beginning of the Sonata's narrative while the first movement functions structurally as a summation
rather than an exposition – it states material from all the other
movements.

I. Moderato The contrast of instruments in sound and time appears
immediately. The piano is a machine, ticking away at a regular pulse
of MM 112. The cello sustains an expressive melodic line whose notes
never coincide rhythmically with the piano's pulse. There are three long

phrases. The first, lasting sixty-eight bars, extends each instrument's distinctive character with mounting tension. The piano's pulse continues relentlessly, compounding its force with additional strata of pulsed contrapuntal lines (Ex. 30). The cello is equally unrelenting in its own

Cello Sonata
© 1953 Associated Music Publishers, Inc. Used by permission

Ex. 30

pursuits, but is more fanciful and discovers more varied material (the third movement is anticipated at bar 38; the second at 43). All that unites the two instruments is the shape of two rising major seconds heard in the cello in bars 18–20 and then in the piano at 20–2. The piano, significantly, tends to give musical shapes definite, motivic form – there are several recurring mottos in its part including a Hauptrhythmus pattern derived from the opening bars. The cello, by contrast, never articulates clear motifs; its character is freer than the piano's.

The second phrase (bars 68–103) contrasts sharply with the first. The cello begins alone with quiet, flowing music that is gradually taken up by the piano. The instruments achieve a climactic intersection at bars 95–100. Although they both play at the same speed at this point, their directions diverge and their phrases do not correspond. The instruments never unite. They collide and then bounce away from each other.

The third phrase begins like the first; but it is a reversal not a recapitulation. Instead of intensifying, the music gradually fades away to the interval of the minor third. The instrumental characters are neutralized as their phrases break into fragments.

II. Vivace, molto leggero   Carter has pointed out that where the Moderato is an abstraction of jazz textures, the Vivace approaches jazz and pop music stylistically. In form and harmony the Vivace is close to *The Minotaur*'s *pas de deux*. Two sections alternate in an A B A B A design, whose proportions suggest a ternary form with coda. Unlike the usual ternary forms of scherzo movements, the middle section here is more intense in feeling than the opening. A and B are in a tempo ratio of 3:4 obtained by maintaining a constant value for the eighth note. The pulse of B is identical with the tempo of the first movement, though this relationship is not made explicit by any thematic recall or allusion.

Harmonically, the second movement – the last Carter was to write with a key signature – contrasts B major and B flat minor, an opposition stated in the first two measures. Carter had explored this polarity in the Piano Sonata and Emblems; here, however, the fluctuations between keys are far more rapid than before and moments of diatonic simplicity sound ironic rather than affirmative – Carter has described the more tonal parts of the movement as parodies of 'pop' music (see bars 37–40, for example). The contrasted tonalities of this movement tend to form chromatic figurations that emphasize the minor third, and in retrospect the listener may note that the apparent tonal opposition is in fact derived from the six-note cell heard at the beginning of the first movement. Minor thirds, often complemented by perfect fourths to form the 'key' four-note chord of the Sonata, dominate both the harmonic and thematic materials of the movement. The repeated downward thirds of the 'pop' tune phrases of A, are transformed in B into rapidly oscillating quintuplets and also into a 'Dies Irae'-like motif that dominates the central section of the movement (Ex. 31). The composer does not recall his reasons for making this allusion, but the darkening of mood is unmistakable. The change in tone from the jazzy scherzando of the opening to the more impassioned, complex, and menacing expression of the B section seems crucial to the second movement's design and its relation to the other movements. As the Sonata continues, its character becomes increasingly provocative and unsettled.

III. Adagio   The interaction of tempo and form tried out in the Vivace now yields a more complex pattern. The opening tempo is proportionally

Cello Sonata
© 1953 Associated Music Publishers, Inc. Used by permission

Ex. 31 Dies Irae allusion (?)

related to the tempo of the B sections of the Vivace. The cello's sixty-fourth notes at the opening of the Adagio are at the same speed as the piano's quintuplet eighths of bars 198–203 of the Vivace. The cello makes this relation explicit by quoting the piano's oscillating minor thirds – the repetition is also a transformation, however; the piano's softly rocking motif becomes a ruggedly expressive ornament in a slow recitative. The change in character is further emphasized by the sharp contrast in speed, character and harmony between the cello's passionate lament and the calmly rising line in the piano. In terms of tempo the movement might be described as having the form ABCACD. The tempo of each section is:

A MM 70
B MM 60
C MM 80
D MM 48

The A sections develop the wavering minor third motif of the opening. The B section stresses the semitone relation of D and E flat. The C section is an intensified variation of B. The D section is a coda. Unlike the second movement, the contrast between sections is obscured so that the music seems to change tempo gradually. The piano's inability to compete with the cello's melodic intensity distances the two instruments much more distinctly than in the previous movement. By the end of the Adagio, their melodic shapes and gestures have become more dramatically opposed.

IV. Allegro   The piano begins by repeating part of the cello's concluding phrase from the Adagio (Ex. 32). The speed of the cello's quintuplet thirty-seconds is renotated as sixteenths to give a new tempo of MM 120, related to the B sections of the Adagio; the tempo structure of the Allegro is a

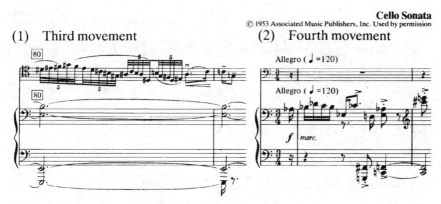

(1)   Third movement   (2)   Fourth movement

Ex. 32 Motive transferred from cello to piano

mutation of the Adagio. Again there are four tempi: 120, 140, 160, 112. The form of the movement might suggest a very developed rondo, but a more appropriate account of the music would note that the rapid opening of the Allegro is deflected by the echoes of the second and third movements, resisting their backward pull successfully until it is suddenly transformed into the tempo of the first movement. The return of the piano's MM 112 pulse at bar 147 is the climax of the entire Sonata and its first full realization of the poetic and structural possibilities of Carter's new idiom (Ex. 33). Whereas earlier in the Sonata proportional tempo changes had linked distinct sections, here the musical high point is achieved at the very moment of transformation through a superimposition of tempos. The massive and imposing character that marks so much of the Sonata here finally takes flight as the music seems suddenly to discover unforeseen possibilities.

Sonata for Flute, Oboe, Cello and Harpsichord

The Sonata was commissioned by Sylvia Marlowe for her Harpsichord Quartet of New York in 1952, and first performed by that group at Carnegie Recital Hall, New York, 19 November 1953. Because Miss Marlowe was not known as a champion of advanced music and the First Quartet had yet to be performed at the time, Carter avoided, at least in the first two movements, the rhythmic complexities of the Quartet. The Sonata, however, was not a step backwards. The First Quartet had demanded three years of experiment and sketching for its composition. Carter was now able to use his new idiom in a relaxed and improvisatory manner. The Harpsichord Sonata also extends the researches of the Quartet. The third

Ex. 33 Climax

movement is as complex in its tempo modulations as the Fantasia of the Quartet, and the form of the Sonata is even more original than the Quartet's, for here process replaces motivic development as the basis of form. Carter has said that the rhythmic simplification of the first two movements was deliberate: he wanted to show that his new approach to musical form was broader in implication than the specific procedures used in the Quartet.

The idiom of the Sonata consolidates the achievements of Carter's works since the Cello Sonata. Its harmonies derive from the opening bars of the harpsichord (Chart 17).

The rhythms, particularly in the first movement, are simpler than those of the Quartet; and yet they sound freer. The Sonata's form was determined by its instrumentation:

> My idea was to stress as much as possible the vast and wonderful array of tone-colors available on the modern harpsichord ... The three other instruments were used for the most part as a frame for the harpsichord. This aim of using the wide variety of the harpsichord involved many tone-colors which can only be produced very softly and therefore conditioned very drastically the type and range of musical expression, all the details of shape, phrasing, rhythm,

Chart 17 Sonata for Flute, Oboe, Cello, and Harpsichord: harmonic scheme

texture, as well as the large form. At that time (in 1952, before the harpsichord had made its way into pop) it seemed very important to have the harpsichord speak in a new voice, expressing characters unfamiliar to its extensive Baroque repertory.[1]

Carter had little interest in reviving elements of eighteenth-century style; his use of the harpsichord is more reminiscent of Nancarrow's player pianos than of Rameau's clavecin. He derived the substance and style of the work from the particular sonorities of the instrument. The main characteristic of the harpsichord's sound is its sharp, percussive attack and rapid decay – the first movement is derived from this property. The 'modern' harpsichord with its double manual, pedal stops, and – in the case of the Challis Carter wrote for – half-hitches for all stops, is also capable of many small differentiations in tone color. The second movement explores these possibilities. (The 'modern' harpsichord has gone out of fashion now as Baroque specialists have come to prefer instruments closer to historical models, which, unfortunately, are not well suited for the Sonata or the Double Concerto.)

The first movement starts with a 'splashing dramatic gesture whose subsiding ripples form the rest of the movement.' The form of the movement is the attack–decay contour of the harpsichord shown in slow motion. The three other instruments sustain the upper harmonics of the harpsichord – the cello plays intensely at the very top of its register. There are no themes; only ripples and waves from the primal splash in subsiding motion. The style of playing at first is rubato: the initial energy stretches and compresses the musical phrases. The harpsichord, however, gradually becomes clock-like in its gestures – true to its mechanistic form – as the

Sonata for Flute, Oboe, Cello, and Harpsichord

Ex. 34 Fade-out

other instruments continue to play freely. At bar 30 the mechanical tendency of the harpsichord yields a steady pulse rhythm, its phrases reiterated in expanding cycles against fragments of rubato material in the other instruments. The steady ticking of the harpsichord, however, also serves to sustain its overtones – a function shared by flute, oboe and cello at the convergence of bars 45–50. Gradually the harpsichord moves outwards across its musical space, subduing the last fragments of the initial burst. The reinforcements and cancellations of the harpsichord's vibrating strings form nodal pulses which the regular rhythmic pulse makes explicit. When the entire range of the keyboard vibrates the pulses cancel each other out and the music stops (Ex. 34). As in the Cello Sonata, the music appears to begin in the middle of an action, and the 'end' occurs at the very center of the work. As in the First Quartet, the formal process of the music stems from a double time-scheme. The real time of attack-and-decay is projected into slow-motion illusionistic time.

The conceptual double time-scheme of the first movement continues in the second movement, but in a new form. The movement begins as a one-note study, like the seventh Etude. The opening G, however, is the turning-point of the Sonata, the low point of its formal curve. The instrumental trio and the harpsichord begin to bring the music back to life with two streams of free association. These are fragmented and cross-cut without overlaps. Frequent cross-cutting exposes two contrasting developmental processes and allows all the changes in harpsichord registration to be heard. The form of the music again springs directly from the nature of the harpsichord – the movement is a study in alternating registration, with the other instruments stressing their unique ability to 'sneak' changes against the harpsichord's sudden shifts. The harpsichord's continuity is abrupt and dramatic, while the others carry on a more sustained line of thought. As usually happens in Carter's music, the overall form is projected by changing degrees of similarity and contrast, as delicate moments of convergence alternate with dramatic or humorous non-cooperation as at bars 120–4.

At bar 155 fast music suddenly bursts forth from all four instruments. This jazzy interlude sounds like a compression of the music that has preceded it – note the rapid alternations in color by all four instruments, particularly at bar 175 (Ex. 35). The entire passage may also be regarded as a new 'registration' of the ensemble, extending the juxtaposition of registers to a more complex formal level. The rapid motion of this passage can also be heard as an intersection with other time-planes of the piece; it

Sonata for Flute, Oboe, Cello, and Harpsichord

Ex. 35 Tone-color melody

echoes the opening of the first movement, though now with expanding rather than subsiding force. Perhaps this passage is the primal sound event of which the work's opening is just a reverberation. The interlude also prefigures the final movement – compare II bars 176–8 with III bars 283–6. Even after the harpsichord restores the original pattern of the second movement at bar 179, both the cello and harpsichord continue with anticipations of the next movement. The final fortissimo G's, starting with a six octave doubling in the harpsichord, then four in the instruments, then three in the instruments, then in unison, are a barrier which the new stream of motion overcomes.

The alternating time-strata of the second movement converge in the third, which presents a dizzying series of tempo modulations. The music begins in the gentle rhythm of a forlana but bursts beyond the limits of baroque style, as the harpsichord superimposes a faster tempo in a cross rhythm that points to the influence of Nancarrow. The music now becomes a study in motion and color. The original forlana pattern is broken down into its polyrhythmically components, a trochee and a pulse. The trochee rhythm turns into a fast jig, while the pulse gives rise to many contrasted speeds of uniform motion, focused in two brilliant cadenza-like passages for the harpsichord. The continuity of the movement is 'cross-cut like a movie – at times it superimposes one dance on another.'[2] The collage technique of the second movement is thus combined with the overlapping design of the first, with faster and slower pulse strata added to the motion as it proceeds. The second cadenza sweeps upwards across the harpsichord's range, against fragments in the other instruments that reach their fastest speed (675) after bar 445. The last flash of rapid music resonates as an echo in the beautiful closing bars. This last gesture recalls the end of Ives's *The Housatonic at Stockbridge*.

Duo for Violin and Piano

Commissioned by the McKim Fund in the Library of Congress and dedicated to the composer's wife, the Duo was completed on 27 April 1974 after a long gestation. It was first performed by Paul Zukofsky, violin, and Gilbert Kalish, piano, at a New York Philharmonic Prospective Encounter Concert at Cooper Union, New York, 21 March 1975. It was played twice on that occasion with violin and piano placed about thirty feet apart – not the composer's idea but a dramatic visual image of the musical design, in which the two ill-matched protagonists play equal but contrasting roles. The Duo was soon taken up by other violinists including Rolf Schulte, Robert Mann, Otto Armin, Regis Pasquier, Linda Quan and Ole Böhn.

Carter has written that the Duo 'draws its basic character primarily from the contrast between the sounds made by stroking the violin with a bow, that can be sensitively controlled during their duration and the sounds made by striking the piano that, once produced, die away and can only be controlled by being cut short.'[3] The contrast in sound is extended to every element of composition. The instruments are stratified not only in their material – as in the Third Quartet – but also in their way of developing. The piano's music is textural. It is made of long, contrasted episodes built out of complex cross-pulse designs; its polyphony emphasizes the contrast of lines, harmonic density and the variety of ways of striking the keyboard: legato, semi-staccato, staccato, martellato. The violin's music, by contrast, is expressive and sensitive. It contrasts many characters, not as 'movements,' but in short phrases of a continuously developing line. The two instruments articulate different formal processes. This opposition appears at the very opening of the work. Against an impassive, terrifyingly slow polyrhythmic exposition in the piano the violin plays a rough and passionate recitative, rapidly contrasting all of its expressive characters – appassionato, tenero, ruvido, espressivo – in mercurial, nervous phrases. Carter has compared this passage to a man climbing a glacier.

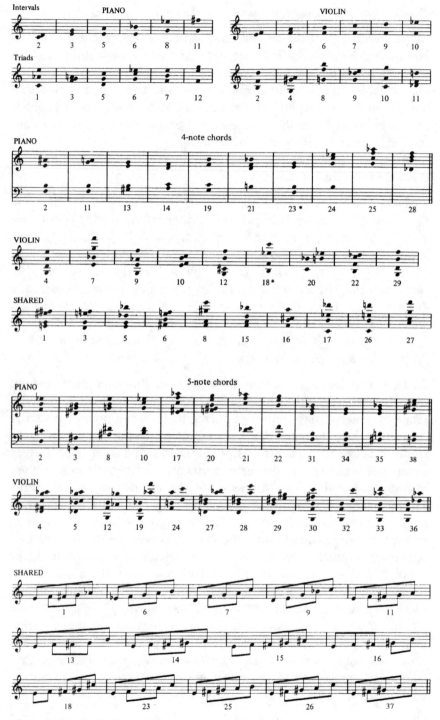

Chart 18 Duo for Violin and Piano: harmonic scheme

Intervals and three-note chords are stratified between the two instruments. Four- and five-note chords are split three ways, with a group of the most dissonant and most consonant harmonies reserved for connecting the violin and piano (see Chart 18). (Carter's objection to the spatial separation of the two instruments at the Duo's première sprang from a concern that these linking harmonies would be obscured.) As explained above, the form of the work is also stratified; the listener must perceive two formal processes at once. The piano has a series of contrasted movements: a slow polyrhythm of intervals and chords (see Chart 19); a gradually

$$
\begin{aligned}
\text{minor 3rd} &= 72 \; \flat = \text{MM4.666} \\
\text{major 9th} &= 75 \; \flat = \quad 4.48 \\
\text{tritone or} \atop (046) &= 73 \; \flat = \quad 4.603 \\
\text{minor 6th} &= 69 \; \flat = \quad 4.869 \\
\text{5-note chords} &= 56 \; \flat = \quad 6
\end{aligned}
$$

Chart 19 Duo for Violin and Piano: opening polyrhythm in piano

accelerating scherzando built out of flowing cross-pulsed lines in contrasted articulations (102–215, with significant interruptions); a pointillistic section based on a three-level polyrhythm of the bottom, middle and top of the piano's range (235–57); a delicate cantabile passage (266–89); a climactic relentless, martellato polyrhythm, summing up all the piano's harmonic and pulse materials; and a coda, combining previously heard material in a continuous fade-out, whose final, silence-fragmented tones dimly echo the work's opening.

Against these highly contrasted episodes the violin's music gradually evolves out of the opening recitative. Despite many flights of virtuosity – double-stopped harmonics, rapidly-changing chords – the violin's music is not coloristic but spatial in conception. The violin sweeps through its whole range in arching phrases, emphasizing its intensity of sound, against the piano's greater but less vibrant range. As the work continues, the violin's phrases grow longer, almost imperceptibly, so that it gradually takes over from the piano. From bar 315 onwards the violin builds to a climactic fusion of its materials, leading to an onset of fast music so rhapsodically irregular that it is only approximately co-ordinated with the piano. In the course of the violin's free flight the piano begins its fade-out, so that the last forty bars of the work are dominated by the violin with an unbroken phrase of heroic eloquence and poignant tenderness.

Carter has described the Duo as a series of ironic interactions. Throughout the work, violin and piano contrast sharply in mood. Yet the Duo introduces an irony beyond contrast. From time to time the protagonists seem to come together, as if by chance. Suddenly they find themselves occupying the same terrain (usually a fixed-pitch twelve-note chord); they listen to each other calmly, exchanging pitches while retaining their own harmonies. (See bars 84–94 and 218–31 for example.) In the polarized context of the Duo these quiet interchanges seem as ironic as the most extreme contrasts; they arise from the natural and opposed continuities of each instrument and seem to have no influence on the course of events, and yet they reveal the possibilities of communion.

Triple Duo

For Flute (Piccolo), Clarinet in B flat (Clarinet in E flat and Bass Clarinet); percussion and piano; violin and cello. 'Commissioned by the British Broadcasting Corporation for the Fires of London and affectionately dedicated to that ensemble and its prime mover, Peter Maxwell Davies.' Completed 7 February 1983. Première 23 April 1983 at Symphony Space in New York City. Recorded by Fires of London for Nonesuch and Thomas Demenga for ECM

Triple Duo begins with a joke – the instruments sound like they are caught in the act of warming up – and its high spirits and slapstick pacing never let up. Carter wrote it for the Pierrot + percussion combination common to many contemporary music groups, and in particular for the resources of the Fires of London; the two octaves of crotales, which play an unusually important role, was an identifying signature of the English ensemble at the time. In retrospect, though, while the commission of the work was British, the style is very much New York 'new music'. (The contrast was apparent at the New York première which also featured Maxwell Davies's *A Mirror of Whitening Light*, written for the same instruments but utterly different in mood.) This style reflects the performance manner of the original Speculum Musicae, especially violinist Rolf Schulte, cellist Fred Sherry, and pianist Ursula Oppens, all of whom had performed many of Carter's works in the preceding decade. The music of *Triple Duo* is edgy, aggressive, in-your-face – but also, at times, wistful, serene, playful, and elegant.

Although written for three strictly delineated duos the work is not a collage like the Third Quartet. The structural forces linking the duos are stronger than those that divide them, and in the final section of the piece the divided forces come together in a common pursuit that was implied throughout. The duos are differentiated in color, character, harmonic vocabulary, and rhythmic speeds (Chart 20). Listeners will first note the contrast of characters: the woodwinds gurgle, shriek and coo like a pair of amorous birds, the strings scrape and pluck comically, and the percussion and piano evoke the more angular variety of free jazz. It's a raucous band. The character contrast between the duos stems from a division of intervals: the sweet thirds of the winds, spiky fourths and sevenths of the piano, and sardonic major seconds in the strings fit their dramatic personalities. Players will immediately notice the rhythmic contrast of 3 against 4 against 5 (winds, strings, piano-percussion) that runs throughout the work. Less obvious are the patterns of harmonic combination, a systematic division three-, four- and six-note chords for each duo and for the

Woodwinds

intervals: 3, 4, 6, 11
three-note chords: 1, 6, 8, 11
four-note chords: 9, 13, 14, 16, 21, 23, 28
six-note chords: 1, 8, 9, 12, 13, 14, 22, 29, 31, 37, 42, 50
$3/91(7 \times 13)$ $\downarrow$ = **50.05** M. 1.65
(in other words – pulse on every ninety-first triplet quarter note at metronome speed of 50.5 to the half. 50.05. $50.05 \times 3 = 150.15$. $150.15/91 = 1.65$.)

Piano-Percussion

intervals: 1, 5, 8, 10
three-note chords: 3, 4, 5, 9
four-note chords: 6, 17, 19, 20, 22, 24, 27
six-note chords: 3, 4, 7, 10, 11, 20, 23, 25, 33, 35, 38, 41, 48
$5/77 (7 \times 11)$ M. = 3.25.

Strings

intervals: 1, 2, 6, 7, 9
three-note chords: 2, 7, 10, 12
four-note chords: 1, 3, 4, 5, 7, 12, 29
six-note chords: 15, 17, 18, 19, 27, 28, 30, 32, 44, 45, 47
$8/143 (11 \times 13)$ M. 2.8

Combinations of Duos

four-note chords: 2, 8, 10, 11, 15, 18, 25, 26
six-note chords: 2, 5, 6, 16, 21, 24, 26, 34, 36, 39, 40, 43, 46, 49

Chart 20 Triple Duo: stratification of intervals, chords and pulses

harmony created between them. Subtlest of all the technical features is the structural polyrhythm which begins on the downbeat of bar 5 and ends on the downbeat of bar 533 – the only two simultaneous tutti attacks in the entire work.

While the patterns of the polyrhythms are not audible, the unified rhythmic substructure holds the piece together. A conductor – and the piece needs one – will soon realize that though there are eight tempi in the piece they all are closely related to the basic tempo of MM 100 to the quarter (Chart 21). Carter achieves a rhythmic design here comparable to the tonal structures Schoenberg describes as 'monotonal'; the piece moves from a home tempo through many related regions, but it has a strong sense of a constant pulse running from beginning to end.

Basic tempo ♩ = *100*

Related tempi:
100 × 2/3 = 67
100 × 3/2 = 150
100 × 5/4 = 125
100 × 3/4 = 75
100 × 5/6 = 84 –

Chart 21 Triple Duo: tempo relationships

Triple Duo is performed as a one-movement piece but is constructed out of many short contrasting episodes which involve ever-changing combinations of instruments. Each of the duos has a repertory of fast, moderate, and slow material, and they appear in isolation and in changing combinations. These 'quarries' of musical elements emphasize the contrasting sounds of the instruments. The sustained woodwind passages, for instance, dramatize the role of breath, the sustained double stops which mark the slow material of the strings call attention to the pressure of the bow, and the bell-like sounds of the piano/percussion duo's slow material derive from the resonance of struck surfaces. This intense focus on the way sounds are produced gives the *Triple Duo* its engagingly tactile quality.

At the opening the piano comes to the fore with a brilliant toccata, as if it were launching a sustained fast movement, but it is suddenly interrupted at bar 23 by a tranquil duet in the woodwinds, and the cross-cutting structure of the work now takes the place of a continuous unfolding. It sounds as if the traditional first three movements of a sonata, Allegro, Adagio, Scherzo, were chopped up and pasted together, a fine example of cinematic influence. By contrast with the Third Quartet, however, the formal sections of the opposed forces do not sound super-imposed; instead of a three-tiered unfolding, we hear a series of short events built out of different combinations of the thematic elements of the duos. Although the episodes usually mismatch a contrast of characters, the duos also come together, as in the trio for bass clarinet, piano, and cello, all moving rapidly in the bass register, at bar 100, or in the sustained slow section from 247 to 288, a crystalline, music-of-the-spheres passage in the upper register of all the instruments which forms the whirling work's still center.

Although each of the duos has its own 'spotlight' episodes, the duets of the piano-percussion pair form the structural spine of the work: a glockenspiel/piano duet at 175; the crotales/piano episode at 257; the Maestoso piano solo at 390; and the scherzoso marimba/piano duet at 425. This last duet leads directly to the Allegro Fantastico, the finale of the work, which alters its formal strategy. The texture of the finale resembles that of Schoenberg's op. 16, No. 5, 'The Obbligato Recitative'. Beginning with the violin in bar 442, the instruments take turns spinning out a long melodic line, expressive and supple. As they take up the line from the previous instrument, they often begin with the same group of pitches but reorder them to produce their own characteristic intervals – see clarinet and violin in bars 447–449. Against this melodic line, a second contra-puntal line also appears, similarly traveling around the ensemble. It is a series of staccato pulses that gradually increase in speed. And against these two strictly defined elements Carter weaves a floridly fantastic back-ground, all of which still follow the strict harmonic rules of the piece. The texture of this finale, built out of feverish lyrical expression, a driving pulse and improvisatory arabesques, is an abstraction and magnification of jazz: ultra-bop. As the lyricism of the melodic line heats up and the pulses get closer and closer, the music flows with an increasing intensity, reaching an ecstatic climax at 517 with a dazzling piano cascade accom-panied by the crotales, and then rushing to the consummate tutti at 533. Carter has never written a more joyous passage.

Some performance thoughts: Although *Triple Duo* premièred without a conductor, the distance between piano and percussion make co-ordination difficult without a conductor's assistance. With a conductor, and the required quality of players, the piece can be well-assembled in four three-hour rehearsals, the first of which might be divided into sectionals (I have found this particularly useful). Unlike some of Carter's other oppositional pieces, the *Triple Duo* does not really require an unusual degree of spatial separation between the duos; too much separation obscures the important connections between them. The notation is occasionally confusing because it is not clear whether the music should be conducted in quarters, halves or dotted halves. My own experience with the piece suggests that once the players have mastered their parts a slow beat is actually more effective in shaping and phrasing the music and brings out the long line. Therefore passages in 2/2 or 6/4 are best conducted in a slow two, although some of the 6/4 bars are better conducted in 3/2. There is an important letter from Carter to Oliver Knussen about performance of the piece in the Sacher Stiftung, one of the few documents of Carter's own performance preferences. Carter encourages Knussen to bring out the quirky, comic aspects of the music.

Quintet for Piano and Winds
(Oboe, Clarinet in B flat and E flat, Bassoon, Horn in F)

'For Heinz Holliger and KölnMusik'. Composed 'during the summer of 1991 in Southbury, Connecticut' though the sketches go back to December 1990. Première 13 September 1992 at the Kölner Philharmonie, Cologne, Germany by Heinz Holliger, oboe; Elmar Schmid, clarinet; Klaus Thunemann, bassoon; Radovan Vlatkovic, horn; Andras Schiff, piano.

The musicologist Carl Dahlhaus noted that Beethoven the composer of symphonies was equally the composer of serenades, particularly for wind instruments. Although Carter's critics, like Virgil Thomson, have accused him of writing only in the genre chef-d'oeuvre, he has amassed a sizable oeuvre in the genre divertissement. The Quintet for Piano and Winds crowns this series and in some ways bridges the gap between Carter's most recent technical concerns and the Parisian neo-Classicism in which he was trained.

Carter notes that he thought about the Quintet by Mozart (which Mozart called his finest work) when composing for the same combination; but he may have been thinking as well of his own *Triple Duo* and how to write a piece for similar forces in a different way. The Quintet is more introverted than *Triple Duo*, more chamber music-like and less concertante. Like the *Triple Duo*, the Quintet divides its forces in three. Here, however, the three woodwinds form one unit; the horn, a second; the piano, the third. At the outset of the piece their contrasting characters are made clear. The woodwinds are nervous and whimsical, each in its own way; the horn is lyrical; the piano is agitated and dramatic. There is also, however, a twofold contrast between the piano and the four winds, since the horn also joins ranks with the oboe, clarinet and bassoon to form a wind choir. The sustained sounds of the winds play off against the staccato piano writing. The form mirrors this acoustical contrast: the piano, with the sharpest attack sound and fastest fade, dominates the very opening of the piece and very gradually drops back as the winds take on greater importance. For much of the middle section of the piece the piano merely 'comps,' playing sparsely and sometimes disappearing altogether, though it returns to importance in the last part of the work. As one might expect, the writing for all the instruments is superbly idiomatic. Surprisingly, given the dedication of the Quintet, it makes no use of the extended techniques favored by Holliger; indeed, the oboe has the least showy part. But the Quintet is more about ensemble than solos, and despite its internal oppositions, the work is most remarkable for its rich sonority and its constant inventiveness in color and texture.

Of all the works of the nineties, the Quintet shows the most elaborate pre-compositional scheme, with a complex rhythmic and harmonic framework, and a detailed calculation of all the possible combinations of instruments. Carter divides the ensemble rhythmically into three units: woodwinds, horn and piano. The winds play rhythms based on sixteenth notes, which often give them a jazzy character reminiscent of the Woodwind Quintet; the horn plays quintuplets; the piano, sextuplets. Carter worked out a five way polyrhythm based on metronomic speeds of MM 7 for the oboe, 6.75 for the clarinet, 7.56 for the bassoon, 8.859 for the piano and 7.5 for the horn. The harmonic structure derives from hexachords nos. 11, 23 and 35. The division of intervals is shown in Chart 22.

Oboe:	1			4	5				10		
Clar.:		2					8	9			
Bassoon:			3			7				11	
Horn:	1	2	3		5		8				
Piano:				4		7		9	10	11	

Chart 22 Quintet: P&W interval assignments

Unlike Carter's older practice, the instruments share intervals. But more importantly, Carter calculates the intervals of each instrument in relation to one of the three hexachords. For instance, the piano's intervals appear in hexachord II in the intervallic ordering 9 4 7 II 10, and in hexachord number 35, II 7 10 4 9.

Carter's intense study of the harmonic possibilities shows that he viewed the medium of piano and winds as harmonic in essence, as opposed to the *Triple Duo*, whose forces were differentiated melodically. The sonority of much of the piece opposes harshly struck chords in the piano with held harmonies in the winds, as if the winds were functioning as a sustaining pedal for the piano. Although there are extended solos for each of the winds, much of the piece treats them as a harmonic choir.

The Quintet is in a single movement divided into several sections, but its formal scheme is difficult to classify. Each of the instruments has a solo somewhere in the piece, but in no predictable pattern. The phrase structure is rather different from the short, contrasting episodes of *Triple Duo*. Here the phrases have a Schubertian spaciousness, unique in Carter's output. We might outline the form as follows:

bars 1–71   Agitato piano solo played against tranquillo sustained winds with occasional outbursts of melodic ideas in the winds which become longer as the piano's phrases become shorter

71–93   Duets for the winds against sporadic piano punctuation

93–116   Horn solo against sustained notes in all other instruments

117–167   Four-part wind 'chorale' against piano staccato pulses and outbursts

168–198   Bassoon solo, cantabile, espressivo, with ironic asides

199–295   Increasingly appasionato wind solos against sparse piano notes

295–355   Tranquillo slow movement for sparse winds, sparser piano

356–439   Scherzando centered on E flat clarinet solo (363–399)

440–542   Quasi-recapitulation of opening: return and development of piano solo; second horn solo (497–542)

543–612   Coda; accelerating pulses; sostenuto; a final explosion.

The long phrases and rich texture give the Quintet a less dynamic sense of momentum than in *Triple Duo*; ideas unfold more expansively and there are few sudden contrasts. Carter here seems less interested in moving the listener along in the piece, more interested in luxuriating in the wind sonorities. Despite the obvious stylistic differences, the sensuousness of the work and its delight in its own sounds connects it with Mozart's great example.

Quintet for Piano and Strings

Commissioned by the Library of Congress; completed on 14 April 1997; première by Ursula Oppens and the Arditti Quartet, 20 November 1998 in Washington.

Like the Fifth Quartet, the Quintet for Piano and Strings has the quality of mature retrospection. As in the quartet and the Clarinet Concerto, Carter returned to the systematic use of the two all-interval hexachords that he had charted for the Second Quartet and Double Concerto; it is as if he had decided to re-explore his most characteristic harmonic world. The Quintet, however, goes even further in search of the composer's past, for it revives the long melodic lines built of notes of even duration that defined the texture of the First Quartet. In the opening section of the Quintet each of the strings plays such a line as a ghostly cantus firmus behind more expressive phrases in the other strings and the interjections of the piano. Also reminiscent of the First Quartet is the circular form: the last staccato G sharp of the piano could lead right back to the work's beginning.

Compared to *Triple Duo* or the Quintet for Piano and Winds, the present Quintet presents a clearer and more sustained series of dramatic contrasts. Although each string instrument has its own intervallic vocabulary (see Chart 23), the music pursues a binary opposition of strings against piano.

Vl. I:	1			4	5			9		
Vl. II:		2		4			7			11
Vla:		2	3		5	6				
Vc:	1				6		8		10	

Chart 23 Quintet for Piano and Strings: interval assignments

The Quintet falls into six main sections (which could be labeled Opening, Scherzo I, Slow Movement, Scherzo II, Finale, Coda) played without pause. In the opening bars (1–96) the strings weave a polyphony out of long melodic lines and shorter expressive phrases while the piano plays staccato pulses that gradually become faster; every once in a while the piano interrupts the strings with bursts of rapid music that finally seems to emerge at bar 96. At this point, however, the piano and strings engage in a dramatic exchange of gestures, as if they were trying to converse. This dialogue serves as a transition to the next section (bars 129–191) which is a fragmented scherzando, mainly for the strings, reminiscent of the First Quartet in its mosaic texture. The scherzo breaks off dramatically at bar

191, and a slow movement begins (bars 192–248) with sustained, swelling harmonies in the strings against sustained chords in the piano. At the center of this movement, the viola recalls the expressive melodic lines of the opening. At bar 246 the piano suddenly launches a second scherzo while the strings continue the slow movement. From 275–325 the strings accompany the scherzo with occasional accents, but at 325 they return to the sustained notes of the slow movement which now form a striking contrast against the nervously darting motion of the piano. At bar 355 the Finale begins with quiet string tremolandi that occasionally turn into expressive melodic phrases. As in the opening section the piano interrupts the string texture from time to time, but otherwise sits silent; at the end of the movement (bars 425–436) the two parties state an antiphonal climax. In the brief Coda, the strings play their basic harmonic and melodic ideas against staccato notes in the piano which lead the music back to its opening.

Luimen

Scored for Trumpet, Trombone, Harp, Mandolin, Guitar, Vibraphone. Commisioned by the Nieuw Ensemble of Amsterdam. Completed 7 July 1997. Première 31 March 1998 in Amsterdam by the Nieuw Ensemble, Ed Spanjaard, conductor.

Carter waited nearly eighty-nine years before writing for the mandolin; the jingling ensemble of *Luimen* springs from the Dutch ensemble for whom it was written. The ensemble also gave the work its title, an old Dutch word (virtually unpronounceable by the non-Dutch) meaning 'whimsical moods'; the word corresponds to the German 'Grillen' used by Schumann.

In composing this work, Carter, following several examples of Berio, did something he had never done before; he built it around a previously completed piece, the guitar solo, *Shard*. The harp, mandolin and vibraphone are thus mirrors and extensions of the guitar, while the brass duo mainly punctuates and sustains the musical fabric. The harmonies of the work, like others of Carter's latest phase, stem from the two all-interval tetrachords.

The piece, which lasts about eight minutes, is in four continuous sections. The opening section (bars 1–68) contrasts shimmering textures with short solo phrases by each instrument, culminating in an extended harp solo. In the next section (bars 69–125), a sort of figured chorale, slowly moving intervals in the harp and brass form a backdrop to fleeting staccato figures in the mandolin, guitar and vibraphone. In bars 126–197 the guitar plays the gradually accelerating *Shard* to a light accompaniment. At bar 198 the closing section begins, finally bringing the brass to the fore against an apotheosis of plucking by the harp, guitar and mandolin.

Notes

1 CEL, p. 231.
2 Ibid.
3 CEL, p. 259.

4 Short Instrumental Works

Canonic Suite

The Canonic Suite stems from contrapuntal exercises Carter wrote for Nadia Boulanger. These pieces originally formed three of four 'Musical Studies' that were composed without any specific instrumentation or even any intention of performance. For a BMI competition in 1939, Carter arranged them for the unlikely but required combination of four alto saxophones, and in 1956 he rescored them, with slight revisions, for four clarinets (though they might work equally well if arranged for four violas or even four marimbas). In 1981 Carter made a re-revised edition for saxophones. The canons have a charm that belies their rigorous mechanisms.

The first, Fanfare, is a four-part canon at the unison, at the distance of a brisk quarter note. The stretto masks the canonic imitation. The listener hears a texture that evolves mysteriously. The second piece, Nocturne, also grows out of an unusual canonic design. It simultaneously unfolds an original line, its diatonic inversion, retrograde and retrograde inversion. Harmonic motion, from modal diatonicism through enharmonic modulations and back again, matches the counterpoint in subtlety. The third piece, a Tarantella, is a strict four-part canon, with each entrance a second higher than the one before. Formally it is a ternary design with a contrasting lyrical midsection. A fourth study, an Andante espressivo in the form of a double canon in inversion, was not published. It contrasts a flowing line with rests and long isolated notes, creating a polyphony of contrasted motion in time, a texture prophetic of later Carter.

Elegy

The *Elegy* exists in a variety of arrangements. It was composed in 1939 for cello and piano. Carter was never pleased with the original scoring, and rearranged the work for a string quartet he met while on vacation in Maine in 1946, and again for string orchestra in 1952. In 1961 a final revision was made, now for viola and piano. The viola version introduces a great deal of written out rubato to separate the two instruments polyphonically, and also ends in tonal ambiguity, unlike the older quartet and string orchestra versions. Thematically the piece is closely related to the slow movement of the Symphony No. 1 and the song *Voyage*, which it resembles in expressive mood and fluid continuity.

Pastoral

The *Pastoral* was written in 1940 for the oboist and English horn player Josef Marx. Although published – at Henry Cowell's insistence – as a viola piece with alternative parts for clarinet and English horn, Carter composed it for this last instrument and prefers that version. The Pastoral, together with the Elegy, the Frost songs and the Symphony No. 1 represents a brief bucolic phase in Carter's development. These works share a wistful mood. Unlike many of his later pieces, they are not difficult to play, and so make a good, if hardly typical, introduction to Carter for amateur performers.

Carter calls the *Pastoral* his Walter Piston piece.[1] Its mild manner ('like a conversation in country surroundings') is more characteristic of his Harvard teacher than of himself. Piston's influence on Carter, however, should not be underestimated. Piston encouraged him to study with Nadia Boulanger, and his music, which Carter began to know in the 1920s, forcefully illustrated the strengths of the new classicism. In 1978, for one of the concerts honoring his seventieth birthday, Carter asked that Piston's *Three Pieces* for flute, clarinet and bassoon of 1923 be played, together with Leo Ornstein's Violin Sonata (1917). The wit, clarity and inventiveness of Piston's music still seemed like a gust of fresh air compared to Ornstein's post-Scriabin haze. The linear counterpoint of the *Pastoral* and its elegantly restrained use of jazz both derive from Piston. The work opens, however, with a Carterian signature: the rising fifth motif from the Seikilos Song that he also uses in *Philoctetes*, *The Minotaur*, and 'Anaphora.'

The *Pastoral* already indicates some directions that Carter would follow in the Cello Sonata, and even in the Duo of 1974. Carter builds the piece out of contrasted sonorities. The formal plan bypasses classical procedures for an open form inspired by jazz improvisation. The work opens by defining the piano's sonority: a combination of sharp staccato attack and sustained decay sound which colors the piano part throughout. The soloist enters with a pentatonic, lyrical theme, while the piano continues its material. The meter is 5/8, as in *The Rose Family*, and this rhythmic pattern, which can be a straitjacket, is treated here with flexibility. As the *Pastoral* develops, syncopated sixteenth-note motion gradually develops out of the opening material. By fig. 106 this new motion turns into a jazzy 'second theme' that has really been present for some time in incomplete form. The two basic elements then alternate, leading to solo cadenzas and an accelerando conclusion.

In 1988, at the request of Heinz Holliger, Carter arranged the *Pastoral* for English horn, strings and marimba.

Eight Pieces for Timpani

In 1950 Carter wrote six studies for timpani. They were intended as compositional studies mainly in tempo modulation, but also in the manipulation of some of the four-note chords he was now using as a means of harmonic organization. He showed the pieces to New York percussionists at the time – and was not pleased with the way they sounded. Only two, the Recitative and Improvisation, were published (in 1960) but the others circulated widely in photocopy and were often played. In the mid-sixties, Carter revised the pieces with the aid of the percussionist Jan Williams, in order to make them more effective in performance. He composed two additional pieces, Adagio and Canto, at this time, and dedicated them to Williams; these are the only two that require pedal timpani. The entire set of eight pieces was published in 1968, with the older ones dedicated to many of the percussionists who played them in the fifties. The eight pieces are an anthology, not a suite; the composer specifies that not more than four of them should be played as a suite in public.

Whatever Carter's reservations about these pieces may have been, in their revised form they are equally compelling as formal designs and as instrumental vehicles. As with the *Eight Etudes*, the reduction of means was part of a search for new ways of putting music together. Carter later refined the music for performance by stressing the many possible contrasts in timbre, range, dynamics and character. Each piece presents a specific rhythmic and timbral problem.

Saëta (dedicated to Al Howard) 'An Andalusian song of improvisatory character sung during an outdoor religious procession, usually at Easter, said to be the descendant of a rain ceremony during which an arrow (saëta) was shot into the clouds to release the rain' (Composer's note). Saëta is both improvisatory and ritualistic in character. It is framed by a freely accelerating figure. The strictly notated rhythms within the frame gradually accelerate by means of tempo modulation, so that the process of the piece is the same as that of the frame, but in slow motion. The slowed motion also allows the polyphony of pulses to be articulated by contrasting dynamics and timbre, as in bars 20–4 (Ex. 36).

Ex. 36 Pulse polyphony

Moto perpetuo (to Paul Price)   An unbroken pulse of 480 is articulated in changing accentual groups, mostly in a soft dynamic.

Special cloth-covered rattan sticks are required to produce the desired light tone quality. The tone colour changes with the accentuation as the drums are struck in different places. The overall effect is of a sustained sound rapidly flickering in colour. The four drums are tuned close together to produce this unbroken effect. The four pitches – B sharp, C sharp, D sharp, E – form the four-note chord which figures prominently in the *Eight Etudes.*

Adagio (to Jan Williams)   Written in 1966 and closely related to the timpani parts in the Piano Concerto, this study exploits pedal timpani to produce glissandi, vibratos, harmonics and sympathetic vibrations. Most of these effects are very quiet; they are heard as the decay of a few, dramatic sharp attacks. The piece focuses attention on several aspects of timpani playing – change of pitch, resonances – usually regarded as peripheral 'noise.'

Recitative (to Morris Lang)   Marked Adagio drammatico, this piece contrasts three ideas whose independent developments are cross-cut: a dramatic tremolo, a bolero rhythm, and an irregular heart-murmur pulse.

The three converge and intersect in different ways. The heartbeat comes out of the opening tremolo; the tremolo grows increasingly explosive and merges with the bolero figure. The heart pulse then takes over as the other figures fade away in fragments. The drums are tuned to G sharp, A sharp, C sharp and D, the all-interval chord used in the First Quartet. The complete range of intervals serves to define harmonic motion even with four unchanging pitches.

Improvisation (to Paul Price) A study in tempo modulation and free continuity. The tuning uses the same chord as the Moto perpetuo but it is now widely spaced to allow greater contrasts in sound. The work is based on the cross-cutting of speeding and slowing materials. The illusion of improvised speed change is created through six co-ordinated tempi.

Canto (to Jan Williams) Written in 1966, this study for pedal timpani has a distinctive tone colour because of the combined effects of glissandi and snare-drum sticks used to create an unbroken 'song.' Like the Adagio, the Canto brings to the fore the resonances and pitches that lie between the normal sounds of the timpani. The use of snare-drum sticks and rim shots brings out the higher overtones of the drums.

Canaries (to Raymond Des Roches) The title is a reference to a Renaissance dance imported from the 'wild men' of the Canary Islands – and not chirping birds, though the pun is probably intended. The music is a study in 6/8 rhythms that anticipates the jig figures of the First Quartet and the Forlana of the Harpsichord Sonata. The dactyllic rhythm of the old dance serves as a contrast to the even pulses of many of Carter's rhythms and at the same time implies a polyrhythmic pattern that is exploited here in numerous ways. The different possible long-short patterns within the opening motif appear quickly, speeding up the pulse of the music so that within its first twenty bars the tempo has doubled. Later a constant pulse and an accelerating one are superimposed, and towards the end the multiple speed layers of the piece are both combined polyrhythmically and cross-cut. The tuning once again uses the all-interval chord, now in a wide spacing.

March (to Saul Goodman) The last piece is a bit of Ivesian humor, which some drummers also hear as a portrait of the New York Philharmonic's timpanist for fifty years – his conservative manner may be reflected in the one-five tuning of the piece. There are two marches, each at its own speed, one played with the heads of the sticks, the other with the butts (Ex. 37). The contrapuntal play of the two turns the timpanist into a baton twirler, flipping the sticks from one end to the other. The shape of the piece suggests a hypothetical scenario which only those who have played in an American marching band could understand. Two drummers approach each other playing at different speeds. They meet and 'challenge' each other, imitating each other's figures and outdoing one another in virtuosity. Having established their equal credentials they then march away at different speeds. The compositional legerdemain involved in constructing this little scene has to be matched by that of the player who takes both roles. The humour of this piece foreshadows 'A View of the Capitol from the Library of Congress.' (After a 'contemporary' concert in New York which ended with a selection of ragtimes and marches, Carter told me, 'I always forget what a good composer John Philip Sousa was!')

March (Eight Pieces for Four Timpani)
© 1969 Associated Music Publishers, Inc. Used by permission

Ex. 37 Double march

Canon for 3
Igor Stravinsky In Memoriam (1971)

Written as a memorial to Stravinsky, *Canon for 3* first appeared in *Tempo* No. 98, one of two issues of tributes by composers. It is written for 'three equal instrumental voices.' Performances have been given with three trumpets, flugelhorn, cornet and trumpet, and oboe, clarinet and trumpet. Other combinations are certainly possible.

   The short work is a strict canon, with the second voice in inversion at the tritone; the third voice repeats the first exactly. After the third voice has restated the subject, the continuing canonic motion of all three parts produces first the inversion at the tritone and then the original subject as a *Klangfarbenmelodie* formed by the three lines. The voices thus merge, and independence gives way to unity. The *Canon* combines Renaissance and twentieth-century techniques, a feat that Stravinsky would have appreciated.

A Fantasy around Purcell's 'Fantasy on One Note' for Brass Quintet (1974)

A Fantasy was written as a Christmas present for the American Brass Quintet who had just given the première of the Brass Quintet. Carter has long admired Purcell's music, and in particular the fantasias for viols which were an important inspiration for the First Quartet. The 'Fantasia upon One Note' has a special appeal because of its contrapuntal ingenuity, and because of the rhythmic structure which doubles and then redoubles the pulse-rate of the music against the constant durations of the drone. In arranging the piece Carter strove to keep the drone audible, which it rarely is when performed on viols, and to articulate and phrase the music so that its contrapuntal structure would be clear. Carter's Fantasy transforms Purcell's sustained drone into a tolling bell-like *Klangfarbenmelodie*, which passes from instrument to instrument.

Birthday Fanfare for Sir William Glock's 70th, 3 May 1978 (Unpublished)

One of Carter's two birthday cakes (see *Birthday Flourish* below), *Birthday Fanfare* is scored for three trumpets, vibraphone and bells – as befitted its occasion. Carter decided that the piece was strictly occasional.

Changes, for Guitar Solo

Commissioned by and dedicated to David Starobin, who gave the première in New York on Carter's seventy-fifth birthday, 11 December 1983. Completed 8 September 1983.

Changes began as a four-minute study, but David Starobin urged the composer to expand the work and eventually it more than doubled in length. *Changes* is the heir of the guitar part in *Syringa*, which Starobin had performed. The sketches of *Changes* in the Sacher Stiftung are a fascinating document of the interaction between composer and performer. They reveal Starobin's ingenuity in solving technical challenges, and also Carter's willingness to simplify passages when necessary to make them more effective. They also show how Carter could expand a work of highly structured episodes by adding more freely composed passages without diminishing the musical unity. Most interesting, perhaps, is the way a rather introverted study gradually turned into a *tour de force*.

To the listener, *Changes* sounds like an improvised journey through the colors of the guitar. Passages of flamenco strumming, bell-like harmonics,

ponticello, rapid arpeggiation, intricate counterpoint alternate unpredictably, yet with an inner coherence. As with other works of this period, that
subliminal unity stems from a rhythmic and harmonic pattern, although
Carter altered some aspects of the pattern as the piece grew. Originally he
built the work on a 75:56 polyrhythm, but he let out the seams of this
structure to expand the piece, particularly in the scherzando passage from
89–109. The six strings of the guitar led Carter to a harmonic design
based on hexachords. There are two types of hexachordal harmonies in
the work. The all-triad hexachord (Carter's number 35) is the most
important harmony in the work and occurs throughout, as a strummed
six-note chord, or a pair of triads. Contrasting with the all-triad chord are
hexachords, such as the kind that Carter had used in *Night Fantasies* and
In Sleep, In Thunder, that can be arranged to make up half of a symmetrical all-interval twelve-note chord. Carter's 6-note chord number 3
appears at the very opening of the work; bars 12 and 13 are based on
Carter hexachord number 4. Several passages of the work hold pitches in
a fixed position, sounding them in changing orders. This aspect of the
work ultimately gave it its title, although it was named after it was composed. Bars 9–13 give the earliest example of such a passage of ringing
changes; the serene coda of the work, bars 131–150, is another (Ex. 38).
Because it is exclusively based on hexachordal harmony rather than the
intervallic stratification *Changes* is, apart from its effectiveness as a

Changes
© 1983 Hendon Music Inc.

Ex. 38 Ringing changes

display of guitar virtuosity, an excellent introduction to the harmonic procedures which support Carter's later works.

Canon for 4 – Homage to William

For Flute, B flat Bass Clarinet, Violin and Cello. Written 'for the occasion of Sir William Glock's retirement from the Bath Festival which rose to such eminence under his leadership, June 3, 1984.' Dedicated to Sir William Glock. Completed in New York, 19 April 1984.

Canon for 4 combines two devices of Carter's previous canons. Like the central movement of the Canonic Suite, it simultaneously states prime [cello], retrograde [bass clarinet], inversion [flute] and retrograde inversion[violin]. The bass clarinet plays the cello part backwards and transposed down a minor third. The flute imitates the cello in inversion, beginning in bar six, with free counterpoint in the first five bars. The violin plays the retrograde of the flute line, including the first five bars, tranposed down a major third. Bars 66–67 mark the midpoint of the canon, and Carter makes the move to retrograde audible as the flute and violin cross paths.

Carter writes that he followed the old tradition of honoring a musical colleague with a demonstration of compositional skill, but that he wanted the piece 'to be interesting and communicative to a listener not pre-occupied with its formal devices.' While the rigorous structure of the piece is barely perceptible, it has an audible form. The cello line, designated as the 'original' can be divided into several contrasting segments: a burst of martellato sixteenth notes; an expressive twenty-six note melodic figure, whose first twelve-notes are a 'row'; a group of accented notes, each four eighths in duration, long held notes and a cadential phrase which first accelerates and then ritards. In the second half of the canon variants of these ideas recur in reversed order, but not in retrograde (which would be superfluous.) The espressivo melody does return in its original form, transposed down a minor seventh. The piece thus sounds like a circle rather than a mirror, returning to its starting-point by means of canonic rigor and thematic variation and repetition. The expressive melody becomes the key feature of the canon, appearing in its four forms at the beginning and end of the piece, but also heard in *Klangfarbenmelodie* at bars 100–105, a device Caster used in *Canon for 3*. Anyone who thinks that such puzzle canons write themselves might inspect the hundreds of pages of sketches Carter needed to arrive at the final version.

Riconoscenza per Goffredo Petrassi

Violin Solo. Dedicated to Petrassi 'in occasione del suo ottantesimo compleanno, con profunda stima e affettuosa amicizia.' Completed 30 April 1984. Première at the 1984 Festival Pontino by Georg Mönch, 15 June 1984.

Carter has often told me that he considered Petrassi to be his best musical friend; *Riconoscenza* is the first of two tributes. Its form recalls the seventh variation of the Variations for orchestra. (The Variations were composed in Rome; Carter may have intended an allusion to his first meeting with Petrassi.) It is an example of temporal counterpoint. Three ideas unfold in small, interspersed episodes, creating the illusion that we are hearing three pieces, expressive, percussive and peaceful, at once. The opening lyrical idea is built out of the intervals of the major second, minor third, tritone and major sixth. The flexible rhythm and expressive cantabile of this material will reappear in the opening viola solo in *Penthode*. The second idea is marked 'giocosamente furioso martellato' – performers should make it sound like a parody of fury, not the real thing. It uses the intervals of minor second, major second, minor sixth, minor seventh and major seventh, in violent scraping passages. The third material is slow and tranquil, built out of major thirds and fifths sustained as double stops, often in a harmonic sequence that produces the all-interval tetrachord.

esprit rude/esprit doux

For Flute and B flat Clarinet. Written 'for the celebration of Pierre Boulez' sixtieth birthday on 31 March 1985 in Baden-Baden.' Dedicated 'pour Pierre Boulez.' Completed in Waccabuc, 2 November 1984. 4 minutes. Première by members of L'Ensemble InterContemporain: Lawrence Beauregard, Flute; Alain Damiens, clarinet.

If the structure of *Canon for 4* recalled the mystification of the old puzzle canons, the dedication of *esprit rude/esprit doux* is something of an in-joke between two classically educated composers. Carter explains in the score how the title derives from the rough-breathing/smooth-breathing dualism of classical Greek pronunciation. The rough and smooth sounds appear in the Greek words transliterated as *hexèkoston etos*, meaning sixtieth year. The piece begins and ends with a motto, B flat C A E based on the B [flat] U[t] L[a] and E of 'Boulez.' However obscure, the title and motto have palpable musical implications. *esprit rude/esprit doux* is built out of contrasts between the rough and smooth sounds produced by the two woodwinds. It opposes different kinds of tonguing and legato, both within each instruments line and between them. The four pitches of the Boulez motto also spell out the all-interval tetrachord number 23. The two all-interval tetrachords appear during the sustained parts of the piece as the harmonic link between the instruments

The duet is reminiscent in character of the music played by the winds in *Triple Duo*, but here the flute and clarinet have contrasting harmonic and rhythmic materials. The division of intervals is based on a twelve-note chord structured like those in *In Sleep, In Thunder*: 1 9 7 2 8 6 11 3 5 10 4. The flute uses the first six intervals, the clarinet the latter six; the tritone is common property. The rhythms grow from a 21:25 polyrhythm which begins on the downbeat of bar 6 and ends on the downbeat of the last bar. At the initial tempo the structural pulses of the flute occur every thirty septuplet divisions of the quarter; the clarinet pulses occur every sixteen beats. The full duration of the structural pulse appears in the flute part in bars 17–20 (the C) and bars 51–64; and in the clarinet in bars 50–61 (Chart 24).

Division of intervals:
Flute: 3, 4, 5, 6, 10, 11.
Clarinet: 1, 2, 6, 7, 8, 9.
based on all-interval twelve-note chord*: 1 9 7 2 8 6 11 3 5 10 4
*#9 for hexachord 18
Structural polyrhythm: 21:25 MM5.25: MM6.25, based on sketch tempo of $\flat$ = 35
Flute pulses 3/20 [35 × 3 = 105; 105/20 = 5.25]
Clarinet pulses 5/28 [35 × 5 = 175; 175/28 = 6.25]

Chart 24 *esprit rude/esprit doux* (rough breathing/smooth breathing)

As in *Triple Duo*, the protagonists each have fast, slow and moderate material which are recombined in short episodes. The fastest material is scorrevole in character, the moderate music is giocoso, the slowest appears either as intensely loud or tranquilly soft. There are also two tremolando passages which emphasize the importance of the all-interval tetrachords as binding harmonies. These ideas are also differentiated in terms of roughness and smoothness. The scorrevole passages are smooth; the giocoso passages, rough. The sustained passages appear in both smooth and rough forms, while the tremolandos combine both qualities. The piece is assembled out of the many possible oppositions between the materials, from extreme difference, to near unanimity. The instruments contrast subtly in speed, rhythmic patterns and harmonic color. In the scorrevole sections, the flute gurgles in thirds while the clarinet slithers in seconds. In the giocoso section the flute plays rhythms based on the 5:4 polyrhythm while the clarinet bases its rhythms on 7:3. The two instruments come closest to communion in the tranquil section beginning at bar 51. Here the harmonic and rhythmic framework are exposed, yet here too the harmonic relation between the two instruments is clearest. Their combined motions complete all-interval tetrachords. The keystone of the piece is the sustained high minor second in bar 59, a kind of near-unison, where, acoustically, the sounds of the two instruments seem to blend. (See Ex. 11, page 47)

Enchanted Preludes 'for Ann Santen's Birthday'

Ann Santen was the programming director of the public radio station in Cincinnati, and played an active and creative role in bringing new music to the public's attention. Commissioned by Harry Santen for his wife, 'and composed in gratitude for their enthusiastic and deeply caring support of American music.' Composed December 1987–January 1988. Completed in New York 13 February 1988. Première by Patricia Spencer, flute, and André Emelianoff, cello, of the Da Capo Chamber Players in New York 16 May 1988.

Carter explains that the title comes from a section of Wallace Stevens's *The Pure Good of Theory* entitled 'All the Preludes to Felicity':

Felicity, ah! Time is the hooded enemy,
The inimical music, the enchantered space
In which the enchanted preludes have their place.

As is often Carter's practice, he chose the title after the piece was composed, though the sketches show that he appended the two-bar cadence after naming the piece. In the sketches he originally called the duet 'Spots of Time,' then 'The Secret Heart of Sound.' He searched through Stevens's complete poems and found no fewer than thirteen possible titles (including 'Scintillant Sizzlings') before arriving at 'Enchanted Preludes.' From the beginning, however, Carter thought of the duet as a Mendelssohnian scherzo.

In its construction *Enchanted Preludes* shows many similarities to *esprit rude/esprit doux*. A 45:56 polyrhythm runs the length of the piece, resulting in a contrast triple rhythms in the flute and quadruple rhythms in the cello. The intervals are divided on the basis of an all-interval twelve-note chord derived from hexachord number 19: 7 4 2 9 11 6 5 8 10 3 1. The cello plays the first five intervals, the flute the last five. This harmonic

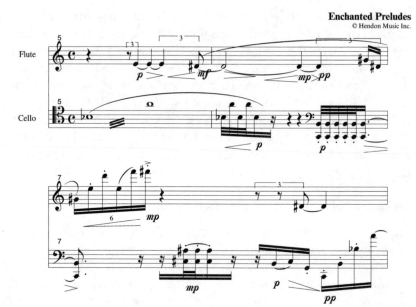

Ex. 39 Harmonic framework

relationship is articulated explicitly in bar 6 (Ex. 39). Carter emphasizes the use of four four-note chords (Nos. 3, 13 and 15) which combine the intervals of each instrument. Because of the brevity of the piece, and because of the very complete set of sketches for it in the Sacher Stiftung, *Enchanted Preludes* would be an excellent work to study for an understanding of Carter's compositional techniques and process. Of particular interest is the way Carter transforms the 'inimical music' of his abstract temporal framework into an unpredictable dance.

Enchanted Preludes is a study in color and mood. In sonority it solves a different problem from that posed by *esprit rude/esprit doux*. There Carter built the piece around subtle contrasts of similar-sounding instruments. Here the task was to bring the alien sonorities of flute and cello into the same sound world, an 'enchanted space.' Most obviously Carter does this by using cello harmonics (or flautando notes) often written higher than the flute line, as pedal tones. Most of the cello part lies very high except for the many pizzicato passages, whose sonority connects to the flute's staccato, and a single agitato phrase (from 101–108) which places the light character of the rest of the music in relief. Flute and cello also come together in their lyrical materials (lovers' duets?) which alternate early in the piece and combine climactically at the middle (61–67).

Birthday Flourish, 'for Helen'

A true 'pièce d'occasion,' *Birthday Flourish* was composed for Helen Carter on her birthday, 4 July 1988. It was originally written for five trumpets, and later transcribed for a brass quintet of two trumpets, horn and two trombones. It alternates quiet passages which unfold a melodic line in *Klangfarbenmelodie* with fanfare-like bursts. The concluding phrase is probably the most recherché arrangement of 'Happy Birthday' ever composed.

Con Leggerezza Pensosa

Omaggio a Italo Calvino. Commissioned by Dr. Raffaele Pozzi, the director of the Istituto di Studi Musicali in Latina, Italy, as a homage to the Italian author Italo Calvino, to be performed in connection with the institute's first annual awards for the best musicological papers of the year. Composed in June 1990 in Waccabuc (the last piece written there). Première 29 September 1990 at the Istituto di Studi Musicali, Latina, Italy, by Ciro Sarponi, clarinet; Jorge Risi, violin; Luigi Lanzillotta, cello.

Carter notes that the title was suggested by a remark Calvino made in his *Six Memos for the Next Millennium*: 'Above all I hope to have shown that there is such a thing as a lightness of thoughtfulness, just as we all know there is a lightness of frivolity. In fact, thoughtful lightness [leggerezza pensosa] can make frivolity seem dull and heavy.'

Carter's little trio compresses a great deal of musical contrast into its five minutes. The instruments divide up and share the intervals in three according to a twelve-note harmony heard in bars 3–6 :9 2 4 5 11 6 3 10 8 7 1 (Ex. 40). The cello plays intervals 9, 2, 4 and 5; the clarinet plays 5, 11, 6, 3, and 10; the violin, 10, 8, 7, and 1. They are also divided rhythmically with the clarinet playing triplets; the violin, sixteenths and the cello quin-tuplets. Carter has said that the funny thing about his use of structural polyrhythms is that they are very hard to find if you don't know where to look. The rhythmic sketches for this piece have not survived, but it may be built on a 50: 48: 45 ratio. The forces of disruption are balanced by a common harmonic goal, the all-triad hexachord which appears most explicitly in the tranquil passages which function as a kind of refrain alternating with the more playful passages.

Ex. 40 Twelve-tone harmony

Scrivo in Vento

For flute alone. 'For Robert Aitken.' Composed Spring 1991. Première 20 July 1991 at the XVIIIe Rencontres de la Chartreuse of the Centre Acanthes at the Festival of Avignon, France, by Robert Aitken. The title comes from Petrarch's Rime Sparse 212: '. . . I plow the waves and found my house on sand and write on the wind.' The première fell on Petrarch's 687th birthday.

Petrarch's sonnet contrasts the blessing of sleep with the turbulence of unrequited love. Carter evokes this contrast with an extravagant opposition of flute registers. The piece probably sets a record for use of the high C sharp, and crosses the register barrier with a couple of D sharps in alt. Harmonically, the dualism of the piece derives from a single source: Carter's hexachord number 20 (0, 1, 2, 3, 5, 7) which contains both all-interval tetrachords (0, 1, 3, 7) and (1, 2, 5, 7). Hexachord number 20 and an inversion contain all twelve tones, a feature Carter exploits at bars 48–49.

Trilogy

Although these three works were composed for separate occasions, and can be played separately, Carter thought of them as a unit from the beginning, a three-part work for Heinz and Ursula Holliger. Carter planned three 'portraits': of the composer and harpist Carlos Salzedo, of the composer Stefan Wolpe, and of the Holligers themselves. The entire *Trilogy* has as its motto the last two stanzas of Rilke's *Sonette an Orpheus*, II, 10:

> Aber noch ist uns das Dasein verzaubert; an hundert
> stellen ist es noch Ursprung. **Ein Spielen von reinen**
> **Kräften**, die keiner berührt, der nich kniet und bewundert.
> **Worte gehen noch zart am Unsäglichen aus** . . .
> Und **die Musik, immer neu**, das den bebendes Steinen,
> baut im unbrauchbaren Raum ihn vergöttliches Haus.
> [But existence is still enchanting for us; in hundreds of places it is still pristine. A play of pure forces, which no one can touch without kneeling and adoring. Words still peter out into what cannot be expressed . . . And music, ever new, builds out of the most tremulous stones her divinely consecrated house in unexploitable space.]

I BARIOLAGE FOR HARP

'For Ursula Holliger.' Motto: Ein Spielen von reines Kräften. Written for a festival of Carter's music in Geneva. Première 23 March 1992 by Ursula Holliger.

Bariolage is a tribute to Carlos Salzedo. Carter met Salzedo in the twenties; the harpist and composer was giving lessons to the sister of Carter's schoolfriend John Bitter. In his essay 'Expressionism and American Music' Carter cited Salzedo's book, *Modern Study of the Harp*, written in 1921, as an example of the development of the resources of instrumental technique in America, noting that Salzedo 'presents a whole new repertory of effects for that instrument that are still not incorporated into our composers' vocabulary.'[2] Carter had employed some of Salzedo's techniques in the harp parts of the Variations for Orchestra and *Penthode*, but Bariolage emphasizes such devices as pedal glissandos, xylophonic sounds and glissando with the back of the fingernail, as well as the more traditional effects of harmonics and playing 'près de la table.'

2 INNER SONG FOR OBOE

'To Heinz Holliger in memory of Stefan Wolpe.' Motto: Worte gehen noch zart am Unsäglichen aus. *Carter notes 'the fascinating friendship with Wolpe is a very treasured memory.' Written for a festival of Wolpe's music in Witten, Germany. Première 25 April 1992 by Heinz Holliger.*

In his sketches Carter refers to Inner Song as 'some thoughts about Wolpe's hexachord.' Wolpe composed his Suite in Hexachord for oboe and clarinet in 1936. Its first three movements use only six pitches: G, A flat, A, B flat, B and C. The remaining pitches enter only in the final Adagio. In his later music Wolpe often would begin a piece, such as *Form* for piano, with a statement of a hexachord which would immediately be subject to variation in register and texture and then introduce a complementary hexachord according to his idea of 'molding opposites into adjacent situations.' Carter knew Wolpe from the early forties, when Wolpe arrived in New York from Palestine. There was always a certain rivalry between the two composers whose personalities contrasted sharply. Driven out of Germany and then Austria as a Jew and a Communist, and suffering in his later years from Parkinson's disease, Wolpe lived a life of many displacements and disappointments. Yet he appeared as an embattled visionary surrounded by a small circle of devoted disciples and students. To pay the rent he would lecture on aesthetic philosophy for composers, painters and jazz musicians, in his apartment, passing the hat afterwards. He felt particularly at home with the rough-and-tumble aesthetic of New York Action Painting and would tell students to look out of the window and compose music based on the sounds of the traffic. Carter was always impressed with Wolpe's compositional daring; after a Wolpe concert he told me 'he does everything wrong and it comes out right.' Carter's choice of the oboe for a Wolpe tribute also honors the American oboist Josef Marx, Wolpe's long-time friend, publisher and performer, who also premièred the *Suite in Hexachord* as well as Carter's *Pastoral* for English horn.

Inner Song begins with the exact hexachord of Wolpe's suite, the chromatic span upward from G to C, but then uses many transpositions to form a slow arching melodic line which is only occasionally punctuated by faster motion. The complementary hexachord is the one from C sharp to F sharp but Carter only juxtaposes these two forms twice in the piece, in bars 33–37 and at the end. Carter's main interest in 'Wolpe's hexachord' is in generating a variety of spacings that unfold five different intervals. These are mainly heard in a series of descending figures that are the most striking feature of the work, and climax with the three descents from high F sharp beginning at bar 76.

3 IMMER NEU FOR OBOE AND HARP

'To Ursula and Heinz Holliger.' Motto: die Musik, immer neu. *Première, at the request of Raffaele Pozzi, at the Pontino Festival 30 June 1992, 'a festival centered around a vision of the new that led so many beside Columbus to explore the world 500 years ago. In this piece each instrument in turn leads the other to a new tempo.'*

Immer neu is a study in metrical modulation, as suggested by Carter's program note. The sketches reveal that, at Heinz Holliger's urging, Carter added many of the virtuosic oboe phrases after a first draft had been completed, so that the piece became more extroverted and dramatic in character.

Gra for B Flat Clarinet

'For Witold Lutosławski's 80th Birthday with admiration and affection.' Composed February–April 1993. First performance 4 June 1993, Pontino Festival, Sermoneta, Italy, by Roland Dury, clarinet.

Lutosławski composed a piece for Carter's eightieth birthday (which featured a huge bass drum) and here Carter returns the favor. The character of the piece is marked by the unusual term 'Ghiribizzo' – whimsically. It is a humorous exploration of the registers of the clarinet and of the all-triad hexachord, which is set out with the coyness of a purring kitten in the opening in the clarinet's low register. An important part of Carter's game is to find ways of restating the six-note figure without having it sound like a six-note figure. The piece juxtaposes legato, staccato and sustained phrases in an improvisatory fashion with no idea lasting longer than four bars before it is interrupted. At the end, beginning at bar 86, Carter introduces a recurring multiphonic E-B as a cadential 'dominant' pedal. Typically of his 'latest phase,' he does not state this chord at a mathematically regular pulse.

Figment for Cello Alone

'To Thomas Demenga.' Composed in Santa Monica, California in December 1993 and January 1994 (work interrupted by a major earthquake) and revised in New York in June 1994 with revisions through January 1995. First performance 8 May 1995, in New York City, by Thomas Demenga.

Over the years several cellists, including Mstislav Rostropovich and Fred Sherry, have asked Carter for a cello concerto. *Figment*, for all its brevity, feels like a cello concerto without orchestra – the orchestra is a figment of the listener's imagination. It is an extravagant, exhibitionistic showcase, taking the cello all over its four octave range in a series of brief, dramatically contrasted phrases.

Carter has described the piece as 'a variety of contrasting, dramatic moments using material derived from a single musical idea.' That idea is hexachord number 35 and it is presented with the opening gesture of the piece (Ex. 41) and then over and over again in changing transpositions,

Figment
© Hendon Music Inc.

Ex. 41 All-triad hexachord

spacings and orderings, though Carter contrives never to state it as a 'theme.'

Fragment for String Quartet

'To the memory of David Huntley.' Première 13 October 1994, Merkin Hall, New York City, by the Kronos Quartet.

This short piece was written for a concert in memory of the director of the New York office of Boosey & Hawkes. It is played entirely as harmonics. Despite its title, it is not part of another piece and is a different work from the Adagio sereno of the Fifth Quartet which is also played in harmonics.

esprit rude/esprit doux II for Flute, Clarinet and Marimba

'Pour Pierre Boulez en célébration de son soixante-dixième anniversaire avec profonde admiration et amitié affectueuse.' First performance 30 March 1995

(Boulez's birthday), Orchestra Hall, Chicago, by Richard Graef, flute, John Yeh, clarinet and James Ross, marimba.

The score indicates that *esprit rude/esprit doux II* may be performed alone or follow *esprit rude/esprit doux I* after a pause, or the two works can be played without interruption by substituting the first bar of *II* for the last bar of *I*. The old title takes on a new significance: the contrast of rough and smooth breathing now relates to the contrasting epsilons in the Greek 'hebdomèkoston etos' or seventieth year. As in the first piece, Carter derives a motto from Boulez's name: B flat, C A E; it appears at the very end. The 'open' form of the piece may itself be a tribute to Boulez who has expanded works like *Eclats* and *explosante/fixe* through similar additions.

Played together, the two Boulez tributes offer a fine contrast of late and later Carter. *er/ed II* has a polyrhythmic substructure like its predecessor. The three parts, which do not begin together, converge on a silent beat before the final chord in a polyrhythm based on every sixty-eighth (17×4) quintuplet sixteenth for the flute, every forty-eighth (16×3) triplet eighth for the clarinet, and every thirty-fifth sixteenth for the marimba. But there is no intervallic partitioning. Instead the three instruments conspire to restate hexachord number 35 in ever-changing fashion. Their parts, therefore have to be heard first harmonically rather than linearly, the reverse of *er/ed I*.

Since *er/ed I* contrasts rough and smooth breathing, the introduction of the marimba, which does not breathe at all, is a bit surprising, but the marimba has its own degrees of roughness and smoothness, and its sonority can blend easily with those of the winds, except when it comes to slow, sustained melody. Carter brings the marimba closest to the winds in tremolando passages; and the winds closest to the marimba in angular staccato sections. But in the second half of the piece the melodic tendency of the winds leads them ever further from the percussion, as they play an expressively melodic duet.

A Six Letter Letter for English Horn

Carter's note:

> *A Six Letter Letter* was composed to be played as a surprise encore at the conclusion of a concert given in Basel, Switzerland 27 April 1996, to celebrate Dr. Paul Sacher's ninetieth birthday and the tenth anniversary of the opening of the Paul Sacher Foundation. As the

concert concluded with a performance by Heinz Holliger of my Oboe Concerto, I decided to write Holliger an encore using his English horn. This short solo was composed in New York during March 1996 and uses only the six pitches associated with the name S A C H E R – E flat, A, C, H (b), E, D (re).

Shard for Solo Guitar

Written for David Starobin in 1997.

Notes

1 See Howard Pollack, *Harvard Composers*, for a thoughtful discussion of Piston's influence on several generations of students.
2 WEC, p. 241.

II *Vocal Music*

5 Choral Works

The majority of Carter's compositions before 1948 are choral works, written for a variety of vocal ensembles. This emphasis may now appear surprising, for after *Emblems* of 1947, Carter never returned to the choral medium. However, because he had conducted and sung in choruses and madrigal choirs at Harvard and in Paris, choral composing was a natural direction for him to take after he returned home from France. In Paris, he had organized choirs for the performance of older music; on his return to the States he transcribed a large number of medieval and Renaissance works from manuscripts and old editions in the New York Public Library. Among these transcriptions are works by Perotin, Machaut, Dufay, Obrecht, Ockeghem, Monte, Gabrieli and Gesualdo.[1]

Tarantella

The *Tarantella*, originally the finale to *Mostellaria*, was first performed by the Harvard Glee Club in April 1937; it remained a favorite of that ensemble for many years. It exists in two versions: with orchestral or four-hand piano accompaniment. The latter version was first published by the Harvard Music Department in 1972, and later by Associated Music Publishers.

The text of the *Tarantella* is from Ovid's *Fasti*, book V, lines 183–99 and 331–77. It describes the Bacchic celebrations of May which were the occasion for performances of Plautus's comedies; Carter's earliest published piece is a rite of spring. It was probably inspired by a different work of Stravinsky, the chorus 'Mulier in vestibulo' from *Oedipus Rex*. Carter's chorus, carefully crafted and sophisticated in its musical style, demonstrates what he had learned in Paris. Although the music may not sound like later Carter, it certainly reflects Harvard in its conspicuous literary erudition and sly musical humor. Carter took much of the melodic material from a book of Neapolitan tarantellas – the chorus of virile Roman youths therefore sings tunes associated with Calabrian peasant women, the kind of music Harvard students would hear in a North End spaghetti joint.

Harmonically, the *Tarantella* is tonal but often highly dissonant – functional harmonies are sounded against appoggiatura chords, usually a half-step away. At the entrance of the chorus, for instance, an F natural in the bass supports an E major triad in the chorus (Carter uses this very harmony near the opening of the First Quartet.) The result is not bitonality, since the harmonic roots are clear, but rather a high level of harmonic tension stemming from the clash of appoggiatura chords with the diatonic vocal lines. Compared to the Stravinsky that it resembles, the *Tarantella* shows a more dynamic tonal structure. The whole piece might be described as a search for the final cadence on D, a search that begins from tonal ambiguity, and is colored by the half-step relationships inherent in the polychords. The final cadence on D is prepared by a penultimate cadence on D flat, followed by a superimposition of E flat on the D major harmonies in the chorus. Throughout the piece, D is approached by these contrary half-step motions.

Unlike much of Carter's music from this period, *Tarantella* had a marked success. Goddard Lieberson (later of Columbia Records) wrote:

> Carter succeeded in writing something that even the Harvard boys couldn't be tight-lipped about! I wish I could convey with words the lift this music gave.'²

It was after hearing this work that Carter's Harvard friend Lincoln Kirstein asked him to become musical director of his new touring company, Ballet Caravan, a position that soon led to the writing of the ballet *Pocahontas*.

Let's Be Gay

In a similar style to the *Tarantella*, but slighter, is *Let's Be Gay*, for women's chorus and two pianos, which was commissioned by Nicholas Nabokov for a production of *The Beggar's Opera* at Wells College in upstate New York. The work continues the melding of popular-style melodic material and tangy polychordal harmonies, once again to express *carpe diem* revelry. Although he has saved the manuscript, Carter feels that this chorus is too inconsequential to merit publication.

To Music

In 1937 Carter organized a madrigal chorus in New York, and made the transcriptions of early music previously described. To complement these older works he began to compose a Madrigal Book. *To Music* was one of two settings of Robert Herrick for a cappella chorus. The other Herrick piece, *Harvest Home*, was performed in 1937 and reviewed by Paul

Rosenfeld who thought that the line 'to the rough sickle, and crook'd scythe' indicated that the song was a leftist anthem – in the thirties, apparently, anything could be politicized. Whatever its political purpose (Carter doesn't recall any such intention), it remained unpublished for sixty years; Carter edited *Harvest Home* for publication and a recording in the spring of 1997.

To Music sets Herrick's poem, 'To Music, To Becalm His Fever.' The poem praises music for its power to ease suffering but its resolution is unclear; the concluding flight to heaven is either a conventional trope for the music of the spheres, or an image of the poet's ultimate relief from worldly suffering. The work won a WPA contest and was performed by Lehman Engel's Madrigal Singers in the spring of 1938, and subsequently by Varèse and his worker's chorus at the Greenwich House Music School. (Carter says Varèse made the music sound like Varèse, which is hard to imagine.)

To Music belongs to a brief neo-Jacobean phase in Carter's music. His Harvard room-mate, the musicologist Stephen Tuttle, had introduced him to the music of William Byrd, and to the Fitzwilliam Virginal Book and the English madrigal composers. In its modal melodic line, elegant melismas and flexible rhythmic accentuation, *To Music* echoes the English madrigalists, as does its melancholy tone, which recalls Dowland and Wilbye. In harmony and texture, however, it was up to date. The texture fans out from four to seven parts and at the end a solo soprano soars above the choral mass in an evocation of the poet's heavenly flight. The work begins in F sharp aeolian, then moves to A aeolian and phrygian. The central stanza, which pictures the poet's feverish sufferings, sounds more chromatic, but actually lies within C sharp minor, exploiting the clash of raised and lowered leading notes that traditionally colors the minor mode. The tonality moves to C sharp major where the consuming fire dies down to a gentle flame. The music then returns to its opening F sharp tonality but the ending – a cadence on B flat, a key that has not previously appeared – is completely unexpected. In traditional theory this tonality might be said to express the Picardy third in F sharp minor, but Carter explains it as a Doppler effect – the B flat follows a preparation on B, and the sinking tonality suggests the poem's motion into the celestial distance. (Ives used a similar device at the close of his song 'West London.')

Heart Not So Heavy As Mine

In his next choral work, *Heart Not So Heavy As Mine*, written in 1938 Carter simplified his technique. Whereas the Herrick chorus sounds at times uncomfortably like an updated madrigal, this setting of Emily Dickinson strikes a new tone. A miniature drama of opposed voices, it is the seed of much later Carter.

The opening third of the work lies within the scale of B flat aeolian (natural minor). Instead of harmonic motion, there is a gradual saturation of a static tonality. The middle section similarly moves within G aeolian and phrygian, but with more ambiguity as to tonal center, creating a growing harmonic tension which is released at the climactic recapitulation of the opening, a sudden return to B flat aeolian, now strongly colored by D flat. The final cadence in B flat major is at once the relative and parallel major of the main tonal areas of the piece, and its shifting major-minor inflection echoes the climactic D flat – all the tonal elements of the piece are brought to final resolution simply and clearly.

Heart Not So Heavy As Mine

Ex. 42 Climactic turning point

The poem contrasts the isolation of the poet with the vitality of an unknown passer-by whistling a tune. Carter superimposes fragments of a lively music on a sustained tolling motif (suggestive of the 'Dies Irae' or of Brahms op. 118, No. 6). Both kinds of music migrate through the four voices. The fact that both ideas share the same pitches serves to heighten their rhythmic and expressive contrast. The form of the work also antici- pates later developments in Carter's music. The climax, occurring at the end of the phrase 'without the knowing why,' overlaps the return of the opening motif. The harmony suddenly moves from C minor to D flat major, precisely at the melodic climax of the work, but is immediately pulled back to B flat minor by the bass (Ex. 42). The climax is at once a point of arrival and a point of departure. This complex gesture is to appear again in the Symphony No. 1 and the Variations for Orchestra.

The Defense of Corinth (1941)

Written in 1941 for the Harvard Glee club when Carter was teaching music, classics and mathematics at St. John's College, Annapolis, this is a comic work with serious overtones. Scored for men's chorus, piano duet and speaker, it combines narration, rhythmic recitation, choral speaking, whispering and hissing, with virtuosic sung polyphony. The inspiration for these effects was Milhaud's *La Mort d'un Tyran*. The work puts these effects to dramatic use: the chorus slowly emerges from the narrator's speaking voice, its music gradually evolving from speech and isolated sung notes to a polyphony of speech and song; speech then drops out and the song mounts to a dense choral fugue, which then fades back into the narrator's words and a bare pianissimo cadence.

The complex form of the work serves an equally complex expressive goal. *The Defense of Corinth* is both comic and cautionary. In choosing Rabelais's account of the tale of Diogenes and his tub (in a delightfully archaic seventeenth-century translation by Urquhart and Motteux) Carter had political motives, for in 1941, before the United States entered the war, this text could be read as a protest against American neutrality, and against the artist's own sense of uselessness at a time of national crisis. The extraordinary sound-world of *The Defense of Corinth* equates Carter's music with Diogenes's tub. The music transforms noise into words and speech into song. The opening choral description of the Corinthians' preparation for the siege uses speech noises as musical sounds. By contrast, the climactic double fugue celebrating Diogenes's downhill slide turns music back into noise, in a splattering of machine-gunned cross-accents.

The Harmony of Morning

Carter's only work for women's chorus and orchestra sets 'Another Music' by Mark Van Doren, a poem neither dense nor modern, nor with any apparent social or political implications. Its subject, however, is central to Carter's work: the relation of music to both sound and thought. To convey the poem's progression from sounds to ideas, Carter chose the form of cantus firmus variation. A seven-note motif rings through the entire work, recurring in varied guises. The accompaniment is an integral part of the drama: the poem's 'rage of the viols' gives rise to an energetic concertino for orchestra at the work's centre. The small instrumental ensemble, woodwind quintet, piano and strings, gives forth a spray of poetic colors – note the two responses to 'sweet keys depressed,' the bell-like sound achieved through pizzicato heterophony at letter T, the pianissimo chime of piano and plucked strings just before the conclusion. The choral sonority is similarly iridescent, particularly in the way it draws musical colors and accents from the sounds of the words; as in the fugato on 'but in the chambers of a brain/Are bells that clap an answer.'

Harmonically, the work sums up the resources of the flexible, diatonic idiom that Carter first used in *Heart Not So Heavy As Mine*, and that he explored on an extensive scale in the Symphony No. 1. *The Harmony of Morning* is saturated with the sound of A major; at the same time it is constantly in harmonic motion. Typically subtle in harmonic function is the chordal frame of the central section of the piece. First stated as a juxtaposition of A major on D minor, it later returns a semitone lower: a section in A flat prepares the return to the central A major tonality. This harmonic progression mirrors the high points in the work's vocal range – G sharp seems to be the highest sustained note, until the octave leap to high A on 'with truth.' The climactic statement of range dramatizes the most striking structural overlap of the work: the orchestra begins the coda with a sharp change in texture while the chorus continues its previous phrase, stretching it to a new climax against the sudden rhythmic burst in the orchestra.

Musicians Wrestle Everywhere

Written in 1945, this five-voice madrigal sets Emily Dickinson at her most dense and ambiguous. The poem is full of intimations of immortality, but its vision is at once vivid and uncertain. Carter employs a cross-accented rhythmic counterpoint. The way the crossed-accents spring from the syllabic stress of the words suggests an updated Renaissance practice.

Harmonically, *Musicians* extends the technique of controlled pandiatonic writing of *Heart Not So Heavy As Mine*. The vertical combinations of notes are more dissonant; the harmonic motion is faster and more unstable. After successive spins through all the sharp and flat keys the music resolves on C major, the one tonality not previously stated. The double ending in simultaneous layers of loud and soft sound dramatically captures the central ambivalence of the poem, making the very purity of the final C major triad provocative and unsettling. Richard Franko Goldman, one of Carter's earliest and most perceptive champions, saw in this work the beginnings of Carter's later music.[3]

Emblems

Written for the Harvard Glee Club, *Emblems* is a serious counterpart to *The Defense of Corinth*. Like *The Defense*, *Emblems* is about the relationship of art and society. Although composed in 1947, it was not performed until 1952 because of its difficulty. The text by Allen Tate was suggested to Carter by his friend, the poet John Berryman.

To an even greater extent than *The Defense of Corinth*, *Emblems* has a distinctive structure and sound. The choral sonority is granitic, filling the total range of the male voice with up to eight-part harmony. The work takes the novel form of a concerto for piano and chorus; the piano is not an accompaniment but an independent element; the opening movement of the piece is entirely a cappella. The piano enters with a bravura burst at the beginning of the second movement. This flourish is a stylized abstraction of a bass-drum roll traditional to a dirge; the movement is a funeral march. The funeral march gradually fades away, continuing in the piano while the chorus begins the fast final section of the work. After briefly joining in the rapid, fugato motion, the piano evaporates, and the piece ends with a massive fortissimo slab of choral sonority, all the more intense for the absence of piano support.

Notes

1 Carter gave these transcriptions to Noah Greenberg, founder of the New York Pro Musica, when Greenberg was copying the parts for the First Quartet.
2 *Modern Music* XIV, 4 (May–June 1937)
3 *MQ* XLIII, 2 (April 1957) p. 156.

6 Songs with Piano (or Guitar)

In his entire career Carter has published just ten songs for voice and piano, all based on American poems; the last five were written after a fifty-year hiatus in this genre. This sparse offering seems odd in a composer whose work gives so much evidence of literary influence, but the songs reveal a certain discomfort with the conventions of the genre. Carter once told me that he admired the late Fauré songs, but found that they were so subtle in the relation between words and music as to be virtually unperformable; any effort the singer might make to put the songs over would violate their aesthetic.

Carter's least typical songs, early settings of Frost, might have been written by Samuel Barber; they share the charm and intimacy that has drawn singers to Barber's songs. But as early as *Warble for Lilac Time* of 1943, Carter set out on a different path. He set a long and shapeless poem of Whitman's in a style that violates the normal limits of art-song style and vocal *fach*. There are numerous melismas, and an operatic use of the upper register that make the song feel more like a Bach aria than a *lied*; but the style does not suggest Bach at all, let alone Richard Strauss whose songs can also be operatic. Similarly the voice implied by the music needs both strength and agility, an unlikely Wagnerian bel-canto, and also, at times, must revert to the intimate scale of lieder singing. *Warble* may seem like an ambitious experiment with mixed results but in its choice of a difficult text and refusal of art-song traditions it sets the pattern for the six songs that follow.

'Tell Me Where is Fancy Bred'

Carter's earliest published song was written at short notice in 1938, as incidental music for a recording of *The Merchant of Venice* by Orson Welles's famed Mercury Theatre. This was also Carter's first piece to be recorded. The song, scored for low voice and guitar, was first published in 1972 with the guitar part edited by the guitarist-composer Stanley Silverman.

The style of the song echoes Campion and Dowland. The modal melody is drawn out in sighing phrases, complemented by simple counterpoint in the guitar – the two parts intersect on the word 'cradle.' This is the finest work of Carter's back-to-Byrd phase.

Three Poems of Robert Frost

Carter began his settings of American poetry with Robert Frost. Three of these songs are now published as a group. *The Line Gang*, not published until 1975, calls for a heavier voice than either *The Dust of Snow* or *The Rose Family* require, and is not up to the artistic level of the other two songs. The Frost songs are the closest Carter ever came to the charming vocal manner of Copland and Barber. *The Dust of Snow* and *The Rose Family* can be sung by a non-virtuoso (who can count) and have often served as encores for a song recital. *The Dust of Snow* contrasts a long, slow-moving melodic line against a darting, staccato, syncopated accompaniment. The pentatonic vocal line captures Frost's matter-of-fact, New England intonation, while the piano's suggestion of sleigh bells sets off the poet's words in the blank spaces of a winter landscape.

The Rose Family is Frost's response to Gertrude Stein. Carter captures the poem's tongue-in-cheek tone by setting it in a fast-moving 5/8 meter, a little frantic, a bit off-center. The subtlety here is harmonic. Carter begins with fifth-dominated pentatonic material that gradually modulates away from its opening tonality and then back to it, traveling all round the circle of fifths in less than a minute. At its half-way point the song has moved from A flat to A major (notated in the voice as B double flat). The implications of this harmonic technique were to be more fully realized in the first movement of the Piano Sonata.

The Line Gang portrays a noisy construction crew breaking through a forest to put up phone and telegraph lines. It was not published until 1975 and seems to fall between the light songs of 1942 and the larger vocal canvases of the following year. The musical punch-line, an imitation of a telegraphic key-punch, though cleverly set up early in the song, suggests a comic attitude not apparent in the text.

Carter arranged the Frost songs for chamber orchestra in 1975.

Warble for Lilac Time (1943)

First performed by Helen Boatwright, soprano, and Helmut Baewald, piano, at the League of Composers, Museum of Modern Art, New York, 16 March 1947; a version with chamber orchestra had been performed the year before, and it is possible that the song was conceived orchestrally. In contrast to the aphorisms of Frost, Carter here set a vast, unruly catalogue poem of Whitman. The poem is a catch-all of springtime reminiscences, in the course of which Whitman eventually transforms himself from outside observer to the voice of nature itself, indistinguishable from the warbling song of the birds. Carter's vocal style, perhaps stimulated by the original orchestral accompaniment, here similarly crosses the stylistic line from simplicity to extravagance. The vocal line sustains long phrases against the fast-flowing stream of the accompaniment.

Harmonically, the song uses the pandiatonic idiom in a fluid way similar to *The Harmony of Morning*. From a simple diatonic opening the music gradually accelerates in harmonic motion; these speeding changes culminate in polychordal clashes. As in other works of this time, a half-step conflict, here between E and E flat, frames the harmony. The harmonic tension climaxes and resolves in the soaring melismatic setting of the words 'to sing,' the climax of the song (Ex. 43).

Warble for Lilac-time
© 1956 Peer International Corp. Used by permission

Ex. 43 Voice of nature

Voyage

Premièred on the same concert as *Warble* and dedicated to John and Hope Kirkpatrick. Arranged for chamber orchestra in 1975 (rev. 1979), *Voyage*, written in 1943 (though the score is dated 1945) may be Carter's earliest masterpiece; both its style and its emotional content are deeply personal and point to the later music, especially to the Piano Sonata which shares its B major tonality. Like *Warble*, it sets a difficult poem in an arioso style, but it seems more focussed in syntax and form. In its stylized, continuous accompaniment, the song and its emotions suggest the influence of such Fauré songs as 'Au cimitière' and 'Prison.' The text, Hart Crane's 'Infinite Consanguinity,' one of a group of poems entitled 'Voyages' published in *White Buildings*, is obscure in syntax and symbolism, but not in its emotion. It is an acceptance of the destructive and renewing power of love. (Carter wrote an *explication de texte* for the song's first edition.) Carter discovered Crane's poetry in the 1920s when *White Buildings* and *The Bridge* first appeared, and he has obviously felt deep affinities with Crane – for all their differences they both were rebellious sons of wealthy families. He portrayed the poet's suicide both in this song and in *A Symphony of Three Orchestras*. (If *Voyage* were sung before a performance of the Piano Sonata, the latter work might appear to have a Crane subtext as well.) The song takes us into a different world from the wistfulness of Carter's early music.

Voyage is simple in conception. The piano weaves a flowing contrapuntal texture based on a six-note motif in quarter notes which moves between slow, parallel outer voices. The motif is a Carter signature of this period; it engenders both the second movement of the Symphony No. 1 and the *Elegy*. With this figure, Carter develops a subtly evolving ostinato, constantly changing in rhythmic shape. The interplay of two strands in the accompaniment and the third element of the voice yields a complex cross-accented texture which evokes the motion of the sea without recourse to conventional tone-painting. The outer lines of the piano part gradually evolve into the dramatically tolling bells – echoing Crane's 'Broken Tower.' The vocal line, preferably sung by a dramatic mezzo or heroic tenor, seems to float slowly on the piano's surface, joining it seemingly only at occasional moments of contact.

Harmonically the song reveals a new side of Carter's pandiatonic practice. The slow parallel thirds of the piano's outer voices give rise to polytonal cross currents that increase in tension until the climactic superimposition of G minor and E major at 'unto your body rocking' (Ex. 44). The final cadence is bitonal – E flat major appears as an overtone of a B major bass. The harmonic conception is motivated by the contrapuntal writing. Each strand has its own tonal center, and their combined motion

Ex. 44 Polytonal harmonies

produces six-and seven-note harmonies which replace tonal triads as the harmonic norm. The harmonic idiom of *Voyage* leads directly to that of the Piano Sonata.

The Difference

The Difference, written in 1944, is an unpublished duet for soprano and baritone with piano accompaniment, to a poem by Mark Van Doren. The poem describes two people whose perception of reality is different – a Carterian situation that the composer felt deserved a more dramatic and contrapuntal treatment than he gave it here. By his later standards the scale of the song is too small for the forces employed, and its working-out too facile; but it is an attractive setting which anticipates in texture and harmony parts of the Cello Sonata written four years later.

Of Challenge and of Love

Written in the last months of 1994. Commissioned by the Aldeburgh Foundation for Lucy Shelton with funding provided by the Rex Foundation. First performed 23 June 1995 at the Aldeburgh Festival by Lucy Shelton, soprano, and John Constable, piano.

More than fifty years after writing *Voyage*, Carter returned to the medium of voice and piano with settings of five poems by John Hollander. Hollander has long shown an interest in the relation of poetry and music; his early scholarly book *The Un-tuning of the Sky* traces the change in the poetic image of music in the seventeenth century. Milton Babbitt set Hollander's verse in *Philomel* and *The Head of the Bed*. In some ways Hollander's poetry is a surprising choice for Carter, for it lacks the dramatic quality and emotional directness found in Bishop and Lowell. (When I studied with Carter, he was uncharacteristically dogmatic about what kinds of poetry were and were not suitable for song; he felt, for instance, that Wallace Stevens's poems lacked the requisite drama and the presence of a clear 'persona.') Hollander's poetry might be termed neo-metaphysical, a modern version of Donne, Herbert or Marvell. It develops complex metaphors and often uses archaic verse forms. In the program note printed in the score Carter states that the character of the poem 'Quatrains from Harp Lake,' with its 'brief, vividly contrasting quatrains that have an undercurrent of irony and deep anxiety,' dictated the choice of the other poems.

Compared to his works for voice and ensemble, the Hollander songs are intimate, though not cozy, and knotty. The songs are not recitations; Carter often stretches the words out in long melismas. The piano and vocal writing is elaborate and intertwined. Often the piano part seems to be developing metaphorical figures of its own, pushing the poet's words in directions they don't seem to want to go. Perhaps the piano accompaniment should be thought of as a 'writerly' reader, to borrow Roland Barthes's term, producing its own textual overlay as a response to the poems.

Technically all five songs are composed 'in hexachord' using the all-triad hexachord 6–35 much as Carter had done in 90+; in the opening bar of 'End of a chapter' the piano plays a 'Link' all-interval chord; the first notes of the voice part are the pitches from the all-triad hexachord contained in the 'Link' chord. In the first three songs, Carter develops a piano sonority suggested by the text. 'High on our Tower' places two lovers on a metaphorical windswept white tower. The rapid figuration of the piano part suggests an equally metaphorical musical wind sweeping around the passionate vocal line. In 'Under the Dome' the poem's echo chamber inspires a study of resonance in the piano part, with the piano sustained almost throughout. In 'Am Klavier,' which provides the title words of Carter's cycle, the poem seems to be addressed to the piano keyboard in its title, although it speaks of the relation between memory and the present. The piano part is an étude in articulation; its contrapuntal texture combines lines with different kinds of touch. The relation of the voice to the piano may be suggested by the phrase: 'thus what we are, being sung against what we come / to be a part of.' This song illustrates well the games Carter often plays with literalness. The word 'pluck' is accompanied by a staccato chord, but 'harp' (a pun in the poem) does not produce an 'arpeggio.' The staccato chord is not a response to the word 'pluck' but part of the piano's repertory of attacks; momentarily the poem's 'story' and the piano's seem to overlap, but just as suddenly they move apart.

The last two songs show a more abstract relation between text and music. Carter was particularly proud of 'Quatrains from Harp Lake' because it presented the biggest musical challenge. The poem is a sequence of nine four-line stanzas; each stanza consists of two sentences of contradictory meaning. The music is likewise a series of reversals, each one different from the previous; only the last stanza is accompanied by a single figure, a tolling of fifths in a regular cross-rhythm of thirteen sixteenths. 'End of a Chapter' is an aphorism, in which Carter seems to undercut Hollander's pomposity. (Hollander's words seem to be a paraphrase of a famous saying of Schoenberg's.) Carter represents 'Beauty' with an ironically bare two-note whole-step motif (Ex. 45). The texture is based on a simple polyrhythmic structure. The piano part is built on

'End of a Chapter' from Challenge and of Love
© Hendon Music Inc.

Ex. 45 Whole-step motif

a skeletal rhythm of every sixteenth triplet eighth; the vocal part, on a rhythmic pattern which sounds every ninth eighth-note. (The analyst following this pattern will discover a little musical joke near the end.) The 'insensitive' piano coda reminds the listener not to take the words too seriously, or perhaps underscores the poet's distinction between the beautiful and the picturesque.

7 Works for Solo Voices and Instruments

In the late 1970s Carter, who had written no vocal music since 1947, turned once again to American poetry. He composed three works for voices and instrumental ensemble: *A Mirror on Which to Dwell* to poems of Elizabeth Bishop, *Syringa*, to a poem by John Ashbery, and *In Sleep, In Thunder* to poems of Robert Lowell; *A Symphony of Three Orchestras*, written in the midst of the poetic trilogy is itself a portrait of Hart Crane. For the sung works Carter chose three contemporary poets with contrasting personalities; each poet presented him with a different expressive problem. For Bishop, Carter's music had to be intimate; for Ashbery, daring; for Lowell, mad.

Carter's approach to vocal writing owes little to the traditions of art-song or opera. He has said that the source of his vocal style was his experience of singing Bach cantatas while he studied with Nadia Boulanger. His works share certain features in common with Bach's arias; they often give a prominent role to an obbligato instrument (the oboe in 'Sandpiper'; the trumpet in 'Across the Yard: La Ignota') and reflect the text in emblematic terms rather than through the devices of lyrical expression. Unlike Bach, or anyone else, Carter imposed two rather stringent conditions on himself. His vocal lines are in a novel arioso style; they are not recitatives but have the quality of a stylized reading in their response to the rhythm of the words: as Lloyd Schwartz has written, 'Carter is breaking down the differences not only between recitative and aria but between recitative and speech. The notes themselves evoke speech inflections, yet they can soar suddenly into high-flying operatic lyricism. Rangy coloratura alternate unpredictably with leaping declamation – it's like Bellini and Wagner at the same time.'[1] Bellini, Wagner, even, at times, Ives.

Carter's second constraint is perhaps more puzzling. He eschews preludes, interludes and postludes. The music begins and ends with the poet's word; Carter does not use instrumental interludes to announce his personal reading of the poems, the way Wolf or Berg do. Such parentheses create a distance between music and the poetry; the tendency in Carter is toward an expressive synthesis. Each of these cycles or cantatas seeks a common ground where the poems and the music can read each other.

A suggestion: *A Mirror, Syringa* and *In Sleep, In Thunder* have been performed together several times, usually in the order: Bishop, Lowell, intermission, Ashbery. Taken together, they form a triple vision of American poetry. In an age when so many different kinds of musical theater are termed opera, Carter's trilogy calls out for a staging which would recognize its proximity to the Monteverdian origins of the form. The four singers might sing *Heart Not So Heavy as Mine* as an overture.

A Mirror on Which to Dwell (six poems of Elizabeth Bishop)

A Mirror was commissioned by Speculum Musicae, in honour of the United States Bicentennial, with grants from the New York State Council on the Arts, the Mellon Foundation, Milton M. Scofield, Murray Socolof, Fred Sherry and Bernard E. Brandes. It is dedicated to the soprano Susan Davenny Wyner and Speculum Musicae, who gave the first performance of A Mirror, *conducted by Richard Fitz, at Hunter College Playhouse, New York City, 24 February 1976.*

The work is scored for nine players; each song has a different instrumentation:

'Anaphora': Alto flute, oboe, clarinet in B flat, vibraphone, piano, violin, viola, cello, bass.
'Argument': Alto flute, bass clarinet, four bongos, piano, cello, bass.
'Sandpiper': Oboe, piano, violin, viola, cello, bass.
'Insomnia': Piccolo, marimba, violin, viola.
'A View of the Capitol': Flute-piccolo, oboe, clarinet B flat and E flat, one percussionist playing snare drum, bass drum, triangle, suspended cymbal, piano, violin, viola, cello, bass.
'O Breath': Alto flute, English horn, bass clarinet, suspended cymbal, bass drum, violin, viola, cello, bass.

Because the songs were commissioned for a soprano, Carter looked for poems by women. Robert Lowell recommended the poetry of Elizabeth Bishop, which had had a profound impact on his own development. Bishop's poems move from the commonplace to the universal. She observes landscapes and domestic scenes with a precise intensity yet her vision also expands outwards:

The world is a mist. And then the world is minute and vast and clear.

('Sandpiper'[2])

Many of Bishop's poems deal with borders, coastlines, beaches – places where opposites meet but are never reconciled, like the lovers' bed in 'O Breath.' The six songs of *A Mirror* are not connected; each has its own technique and color. Carter arranged them so as to reflect two aspects of Elizabeth Bishop's art: the geographical and the personal. Two groups of poems are interlaced. Three describe the relationship between the poet and the world: 'Anaphora,' 'Sandpiper,' 'A View of the Capitol from the Library of Congress.' The other three, appearing second, fourth and sixth, are about love. Both series move from the general to the specific. 'A View of the Capitol' is the most explicitly public and 'O Breath' the most intensely private, almost existing in a world beyond communication where both word and music are reduced to the common factor of breathing. 'Insomnia,' containing the title of the cycle (also a reference to Speculum Musicae, music's mirror) is the emotional center of the music.

'ANAPHORA'

The first poem is the most universal in subject, and receives the most abstract musical treatment. The title refers to a figure of speech in which a word is repeated in different clauses or lines. Its root meaning is 'carrying backwards', suggesting a recessional, and the poem turns a condensed description of a day into a ritual. Lloyd Schwartz points out that the ceremony described in the poem is 'a kind of concert – birds, church bells, factory whistles (the poem was written in Mexico) – that Carter reproduces in a shimmering cacophony ... that the narrative voice has to elbow through.' The poem is a falling progression from the day's primal energy to man's mortal fatigue. The poet, 'the beggar in the park,' reverses the fall through 'stupendous studies' and 'Endless assent.' The pun implied in the last word perhaps suggests the poet's willed, even deceptive, inversion of reality. The poem creates a world and places the hapless poet in its midst to give it meaning.

The musical structure reflects the fundamental theme of the poem. The pitches of the chromatic scale are each given fixed registral positions, forming a twelve-note chord that lies within the range of the soprano (see Chart 25). These are the only pitches used in the song. The entire twelve-note chord, however, rarely appears. The six-note all-triad chord, 5–35 (0, 1, 2, 4, 7, 8) is the recurrent harmonic unit. In changing transpositions, the chord is mapped on to the fixed twelve-note structure, assuming

Chart 25 'Anaphora': harmonic and rhythmic schemes

ever-changing intervallic and triadic shapes. (See the piano and vibraphone from bar 59 to the end (Ex. 46).)

The resulting texture is both rigid and free. Despite the drastic limitations in pitch-content, the twenty-four possible transpositions of the
hexachord in prime and inverted forms and their changing triadic presentation create a harmony of subtly shifting colors. The vocal line illumin-
ates the resources of the harmonic matrix by emphasizing one interval
after another – perfect fifths, major and minor thirds, minor sevenths,
and, climactically major ninths. The rhythm of the song is as structurally
conceived as its harmony. A rhythmic backbone is formed by a cross-pulse
between piano and vibraphone (sometimes passing to the other instruments) in a pulse ratio of 65:69. The two instruments coincide only once,
at bar 23, the poem's still center. Against this constant polyrhythm the
voice, beginning with a line of limitless energy and sweep, gradually slows
and fades and then regains its initial impetus.

The music's harmonic and rhythmic structures serve to evoke and
elucidate the text. The constant repetition of pitches in ever-new chordal
transpositions and inversions is musical anaphora. The vocal trajectory
mirrors the poem's theme of faded and recreated energies; the unique
coincidence of the two crossed pulses occurs at the low point of the ebbing

Anaphora (A Mirror on Which to Dwell)

Ex. 46 Cross pulses and triads

initial burst, just before the poet's entrance. The shared pulse is thus a
turning point, marking the birth of a new vision, the artist's reconstruc-
tion of life's primal force in 'stupendous studies.' The setting of 'stupendous' is climactic – and characteristic in its union of the literal and the
structural. The voice leaps downwards nearly two octaves. A stupendous
jump, to be sure, but also the only melodic delineation of the song's
harmonic extremes and the only time the voice articulates the two
structural pulses.

'ARGUMENT'

At once abstract and personal, 'Argument' portrays a lovers' quarrel, as a struggle between 'days' and 'distance,' space and time – the basic categories of human separation. The unified ensemble of 'Anaphora' splits in two, superimposing two arguments. The voice, supported by alto flute and bass clarinet, is shadowed by the double bass, which plays an expressive, grotesque anti-song aided by the cello. The vast space between soprano and bass is filled in by a counter dialogue between piano and bongos. Each argument has its own harmonic and rhythmic design. The voice–bass viol dispute is associated with chord 5–38 (0, 1, 2, 5, 8, 9) and rubato rhythms.

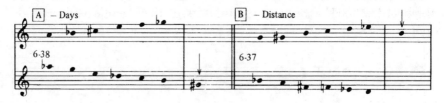

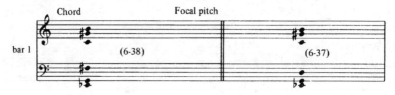

Chart 26 'Argument': harmonic scheme and materials

The piano-bongo skirmish uses chord 5–37 (0, 1, 3, 4, 7, 8) and fast pulse rhythms (Chart 26). The piano plays in nonuplets at the speed of MM 756 while the bongo superimposes triplet and quintuplet divisions of the MM 84 beat. The dual structure of the song is emphasized in the voice by two recurring pitches: G sharp heard with 'days' and B with 'distance.' The climactic montage of all these elements comes at bars 27–32.

The opposed strata more than illustrate the words; the words seem themselves to be an image of Carter's music, built out of arguments. Yet both poem and music suggest a reconciliation. Toward the conclusion the music takes on a more intimate coloring as the piano – which has gradually ascended throughout the song – tinkles away at the top of the keyboard, echoed by the bongos. The lovers, on their 'gentle battleground,' put aside their differences.

'SANDPIPER'

The Sandpiper is 'a student of Blake,' a poet obsessively seeking the world in a grain of sand. In the music the sandpiper appears as a frantic oboe pecking away at staccato half-steps interspersed with multiphonic screeches. If the poem's bird is a self-parody of the poet, the oboe parodistically represents the composer fanatically choosing and placing notes, trying to impose order on a chaotic world (Carter studied the oboe while at Harvard).

The music meshes two elements. The oboe plays at the same speed throughout, MM 525, using the intervals of half-step, minor third and perfect fifth. The strings and piano, evoking hissing sands and breaking surf, play spacious harmonies derived from minor sixths, major sevenths and major ninths. The string rhythm is fluid, with frequent changes of tempo, all coordinated with the constant motion of the oboe (Chart 27).

A — Oboe: same note-lengths throughout ♪=M 525

semitones, minor thirds, perfect fifths

B — Strings and Piano: rubato – many changes in tempo

Harmonies

Chart 27 'Sandpiper': two elements

The voice mediates between both elements, sometimes calm and spacious – 'the world is a mist' – elsewhere as jumpy as the oboe, as in their Bach-like duet at bars 49–54.

'INSOMNIA'

All the songs in *A Mirror* are remarkably lucid; 'Insomnia' is the simplest of them all. No other work of Carter's achieves so much with such spare strokes; the inverted thirds at:

where left is always right

are exquisitely mimetic. Yet even the sparse texture of the song, scored for four instruments, suggests several layers of feelings. The high slow-moving lines of piccolo and violin contrast with the nervous rattle of the marimba and viola, reflecting the poem's contrast of an insomniac with the reflected moon. Piccolo and violin outline a cross-pulse of 84:85 (every fourteenth quintuplet against every seventeenth sextuplet of the

B   Piccolo + Violin: polyrhythm of 85: 84

$$17 \quad \flat^6 \quad : \quad 14 \quad \flat^5$$

C   Voice-palindromes to suggest Mirror

Motif of C :

Chords

Chart 28 'Insomnia': three elements

slow MM 54 pulse). Marimba and viola play at steady speeds of MM 648, 432 and 324, until bar 23 where they join the flute and violin as the singer describes the 'inverted' world dwelling on the mirror. All the harmonic material of the song is derived from the first four pitches of the voice and their inversion which immediately follows (Chart 28). The ease with which the song evokes the thoughts of an active mind in the still hours of the night may be explained, in part, by noting that the composer has recurring bouts of insomnia himself, which he usually tries to fight off by conjugating irregular Italian, German or Greek verbs.

'A VIEW OF THE CAPITOL FROM THE LIBRARY OF CONGRESS'

A Mirror was a Bicentennial commission and 'A View' responds to the occasion, portraying the relation of artist and government comically (how else?). The poet's irreverent images of the Capitol inspired an Ivesian texture. Again there are two elements (Chart 29). The maestoso opening describes the giant trees which block the view of the Capitol dome and muffle the sound of the Air Force band – the Library of Congress is directly east of the Capitol. The band's Sousa-like small-interval fragments

Chart 29 'A View of the Capitol': two elements

are projected against majestic major ninths. The rhythmic structure inverts the expected confrontation. The opening tempo remains constant in the voice and the viola, which plays an important obbligato. The band music by contrast is unsteady and out of phase. The song's tone is just slightly menacing, for all its comedy. At the close, 'the gathered brasses want to go boom-boom' drops an ominous Cold War hint that Carter underscores by having the 'booms' intensely whispered against 'angry' notes in the strings.

'O BREATH'

The poet looks at her sleeping lover and finds that all that unites them is breathing. Each of the poems in *A Mirror* is about the attempt to cross a boundary. 'O Breath' is the ultimate statement of this theme in its most intimate human form. The music counterposes two kinds of breathing. The soprano sings asthmatic fragments, as if out of breath. Her florid line ('an unsettling mixture of Viennese expressionism and Italian bel canto,' as Lloyd Schwartz says) is punctured with rests which mirror the split lines of the poem. The vocal line uses every interval except the perfect fifth and minor seventh. These two intervals dominate the slow, swelling chords heard in the orchestra. The instrumental texture suggests the rise and fall of a deep sleeper's breath; it is based on a three-part polyrhythm of every forty-third sixth of a beat, every thirty-seventh fifth of a beat and every sixty-fifth ninth of a beat. This pattern is not meant to be recognized; the complex cross-play of very slow pulses (MM 8.372, 8.108 and 8.308) gives the impression of a regular pulse surrounded by slightly irregular swelling and fading. By contrast the soprano's rhythm is erratic.

Without any Bergian demands for empathy, the song evokes an unnamed emotion somewhere between acceptance and despair.

Syringa

Dedicated to Sir William and Lady Glock, Syringa was made possible by a Composer-Librettist Grant from the National Endowment for the Arts. It was first performed at Alice Tully Hall, Lincoln Center on 10 December 1978, the eve of Carter's seventieth birthday, as the central focus of a year-long retrospective festival of his music by New York's contemporary music ensembles. The first performers were Jan de Gaetani, mezzo-soprano, Thomas Paul, bass, and Speculum Musicae conducted by Harvey Sollberger. The prominent guitar part was played by Scott Kuney. Syringa is scored for mezzo-soprano, bass, guitar, alto flute, English horn, bass clarinet (doubling B♭ clarinet), trombone, percussion (marimba, vibraphone, bongos, tom-toms), violin, viola, cello, bass, and piano.

John Ashbery, born in 1927, is the most important poet of the New York School. Influenced both by the dreamlike collage of French surrealism and by the open-ended philosophical discourse of Wallace Stevens, his poetry blends deadpan irony, camp humor and exquisite lyricism. For Ashbery, the act of writing poetry often seems absurd, merely a matter of random inclusions and exclusions. Not surprisingly, his work has been influenced by John Cage; his long poem 'Europe' reads like a transcription of a performance of Cage's piece for twelve radios. Ashbery has also cited the influence of Carter's music on *Three Poems* and *The Skaters*. He approached Carter with the idea of a collaboration; he may have been nonplussed by Carter's decision to surround his poem with Greek texts.[3]

For Carter, Ashbery's poetry presented novel challenges and difficulties; its jokiness and irony and its jolting shifts in diction from the lofty to the vernacular were qualities not found in Carter's earlier music. Ashbery reads his poetry in a flat, common-sensical way, as if his wildest flights of syntactical fancy were perfectly obvious in their meaning. What is not said in Ashbery's poems is often as important as the printed text. Their relentless irony is a strategy of understatement. The poems are rent by silences and cut-off phrases, implying realms of experience too painful to mention.

After reading through all of Ashbery's published and unpublished poems, Carter decided to use two singers as in Cavalieri's *Rappresenszione di anima e di corpo*, which he showed me at a lesson one day, exclaiming 'I've found the solution!' The work-in-progress would not be a song cycle like *A Mirror* but a new genre: a polytextural motet, a cantata, a chamber opera, a vocal double concerto – all in one. The text of Ashbery's poem would be superimposed on its implied subtext.

Carter labored at the Greek text, both in its selection and its scansion, starting with his classics textbooks from Harvard, and later doing research at the British Museum. He interrupted work to take a short vacation in Morocco where he visited the ruins of the Roman city of Volubilis. There he came upon the 'house of Orpheus' where there was a large circular mosaic of Orpheus playing his lyre surrounded by a small concert audience of birds and beasts. It suggested to him the idea of Orpheus singing and playing, attracting his audience one by one. *Syringa* starts with the bass singer and guitar alone and one by one each of the instruments, the conductor and the mezzo are drawn in by the spell of the music. Carter later learned that Ashbery had written *Syringa* while listening to Monteverdi's *Orfeo*. He saw this as a further justification for a texture something like a Monteverdi madrigal for two voices and accompaniment with a formal looseness similar to Monteverdi's 'arioso.'

John Ashbery's *Syringa* is an oblique retelling of the Orpheus story. In Carter's setting, the mezzo-soprano sings Ashbery's words in a flat patter remarkably close to the poet's own inflection. The bass sings a text in classical Greek, made up of fragments chosen by Carter to suggest the contrasts implied by the poem 'in whose tales are hidden syllables/Of

what happened so long before.' What Ashbery mainly leaves unsaid is
Orpheus's passion. His Orpheus is a very modern poet, too aware of the
futility of his art. Apollo, no less, tells him:

> 'Leave it all on earth
> Your lute, what point? Why pick at a dull pavan few care to
> Follow, except a few birds of dusty feather,
> Not vivid performances of the past.'[4]

The whole poem is a response to the god's academic despair, celebrating
the discoveries of the present moment against the claims of a lost past.
The bass gives a vivid performance, intense and emotional, but in words
whose meaning is lost. Carter assembled a collage of classical Greek texts
mostly dealing with aspects of the Orphic cult which developed, Carter
enjoys saying, when, after his dismemberment, Orpheus's head floated
across the Aegean, still singing. In Byzantine phrases of extravagant lyricism, the bass sings of a world of undistanced passion, set in motion by
the demands of Eros.

If Orpheus in Ashbery's poem appears as a self-portrait of the poet,
Carter's music seems like an idealized embodiment of all those expressive
qualities most personal to the composer. He has often said that the true
medium of musical composition is not sound but time. *Syringa* celebrates
time; Ashbery and Carter honor the quality of temporal passage, and its
inherent nexus of the destructive and the creative:

6-35 (0 1 2 4 7 8)-all-triad hexachord

7-4 (0 1 2 4 6 7 8)

triads stated twice

3-4   3-5   3-7   3-9

7-34 (0 1 2 4 7 8 9)

3-4   3-7   3-8   3-9

Chart 30 *Syringa*: harmonic basis

                       . . . music passes, emblematic
Of life and how you cannot isolate a note of it
And say it is good or bad . . .
For although memories of a season, for example,
Melt into a single snapshot, one cannot guard, treasure
That stalled moment. It too is flowing, fleeting.
It is a picture of flowing scenery, though living, mortal.
Over which an abstract action is laid out in blunt,
Harsh strokes.

Or as Heraclitus says in the Greek text, 'What is is like the current of a river.'

The two texts contain the whole of time, from creation – 'Time gave birth to the egg' – to a distant future, 'When all record of these people and their lives/Has disappeared into libraries, onto microfilm.' Each text evokes motion in time. In Ashbery's poem all experience seems to vanish like Eurydice into *les temps perdus*. The words are merely a record of pebbles along the way. The Greek text portrays a world ravished by time: 'Eros has shaken my soul like the wind which comes from the mountains and fells trees.' Ashbery's irony and the Greeks' daemonic passion are superimposed by Carter as related aspects of temporal experience: the very sense of time lost stems from the violent intensity of each present moment.

The two singers spin forth contrasted musical characters and continuities, whose intersections are sometimes ironic, sometimes revelatory. The main structural contrast between the voices is the size of their intervals. Carter built the work on six seven-note chords, all of which fulfill two conditions: they contain the all-triad hexachord, 5–35 (0, 1, 2, 4, 7, 8) and they contain two statements of a triad (Chart 30). Soprano and bass thus often sing notes based on the same three-note chord, with the soprano in close position and the bass in open, as at bars 24–5 (Ex. 47). One of the main chords used is 7–4 (0, 1, 2, 4, 6, 7, 8), containing not only 6–35 in two versions but also 6–7 (0, 1, 2, 6, 7, 8), which can be spaced in such a

Syringa
©1980 Associated Music Publishers, Inc. Used by permission

Ex. 47 Contrast of intervals

way as to make a triad built of fourths (0, 5, 10) superimposed on one built of fifths (0, 7, 14). This chord with its relation to the open strings of the guitar appears all through the work and is featured at the moment when the bass sings that Orpheus was only a musician (*kitharodos*), at bars 299–300 (Ex. 48).

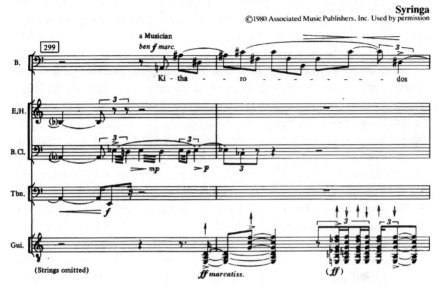

Syringa
©1980 Associated Music Publishers, Inc. Used by permission

Ex. 48

The soprano sings throughout in simple pulse rhythms that contrast with the rhapsodic phrases of the bass. As in *A Symphony of Three Orchestras*, however, the musical events go by too fast for the structural contrasts to be perceived. The listener hears a series of intense sound-images that emerge and disappear into the musical flow. The music finds a strikingly evocative correlatives to the words, from the opening bars where creation is heard in the sound of sharply plucked guitar strings, to Apollo's sudden appearance announced by English horn and vibraphone, to the beautiful melodic descent 'at the way music passes,' and the ravishing guitar arabesque, set off against the vibraphone, at 'a bluish cloud.' Because of the music's identification with the text – each seems to describe the other – the best approach to the form of the piece for the listener is to follow the double text. Here is an assemblage of both texts, roughly indicating their temporal relation as well as indications of the Greek sources, identified at the end:

bar
numbers

 5 *Chronos (Time) gave birth to the world-egg*
   Fair, gowing Ocean was the first to marry
   and he wedded his sister Tethys,[1]

21 Orpheus liked the glad personal quality
   Of the things beneath the sky. Of course, Eurydice was a part
   Of this.
   daughter of the same mother

28 *Then Eros fairest among the immortal gods, who unloosens the*
   body

37 *(exclamations of despair)*[2]

25 Then one day, everything changed.

40 *For you, oh, only one, oh, dear wife*
   Woe, alas, oh fate!
   He rends
   Rocks into fissures with lament.

56 *drops of poison flow in exchange for my heart's grief.*[3]
   Gullies, hummocks

55 Can't withstand it. The sky shudders from one horizon
   To the other
   O, evil, alas
   almost ready to give up wholeness.

58 *For, doom, fathomless, approoches*[4]

61 Then Apollo quietly told him: 'Leave it all on earth.
   Your lute, what point? Why pick at a dull pavan few care to
   Follow, except a few birds of dusty feather,
   Not vivid performances of the past.'

71 *But what life would there be, what joy without golden Aphrodite?*
   But why not?
   All other things must change too.
   The seasons are no longer what they once were,
   But it is the nature of things to be seen only once
   As they happen along, bumping into other things, getting along
   May I die when I am no longer concerned with secret love
   and gentle gifts[5]
   Somehow. That's where Orpheus made his mistake.

87 Of course Eurydice vanished into the shade;
   She would have even if he hadn't turned around.

90　*There can be nothing unexpected, nothing impossible, nothing*
　　marvellous since Zeus, Olympian father out of midday made night,
　　obscuring the light of the sun.[6]

104　No use standing there like a gray stone toga as the whole wheel
　　Of recorded history flashes past, struck dumb, unable to utter an
　　intelligent
　　Comment on the most thought-provoking element in its train.

110　*Dream in the black night, Eros, sweet god.*[7]

117　Only love stays on the brain, and something these people,
　　These other ones, call life.

129　*Eros has shaken my soul like the wind which comes from the*
　　mountains and fells trees[8]
　　Singing accurately

138　So that the notes mount straight up out of the well of
　　If I catch a brief glimpse of you
　　Dim noon and rival the tiny, sparkling yellow flowers
　　Growing around the brink of the quarry, encapsulizes
　　I can't say a word, my tongue is torn
　　The different weights of the things.
　　and under my skin a subtle fire runs, my eyes don't see and my
　　ears buzz.[9] Once again Eros, who unloosens my body

162　　　　　　　　　　　But it isn't enough
　　To just go on singing. Orpheus realized this
　　And didn't mind so much about his reward being in heaven
　　torments me – bitter-sweet, invincible monster[10]
　　After the Bacchantes had torn him apart, driven
　　Half out of their minds by his music, what it was doing to them.

178　*Saving the seed of fire*[11]
　　Some say it was for his treatment of Eurydice.
　　But probably the music had more to do with it, and

187　The way music passes, emblematic
　　Of life and how you cannot isolate a note of it

190　*Cool waters from above sing as they flow through the*
　　apple orchard
　　And say it is good or bad. You must
　　Wait till it's over. 'The end crowns all,'
　　and from the trembling leaves sleep falls down.[12]
　　Meaning also that the tableau
　　Is wrong. For although memories, of a season, for example,

Melt into a single snapshot, one cannot guard, treasure

212 That stalled moment. It too is flowing, fleeting:

211 *In the spring quinces and pomegranates are watered by the river*

It is a picture of flowing scenery, though living, mortal,

Over which an abstract action is laid out in blunt,

221 Harsh strokes.

in the undefiled maidens' garden

And to ask more than this

Is to become the tossing reed of that slow,

vines grow with shading vine-leaves.

Powerful stream, the trailing grasses

Playfully tugged at, but to participate in the action

For me however Eros never sleeps

No more than this.

but by burning lightning and freezing wind a scorching frenzy

sent by the Cyprian has captured my heart since childhood.[13]

Then in the lowering gentian sky

250 Electric twitches are faintly apparent first, then burst forth

Into a shower of fixed, cream-colored flares. The horses

259 Have each seen a share of the truth, though each thinks,

'I'm a maverick. Nothing of this is happening to me,

Though I can understand the language of birds, and

The itinerary of the lights caught in the storm is fully apparent to

me.

272 *Orpheus, unrewarded, they sent back from Hades,*

274 Their jousting ends in music much

As trees move more easily in the wind after a summer storm

And is happening in lacy shadows of shore-trees, now, day after

day.'

They showed only a phantom of the wife for whom he came;

her real self they would not bestow; for he was considered a coward

since he was a musician, and would not have the heart to die of

love.[14]

301 But how late to be regretting all this, even

Bearing in mind that regrets are always late, too late!

To which Orpheus, a bluish cloud with white contours,

Replies that these are of course not regrets at all,

322 *All things change;*

Merely a careful, scholarly setting down of

> *You cannot step twice into the same river*
> Unquestioned facts, a record of pebbles along the way.

333 What is is like the current of a river.[15]

330 And no matter how all this disappeared,
Or got where it was going, it is no longer
Material for a poem. Its subject

340 Matters too much, and not enough, standing there helplessly
While the poem streaked by, its tail afire, a bad

346 *soon, clearly and sweetly he played on his lyre,*
Comet screaming hate and disaster, but so turned inward
*he lifted up his voice and sang, and lovely was the sound of his voice
that followed.*
That the meaning, good or other, can never Become known. The
singer thinks
He sang the story of the immortal gods

359 Constructively, builds up his chant in progressive stages
Like a skyscraper, but
*and of the dark earth, how the first was born and how a task was
allotted to each.*
　　　　　　at the last minute turns away.
The song is engulfed in an instant in blackness

372 *First among the gods he honored Mnemosyne (Memory), mother of
the Muses in his song . . .* [16]
Which must in turn flood the whole continent
With blackness, for it cannot see. The singer

377 Must then pass out of sight, not even relieved
Of the evil burthen of the words.

389 *Apollo, Apollo, guardian, destroying me, you have crushed me
utterly,* [17]

406 *Begone, go away, save your present mind.* [18]
　　　　　　Stellification

412 Is for the few, and comes about much later
Alas, woe! [19]
When all record of these people and their lives

413 *The body is the sign (tomb) of the soul.* [20]
Has disappeared into libraries, onto microfilm.

416 *saving the seed of fire*
A few are still interested in them. 'But what about
So-and-so?' is still asked on occasion. But they lie

420 *Of Ge (Earth) and Uranus (Sky) were born the children Oceanus*
      and Tethys

422 Frozen and out of touch until an arbitrary chorus
      Speaks of a totally different incident with a similar name
      In whose tale are hidden syllables
      Of what happened so long before that

431 body, sign (*soma, sema*)[21]
      In some small town, one indifferent summer.

Sources of Greek texts:

1   Otto Kern, *Orphicorum fragmenta*, Berlin 1922, No. 54.
2   Quoted by Plato (Socrates) in *Cratylus*, 402C as being part of an actual poem by Orpheus.
3   Hesiod, *Theogony*, 120
4   Exclamatory passages from Aeschylus, mostly from Cassandra's lines in *Agamemnon*; except for bar 40 and bar 58 which are from Euripides's *Alcestis*.
5   Mimnermus-Diehl, 1 (E. Diehl, *Anthologia Lyrica*, Leipzig, 1922.)
6   Archilochus-Diehl, 74.
7   Sappho-Diehl, 67.
8   Sappho-Diehl, 44.
9   Sappho-Diehl, 2 (excerpt).
10 Sappho-Diehl, 137.
11 Homer, *Odyssey*, Book V, 49.
12 Sappho-Diehl, 5.
13 Ibycus-Diehl, 6.
14 Plato, *Symposium*.
15 Plato, *Cratylus*, 402Λ (quoted from Heraclitus).
16 Homeric Hymn IV, To Hermes, 425–30.
17 Aeschylus, *Agamemnon*, 1091–2.
18 Aeschylus, *Prometheus Bound*, 392.
19 Aeschylus, *Agamemnon*, 1307, 1072.
20 Orphic saying, discussed by Plato, *Cratylus*, 400 C.
21 Plato, *Timaeus*, 40 E.

Carter first used his college text book. *Greek Lyric Poets* by M. H. Morgan, revised by C. B. Gulick (Harvard University Press, 1929). Although he later found that classical scholarship has improved some of the texts chosen, he decided to use the version in the Harvard text.

The intersections of the two layers of text are sometimes close in meaning, at other times distant. Often they are related by sound, not meaning. The Greek *Pheou*, an exclamation of despair, echoes 'Orpheus'; *Stellou*, 'be gone,' sets off 'Stellification is for the few,' Ashbery's conflation of Orpheus and Chaucer's Troilus. 'One indifferent summer,' the final phrase in English, echoes the Orphic cult words, *soma, sema* that conclude the Greek.

The orchestra cloaks these linguistic confrontations in a glowing double-aegis of sound. It is not divided into opposed ensembles, but is protean in color, volume and density, ranging from the exquisite interplay of guitar and vibraphone to violent outbursts in the drums, piano and trombone.

Carter describes the form of *Syringa* as a series of short vocal pieces by the bass with commentary by the mezzo. The bass's music is sectional while the mezzo's is free-associational in development. The sections of the bass part are:

1 (bars 1–35) Creation myth. The bass breaks down on the word 'athanatoisi', immortal.
2 (36–59) Lament for Eurydice. This is interrupted by Apollo as music critic.
3 (71–113) Songs about Eros.
4 (116–265) Songs of the power of love, its pleasures and torments.
5 (272–309) Orpheus's story as seen by Socrates (Plato).
6 (322–80) Heraclitus on time and a description of Hermes, who made the lyre, demonstrating its use to Apollo.
7 (389–412) Cassandra's curse, and Prometheus's warning – both criticisms of Apollo.
8 (413–end) Recall of opening texts and Orphic sayings.

There are no musical recurrences. *Syringa* allows its listeners no formal guides or fixed landmarks. It demands that we, too, plunge into the river of time:

But it is the nature of things to be seen only once
As they happen along, bumping into other things, getting along
Somehow.

In Sleep, In Thunder

Six Poems of Robert Lowell for Tenor and Fourteen Instruments. Commissioned by the London Sinfonietta. Dedicated 'in memory of the Poet and Friend.' Completed 11 December 1981; première 26 October 1982 with Martyn Hill, tenor, with the London Sinfonietta conducted by Oliver Knussen. Recorded by these players for Nonesuch (out of print). Recording for Bridge Records (with a superb analytic essay by Lloyd Schwartz) by Jon Garrison, tenor, and Speculum Musicae, conducted by Robert Black.

With this song cycle for tenor and fourteen instruments, Carter completed his trilogy of American poems. Although none of the works was meant for the stage, they all imply dramatic situations. *In Sleep, In Thunder*, an extended mad scene, is perhaps the most operatic of the three. Randall Jarrell called Lowell a 'poet of shock'; Carter's musical portrait of Lowell amplifies every jolt.

Although Carter and Lowell were both Harvard men, they were of different generations. The Carters came to know Lowell and his second wife Elizabeth Hardwick during the sixties when the Lowells moved from Boston to New York and became involved with the founding of the *New York Review of Books*. Lowell had begun to work as a playwright with his trilogy *The Old Glory*, and he approached Carter about an operatic setting of a new translation of Racine's tragedy *Phèdre*. The collaboration did not work out; ultimately Benjamin Britten set some of Lowell's translation as a concert aria that was one of his last works. But Carter chose to begin *In Sleep, In Thunder* with a poem, 'Dolphin,' which refers to Racine and *Phèdre* (thereby implicating himself in Lowell's 'fish-net.')

Robert Lowell's poetry may be divided into three periods. He first came to prominence in 1946 with the publication of *Lord Weary's Castle*. His densely written early poems were strongly influenced by T. S. Eliot, John Crowe Ransome and Allen Tate. Then with *Life Studies* in the fifties he began to write confessional poems, revealing the intimate anxieties of his marriage and his mental condition in a sharply edged contemporary language which abolished the proprieties of Eliot's classicism or Tate's gentility. In the late sixties Lowell was a prominent figure in the anti-war movement and produced a series of sonnet-length poems, published as *Notebooks*, which juxtaposed the growing crisis in American society with the course of world history and with his own continuing personal turmoil. In the early seventies, Lowell recast many of these poems in the volume *History*, often in a way which confused or even contradicted their original sense. Lowell was increasingly subject to attacks of mental illness; much of his life he suffered from manic depression, or bipolar condition in which his mental capacities would race forward from brilliance to mania to collapse. According to one account in Ian Hamilton's biography, as early as 1961, Lowell would begin to revise his poetry 'furiously and with a kind of crooked brilliance, and talk about himself in connection with Achilles, Alexander, Hart Crane, Hitler and Christ.'[5]

In 1970 Lowell was appointed a visiting professor of All Souls' College, Oxford. When he arrived in London in April he invited Lady Caroline Blackwood to a party; they had met seven years earlier in New York, in a period of Lowell's mental illness. After the party Lowell moved into Blackwood's apartment. He decided to leave his wife, Elizabeth Hardwick, and their daughter Harriet. By February 1971 Blackwood was pregnant with Lowell's son Sheridan. In October 1972 they married 'for technical reasons.' Lowell, in his confessional mode, recounted the affair in his book *The Dolphin*. Friends of Elizabeth Hardwick's, including Lowell's close friend Elizabeth Bishop, were appalled not merely by his willingness to expose this intimate family business in public, but by the use of his former wife's letters, barely changed, in his own poems. Bishop wrote to Lowell: 'It's not being "gentle" to use personal, tragic, anguished letters that way – it's cruel.'[6] Lowell's mental condition continued to decline, and his new marriage began to unravel. He died in New York City on September 12, 1977. He had collapsed in a cab from the airport to Elizabeth Hardwick's apartment; he was holding a parcel which contained a portrait of Caroline Blackwood by her former husband Lucian Freud.

At the time of his death, and since, Lowell's late poems were highly controversial; they seemed to some readers more pathology than art. Daringly, both for artistic and personal reasons, Carter selected poems from Lowell's late volumes, rather than such anthology pieces from *Life Studies* as 'Man and Wife' and 'Skunk Hour,' catching the poet mid-ocean, between marriages, continents and mental states. In beginning his cycle with the closing poem of *Dolphin*, however, Carter reversed the direction of Lowell's volume *The Dolphin*, which told the story of his marriage to Caroline Blackwood and the crises associated with it but achieved, in its last poem, a resolution in which the poet and his muse become one. Carter's cycle moves away from this resolution toward a violent dénouement. The sketches reveal that Carter considered a large number of poems and even began setting several ('Will Not Come Back,' 'Obit,' 'Stairwell,' 'Seals') that were not included in the final version. These initial choices show that Carter at first was looking for explicit statements of the transatlantic theme. In 'New York,' Lowell wrote that 'the language of New Yorkers, unlike English, / doesn't make me fear I am going deaf.' And in 'New York Again' he found his old city 'austerity assuaged with melodrama.' Carter told me that he was also influenced by the poem 'In the Ward' which tells of a hospital visit to the bedside of the composer Israel Citkowitz (a composer whose work Carter had praised in a 1937 *Modern*

Music article, and a former husband of Blackwood's) who, Lowell writes, invited young friends to his flat

> to explore the precision
> and daimonic lawlessness
> of Arnold Schoenberg born
> when music was still imperfect science-
> Music,
> its ever retreating borderlines of being,
> as treacherous, perhaps, to systems,
> to fecundity, as to silence.

The poem is a double elegy: for a composer and for modern music, and it provides a suggestive subtext for the musical rage of the cycle. Carter thought it might be read before or after a performance of the cycle.

Carter finally settled on a six-poem series:

1. 'Dolphin' (from *The Dolphin*, 1973)
2. 'Across the Yard: La Ignota' (from *History*, 1973; revision of poem in *Notebook*)
3. 'Harriet' (from *For Lizzie and Harriet*, 1973)
4. 'Dies Irae' (from *History*; an earlier version, 'Dies Irae, A Hope,' appears in *Notebook* as does a related poem, 'Helltime')
5. 'Careless Night' (from *The Dolphin*)
6. 'In Genesis' (from *History*)

'There are three poems about women (songs 1, 3 and 5) and three about God,' (2, 4 and 6.) Carter has said. But there are other connections and contrasts. The Dolphin of the first song (Caroline Blackwood) contrasts as a muse with La Ignota, a fading soprano in Harvard Yard. Harriet, Lowell's daughter, is the subject of the third poem; Sheridan, his son, appears in the fifth. The Cambridge, Massachusetts setting of the second poem contrasts with the English suburbia, with sheep meadows, in the fifth. The theme of madness surfaces in the first and third songs and explodes in violence in the fourth and sixth. In the last poem God and Orpheus fuse into a tyrant father, murdered and eaten by his sons, who dance around the barbecue, or 'cookout,' to use Lowell's last word. Flatulent blasts in the brass bring the patricidal binge to an all-too-realistic close. Carter out-shocks Lowell.[7]

Given the sensational element in the poetry, it may be surprising that Carter seems to follow the formal pattern he had used for the very different expressive world of Elizabeth Bishop. Again there are six separate movements with no overt thematic connections. There are no preludes, interludes, or afterthoughts, no room for the composer to comment on the poems. And, again, there are only the most submerged suggestions of 'Americana.' Carter uses instrumental color emblematically, even realistically – or surrealistically. The strings of 'Dolphin' suggest a slippery fish and the fish-net in which it is caught. In 'Across the Yard: La Ignota,' an obbligato trumpet stands in for the sound of a soprano – a complex musical metaphor. In 'Careless Night,' the mention of 'smudge sheep' evokes brass flutter tonguing à la Strauss – but it is not clear if the sheep here are real or delusional, which only strengthens the musical allusion to *Don Quixote*. Elsewhere, Carter takes advantage of the larger instrumental ensemble (four woodwinds, three brass, piano, percussion and string quintet) to contrast delicate chamber combinations with brutal orchestral tuttis. Typically of Carter, the voice type defies traditional categories of *fach*. It swings through a perilously large tenor range of two octaves (b to b) and from Tom Rakewell lyricism to Otello's (or Grimes's) dramatic weight.

Despite apparent similarities, the dramatic sequence of movements feels different from the Bishop cycle. By using only a string accompaniment in the first song, Carter makes it an invocation to the muse, a portico, an overture which hints at all the themes to come.[8] The introductory function of 'Dolphin' places 'Dies Irae,' the fourth song, at the center of a five movement structure – the madscene within the madscene. Like the Bishop cycle, *In Sleep, In Thunder* is a secular cantata, modeled on Bach's cantatas and passions, but where the songs of *A Mirror* were crystalline in their structure, elegantly balancing opposed elements, the Lowell songs are volatile, full of sudden reversals of mood and texture. Ironically, these constant reversals give the cycle a continuous dramatic line.

The harmonic language of the cycle subtly unifies the six songs. Intentionally or not, the technique of the cycle is an emblem of mental bipolarity. The listener will notice the constant opposition of major and minor thirds and of large and small intervals. These contrasts spring from a source repertory of hexachords which complete the twelve-tone scale through transposition at the tritone (see Chart 31). These hexachords can be arranged spatially to form all-interval twelve-note chords with complementary intervals arranged symmetrically around a central tritone. The highest and lowest notes also form a tritone. Such a chord appears in bar 4 of the first song and later throughout the cycle. Often

Chart 31 *In Sleep, In Thunder*: harmony

Carter juxtaposes the two halves of a twelve-tone chord in sudden contrasts of register and intervallic spacing. The opposition of close and open voicings of these hexachords provides a useful texture for framing the vocal line and for contrast between the voice and the accompaniment.

I 'DOLPHIN'

(erroneously printed as Dolphins in the score, thereby confusing the text with a different one in the same collection, *The Dolphin*)

Lowell's poem turns on the multiple meanings of the word 'collaborating' and so serves as a bridge between poet and composer. Collaboration implies both fusion and treachery, inspiration and entrapment:

> I have sat and listened to too many
> words of the collaborating muse
> and plotted perhaps too freely with my life . . .

'Plotted' extends the ambiguities of collaboration: charted, conspired, buried. Lowell's muse appears as a half-fictional sea-creature, dolphin or mermaid. The poet's lines are like an eel net, but also the 'hangman's knot of sinking lines' that mark his ageing body. The poem is likened to a trap – but it is the poet who is lured into its 'iron composition' by the muse's voice. Subject and object, male and female bodies, hunter and prey fuse to the poet's own amazement: 'my eyes have seen what my hand did.'

Perhaps reacting to the phrase 'the glassy bowing and scraping of my will' with its pun on 'bowing,' Carter finds the emblem for Lowell's muse in his own favored medium – the string quartet, here augmented by the bass. The strings slither and glide around the vocal line, which struggles to escape from its small intervals, finally exploding heroically in the last line (Ex. 49).

Ex. 49 'Dolphin' ending

2 'ACROSS THE YARD: LA IGNOTA'

The poem is a double portrait of two artists, the young poet and an over-the-hill soprano (and thus appears as a reconfiguration of the poet/muse relation in 'Dolphin'). The poet's state of ignorance corresponds to the soprano's *Götterdämmerung*, not only the downfall of a career that once took her to Munich, but the twilight of a Christian deity whom Lowell conflates with Wotan and Kennedy, just as he confuses the biblical God with Orpheus and Satan elsewhere in the cycle. The poem also celebrates, albeit comically, the persistence of high European art amidst American squalor.

For this song, Carter asks the solo trumpet to stand behind the ensemble at the opposite side of the stage from the singer. The vocal line becomes a commentary on the trumpet obbligato. Although Carter based the trumpet line on a study of vocalizes, it contains other elements: allusions to Siegfried's horncall and an element of jazz which comes to the fore behind the words 'she flings her high aria to the trash like roses.' Typically of Carter's emblematic imagery, the transformation of Wagner into bebop also inverts the high art/low art polarity of the poem.[9]

3 'HARRIET'

Despite its title this poem is also a double portrait, of the poet and his daughter, and the listener begins to see how Lowell's unbounded sense of self entraps all around him in his private obsessions. Because of Carter's arrangement of texts, the poet's Polonius-like advice to his daughter links this song to the first:

> . . . one choice not two is all you're given,
> health beyond the measure, dangerous
> to yourself, more dangerous to others?

echoes his own confessional in 'Dolphin':

> not avoiding injury to others
> not avoiding injury to myself . . .

These lines also echo the legal definition of insanity, the line Lowell would cross before being committed. The poem is, or at least tries to be, a celebration of his daughter's approaching womanhood, 'three years from Juliet, half Juliet' and a clinical elegy of the poet's premature ageing: 'we . . . change our mouse-brown to white lion's mane, thin white fading to a freckled, knuckled skull.' But the daughter seems like a stage prop for the father's self-pity.

Carter's setting, scored for woodwinds, piano, marimba and strings, mirrors the poems double focus by juxtaposing sections marked 'Teneramente' with those marked 'Ironico' but the nervous staccato of the ironic sections and the sustained lyricism of the tender ones, are both present at all times, only switching in importance. The central subject of the poem – the poet's own anxiety – however suddenly emerges with the words 'health beyond measure' which are framed by clangorous twelve-note chords and which are an abrupt anticipation of the next song: 'Dies Irae.'

4 'DIES IRAE'

Lowell's poem reads like a collaged rant, mingling God and Satan, Old and New testaments, lines from other poems and two popular hymn tunes (whose melodies Carter does not quote). Lowell portrays himself simultaneously saved and betrayed by a God who once saw the world was good. Carter's seismic setting of this poem, punctuated by furious twelve-note chords and scampering polyrhythmic clashes, demonstrates what he might have done with King Lear. The unfettered brass and percussion force the tenor to sing against a storm. After the line 'he strips the wind and gravel from my mouth' the trombone takes over the voice line as the poet is stripped naked. As in 'Harriet,' two moods alternate and co-mingle, an agitato for the poet's fury, and maestoso for his moments of connection with the deity. At the words 'Once our Lord looked down and saw the world was good,' Carter implies a kind of hymn in *Klangfarbenmelodie*, perhaps an emblem of transcendence, or an imitation of the sound of an organ (Ex. 50). After all the tumult, the last line, 'everything points to non-existence except existence,' which is framed by a quietly sustained twelve-note harmony sounds more like an expression of exhaustion than of faith.

5 'CARELESS NIGHT'

The poem turns on the ambiguity of 'careless': without worry and accidental. It begins in a pastoral mood, with the poet and his wife taking a walk in the country. But the rustic peace is an illusion; this is suburbia with encroaching neighbors.[10] The mood turns paranoid. Instead of Christ-child surrounded by shepherds, two ageing parents, measuring their own mortality, must console themselves with an unexpected child. Carter matches the unsettled mood by scoring the song for winds, muted brass, quietly rolled metallic percussion, and strings. A flute solo sounds the pastorale tone, and flutter-tongued brass evoke the sheep and the poet's quixotic mood; but the picturesque effects vanish at the lines of crisis, leaving the poet naked with his pain:

Ex. 50 'Dies Irae': organ effect
By kind permission of *Tempo* magazine, Issue 142, September 1982

    nothing's out of earshot in this daylong night
    nothing can be human without man.

6 'IN GENESIS'

The poet reduces his religious obsessions to black comedy. A retelling of Freud's *Totem and Taboo*, the poem imagines a tyrant god (who is also the poet Orpheus) killed and devoured by his sons – the prototype of Christian communion. Lloyd Schwartz points out that Lowell changed the first word from 'tank' to 'blank,' thereby comparing God's botched creation to a writer's block.

Carter's strategy of subversive collaboration cuts several ways here. He places the beginning last, just as he had placed the conclusion of *The Dolphin* first. He also re-established his identification with Lowell through the allusion to Orpheus, protagonist of *Syringa*. Musically, however, the song is linked to 'Dies Irae,' reducing its violence to a parody, or a 'silly symphony' as Schwartz describes it. Musically it is built on a series of obstinately repeated notes, a G sharp in bars 1–11, a C sharp in 26–36, and on widely spaced fifths. (Ironically, Carter uses the most consonant interval to frame his most grotesque scene.) Against this bleak accompaniment, the voice suddenly becomes melismatic, an attractive gesture which turns ugly when it is revealed as a method of seducing young girls. With its protagonist killed, divided and eaten, the cycle closes on an abrupt, not to say rude, note.

In Sleep, In Thunder may be one of Carter's most forbidding works, but also one of his most daring. Placing the listener within the mind of a contemporary *poète maudit*, it is an unmediated vision of the way we live now. The poems, as Carter arranged them, tell a personal story but also a generic one about the fate of the artist in America. Lowell's family lineage and poetic voice seemed to prepare him for a public role, which he tried to play out during World War II, as a conscientious objector, and during the Vietnam war where his disheveled presence lent prestige, if not coherence, to many peace rallies – yet instead his poetry was trapped within the private confines of his family and his mania. As he had done in *A Symphony of Three Orchestras*, Carter takes on a persona to explore and exorcize his own feelings of isolation and anger.

Notes

1 'Elliott Carter and American Poetry.' Liner notes for CD, Elliott Carter, *The Vocal Works*, Bridge BCD 9014.

2 Elizabeth Bishop, *Complete Poems* (New York; Farrar, Straus and Giroux, 1969).

3 For an extended discussion of the relationship between Carter and Ashbery, see Lawrence Kramer, *Music and Poetry: the Nineteenth Century and After*.

4 John Ashbery, *Houseboat Days* (New York, Penguin, 1977), pp. 69–71.

5 Hamilton, *Robert Lowell* (New York, 1982), p. 285.

6 Ibid, p. 423.

7 I should note that whenever I have spoken of the cycle as 'six songs of a mad poet' Carter has taken me to task and said, 'Cal Lowell was a very nice man and a good friend. We always found him very good company, very amusing.' Cal was an early nickname for Lowell – short for Caligula.

8 The string material for this movement may have originated with sketches for a string quartet which Carter was working on at the time, but which he abandoned after the documentary film-maker Jill Godmilow asked him to compose on camera. Her film was never completed.

9 A note to British performers: 'janitor' is everyday American for 'caretaker' and should not be pronounced as if it were Latin or Italian.

10 It always reminds me of Helen Carter's annoyance with the sounds coming from a Waccabuc neighbor's unseen tennis court.

III *Piano Music*

Piano Sonata

The Piano Sonata written in 1945 and 1946 is the greatest achievement of Carter's early years. It looks back to Copland, Debussy and Stravinsky, forwards to the First Quartet and beyond. The harmonic idiom of the Sonata sums up the possibilities of pandiatonicism. Its fugal second movement consolidates Carter's studies in traditional counterpoint. In its synthesis of instrumental treatment and temporal design, however, it leads directly to the concerns and discoveries of the works of Carter's maturity.

According to Carter's notes:

> The work takes as its departure technically the sonority of the modern piano and is thought of as being completely idiomatic of that instrument, with little or no imitation of other instruments or the orchestra. I have in this work attempted to translate into a special virtuoso style my general musical outlook. I approached writing for the piano as if it were an art all of its own requiring a special musical vocabulary and a particular character unrelated to other kinds of music. There are many features in this work, particularly rhythmic ones, that would be impossible in anything but a solo work. There are melodic conceptions, figurations that are only thinkable on the piano.

The basic premise of the Sonata is the interaction of a virtuoso soloist with the modern grand piano. Free from the constraints of ensemble playing, the Sonata pursues a rhythmic idiom that is complex in its metrical design and improvisatory in its manner of execution. Carter also wanted to move away from the neo-Classical piano writing of Stravinsky and Hindemith and sought to renew the grand piano sonority of nineteenth-century piano writing. While working on the Sonata he discussed his concern for the development of a new grand piano style with Samuel Barber who was writing his Sonata at the same time and had similar goals.

The style and technique of the Sonata seem at times to invoke Copland and Debussy. The opening phrases of both movements suggest Copland's Piano Sonata which predates Carter's by four years. Carter also cites, in

Piano Sonata
© 1948 Mercury Music, Inc. Used by permission

(2)

Piano Variations *(Aaron Copland)*
© Copyright 1932 by Arrow Music Press Inc
Copyright assigned to Aaron Copland
Sole Publishers Boosey & Hawkes Inc

Ex. 51

passing, Copland's Piano Variations: these echoes I believe were intended as a tribute (Ex. 51). Carter wrote the Sonata in the tradition of Copland's piano music but surrounded Copland's gestures with a greater variety of moods and textures, and a greater contrapuntal density. Debussy's influence is less explicit, though the listener may hear echoes of *Les collines d'Anacapri* and *Jardins sous la pluie* in the first movement. Debussy's influence, however, is felt more in the realm of structure; the first movement pursues an improvisatory-sounding style. Although there are many themes, these are generated by abstract material – intervals, chords, arpeggios – out of which the music derives new variations. The combination of an improvisatory surface and a sophisticated system of hidden connections is new in Carter's music and would become even more important in his later works.

The Piano Sonata is in two movements, both of them containing fast and slow music. The first movement has vestigial outlines of sonata allegro design; the second is a portmanteau of slow movement and fugue. The two movements are united by an overall harmonic design and by a cross-network of anticipations and flashbacks. The cross-references indicate an underlying deep structure made explicit only in the final coda.

The most obvious innovation of the first movement is its rhythm; the metre changed so often that Carter eliminated time signatures from the score. The use of rapid sixteenths as the basic unit of speed makes the syncopations of the music about twice as fast as similar rhythmic dislocations in Copland. The more thoroughgoing rhythmic discovery of this movement is the connection between slow and fast tempi. The music ranges in speed from the fastest possible keyboard figuration to the longest possible sounding-board resonance. The tempos of the opening Maestoso and the rapid scorrevole passages are based on the same pulse, sixteenth = MM 528. The scorrevole sections of the first movement display the fast

Piano Sonata
© 1948 Mercury Music, Inc. Used by permission

Ex. 52 Echoes of Copland

motion (Ex. 52) while the Maestoso passages present the sustained resonating material (Ex. 53). Mediating between these two extremes is a third tempo, espressivo, derived not from the nature of the instrument but from the expressive gestures of the performer (Ex. 54).

The harmonic structure is similarly derived from two extremes and a mediator. The harmonic poles of the work are the resonances of the overtone series and the cancellation of resonance caused by the sounding of

Ex. 53 Resonance

Ex. 54 Expressive theme

half-steps. The bright overtone-series harmonies and the dark, chromatic semitones are linked by a cycle of fifths, stated as a rapid arpeggio. A sequence of fifths can generate the entire twelve-note spectrum. It can also generate pentatonic scales and the pitches of the diatonic scale. These properties are realized here in a relation between the pitches B and A sharp:

B major
E B F sharp C sharp G sharp D sharp A sharp = B flat F C G D A,
B flat major

The pitches B and A sharp and the tonalities of B major and B flat major determine the harmonic organization of the Sonata.

According to the composer's notes, the 'genetic' elements of the work are embodied in five ideas heard in the introduction (Ex. 55):

Ex. 55 Genetic material

Ex. 55 (*contd*)

1. Initial jump from low B to much higher B – outlining of the sonorous expanse of the work.
2. Theme in thirds with downward leap of octave. This theme is later often played in 'harmonics' especially near the end of the whole work.
3. The rapid arpeggio figure which appears as an ornament to the above. This is confined to the first movement but fulfills a capacity of binding all the arpeggio material together.
4. Before the first rapid flight of arpeggios, a short motif A sharp– A sharp–G sharp in dotted rhythm appears with chordal harmonies. This is cyclical and appears in many places throughout the work.
5. At the conclusion of the first flight of arpeggios a rising motif in octaves, marcato, in the bass, which occasionally occurs in the first movement and at the end of the slow section before the beginning of the misterioso in the second movement.

The Sonata presents two conflicting formal ideals. Carter claimed that it contained 'no true development in the classical sense . . . all the ideas are in a constant state of change, expansion, contraction, intensification.' Yet at the same time the Sonata displays a conspicuously sophisticated approach to the classical forms of sonata-allegro and fugue. The merger of an improvisatory style with classical structures does not feel strained or artificial. If Carter's aim was to achieve the poetic complexity of Ives's

Concord Sonata through abstract means rather than programatically as Ives had done, he succeeded.

The first movement can be divided into an exposition (with two thematic groups), development and recapitulation, but with a number of escape clauses. It begins with a slow maestoso introduction that returns at several points in the movement; bars 24–32, 123–128 (in harmonics), 251–263. Each recurrence has a different function. The first return interrupts the initial fast theme; the second marks the beginning of the development, and the third comes in the middle of the recapitulation, between the two theme groups rather than as an introduction to the first. The 'first group' of the exposition suggests a jazzy toccata; Carter has cited the influence of Fats Waller and Art Tatum. It consists of two main ideas, a rapid figuration in sixteenth notes and a syncopated motif built on fourths; these two ideas interact playfully and are also interrupted by a gnomic cyclical figure that appeared in the bass of bars 20–22 and in the introduction of the second movement. The device of unexpected interruptions gives the music its improvisatory quality. The 'second group' is anticipated in bars 71–75 with a slowing of the pace, but again a linear approach is counteracted by the sudden return of the initial tempo in an emphatic cadence. The 'second group' is also made up of several elements. It begins by elaborating a nine-note motif, seems to lose interest in it, restates it and then suddenly arrives at a related, but different idea at bar 102; the 'real' second theme seems to arrive unanticipated. The first emphatic statement of this theme immediately gives way to a contrasting counterstatement, a three-part canon in inversion.

The development makes use of the motives of the 'first group'; the nine-note motive of the 'second group' appears at 156–161, but 'is rejected' as Carter's notes put it. After an extended exploration of the toccata figure the music is again interrupted, but instead of a return to the maestoso, which we might expect, a new theme appears in D minor – a flash-forward to the opening of the second movement. This new motif contains a contrapuntal conundrum: the melody in the inner voice is an augmentation of part of the 'second group' – see bar 87. After this mysterious portent the toccata is taken up again, somewhere (it is hard to say exactly where) turning into a free and condensed recapitulation of the first group. Following the inserted reprise of the introductory five bars of the canon the 'second group' returns. A short transition leads to a brilliant coda based on the toccata material. Carter however undermines the applause-inducing virtuosity of the passage by putting the final cadence a half-step low, on B flat rather than B natural.

The second movement, Andante, begins with a bell-like motif whose new tonality of D minor still stresses the conflict between B and B flat. A lyrical melody gradually expands over an ostinato derived from the opening motif. After an intense development of the interplay of ostinato and cantilena, the bell motif returns, interrupted by a rising third that alludes to the first movement and to the coming fugue subject. After a transition recalling the first movement's introduction, there is a rapid, misterioso passage preparing for the statement of the fugue subject.

The design of the fugue is ingenious. The fugal exposition is followed by a series of episodes, each based on a contraction of the fugue subject (Chart 32).

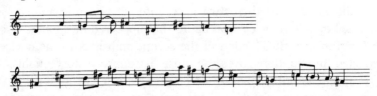

Chart 32 Piano Sonata: shortening of fugue subject

The episodes are sometimes free, sometimes strict, with close three-and four-part canonic writing. A jazzy, white-note episode, sounding distant from the subject, is actually a strict isorhythmic variation, combining the rhythmic shape of the subject with a pentatonic melodic 'row' (Chart 33). In the next episode the complete subject is gradually reassembled out of fragments. There now takes place an exposition in reverse, with fewer and fewer voices until the subject alone is stated in octaves. Along the way, important motives from two of the episodes return, including the white-note motif which appears in augmentation. Harmonically the fugue moves upwards by half-steps from B flat to C sharp. After the octave statement of the subject the opening material of the movement suddenly reappears – but in E flat rather than the original D, preparing for one final harmonic resolution on B. The cantilena returns (shorn of its first eight bars) in an intensified form, leading to a climax which states the entire range and harmonic design of the Sonata, from the lowest B flat to the highest B of the piano. This monumental sonority continues to ring as overtones to a held D sharp–F sharp, a minor third at the very center of the keyboard – the core-sonority, it suddenly seems, of the entire work. In the coda, a kind of recessional that gradually fades away, the basic

Chart 33 Piano Sonata: isorhythmic fugue episode

elements of both movements fuse. The final chord is a glowing emanation of overtones from a primal three-octave B (the opening sound of the Sonata transposed by one octave) whose dying reverberations bring the work to a serene close.

Night Fantasies

Carter's first work for solo piano since the Piano Sonata of 1946 was composed in Waccabuc and at the American Academy in Rome between June 1979 and 12 April 1980. It was commissioned by, and dedicated to, four New York pianists: Paul Jacobs, Gilbert Kalish, Ursula Oppens, and Charles Rosen. The commission was made possible by the American Music Center in New York. Miss Oppens gave the world première of Night Fantasies *at the Bath Festival on 2 June 1980.*

Carter wrote *Night Fantasies* for four pianists who were experienced performers of his music. Paul Jacobs recorded the Cello Sonata, the Sonata for Flute, Oboe, Cello and Harpsichord, and the Double Concerto (playing the harpsichord). As pianist of the New York Philharmonic, he also recorded the virtuoso piano parts written especially for him in the Concerto for Orchestra and *A Symphony of Three Orchestras*. Gilbert Kalish has recorded the Double Concerto (at the piano) and the Duo, which he premièred with Paul Zukofsky. Charles Rosen was the first piano soloist of the Double Concerto. He has recorded that work twice and performed it many times over the last twenty years. The Piano Sonata has been in his active repertory for over a quarter of a century, and in recent years he has also played the Piano Concerto. Ursula Oppens has performed both solo parts of the Double Concerto and has made two recordings of the Piano Concerto.

The title deliberately evokes Schumann; Carter has called the work a 'sort of contemporary *Kreisleriana*.' The link with *Kreisleriana* is conceptual. Carter set out to write a large-scale work whose form would be as different as possible from that of a sonata. Schumann had discovered just such a principle in *Papillons*, *Carnaval* and his other sequences of short character pieces. These compositions are not sonatas, suites or anthologies. They are song cycles without words. They imply a large dramatic argument through the juxtaposition of contrasting moods rather than through thematic development or recapitulation. Although each short piece could stand on its own, in context they take on a dramatic resonance. Their contrasting characters interact to form a large design whose 'story' is mysteriously implied but nowhere stated. Links between pieces are achieved not by thematic recurrence or variation but by transformations that give a more ambiguous sense of causality than the more rigorous means of a sonata would. The G-minor movements in *Kreisleriana*, for instance, are all related, but how and why? Mystery is the essence of the form.

Like *Kreisleriana*, *Night Fantasies* is built out of many contrasting episodes. Carter, however, collages fragments of his episodes so that they emerge, evolve and vanish, sometimes growing imperceptibly out of one another, elsewhere appearing suddenly, sharply interrupting the previous mood. Carter has compared the continuity of the music to the unpunctuated poems of Mallarmé or William Carlos Williams where phrases, thoughts and images are ambiguously dovetailed, so that multiple readings are not only possible but inevitable. He has also likened the music to the unclear thoughts of an insomniac on a wakeful night, a condition he found sharply etched in Robert Lowell's poem 'Myopia: a Night.'[1]

Bed, glasses off, and all's
ramshackle, streaky, weird
for the near-sighted, just
a foot away.
                The light's
still on an instant. Here
are the blurred titles, here
the books are blue hills, browns,
greens, fields, or color.
                This
is the departure strip,
the dream road.

Schumann, Mallarmé, Lowell – despite these 'clues,' *Night Fantasies* springs from Carter's own world. It continues the improvisational and spontaneous manner of the Duo and *Syringa* – a *Syringa* without words, or a Duo whose external instrumental conflict has been internalized, absorbed by a single instrument and a single performer. The piano here is a mirror of the mind (as it often is in Schumann), a mind in a state of semi-conscious meditation. The music is at once calm and nervous, sustained and unstable. The unpredictable rate of change and the deliberate ambiguity of gesture are the essential elements of the music's poetic world – and they are also Carter's creative response to his commission. For *Night Fantasies* in its succession of fugitive visions creates a musical ambience that amplifies the tiniest facet of each interpreter's musical personality. The music is not a portrait of the performers, but it is composed so that each interpretation will be a self-portrait.

In writing for solo piano, Carter denied himself the opposition of protagonists that has become habitual in his recent scores. These oppositions are here absorbed into the musical space of a single instrument. Instead of the lateral contrasts of singers and texts in *Syringa*, the conflicts within *Night Fantasies* are vertical. The surface of the music is an ambiguous reflection of its hidden content. Its foundation is rigorous and regular; its musical surface is improvisatory and changeable. As was already clear in the Piano Sonata, the piano for Carter is the spatial instrument par excellence. It has a huge range that is unified by a consistent mode of attack and by the resonance made possible by the pedals. In the Sonata, Carter emphasized the role of the overtone series in the piano's musical space, and used a few elemental contrasts of materials and textures: fast, slow and moderate materials in the first movement; arioso and fugue in the second. In *Night Fantasies*, he sought a much greater variety of sounds and textures. Quite early in the course of composing the work he told me that he had already written fifty different kinds of piano music, and was now looking for ways to bring them together.[2] The variety of textures in the work is remarkable, especially considering the absence of imitative textures such as canons or fugatos. The performer is called upon to use a great range of dynamics and touch – from leggerissimo to marcatissimo, from staccato to cantabile. The music covers the spectrum of the keyboard in ever-changing configurations, so that the resultant tone color continually varies.

Carter connects the many textures of the work through a systematic organization of the space of the keyboard. The framework for the music is provided by eighty-eight all-interval twelve-note chords. These chords share a structural property: each interval is paired symmetrically with its inversional equivalent (minor second with major seventh, major second with minor seventh, minor third with major sixth, major third with minor sixth, perfect fourth with perfect fifth) around a central non-invertible tritone (Chart 34). The frequent pairing of inversionally-related intervals

(used in bars 3-14)

Chart 34 *Night Fantasies*: principal one of 88 all-interval chords

in the music stems from this chordal property as does the texture of the 'recitative collerico' at bar 235 with its centrally located tritones framed by a chordal accompaniment. The eighty-eight chords are further related because they all derive from just four hexachords (numbers 3–6) that contain every interval except the tritone.

The harmonic technique of *Night Fantasies* marks a breakthrough in Carter's exploration of all-interval chords. Instead of using a few such chords as 'tonic' sonorities, the distinctive spacing of this large chordal constellation informs the entire work. The sonority of the all-interval twelve-note chords is complex, but this very complexity is a source of their structural clarity – no other chords sound like them. Two aspects of the chordal structure will be most apparent to the listener. Carter emphasizes the opposition of large and small intervals. This opposition is at once the constant structure of the work's harmony and the source of its ever-changing sound. Throughout the work, close and open spacings are contrasted, and as these spacings change position relative to the keyboard the sonority of the piano changes accordingly. Close chords in the bass paired with wide-spaced notes in the treble have a very different resonance from their inversion. Carter employs every possible gradation of spatial contrast (within the limits of the chordal structure) so that in the course of the work the total spectrum has been explored. At first the listener will notice mainly the heightened contrasts of registers and spacings; later the many connections established between these contrasts will become apparent. As in his other music, Carter often uses the familiar linkage of common notes to connect his uncommon chords. A few pitches may be sustained, for instance, as a kind of pedal throughout a passage, and many different chords containing these pitches are sounded against them. This method appears most clearly in the last pages of the work, where a four-note chord (pairing major seventh and minor ninth) is sounded repeatedly against fragments of all the twelve-note chords that include it. This four-note chord tolls seventeen times, gradually fading and seeming to absorb all the fragments of the work until its final appearance silences them. (Perhaps this final cadence is also an echo of the quiet G-minor conclusion of *Kreisleriana*; it is also remarkably similar in effect to the ending of Ravel's *Valses nobles et sentimentales*.)

The second compositional property of the all-interval twelve-note chords is their ability to transform smaller intervallic structures. Carter explored this property in 'Anaphora' by projecting many transpositions of one six-note chord on a fixed twelve-note chord. In *Night Fantasies* the procedure is far more varied, for a large number of chords and intervals are projected on the vast array of all-interval chords. Sometimes a single class of intervals is emphasized: the fourths and fifths of the opening tranquillo music, or the minor thirds and major sixths from bars 15–26, or the ninths and sevenths near the end. Elsewhere three-note chords come to the fore: (0, 2, 5) at bars 70–9 or (0, 1, 5) in the capriccioso material beginning at 195. Still elsewhere, four-note chords are stressed, notably Carter's old favorite (0, 1, 4, 6) at 123–8. By contrast with Carter's other music, however, these relatively discrete harmonies are not the main elements of the musical design. Instead, they serve to reveal different aspects of the all-interval chords that form the music's underlying spatial structure. Consequently, clear intervallic or chordal material often appears mixed with less clearly-defined harmonies. At bar 27, for example, the minor thirds of the previous passage suddenly become part of a chord (0, 1, 4) which itself is used to introduce the region of a new all-interval chord in bars 32–6. The music next becomes dominated by the major third, the sum of the previously stressed intervals. Thirds and seconds are then combined into four-note chords in the important passage from 42 to 55 that returns in altered but recognizable form at 417 to 431. By frequently changing his focus from simple intervallic patterns to the all-interval patterns of the deep structure, Carter achieves the ambiguity of character that is the distinctive expressive domain of the work.

The rhythmic structure of *Night Fantasies* displays an internal conflict parallel to that of its harmonic design. Carter began with a desire to write many contrasting types of music, and, as in the harmony, he sought a temporal design that would link these episodes in a coherent sequence. Unlike the Third Quartet and *A Symphony of Three Orchestras*, *Night Fantasies* does not obey a constructivist scheme of musical return. Some episodes come back in clearly recognizable form: the four-note chords at bars 42 and 417, for example, or the capriccioso music whose speed, harmony and tessitura remain constant throughout. Other material returns but in a transformed manner: the recitativo collerico, for instance, spawns a number of episodes clearly related to it in gesture and texture, and yet different in intervallic make-up and melodic contour. Some episodes return only briefly and in altered states: the mechanical nightingale of bars 157–67 is echoed in a quite different context at bars 215–16. Still other episodes are gradually replaced by their opposites: the spacious fifths of the opening correspond structurally to the clangorous ninths of the close. The various episodes of *Night Fantasies* might thus be said to possess contrasting half-lives. Some of them change slowly, some more quickly, others decay even as they are sounded. These juxtaposed rates of transformation again contribute to the ambiguous climate of the music, for as the materials change their contrasts and connections change as well.

Although *Night Fantasies* avoids articulating large points of arrival along its path, the overall shape of the piece creates a context for the many small events that flash by. Carter describes the work as a fast movement interrupted (as in Schumann) by slow 'trios' that gradually turns into a slow movement interrupted by fast 'trios.' Fast and slow episodes thus gradually exchange roles of foreground and background – a difference the performer should make clear. The characters of both fast and slow music also evolve in the course of the work. Several distinct types of fast music (fantastico, marcato, cantabile, leggero, appassionato) are heard before the most sustained fast section (capriccioso leggerissimo) appears. These all return as 'trios' during the second half of the piece, with the marcato passages becoming increasingly prominent. Similarly the slow music changes in character from the barely audible tranquillo opening, floating chords, and brief, static ostinati, to increasingly intense lyrical utterances, most clearly heard in the extravagant beauty of the melodic line at bars 377–87. Typical of the work's reversals of focus is the way this passage returns at bar 417 with its melodic line 'erased' and its chordal accompaniment now the dominant event. Slow and fast materials finally merge at their points of greatest intensity with the harsh chords of bar 472 and following; from this climax of fusion the music gradually subsides.

In order to ensure the coherence of the music in time, Carter quite early in its composition constructed a system of pulses that runs from the beginning to the end. There are two pulse rates, MM 10.8 and 8.75; they coincide only at the downbeat of bar 3 and on the final notes of the piece. The polyrhythm formed is 216:175, and every pulse of both rates is played, though they rarely appear in isolation. Thus, just as Carter composed the musical space of the work, he also composed its 'real' time; this rhythmic design moreover corresponds to the chordal substructure in its poetic function. It is at once hidden and controlling. The relentless pulses might be compared to a clock in an insomniac's room, its ticking passing in and out of the listener's consciousness. Never before had Carter systematically composed real time into a piece of these dimensions with such absolute rigor, and never before had the contrast of clock time and psychological time been presented structurally rather than dramatically – though for the insomniac the glowing face of a clock can become the most terrifying of dramatic personae. Although the cross-pulse is mostly hidden in the faster motion of the musical surface, many of the events of the music owe their drama to the partially revealed deep structure of musical time: all that remains of the erased recitative at bar 419, for example, is the underlying pulse whose isolated notes now bear the expressive burden of the vanished melody. The slower pulse becomes most audible towards the close when it is heard in the repeated four-note chord that gradually extinguishes the music.

The relation of surface events to the underlying polyrhythm is mostly hidden, but its role in the piece is decisive. Having chosen the two pulse rates, Carter could use only those tempi that would allow every pulse to be precisely notated. The slow pulses thus determined an entire field of tempi and generated all the faster speeds and polyrhythms used in the piece (Chart 35). Needless to say, in performance the many gradations of speed must be rigorously observed to ensure both the steadiness of the underlying pulses and the temporal variety of the musical surface.

Apart from its technical demands and its structural originality, *Night Fantasies* has a meditative character rather different from the dramatic mode of most of Carter's music. American composers, who often feel isolated, have produced a uniquely private genre of piano music. Though often difficult to play, works in this genre are soliloquies, intense acts of self-communion. One thinks of Ives's 'Thoreau,' of Ruggles's *Evocations*, or the closing pages of Copland's Piano Sonata, and of his Piano Fantasy and *Night Thoughts*. *Night Fantasies* reaffirms and extends this meditative tradition.

90+

'mille e novanta auguri a caro Goffredo'. Composed in March 1994 to celebrate the ninetieth birthday 'of my dear and much admired friend, Goffredo Petrassi, Italy's leading composer of his generation. Première 11 June 1994 by Giuseppe Scotese at the Pontino Music Festival dedicated to Petrassi's birthday.'

Carter notes that 90+ 'is built around ninety short, accented notes played in a regular beat. Against these the context changes character continually.' His working title was 'novanta suoni sparsi.' In the score Carter numbers the first ten beats and the final 86–90 which are followed by a series of extra notes 'to grow on' which speed up and fade out. Anyone who wants to understand the way tempo proportions work can track down the other 'auguri' as they make their way through several tempo changes. At the opening the tempo is quarter = 96; the staccato notes appear every sixteen triplet eighths or at a metronomic speed of 18 beats per minute. At bar 15 the tempo increases by a ratio of 5:4 to quarter = 120; the staccato notes now appear every twenty triplet eighths. At bar 37 the tempo slows by a ratio of 3: 5 to quarter = 72; the staccato pulses now fall every twelve triplet eighths (or every four quarter notes.) From bar 50

Tempi	Pulses	Surface speed
MM 94.5=♩	5/54=8.75*	♪^{5}=472.5
	4/35=10.8	♪=378
MM 47.25=♩	5/27=8.75	♪^{5}=236.25
	8/35=10.8	♪=378
MM 42=♩.	5/24=8.75	♪.^{5}=210
	9/35=10.8	♪^{3}=378
MM 63=♩	5/36=8.75	♪^{5}=315
	6/35=10.8	♪=378
MM 126=♩	5/72=8.75	♪=630
	3/35=10.8	♪^{3}=378
MM 90=♩.	7/72=8.75	♪.^{7}=630
	3/25=10.8	♪=270
MM 45=♩	7/36=8.75	♪^{7}=315
	6/25=10.8	♪^{3}=270
MM 30=♩.	7/24=8.75	♪.^{7}=210
	9/25=10.8	♪^{3}=270
MM 67.5=♩	7/54=8.75	♪^{7}=472.5
	4/25=10.8	♪=270
MM 78.75=♩.	1/9=8.75	♩.=78.75
	24/175=10.8	♪=1890

*The fraction means that the pulse rate is equal to fifty-four quintuplets

Chart 35 *Night Fantasies*: tempo field

to 85 it appears regularly as the second half of the second beat of the bar. At bar 90 the tempo returns to quarter = 120.

Harmonically, 90+ is an exploration of hexachord number 35. The opening five bars present the all-triad hexachord in a fixed pitch spacing, with changing combinations of intervals and tetrachords and of pairs of triads. In bar 6 the complementary pitches appear, unfolding hexachord number 36 which plays a subsidiary role in the piece to set in relief the constant restatements of hexachord number 35.

90+ is constructed in a series of large phrases that contrast the staccato pulse alternatively with other regular cross pulses or with expressive, rubato rhythms. Bars 1–20 contrast a succession of sustained chords, at a cross pulse of seventeen sixteenth notes with darting rapid figures based on quintuplet rhythms. In bars 21–32 the rapid figures come to the fore in an upper register scorrevole. In bars 37–48 the music takes on a pesante character in the lower registers as it contrasts changing four-note chords, at a regular cross rhythm of nine sixteenths, against repeated intervallic figures. Bars 48–68 are a fragmented scherzando section, marked 'staccato giocoso' which ranges over the entire keyboard. In this section the staccato pulses no longer contrast with other ideas but are camouflaged by the sparse texture. With the upbeat to bar 69 a long rubato melody begins to unfold in the right hand, accelerating against a rhythmically independent staccato accompaniment in the left, a continuation of the previous section; bars 78–81 almost sound like Art Tatum. In bars 82–88 this melody slows down and dissolves. The concluding section, bars 90–113 begins as a fixed register ringing of changes, based on a cross rhythm of seven sixteenths, which moves toward a climactic harmonic statement in bars 110–112. The harmony of bars 92–105 is based on a symmetrical twelve-note chord whose close spacing and hexachordal make-up is rather different in character from that heard elsewhere in the piece. The two hexachords derive from hexachord number 3 (0, 1, 2, 4, 5, 8) which differs from hexachord number 35 by one note. The codetta consists of the infinite extra 'wishes.'

Pianists will find 90+ to be an attractive and compact alternative to *Night Fantasies*. The logic behind its textures and chords become clearer if the performer locates all 90+ staccato notes and also begins to look for hexachord number 35. The most apparently esoteric part of the piece may be the scattered scherzo in bars 48–68. These seemingly random sprays of notes are in fact based on the 'Link' chords, the all-interval twelve note chords which contain hexachord number 35 in a contiguous spacing which theorist John Link assembled for the composer. Only once in this passage does Carter state hexachord number 35 linearly (from the last beat of 62 through the second beat of 64) but all the spacings are determined by the hexachord. 'Link' spacings occur throughout the piece, climactically at bars 108–112.

Notes

1 Robert Lowell, *Selected Poems* (New York: Farrar, Straus and Giroux, 1977), p. 114.
2 See John F. Link, 'The Composition of Carter's *Night Fantasies*.'

IV Orchestral Music

8 Ballets

Pocahontas

Pocahontas was commissioned by Lincoln Kirstein for a touring company called Ballet Caravan. Kirstein wrote the scenario for *Pocahontas*; his original program notes are reprinted in the published score:

> When the English adventurers sailed into the bay by the outlet of the Virginia rivers they still thought of the strange new land not as a new continent but as a part of the East Indies Spice Isles. The people they found, subject to King Powhatan, were by no means the red nomads of the Western plains, but rather the gold-brown village-dwelling hunters and farmers – a race which has since disappeared completely.
>
> Upon his arrival in the new land, the English explorer John Smith – now middle aged, a veteran of the Turkish wars and an experienced adventurer – accepted the cruelties of Powhatan's braves as the price of yet another adventure.
>
> But the character of the young Indian princess Pocahontas was unexpected. Her capricious pity for him in rescuing Smith from the tortures of her kinsmen, her disgust with their savagery and her instinctive feeling for another civilization were something new. And yet the white man's gifts were scarcely an improvement: firearms and firewater instead of tobacco and tomahawk. Guns and whiskey purchased the Indians and a handful of English seized America.
>
> Symbolizing the naive trust and inherent tragedy of the original Americans, Pocahontas died in childbirth in England following her marriage to John Rolfe, Smith's protegé, and her presentation at the court of James I. The idea and character of this ballet were suggested by 'Powhatan's Daughter', the second section of Hart Crane's poem *The Bridge*.

The original version of *Pocahontas* was premièred on 17 August 1936 in Keene, New Hampshire, with choreography by Lew Christensen, and a cast including Lew Christensen, Ruthanna Boris, Charles Laskey, Harold Christensen and Erick Hawkins. This version had only piano accompaniment.

By 1939, when Ballet Caravan gave a New York season, *Pocahontas* was greatly revised and expanded. The biggest change in the music was the excision and replacement of material that later became the last movement of the Symphony No. 1 – and which with its jaunty diatonicism sounded out of place among the rugged features of the rest of the score. The final version of the ballet was first performed on 24 May 1939 at the Martin Beck Theatre in New York, with Leda Anchutina, Erick Hawkins, Eugene Loring and Harold Christensen (doubling the role of John Smith with Todd Bolender). *Pocahontas* shared the program with *Billy the Kid*. The Suite from the ballet, which includes most of the full score, was published in two different versions. In 1941 the work won the Juilliard Publication Award and was printed in a deceptively attractive edition studded with errors – Carter's errata list is twenty-five pages long. For a performance conducted in 1960 by Jacques-Louis Monod, Carter made a thorough revision of the score. The revised version was recorded by Monod and published in 1969.

Very little of *Pocahontas* sounds like later Carter – not in style, rhythm, harmony or orchestration. The shape of the Suite, however, is Carterian. The gradually subsiding motion from an opening explosion is a Carter fingerprint and is achieved with memorable poignancy, as John Smith and John Rolfe are gradually enveloped by the forest of the New World. The opening, explosive material sounds rather like Milhaud (as Ernst Krenek once pointed out to Carter) and the calmer music starts out like Hindemith, before it begins to fade away. There are, however, moments of lyrical beauty in these opening sections that sound personal and original, from fig. 20 to the end of the second section, for example. Interestingly, these less derivative passages are also more characteristic of Carter in their counterpoint, which contrasts layers of different motion; at fig. 17 Carter superimposes a mysterious augmentation of *Pocahontas*'s as-yet unstated motif on top of the 9/8 trot of the Smith–Rolfe material. At fig. 18 there is also an intriguing quotation in advance of a motif from the second movement of the Symphony No. 1, suggesting much interaction between the two scores in their formative stages. The motif, though prominently stated here, plays no important role elsewhere in the ballet.

The music for 'Princess Pocahontas and her Ladies' uses the exotic *Pocahontas*-motif as a frame for an un-Indian pop tune. At fig. 31, however, another section of tender lyricism appears – one of the few passages in Carter that bring Mahler to mind: note the interplay of violas and harp which supports the texture. The clarinet cadenzas here foreshadow more effective passages in the Symphony No. 1; but the orchestration of the last five bars of this section is inspired and well crafted.

The music for the 'Torture of John Smith' is the most uneven part of an uneven score. The basic shape is again distinctly personal, a tremendous build-up of violence released by a pianissimo echo – the barely audible resonance of harp and piano continues to ring after a sharp climactic chord for the whole orchestra. This effect is Carter's first use of a characteristically Ivesian gesture; indeed, fig. 53 to 54 is Carter's only music of this period that looks like Ives on the page. Even at this stage, though, Carter redefines the gesture; the resonating piano and harp begin a new strand of music, taking the listener beyond the immediately shocking juxtaposition in volume. The Pavane that concludes *Pocahontas* is a double homage to Stravinsky's *Apollo* (at the request of Kirstein) and the *Fitzwilliam Virginal Book*.

The Minotaur

A decade after the first *Pocahontas*, Lincoln Kirstein again commissioned Carter to write a ballet, this time for Ballet Society, the immediate predecessor of the New York City Ballet. Ballet Society was as artistically élitist in character as Ballet Caravan had been populist – even the press had difficulty in getting into its exclusive performances held incongruously at the High School of Needle Trades in New York. Among its productions were Ravel's *L'enfant et les sortilèges*, Balanchine's path-breaking choreography for Hindemith's *The Four Temperaments*, *The Seasons* (the first collaboration between John Cage and Merce Cunningham), and the Balanchine–Noguchi–Stravinsky landmark, *Orpheus*.

The Minotaur started out as a collaboration between Carter and Balanchine, who carefully worked out a scenario including the musical and scenic idea of transforming Pasiphae's heartbeats into the hammer blows of workers building the labyrinth. The published score of the Suite contains the following synopsis:

Overture
Scene I – Pasiphae's apartments in the royal palace.
Pasiphae prepares secretly with her attendants for a tryst with the white bull.
Entrance of the bulls, summoned by the horn calls of Pasiphae's attendants. With a few companions, the white bull rushes in and a frantic Bull's Dance with Pasiphae takes place. Blackout.

(Omitted in the Suite: Music during the change of scene suggesting the excited beat of Pasiphae's heart. When the curtain rises on the next scene, this beat turns into the pounding of hammers of stone cutters.)

Scene II – Before the Labyrinth. Some years later.

(Omitted in the Suite: *The Minotaur* is being imprisoned in a labyrinth as his mother, Pasiphae, tries to keep the workmen from building the walls. King Minos and Ariadne enter with Theseus leading a group of Greek captives who are to be sacrificed to the man-eating monster.)

Ariadne and Theseus are attracted to each other and dance a *pas de deux*. Despite Ariadne's pleading, her father commands that Theseus and his men be driven into

The Labyrinth.

Meanwhile Ariadne gives Theseus the end of a thread which is to lead him and his companions safely out of the maze.

Theseus's farewell on entering the labyrinth.

(Omitted in the Suite: Ariadne cautiously unwinds her thread from its spindle as Theseus enters the labyrinth pulling the thread after him.)

Theseus fights and kills the Minotaur, each gesture being transmitted to Ariadne through the thread.

Ariadne unwinds her thread to lead Theseus and his companions out of the maze. To her great dismay, the thread breaks.

Theseus and the Greeks emerge from the labyrinth and rejoice at their success. Then, carrying oars and raising sails, but forgetting Ariadne, Theseus and the Greeks prepare to leave Crete as the curtain falls.

Before Balanchine could choreograph the ballet, however, he left New York – and Ballet Society – for Paris, in an unsuccessful attempt to take over the Paris Ballet after the dismissal of Serge Lifar. Lifar was soon cleared of collaborationist charges and reinstated as director; Balanchine returned to New York in 1948, but meanwhile the choreography of *The Minotaur* had been assigned to his young assistant John Taras. The sets and costumes were by Joan Junyer, and the cast included Elise Reiman, Francisco Moncion, Edward Bigelow and Tanaquil LeClerq as Ariadne. The première took place on 26 March 1947. The ballet received mixed reviews: LeClerq made a great impression, as did Junyer's sets, but the choreography was considered tentative and uneven. The dance critics found the music opaque but the music reviewers praised it: 'One could marvel at the extent of the work and complexity of thought that went into the process,' wrote Arthur Berger in the *Herald Tribune*. After two seasons *The Minotaur* was dropped and was never revived by the New York City Ballet. A new choreography by John Butler to the music from the Suite was staged in Boston in 1970. The Suite, which omits about one-third of the music, was recorded by Howard Hanson and the Eastman-Rochester Symphony Orchestra in 1956. (For several years this was the only orchestral work of Carter's available on disc.) The recording was well received, but critics tended to label Carter a neo-Classicist on the basis of the score – at the very time when his style had left neo-Classicism far behind.

Perhaps more than any other work, *The Minotaur* presents problems for anyone attempting to trace Carter's development. Richard Franko Goldman, in a pioneering article on the First Quartet, went so far as to advise readers not to listen to *The Minotaur*, because of the misleading impression it would give of the composer's work:

> *The Minotaur* is a good score, of which almost any American composer might be proud, but it is not altogether representative of the essential Carter style.[1]

Like the Piano Sonata, *The Minotaur* is a work of lyrical beauty, rhythmic force and emotional depth; but whereas the Sonata points in the direction of Carter's later music, *The Minotaur* looks backwards. If *Pocahontas* seemed to contain echoes of many other composers in a way natural to a young artist just beginning to seek his own style, *The Minotaur* seems perversely Stravinskian, deliberately suppressing many of the personal traits Carter's music had developed by 1947. Passages such as figs. 73 to 75, or, even more, 107 to 109, seem like intentional allusions to Stravinsky's works – the spiccato strings and solo clarinet in an unmodulated mezzoforte are as characteristic of Stravinsky as they are unusual for Carter. The structural formations of the music, from the framing maestoso whose horn duet pays homage to Stravinsky's recent *Scènes de Ballet*, to the clearly juxtaposed sections of the Bull's Dance and *pas de deux*, also sound uncharacteristically close to the Russian master.

The derivative impression the score has made on some listeners, however, is somewhat deceptive. The occasional violence of the music in the Bull's Dance and the building of the Labyrinth break through the general air of neo-Classical restraint; but the structure of the music already employs devices which would allow Carter to abandon neo-Classicism in his next work, the Cello Sonata. *The Minotaur* might be thought of as an example of Carter's agonism; he had taken on Copland in the Piano Sonata and he now confronted Stravinsky, the composer whose influence had paralyzed so many of Carter's contemporaries.

Before analyzing the score it is necessary to say how the Suite differs from the complete ballet. The Suite omits two crucial structural events in the transformation of Pasiphae's heartbeats into hammer blows, and the first statement of the music to which Ariadne unwinds her thread, music that is superimposed on a passacaglia bass when she rewinds the thread and it breaks. Although Carter may have felt that these events were too specifically theatrical to warrant inclusion in the Suite, they are necessary to the dramatic shape of the complete score. Two other omissions – a short, strange ostinato before the White Bull enters, and the long entrance march of Minos – are structurally less important, and musically less interesting than the rest of the music; they do contain bits of recapitulation which may have mirrored the dance, but seem redundant without it.

Two movements of the ballet are constructed on polyrhythmic principles. The propulsive Bull's Dance pits quarter notes at MM 160 against dotted quarters at 106–7. This is the familiar hemiola relationship of 3:2. What is new here is the weakened hierarchy between the two pulses. This passage almost crosses into the new rhythmic world of the First Quartet – but not quite; it sounds like a neo-Classical reinterpretation of the Dance to the Earth at the end of the first part of *Le Sacre*.

The Chabrier-inspired *pas de deux* is also based on two tempi, MM 120 and MM 80, that are related in a 3:2 ratio. The dance alternates large sections built on each of these tempi, thereby creating a structure analogous to, but different from, the traditional and Stravinskian form of introduction, solo variations and concluding duet. In Carter's conclusion the two tempi fuse through cross-cutting. Alternating bars are built on the two different pulses. The composite pattern of the two tempi sounds at first like Stravinsky's shifting accentuation, but its structural source is the conflicting claims of the two pulses rather than the irregular accentuation of a single pulse unit.

The pulse rate of the *pas de deux* reappears structurally in later parts of the ballet. The passacaglia to which Ariadne rewinds her thread moves at quarter = 60, so that it can allude to the *pas de deux*, restating its quaver ostinato exactly by renotating in halved values. The pulse of MM 60 appears climactically at fig. 105 when a cross-accented grouping of five quavers sounds the pulse at the center of a transformation in tempo from dotted quarter = 152 to quarter = 76; the sixteenths at fig. 107 are at the same speed as the dotted eighths at fig. 101.

Carter was composing 'Stravinsky' by hidden Carterian means; the deceptively irregular accents and the major-minor dissonances of the music's surface are produced by coherent, hidden structural principles which never receive explicit thematic form; all the elements of the work are emanations from a hidden core. Most of the melodic shapes of *The Minotaur*, for example, were derived from the Seikilos Song – one of the few transcribed fragments of Greek music. But although Carter originally quoted (Ex. 56) this theme after fig. 104, he later cut the quotation out of the music, leaving variations without a stated theme and hiding the pervasive source of melodic unity.

Seikilos Song (The Minotaur)
© 1956 Associated Music Publishers Inc.

Ex. 56 Hidden source

The harmonic structure of the work grows from a similar submerged principle. The harmonies of *The Minotaur* sound more chromatic and dissonant than those of the Piano Sonata, because there are few of the pentatonic, pandiatonic, fifth-derived sounds of the Sonata. The tonal conflict is controlled by a set of four-note chords based on thirds and minor seconds, the semitones giving the work its distinctive color. By combining pairs of thirds at the distance of a semitone, Carter derives the following seven source chords (Chart 36).

Chart 36 Chords in *The Minotaur*

These four-note groups control the harmonic and melodic idiom of *The Minotaur* with great consistency, though not with the relentless logic of similar practice in the Cello Sonata and later works, for the work is clearly organized in tonal terms as well.

The formal structure of the ballet summarizes the strategies by which Carter undermines the deceptively Stravinskian surface. Most of Stravinsky's neo-Classical ballets are suites of separate dances. In *The Minotaur* clearly demarcated sections turn out on closer inspection to overlap.

Because of the tightly controlled harmonic and rhythmic schemes, motivic cross-references abound – so much so that the listener hears a continuous, integrated permutation of materials rather than linear thematic development, or leitmotivic allusion. Behind many of these relationships is the Seikilos Song: the rising fifths that introduce the Bull's Dance (Ex. 57) state the opening motif of this melody most obviously, but other, veiled allusions abound, as in the cello line at fig. 10 (Ex. 58). This

The Minotaur
© 1956 Associated Music Publishers, Inc. Used by permission

Ex. 57 'Seikilos' motif

The Minotaur
© 1956 Associated Music Publishers, Inc. Used by permission

Ex. 58 Hidden 'Seikilos'

passage in turn anticipates fig. 25; the oboe outline before fig. 27 similarly returns as an accompaniment to the flute solo of the *pas de deux*. The Bull's pounding dotted quarter motif returns in a lyrical guise in the 6/8 sections of the *pas de deux*. Balanchine's first idea, the heartbeat/hammer blow transformation, may have been the source for this continuous process of thematic metamorphosis, much as, in the scenario, Ariadne and Theseus represent a mythical transformation of Pasiphae and the Bull.

In the closing sections of the ballet, contrasting material is gathered up by superimposition. A fugue announces the entrance of the Greek prisoners into the labyrinth; this is followed by a flute solo on a pedal point as Ariadne unwinds her thread. Fugue and pedal point are Stravinskian; but Carter superimposes these two textures as Ariadne follows Theseus's movements as they are transmitted through the thread. When she rewinds the thread the flute solo is now placed over a ground bass, on top of which the fast, violent music of Theseus's struggle is later added. When the Greeks emerge from the labyrinth a new semitone motif appears – deceptively new, for it is the inversion of Pasiphae's music at the beginning of the score. The Greeks' rapid music is transmuted into a background for yet another flute solo at fig. 107. The Stravinsky-sounding strings here are in fact part of a Carterian textural and rhythmic modulation. The flute solo itself, though it sounds like Ariadne's earlier flute music, in fact states the horn theme of the Bull's Dance. To conclude the ballet, the ground bass returns, bringing all the materials of the work to a climactic focus, which then fades away to a return of the opening maestoso, the typical static frame of a Stravinskian collage, but equally the ending and starting point of a typically Carterian cycle.

Notes

1 RFG, p. 40.

9 Concertos

Given the dramatic character of Carter's music, it is not surprising that he has written five concertos; and yet the traditions of this form have also made it somewhat alien to him. The concerto, perhaps more than any other form, represents those glittering aspects of the classical music world with which Carter has had little involvement. Each of Carter's concertos is a subversive anti-concerto in its own way. Carter inverts the heroic stance of the traditional concerto; his soloists are anti-heros. If the fictitious Adrian Leverkuhn took back the Ninth Symphony, Carter, in his Piano Concerto stood the *Emperor* Concerto on its head. (The Double Concerto stands apart from the others, because, like an augmented version of Stravinsky's Concerto for Two Solo Pianos, it pits its soloists against each other, not against the orchestra.)

The concertos form a special case of Carter's divided ensemble; here the protagonists are separate but not equal; the soloist is usually cast in the role of the underdog. The alienation of the soloists from the orchestra is absolute. The soloist is 'a lone swimmer on the ocean' as Carter has said about the protagonist of his Violin Concerto. The soloists are cut off from orchestral sustenance or reinforcement; the opposed elements lack any technical means for finding a common ground. If we add to these technical points the more obvious observation that Carter's concertos lack the thematic structure and lyrical melodies that distinguish the concertos of the concert repertory, it is clear that Carter approaches the form with a quixotic disregard for its conventions; yet by throwing the concerto tradition away and beginning anew, Carter has rediscovered the tragic implications inherent in the form.

Double Concerto for Harpsichord and Piano with Two Chamber Orchestras

Score dated 'Waccabuc, N.Y. August 1961.' Dedicated: 'To Paul Fromm.' Commissioned by the Fromm Musical Foundation. Première 6 September 1961 in Grace Rainey Rogers Auditorium, New York, at a concert of new American music presented at the Eighth Congress of the International Society for Musicology. The soloists were Ralph Kirkpatrick, harpsichord; Charles Rosen, piano; conductor, Gustav Meier.[1]

The idea of a piece for piano and harpsichord originated with Ralph

Kirkpatrick. Carter may have been attracted to a double keyboard concerto because of his admiration for Stravinsky's Concerto for two Solo Pianos and Bartók's Sonata for Two Pianos and Percussion. He worked on the Double Concerto from 1956 to 1961; the Second Quartet was also written during this time. The long gestation points to a sharp change in Carter's idiom. The two works abandon the thematic techniques of the First Quartet and Variations in favor of the more abstract and disjunct idea of musical 'characters'; their harmonic idiom also sheds any connection to tonality. Both works develop a harmonic language based on a partitioning of intervals between protagonists; and both works are far more intricate in their rhythms than Carter's previous music.

Carter spent much of the fifties in Europe and came in contact with the music of the Darmstadt avant-garde. The Second Quartet and Double Concerto reflect many aspects of the new European music, some of which, however, were familiar to Carter from ultramodernist American sources. Rhythmic serialization, made famous by Boulez's *Structures*, was implied in Cowell's *New Musical Resources*. Stereophony, exploited in Stockhausen's *Gruppen*, had appeared in the music of Ives and Henry Brant. The greater role given percussion instruments had already been accomplished by Varèse. While Carter would make use of all these techniques in the Double Concerto, he made a distinction between his aesthetic project and that of the European avant-garde. The young Europeans were overthrowing the burden of the past, to the point of denying 'the possibility of highly purposeful communication'[2] – in other words they were reviving the attitudes of Dada. Carter claimed that it was meaningless for an American to overthrow the musical tradition, since its presence in the States was so weak. Experimentation in America, he wrote, served 'to broaden the communicative possibilities of music through the human perceptions.'

In making such a claim, Carter was invoking the spirit of Ives (and contradicting the ideas of Cage). In practice, Carter's view of the avant-garde musical situation led him to pursue a path that seemed odd at the time: he composed avant-garde masterpieces. The new works were daring in their harmonic, rhythmic and formal ideas, complex in their continuity and expression, challenging in their demands on players and listeners. But they were not anti-art; in an age which thought of musical events as accidents, Carter constructed his music with a fanatical attention to detail. One illustration of the difference in attitude comes in the area of rhythm. In his First Piano Piece, Karlheinz Stockhausen notates the music in a provocative jumble of polyrhythms. It was understood, however, that the mathematical relations implied by this notation were not to be strictly observed by the performer; the notation instead was a conceptual device, *Augenmusik*, to which the performer would respond intuitively. In the Double Concerto, Carter has many cross rhythms which appear as obscure as Stockhausen's, but they must be performed strictly. Where Stockhausen was undermining the traditional relation of performance to the written score, Carter was expanding older notions of notation in pursuit of a new rhythmic language.

At its appearance, the Double Concerto was also different in style from most advanced American music of the time. In the late fifties many American composers were following Stravinsky's move into serialism; the Double Concerto, though it earned Stravinsky's praise, was neither Stravinskian nor serial. Its textures were much denser than the typical American post-Webern essays of the time; only the music of Stefan Wolpe and Ralph Shapey had a similar intensity.

Despite its disjunct atonal and athematic idiom, the Double Concerto continues many of the ideas of the First Quartet and Variations. As in the First Quartet, speed is treated as a structural element and is often articulated in lines based on a single rhythmic value. As in the Variations, Carter frames the calm center of the work with ritardandos and acclerandos. The Double Concerto, moreover, reaffirms Carter's ultramodernist roots. The introduction is built on a coordination of harmonic intervals and speed suggested by Cowell; the sonority of the two soloists and their complex rhythmic interplay stem from Nancarrow, and the prominent percussion writing, which Carter had not previously explored, is a tribute to Varèse. Only Ives seems absent from this picture, until we realize that the basic concept of a work for two rhythmically and spatially independent ensembles is Ivesian. Carter, however, gave these elements a new unity, in which pitch, rhythm, space and tone color work together; he used this new language to articulate a complex narrative of creation and destruction, order and chaos.

The opposition of harpsichord and piano suggested many technical and stylistic contrasts. The harpsichord is an 'instrument of short duration' as Schoenberg might say. The piano can sustain sounds through resonance. The harpsichord changes colors and dynamics suddenly, through the manipulation of stops; the piano can make gradual changes. A postmodernist like Schnittke might have dramatized these differences through style, Scarlatti against Chopin. Carter, however, redefined the two instruments in terms of abstract 'character-patterns' arising from their harmonic and rhythmic materials. Once he established their characters he was particularly concerned to establish connections between the two solo instruments, rather than exaggerating their differences:

> Since the instruments and highly developed ways of playing them already possess a quality of special experience in and of themselves, frequent exploitation of unusual sound effects or of chance playing was avoided . . . it would have reduced the special quality to the ordinariness and obviousness of chaotic confusion.[3]

As he had done in the Sonata for Flute, Oboe, Cello and Harpsichord, Carter composed the Double Concerto for a 'modern' harpsichord. The Challis he specifies in the score has two manuals: Lower manual: 4, 8', 16' and coupler; Upper manual: 8'. All the stops have full and half positions, and both manuals have mutes. Throughout the work Carter calls for rapid changes of stops; these are most easily achieved on an instrument with pedal stops; a hand-stopped instrument can be used with an assistant. (Carter has said that his knowledge of changing stops stems from an experience of his Boulanger years: Carter and another student changed the stops while the Princess de Polignac, dressed in sneakers and an evening gown, played a Vivaldi organ concerto at her house on the Avenue Henri Martin.) In recent years, the preference of harpsichord players for historical rather than modern instruments has imperiled performances of the Double Concerto. Often it is hard to find an appropriate instrument. A high-tech solution to this problem would be the use of a synthesizer; all the changes in registration could be programmed in advance. Paul Jacobs had a harpsichord built by the Dowd company just for the Concerto. He left it to Yale University with the understanding that Yale would make it available for performances of the work. The piano part should also be played on a modern instrument, but in the interest of balance Carter carefully restricted the use of the full resources of the piano to particularly dramatic moments. In much of the concerto the two soloists alternate phrases, and play in contrasting ranges; the only time the two instruments are superimposed at length is in the climactic double cadenza at the end of the Adagio.[4]

Because the modern piano is inherently louder than the harpsichord,

Carter decided early on to augment each keyboard instrument with its own orchestra:

> To join the piano and harpsichord into one world of music that could have many inner contrasts, I chose two small orchestras, each with two percussion players, and since this was to be an antiphonal piece, the two orchestras contained instruments that would underline the qualities of the soloists they were associated with and, in the case of the harpsichord, add dynamic volume to supplement its lack of dynamic range.[5]

In order to unify these two orchestras, Carter surrounded them with four percussionists. The percussion also served to define one end of the work's color spectrum from non-pitched to pitched instruments. This diapason of sonority locates the keyboard instruments, which combine aspects of percussion and pitch, at the center of its sound world acoustically and spatially. The percussion itself articulates a highly differentiated sound-continuum with the drums, membranophones, forming a 'continuous scale of clearly distinguishable pitch levels, as evenly spaced as possible, starting from the highest available bongo to the lowest available bass drum,' and with metallophones and lignophones similarly arranged from soprano triangle down to low cowbell, from soprano cymbal to contrabass tamtam, and from slap-stick to temple blocks. Carter distributed four members of the cymbal family among all four percussionists to connect them in space, as at bar 5 where a cymbal roll moves around the orchestra counter-clockwise, prefiguring later interactions between sound and space.

Carter scored the two orchestras to amplify each of the soloists. He assigned three of the four brass instruments to the harpsichord's ensemble, so that it could compete in volume with the piano's. The harpsichord's orchestra – flute, horn, trumpet, trombone, viola and double bass – has a 'baroque' sonority that is heightened by a 'dry' percussion section made up predominantly of metallophones (anvil, cowbells, gongs, tamtams) and lignophones (temple blocks, wood blocks and slap-sticks). The piano's orchestra – oboe, clarinet, bassoon, horn, violin and cello – is more expressive and 'classical,' with its 'wet' percussion dominated by membranophones (bongos, snare drums, bass drums) capable of creating swelling dynamic shapes. The instrumentation allowed Carter to treat dynamics as a structural element; in a note Carter has added to his score he requests that 'the dynamic range in performance should be very great':

as loud as possible: beginning of bar 5 middle of 310; end of 616; beginning of 619 (climax of piece); for percussion, especially, middle of 654

as soft as possible: when accompanying the harpsichord particularly in its softer registrations as in 214–6. Orchestra (not piano) from 465 to beginning of 475.

The structural function given to the spectrum of pitch and volume is complemented by a structural activation of space (Chart 37). The two groups of pitched instruments sit as far apart as possible, surrounded by the four evenly spaced percussionists to the rear of the stage and the soloists to the front. This plan is both antiphonal and circular; the music moves from left to right and back, and also clockwise and counter-clockwise in changing patterns.

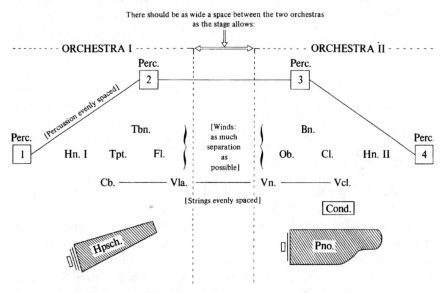

Chart 37 Double Concerto: approximate seating plan

As Carter began working out his overall plan, two literary models suggested themselves: Lucretius's *De Rerum Natura*, and Pope's *Dunciad*. As in Lucretius's poem, the Double Concerto would bring a cosmos into existence by the seemingly random collision of falling atoms:

All things keep on, in everlasting motion,
Out of the infinite come the particles
Speeding above, below, in endless dance . . .

> Surely the atoms never began by forming
> A conscious pact, a treaty with each other,
> Where they should stay apart, where come together
> More likely, being so many, in many ways
> Harassed and driven through the universe
> From an infinity of time, by trying
> All kinds of motion, every combination,
> They came at last into such disposition
> As now established the sum of things.
>   (trans. Rolfe Humphries)

Lucretius expresses the relation of chaos and order in a modern way. As Carter once pointed out to me, there is something particularly hopeless about a genesis where accident gives way to rigidity devoid of a transcendental framework. Carter decided that the end of the Concerto would undo this universe in the manner of Lucretius's 'Destruction of Athens' or the triumph of Chaos at the end of the *Dunciad*:

> Nor public flame, nor private, dares to shine;
> Nor human spark is left, nor glimpse divine!
> Lo! thy dread empire, Chaos! is restored;
> Light dies before thy uncreating word:
> Thy hand, great Anarch! let the curtain fall;
> And universal darkness buries all.

The texts of Lucretius and Pope helped Carter to define the work's dramatic form. He has often looked to non-musical works for strategies of design that differ from traditional musical procedures. The conclusion of the *Dunciad*, 'uncreating' itself in ironic hyperbole, suggested a new kind of musical retrograde. Lucretius and Pope, however, also seem relevant to the expressive coloring of the Double Concerto, its brittle sonority, rapid-fire, explosive continuity, and its avoidance of the lyricism so prevalent in Carter's other works. The Concerto evokes a mood of desperate comedy, as rationality totters on the brink of the irrational. The style of the work might be described as revisionist neo-Classicism: with its paired eighteenth-century protagonists surrounded by a shell of noise, the Concerto evokes the dark side of eighteenth-century rationalism; not the *Encyclopedia* and Dr Johnson's *Dictionary*, but *The Battle of the Books*, *Tristram Shandy*, *Le Neveu de Rameau*, Dr Johnson's madness. The Double Concerto raises comic irony to a prophetic vision. Its polyrhythmic collisions, spiraling spatial trajectory, and geometric fluctuations through the spectrum of sound are a cosmic contraption.

The organizational techniques of the Double Concerto and the Second Quartet are closely related. All eleven intervals are partitioned between the two orchestras, and their harmonic combinations are largely defined by the two all-interval four-note chords – (0, 4, 6, 7) for the harpsichord and (0, 1, 4, 6) for the piano. These chords are then co-ordinated in ways suggested in Chart 38 'in order to provide a somewhat ordered sub-structure (like the triadic harmony of the common practice period, but more freely used because it is not adhered to so strictly) as a source of many degrees of interrelation on several different levels at once.'[6] Because the intervals are divided into two groups rather than four as in the Second

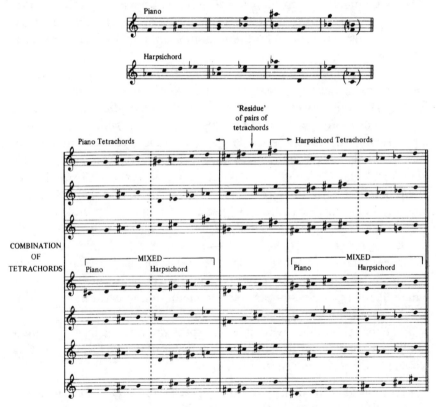

Chart 38 Two all-interval tetrachords, with characteristic intervals used in the Double Concerto

Quartet, the intervallic contrast of the two groups is less immediately apparent; the listener will be aware of a contrast in harmonic colors. The harpsichord's intervals are 'dark'; the piano's 'bright.'

Harpsichord	Piano
Minor second (ninth)	Major second (ninth)
Minor third	Major third
Perfect fourth	Perfect fifth
Tritone	
Minor sixth	Major sixth
Minor seventh	Major seventh

In addition to the recurrent harmonic sonority of the two all-interval four-note chords, a sixteen-note chord shown in the interval chart appears frequently as an all-interval 'tonic' – see bars 39, 147–9, 158, 326–8 (piano) and 615, for literal restatements of this chord; many close mutations, usually related by the prominent major third on top, occur elsewhere.

As in the Second Quartet, the stratification of intervals mirrors the rhythmic organization. Where the Quartet associated intervals with contrasting rhythmic styles, here each interval (except the minor sixth) is given one or more speeds. These speeds divide up the ratio of 2:1 according to two mathematical series. Five speeds are in a ratio of whole numbers – 10:9:8: 7:6:5 – and five are in a ratio of reciprocals 1/10:1/9:1/8: 1/7:1/6:1/5 (see Chart 39). The association of intervals and speeds thus gives each orchestra a rich repertoire of cross-rhythms and tempo modulations. Furthermore each soloist 'specializes' in a polyrhythmic combination: 4:7 for the harpsichord and 3:5 in the piano. These are most clearly heard respectively in the Presto and Allegro scherzando, while the cadenzas for both instruments display the relationships between their contrasting intervallic speeds, most notably in the piano at bars 567–70 where five polyphonic strands, each made of one interval moving at its regular speed, are woven together (Ex. 59).

The chosen ensemble, with its sound-spectrum ranging from seemingly undifferentiated 'noise' to articulated pitch, called forth a formal plan that would project this sonic continuum in time:

> I ... arrived at the idea of unhitched percussion groups, from which everything the two soloists did could be rhythmically derived. According to this notion, a 'primordial rhythm' expressed by the

RATIO	BETWEEN				SPEEDS		METRONOMIC SPEEDS	PIANO	HARPSICHORD
2					1/5	10	35 ⟶		
	81					9	31½ ⟶		
		25			1/6		29 $\frac{1}{6}$ ⟶		
			32			8	28 ⟶		
				50	1/7		25 ⟶		
				49		7	24½ ⟶		
			25		1/8		21 $\frac{7}{8}$ ⟶		
		18				6	21 ⟶		
	50				1/9		19 $\frac{7}{9}$ ⟶		
1					1/10	5	17½ ⟶		

Chart 39 Double Concerto: Interval scheme of Introduction

Double Concerto
© 1964 Associated Music Publishers, Inc. Used by permission

Ex. 59 Polyphony of interval speeds

> unpitched percussion would progressively take on pitches through
> the two resonating solo instruments, whose statements would then
> be elaborated and amplified by two groups of sustaining pitched
> instruments. Finally at the beginning of a 'coda', there would be a
> gong crash, whose vibrating resonances would be 'orchestrated' as it
> died away, which would then be progressively re-absorbed by the
> unpitched percussion.[7]

From the first, sound and structure were to be one; the work would 'get
down to the physical origins of musical sound and . . . take off from there.'

> The form is that of confrontations of diversified action-patterns and
> a presentation of their mutual interreactions, conflicts, and resolu-
> tions, their growth and decay over various stretches of time.[8]

Carter's comments show that he was concerned to build the score on new
formal principals. In the Second Quartet he was inspired by modern
drama; here he looked towards the model of dance. The Concerto grows
from an imaginative 'choreography' of sound in time and space. Carter
has himself pointed out this aspect of the Concerto in noting how the
relation of soloists and ensembles evolves:

> In the central Adagio, the 'choreography' changes; the entire
> wind section, in center stage (although still divided into groups)
> plays slow music, while in the background the two soloists,

strings, and four percussionists surround the winds with accelerating and decelerating patterns that alternately move clockwise and counter-clockwise.[9]

In the Presto, moreover, the 'choreography' changes yet again, as all the sustaining instruments join the harpsichord, leaving the piano in isolation. The music throughout is as carefully composed in space as it is in time; Carter sketched many of the great effects of temporal and spatial choreography visually, without pitches: his notebooks for the Concerto are filled with Cartesian fantasies of colliding lines, curves and waves.

As in the Variations and the Second Quartet, the form of the Double Concerto is at once sectionalized and continuous. It falls into seven sections: Introduction, Cadenza for Harpsichord, Allegro scherzando, Adagio, Presto, two Cadenzas for Piano, Coda – the Adagio serves as keystone. This plan contains the ghost of a traditional three movement fast–slow–fast concerto form. The length and weight of the Introduction and Coda, however, make them far more important to the form than a mere frame. The asymmetrical placing of the cadenzas, one for the harpsichord near the end of the Introduction, and two for the piano during the Presto, counteract the suggestions of a Bartókian arch design. Each movement is based on a distinctive integrative or disintegrative process. The Introduction and Coda are huge polyrhythmic patterns, bringing the atomic intervals of the work into alignment, and back into chaos. The Allegro scherzando is dominated by the piano and its ensemble, with interruptions by the harpsichord group. The Adagio contrasts a sustained chorale in the winds with unstable spirals for the soloists, strings and percussion, culminating in a brilliant duet for piano and harpsichord in which the piano accelerates to its fastest speed and the harpsichord ritards to its slowest. The Presto, featuring the harpsichord and so balancing the Allegro scherzando, is interrupted by the piano, playing maestoso. Instead of the increasing interaction of the two soloists in the Allegro, here they move farther apart, the disintegration of texture being compounded by the percussion which re-enter after the second piano cadenza, and drown the ensemble in a cadenza of their own. The clarity of the Concerto's large scale form is masked or contradicted by its fragmented and constantly varied surface. The music starts and stops unpredictably. Particularly remarkable in this respect are several surprising moments of silence, for at no two places does the cessation of sound have the same grammatical effect. The grand pause before the gong crash at bar 619, where most other composers would have written a grand tutti crescendo, is very typical of the work's surprising dramatic 'logic.'

INTRODUCTION

Carter sets the Double Concerto in motion in a way reminiscent of Berg's *Three Orchestral Pieces*; pitches gradually emerge from percussion. Carter gives the percussion simultaneous accelerations and ritards which converge as a climax at bar 5. As this intersection subsides, two pulses emerge in a ratio of 49:50 (fifteen sextuplet semiquavers against twenty-one quintuplet semiquavers, at metronome speeds of 24.5 and 25 respectively). These nearly indistinguishable pulses, introduced by rolled cymbal and snare drums, begin to be orchestrated at bar 11, as the 24.5 pulse is transformed into a tremolando minor second in the harpsichord's orchestra, and the 25 pulse is heard in a tremolando major second in the piano's orchestra; the intervals sound like overtones of the percussion. Gradually the other intervals are placed in orbit, all emanating from unpitched percussion at widening pulse speed ratios:

Bar			
13–14	Perfect fourth (28)	Major seventh (217/8)	32:25
16–17	Tritone (291/6)	Major sixth (21)	25:18
20–23	Minor third (19 4/9)	Perfect fifth (31.5)	81:50
35–36	Minor seventh (17.5)	Major third (35)	2:1

The soloists enter with tremolandos, gradually building materials and gestures out of the intervallic atoms, but also forming larger character-patterns, forecasting later events. The piano anticipates its Allegro scherzando at bars 23, 29, 35, and 89; the harpsichord pre-figures its Presto at 33 and 50. Meanwhile the twin intervallic systems begin to approach two points of simultaneous accent. The two collisions are prepared by a crescendo, building from bar 41 to 46, and set off by synchronous strokes on tamtam and bass drum (each part of different pulse systems). The two ratio systems approach their rhythmic unisons in different ways. One system of pulses, related by ratios of whole numbers, approaches a unison attack on the downbeat of bar 45. The composite rhythm formed by these pulses produces a pattern of constant acceleration, heard clearly in the piano. The other system of pulses forms a pattern of accelerating acceleration, that is, the rate of acceleration is not constant but increases. These pulses collide at the downbeat of bar 46, and then continue to form a pattern of deceleration played by the harpsichord in bars 47 and 48 (Chart 40). The quiet, widely spaced notes in the piano from 46 on, heard against a fading burst of fast music in the harpsichord, are the continuation of its speed pattern, moving out of phase in regular pulses.

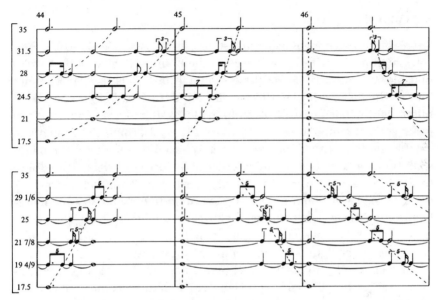

Chart 40 Double Concerto: rhythmic scheme

The second half of the Introduction continues the fading motion from the climax at bar 46, with each orchestra trying to launch its own fast material. The music seems to come to a complete stop at bar 84, as a viola trill fades into a rolled cymbal. After a brief silence, the piano attempts to begin its Allegro movement, only to be overtaken by rhythmic accents in both orchestras, stressing a 4:3 speed ratio. Out of this new clash the harpsichord emerges with its cadenza.

CADENZA FOR HARPSICHORD

Many contrasting characters and the full range of harpsichord stops and mutes appear in fleeting, aphoristic form. This improvisatory-sounding sequence is built on the harpsichord's intervals: minor second at MM 25.5 (bars 105–6), perfect fourth at MM 28 (bars 108–12), minor seventh at MM 17.5 (bars 113–5), tritone at MM 291/6 (bars 120–7), and minor third at 19 4/9 (bars 133–6). The cadenza ends with a fanfare-like burst in the harpsichord's orchestra, which is swallowed up and dissolved rhythmically by the piano's orchestra, leaving the primal chord suspended in slow, quiet motion (bars 147–50). The pitched material once more fades into percussion, and then to a ten-second silence.

ALLEGRO SCHERZANDO

Snare drums and bongos usher in fast, playful music in the piano's orchestra. Rhythmically, this music develops the many possibilities of the relationships of 3:5 heard at the outset in the drums. This ratio appears not only as the polyrhythm of triplets against quintuplets, but also in a large number of related cross-accentual patterns (bars 223 and 224, for instance) and tempo modulations (bars 162–3). Harmonically, the music emphasizes the intervals of major third, perfect fifth, minor second, major sixth (in approximate descending order of importance). The piano draws three of its intervals from the 'primal' chord in bar 158, then rearranges them in the spirit of fantastical improvisation that dominates the movement. Almost everywhere in the Allegro scherzando the piano plays in the upper half of its range and staccato, almost as an overtone of the snare drum and bongo figures which dominate the percussion.

The piano's playful music is cross-cut with slower music in the harpsichord's ensemble. The form of this movement may be compared with the second movement of the Sonata for Flute, Oboe, Cello and Harpsichord. Two independent strands are intertwined, each with its own intervals, chords, speeds and colors. The rhythm of the montage is unpredictable, ranging from the rapid jump cuts at bars 173, 178 and 258 to extensive, sustained statements by each side. In general, the harpsichord, playing mostly in its lower register, attempts to slow down the piano's motion, suggesting a broader temporal universe than the contracted time-world of the piano. The piano 'retaliates' by unleashing its percussion, and itself turning into a percussion instrument, as with the accented clusters, bars 234–8, that are followed by a fast, blurred pedal effect, like a snare-drum roll.

There is frequent overlap between the two musical strands, beginning with the *Klangfarben* effect in bars 172–3, where a chord ricochets across the orchestra; it is transformed en route from one all-interval chord to the other, sustaining common notes through six rapid changes in color. From bars 234 to 251, large polyrhythmic patterns are heard between the two ensembles, all based on the ratio 7:5 that is also heard in fast motion between the soloists (bars 243–5). In the course of the movement overlapping becomes the rule, as if the instruments no longer had the patience to wait for their entrances. After a sustained passage in the low harpsichord and flute, the piano unleashes its most violent explosion, followed by a climactic outbreak by all the percussion (bar 310). The harpsichord, however, in a Chaplinesque gesture, continues on its way and finally begins to impose a general ritard. This ushers in the Adagio as the harpsichord reaches its highest note – the four-foot F that ushers in the crotales, the only pitched percussion instrument in the orchestra.

ADAGIO

Although the tempo, Adagio, is reached at bar 342, the new double configuration that defines this movement begins with the harpsichord ritardando at bar 321, which is countered by an accelerando beginning in the piano at 326. The Adagio combines a slow chorale-like music in the winds with slowing and speeding figures which spin around the winds in space, through the percussion, strings and solo instruments. The winds (whose notes are further sustained by the strings) sound the basic intervals of the work in tranquil, floating motion – the harmony of the spheres. The unstable spinning motion of the soloists and percussion imposes an Einsteinian astronomy on the platonic model of the wind-chorale. Carter reinterprets his own rhythmic invention from the Variations, superimposing the elements of slowing, calm and acceleration that were distinct in the earlier work, in order to produce a more complex, dynamic shape: Ritard, Acceleration, Adagio, Ritard, Acceleration, Adagio, Acceleration. The three kinds of motion are also choreographed in a spatial *Klangfarbenmelodie*. At bar 395 a constantly accelerating pulse moves counterclockwise around the orchestra, with just three or four notes played by each instrument. A clockwise motion is similarly heard in the percussion during the ritarding passages.

The slow wind music evolves gradually from isolated intervals to a climactic superimposition of motifs at 404–6, which is sustained by the barely-audible strings moving at the slowest pulse-speed of the work, MM 9.3 in the viola and bass against MM 7.5 in violin and cello. As the music begins to build again, a new acceleration is launched on the bass drums. As pulses spin around the orchestra, a burst of wooden percussion sparks a duet for the two soloists, accompanied by the last phrases of the chorale in the winds. The rhythmic plan of this duet surpasses everything that has come before in complexity. The harpsichord reaches a stable tempo at bar 433, while the piano continues to accelerate, playing nine increasingly fast beats against eight steady beats in the harpsichord. From bars 436 to 453 both instruments play continuous fast figuration at steady speeds of MM 560 for the harpsichord and MM 630 for the piano – in a ratio of 8:9. Through this crossfire, bassoon and clarinet chant a slow line built on the piano's four-note chord, answered by the piccolo with the harpsichord's harmonic motif. At bar 453 the harpsichord and percussion begin to slow down, while the piano accelerates, uncoordinated with the other instruments. (Charles Rosen has said that the only thing for the pianist to do is not to look at the conductor and just hope that everyone comes out together.) By bar 465 the harpsichord has slowed to silence, and the piano has sped past the vanishing point. The mysterious space evoked by the far-flung ringing of crotales, triangles and tamtam recalls the eerie calm of the First Quartet. As in the Quartet, human expression tries to fill the empty space: the piano enters with a loud, questioning gesture. The question echoes in the metallic stillness and is repeated, remaining unanswered as the harpsichord begins its Presto.

PRESTO

The Presto features the harpsichord, accompanied by all the winds and strings. The sprightly, angular material is based on the intervals of minor ninth, minor third, perfect fourth, minor sixth and minor seventh, which are heard from time to time in clarion bursts (555). The baroque-jazzy dotted rhythms derive from the seven against four polyrhythms, as can be seen at bars 509 to 512. The piano interrupts the Presto with maestoso music, continuing the questioning mood heard at the end of the duet. For the first time in the piece, it plays predominantly in its bass register (while the harpsichord, winds and strings are in the treble) and stresses its most resonant intervals, major seventh and perfect fifth. The contrast of the two soloists is different in mood from that of the Allegro scherzando. There, the piano and harpsichord seemed to move closer together; the light, staccato writing for the piano was an accommodation to the harpsichord, allowing it to compete as an equal. In the Presto the instruments stress their more natural traits – the harpsichord's speed against the piano's weight. There is no interaction between the parties; the oppositions grow ever stronger. The harpsichord answers the piano's brooding prophecies with brilliant cascades of septuplets.

CADENZAS FOR PIANO

Twice the piano expands its interjections into cadenzas. The first (bars 525–39) recalls the mood of the Allegro scherzando, and emphasizes the intervals of major ninth and major third. The second cadenza, introduced by an exquisite intertwining of the two soloists, begins with the scherzando mood, grows more agitated, and reaches a climactic, oracular statement – five intervals moving at the five speeds associated with them in the Introduction. The prophecy gives way to a brilliant display of power, as the piano rapidly resonates its entire musical space (see bar 577), setting off bursts in the percussion.

PRESTO (CONTINUED)

The percussion immerses the music in the destructive element of noise. Piano, harpsichord, winds and strings unite against the drums in futile assertive gestures fractured by percussive bursts. The wind chorale from the Adagio is chopped up and compressed (bars 599–601), finally emerging as the Last Trump at 615 – harmonically a restatement of the primal chord. From bar 603 to 611 the percussion takes over the music in a mounting wave of cross-accents. After final convulsions by strings, soloists and winds, the drums reassert their power – followed by a two-bar silence – a musical blackout.

CODA

The coda begins with an enormous gong crash, orchestrated in a chord unlike any heard earlier in the work – a tower of tritones. The gong crash projected in time becomes the form of the coda:

> like a large gong, [it] dies away over many measures in wave-like patterns, with many diverse tone colors fading and returning – each time slightly different, and each time with less energy – until the work subsides to a quiet close.[10]

The texture of the Coda suggests a huge vibration with many smaller partials, all fading away in complex, periodic motion. As in the Introduction, Carter planned his poetic effect geometrically. There are four simultaneous wave patterns (Chart 41). The main accents come every five bars in the harpsichord's orchestra (MM 5.6) and every seven bars in the piano's (MM 4) with secondary accents every 35 dotted eighth in the

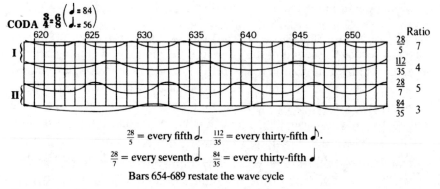

Chart 41 Double Concerto: wave patterns in Coda

harpsichord's orchestra, and every 35 eighths in the piano's. Since the Coda is seventy bars long, the overall 5:7 cycle is heard twice. Comparison bar-by-bar from 654 to the end with 619 to 653 reveals how the second half of the coda is a near-literal echo of the first half. The music no longer expands, it just resonates. Expression fades into physics. By bar 679 all that remains are the rolled cymbals and snare drum heard at the opening of the work. Reversing the sequence in the Introduction, these rolls crescendo into the last phrases of each soloist, then vanish. The piano touches its highest note; the harpsichord sounds a cluster below the range of the piano. A final pitched note on the flute is cut off almost inaudibly by the claves, and the work ends.

Here is what Stravinsky wrote about the Double Concerto:

> I like the mood of Carter's Concerto, first of all. It is full of new-found good spirits, as his quartets were not. But the success of the piece is owing to the listener's eventual involvement and satisfaction in its form. That the Double Concerto should suggest Berg's towering example in general ways is not surprising, but I hear direct references to the Berg in it, too. (Carter is certainly not a naïve composer, but I think these Berg bits are unknowing.) The passage from 432 (the piano entrance here is one of the finest things in the piece) to 460, and especially the flute at 436 and the bassoon at 441, remind me of the Berg, and the architectural plot of the solo instruments – their roles as alternate soloists, duo soloists, parts of ensemble groups – also is reminiscent of the Berg. The Concerto presents many interesting performance problems, not so much in instru-

mental technique – not in the wind and string parts anyway, though the percussion is a different matter – as in rhythm. The score introduces no metrical difficulties, and as the proportionalisms of tempos are easy to hear if the orchestras are reversed from the composer's seating plan so that the conductor stands next to the harpsichord, it is easy to conduct. Incidentally, the most effective example of an interlocking of tempos by a held-over beat pattern is precisely where it is most apparent (loudest): the percussion at measures 143–4. I do not think the chief rhythmic difficulty is in the notation – though I can imagine orchestra players complaining about that, and perhaps fidelity to the writing of the rhythmic series does make the instrumental parts momentarily more difficult to read: I mean, for example, four dotted sixteenths to the dotted quarter rather than 'four for three' without the dots, as I would now do it. The rhythmic problem of the Concerto is the old one common to most contemporary music. The player manages the notes, but cannot count the rests or feel irregular pulsations – or regular ones, but without simple patterns – when he is not playing.

I like not only the shape but also the sense of proportion in the Concerto, and I like the harpsichord and piano writing very much, too. And the intended high point, the coda, is the real climax of the piece. (This section is unclear, though, in the recording, where the rhythm is a blur and the dynamic plan is without profile. The question of dynamics in recording practice must be criticized more strongly than anyone has criticized it so far. The harpsichord is weak in volume by nature, or so the engineer assumes; but this weakness is overcompensated by about ninety percent in the recording.) I cannot comment upon or add to the composer's own analysis, but analysis as little explains a masterpiece or calls it into being as an ontological proof explains or causes the existence of God. There, the word is out. A masterpiece, by an American composer.[11]

Piano Concerto

The Concerto was commissioned by Jacob Lateiner through the Ford Foundations and is dedicated 'To Igor Stravinsky on his 85th birthday with great admiration and friendship.' Carter began work on it in 1963 while he was composer in residence at the American Academy in Rome and continued in Berlin where he was invited by the Ford Foundation and the Berliner Senat to spend the year of 1964. The terms of his residency in Berlin were so generous that Carter invited several of his students including Joel Chadabe, Alvin Curran and Frederic Rzewski to join him. Cold War tensions following the construction of the Berlin Wall left their mark on the Concerto. Carter remembers the constant sound of machine-gun fire from a US Army target range near his studio – a sound that echoes through the second movement. The isolation of Berlin and its hostile surrounding may have suggested the dramatic confrontation of piano and orchestra in the Concerto, although the Concerto may reflect other events in the recent German past as well. It was completed in Waccabuc in 1965 and premièred by Jacob Lateiner and the Boston Symphony Orchestra conducted by Erich Leinsdorf on 6 January 1967.

Reviewing the first performance, Michael Steinberg wrote that 'Carter's Concerto established the most dramatic confrontation of solo and orchestra since Beethoven.' Carter set out to discover a new dramatic meaning for the concerto form. He chose to portray a conflict 'between an individual of many changing moods and thoughts and an orchestra treated more or less monolithically – massed effects pitted against protean figures and expressions.' The soloist is not a hero but an anti-hero in an alien world. (Ursula Oppens, who has recorded the work twice, compares the piano soloist to an operatic heroine.) The Concerto is Carter's most passionate and tragic composition.

As in the Double Concerto, Carter amplifies the soloist with its own orchestra. The piano is surrounded by seven instruments: flute, English horn, bass clarinet, violin, viola, cello, bass. Where possible, this concertino should be spatially separated from the rest of the orchestra – Carter suggests three arrangements in the score. The concertino instruments extend the sounds of the piano but they also have important and difficult solos. This 'partitioning' of difficulty serves a dramatic end. The concertino plays more difficult music than the rest of the orchestra, and its music is also more sensitive, lyrical and imaginative. The orchestra, by contrast, plays deliberately aggressive, massive music. Carter once described American orchestras as 'brontosaurs staggering with inertia and ossification.' In the Piano Concerto the orchestra is a musical brontosaurus; unwittingly it portrays itself. The work can also be seen as a synthesis of the lyrical drama of the Second Quartet and the geometric choreography of the Double Concerto, with the concertino's lyricism and the orchestra's geometry placed on a collision course.

The two instrumental groups specialize in different styles of performance. The piano and its consort are expressive. Carter plays down the mechanical aspect of the piano that was so prominent in the Double Concerto. The solo part is almost always cantabile (even in the scherzando episodes of the first movement). It plays long, expressive lines in changing densities and harmonic colours. The piano writing explores voicings and intervallic distances: note, for instance, the beautiful contraction from widespread minor ninths to a cluster of minor seconds at bars 266–70, or the inventive figuration at 582–3, which, as Charles Rosen told me, reinterprets Chopin's first étude with ninths and sevenths substituting for octaves. The solo instruments serve primarily to amplify the spatial explorations of the piano; the rich timbres of the solo winds, particularly the English horn and bass clarinet, enhance the mood of lyrical meditation. These instruments do not appear in the orchestra and so give the concertino its distinctive coloring. Similarly the solo flute is often set against the metallic glare of piccolos in the orchestra to heighten the concertino's expressive timbre.

The sonority of the concertino is an idealization of chamber music: sensitive, singing, and with much interplay between instruments. By contrast, the orchestra is an insistent, brutal machine. Individual instrumental colors are repressed in favor of dark heterophonic mixtures; the swirling cluster at bar 78 is a typical early manifestation of the orchestral mass, which becomes increasingly menacing as the first movement progresses – note the lava-flow of strings at bar 200, the divided violins at 245, and the climactic dust-storm at 312 with its seventy-note string cluster punctured by massed trills in the winds. (These effects presage the poisonous gas clouds of the second movement.) The dissolution of this texture at bar 321 into wisps of sound is perhaps an even more remarkable invention than the storm itself. These dense textures evolve both internally and in relation to the concertino. In the early sixties Carter was impressed by the 'textural' music of Xenakis, Penderecki, Ligeti and others, at least to the extent of writing that 'the isolation of single notes by pitch, dynamics and timbre . . . is a device that no longer seems to stimulate the writing of interesting music, while the thick, packed, dissonant textures and vivid juxtaposition of whole clusters or constellations of notes seems to lead, these days, to livelier results.'[12] But Carter has said that the inspiration for the string writing in the Concerto was Ives's *Fourth of July*. While composing the second movement, Carter left New York to go to Warsaw for a performance of the Double Concerto. His plane was grounded in London, however, and when he rang up some friends there he found out that at that very moment Frederik Prausnitz was rehearsing his Variations and the *Fourth of July*. Carter arrived just in time to hear the rehearsal of the dense string passages in the Ives, which convinced him that he was on the right track in the Piano Concerto.

The opposed instrumental groups are differentiated in their harmonic make-up. The basic harmonic unit is no longer the interval, as in Carter's earlier music, but the twelve three-note chords. Carter divides these triads between orchestra and concertino, identifying each three-note chord with a dominant interval and limiting the spacing and inversions of each chord in the interest of clear identification (Chart 42). The stratification of

Chart 42 Piano Concerto: harmonic scheme

intervals is similar to that of the Double Concerto, but here the piano is given the darker, more expressive intervals, and both groups share the tritone (found in chords VII and VIII). The tritone functions throughout as a common element, linking the two instrumental groups; its pointed, plangent sound colors the entire work. The tritone's special function appears clearly at bar 18, where orchestra and concertino reiterate the same two pitches, F and B – this important convergence also forecasts, far in advance, the dramatically repeated Fs at bars 605–14. Four triads from each group are combined into two 'key' twelve-note chords that recur frequently and almost literally throughout the first movement and at the beginning of the second. These two chords define the overall harmonic tone color of orchestra and concertino (as clearly contrasted at bars 344–8) and establish harmonic 'landmarks' for the free motion of the work.

Each triad is associated with one to three metronome speeds, which are adhered to strictly in the first movement. These speeds fill in a spectrum between 126 and 42 (3:1) in whole number and reciprocal ratios similar to those used in the Double Concerto (Chart 43). Twenty basic speeds in all

	Tempi – MM						
Chord	Piano	Orchestra	Ratios				
VII	126		21	1/7	18	1/6
II		110.25		1/8		
X	108		18			1/7
II		105			15	
IV	98			1/9	14	
VIII		94.5				1/8
IX	90		15			
VIII		88.2		1/10		
I	84		14		12	1/9
XI		73.5		1/12		
V	72		12			
IX		63		1/14	9	1/12
III		60	10			
XII	58.8			1/15		
VI		56			8	
VI		54	9			1/14
X	50.4					1/15
I	49			1/18	7	
VII	48		8			
VII	42		7	1/21	6	1/18

Chart 43 Piano Concerto: chord-tempi ratios

are defined by this system. Although the Concerto can be played under the given tempo – Charles Rosen reduced the speeds to 5/6 of the given metronome markings – it is imperative that all tempo modulations should be strictly observed so that chordal speeds are maintained, otherwise the distinctive character of each chord will not be heard in the constantly changing polyphonic collage. From bars 62 to 67, for instance, it is essential that chord X should continue straight across the tempo change at a constant pulse of MM 108 – 6/7 of the original tempo of MM 126 and 6/5 of the new tempo of 90. This uninterrupted pulse serves to link a scherzando episode, combining speeds of 108 and 50.4, with a lighter and more delicate passage based on chord V which moves at a speed of MM 72 in bars 68–74.

Throughout the first movement, every triad is associated with a speed and a mode of presentation. Each chord generates a characteristic kind of music, and these characters are combined contrapuntally in changing patterns between and within the concertino and orchestra. At bar 35, for example, the piano elaborates chord VII – its most important chord while the orchestra combines the almost Mahlerian, singing line generated by chord VIII, with the typical square rhythmic shapes of chord IX. By contrast, from bar 68 to 75 the piano contrapuntally combines the delicate character of chord V with the staccato articulation of chord X, while the orchestra sounds the cluster harmonies associated with chord III. The piano's treatment of each chord tends to be imaginative and fanciful. The orchestra's usage is more stereotyped; it tends to restate or intensify previously heard events. The solo instruments of the concertino occasionally act as messengers (as at bars 110–22 and 159–65) attempting to establish points of contact as the large behaviour patterns of piano and orchestra move further and further apart. This underlying divergent tendency, which achieves a climactic formulation at bars 312–23, controls the montage of short episodes in a subliminal way. The two groups seem to respond to each other, or to ignore each other, purely in passing – the larger dramatic pattern of interaction emerges only slowly. The listener's perception of the drama may be said to mirror the piano soloist's evolving self-understanding.

At the time of its première, Carter described the narrative form of the Concerto with a biographical analogy:

> The piano is born, then the orchestra teaches it what to say. The piano learns. Then it learns the orchestra is wrong. They fight and the piano wins – not triumphantly, but with a few, weak, sad notes – sort of Charlie Chaplin humorous.[13]

Taking up Carter's suggestion, the Piano Concerto may be compared with Berg's explicitly programmatic Violin Concerto. Like that work, it is in two parts: the first might be termed childhood, adolescence or education; the second, maturity or self-discovery. Berg's Concerto is based on the specific story of Manon Gropius – her birth, dancing, illness and death. Carter's Concerto seems non-representational; not a biography, perhaps, but a biographical meditation. The drama of the work increases as the piano slowly learns that 'the orchestra is wrong': the first movement can be thought of as the piano's education or 'Bildung' – in the second movement the piano asserts its identity in an increasingly alien world. In Carter's concerto, as in Berg's the scherzando character of the first half gives way to a tragic struggle in the second, with an expanded expressive freedom allotted to the soloist:

> I wanted the second movement to become a very free treatment of materials that in the first movement had been restricted to a more limited pattern of behavior, and to open a broader, more expressive character ... [14]

The two movements are continuous, despite a twenty-second pause, which functions like the breaks in the First Quartet. They differ in their treatment of what Charles Rosen has seen as the major dramatic device of the concerto form:

> The most important fact about concerto form is that the audience waits for the soloist to enter, and when he stops playing they wait for him to begin again.[15]

The first movement is a drama of entrances. The two instrumental groups are cross-cut, with varying degrees of overlap. Entrances are sometimes gradual, sometimes abrupt, continuing ideas from the other group, or interrupting the other's train of thought with sharply contrasting material. At many points the piano will establish a connection with the orchestra through a common note: at bars 79 and 80, the G sharp topping triad III in the clarinet is taken up in triad X by the piano. In the early parts of the first movement the piano's exits are often balletic leaps into the wings, ushering in the orchestra with a virtuoso flourish – bars 22, 36, 74. Later, the dialogue becomes less polite. Contrasting moods interrupt each other with minimal interaction (bars 129–32 or, more intensely, 199–202) or became entangled in polyphonic struggle, as at 174–7. The increasingly sharp contention between orchestra and concertino in the course of the first movement yield a drama of ironic non-cooperation. A fine instance of this can be heard at bars 188–95. Here piano and orchestra cross each other's paths, each playing light, closely spaced three-note chords – chord III in the orchestra at MM 60; chord X in the piano at MM 48. At once distant and related, the two characters engage each other *en passant*; then the orchestra drops the game and the piano moves on. Both the piano soloist and the conductor must be sensitive to the nuances of these delicate, often humorous, moments of failed connection, out of which the larger, darker drama of the first movement grows.

In the second movement, superimposition replaces cross-cutting as the basic structural process. Here, Carter constructs a drama of exits, indeed a drama of annihilation. The piano plays almost continuously, pausing only to let members of the concertino offer their ideas – notably in the three woodwind cadenzas: bass clarinet, bars 438–63, cor anglais, 491–505, and flute, 529–43. Projected behind the concertino are two continuous processes in the orchestra: staccato pulses and dense, sustained chords in the strings. The apparent continuity of these processes is, interestingly, highly illusory. The string chord fades in and out just as the many different pulse layers appear and disappear, seemingly moving in and out of consciousness.

In the second movement, the opposition between the soloist's freedom and the orchestra's tyranny – an opposition that was gradually revealed in the first movement – comes to the fore. After a transition (up to bar 375) during which the piano inverts the figures it was playing at the end of the first movement, as if trying to destroy the technique of that movement, the new, polarized texture emerges. The threatening cloud of strings – Carter terms it a 'suffocating blanket of sound' – is an outgrowth of the clusters built from chord III earlier; now they evolve in harmonic coloring and density, until the musical space is saturated at bar 616. The staccato pulses that were associated in the first movement with chord XI become a giant polyrhythmic mechanism in the second, with many different staccato pulses at speeds from 105/13 to 105 ticking away until they appear to converge at bar 615. Against the orchestra's infernal time-machine, which with its horrific suggestions of machine-gun fire and poisonous gas-clouds can be heard as a sound portrait of the concentration camps, the pianist plays with rhapsodic rhythmical freedom; the entire movement – which can be heard as an expansion of the cello cadenza of the Second Quartet – is Carter's most extended realization of the clash between chronometric and chrono-ametric time-worlds. The pianist seems to be improvising a vast cadenza, using its intervals from the first movement, with the addition of perfect fifths and major sevenths 'stolen' from the orchestra's intervallic repertory. The rhythmic freedom of the piano part constantly threatens to violate notational decency – the hieroglyphic configurations force the player into an agogic, chrono-ametric rhythmic style – and crosses the traditional notational frontier at bar 522 where the concertino accelerates independently of the orchestra. The piano's rhapsodic meditation is interrupted three times by the wood-wind cadenzas – Carter has called the bass clarinet, English horn and flute 'false comforters to the piano's Job.' These cadenzas extend the piano's lyricism to the concertino, but also set off the piano's unbounded expressive freedom from the more restricted lamentations of the 'comforters.'

As the staccato pulses come closer together and the string clusters become increasingly dense, the piano is gradually crowded out; its last foothold is a single F that fades away in accelerating repetition (Ex. 60). A rough blast in the brass, supported by strident tritones in the tim-pani, seems to seal the soloist's doom – but after a terrifying silence the concertino asserts itself with growing force, while sharp thunder claps in the orchestra unleash a cyclone of sound (see bars 656–60). The orchestra seems to be the voice answering Job out of the whirlwind, but the storm passes, and the piano concludes with a short, soft epilogue:

> The piano doesn't beat the orchestra down. It is victorious by being an individual – if there is a victory. Anyway, the orchestra stops before the piano does. Maybe that's a victory. I don't know.[16]

Stravinsky wrote Carter a letter thanking him for the dedication.

Oboe Concerto

'To Paul Sacher.' Commissioned by Paul Sacher for Heinz Holliger. Completed 10 October 1987. Première 17 June, 1987 by Heinz Holliger and the Zurich Collegium Musicum, John Carewe, conductor.

From the music for *Philoctetes* to 'Sandpiper,' the oboe has played a very personal role in Carter's music. Because he studied the instrument him-self, the genre of oboe concerto would have attracted Carter eventually, but the encouragement of Heinz Holliger was a particular incentive. The sketches show that Holliger played an active role in the creation of the Concerto. He provided Carter with a tape of multiphonics and other extended techniques, and with the fingering charts which appear in the score. Carter sent Holliger some initial ideas to see if they were possible. Holliger responded that the sustained, slow lines were more challenging to play than rapid passage work; Carter made these sustained lines, arching

Ex. 60 Asphyxiation

1218
XIXXNORTH WETHERLY DRIVE
HOLLYWOOD 8XXCALIFORNIA
90069

15 June 1968

Mr. Elliott Carter
Mead Street
Waccabuc, New York

Dear Elliott,

My secretary finally found the blueprint
copy of the score and, at last, we listened to the
concerto yesterday. I am more delighted with it than
I can tell you. It is a masterpiece, and I like it
even more than the Double Concerto. I have not listened
to contemporary music lately; a batch of Xennakis a
few weeks ago and some other composers it would not be
very kind to mention. I have been steeped in late
Beethoven quartets, on the other hand, and have not tired
of them. So I came to your concerto with high demands
and quite fresh ears for an old man. I am very honored
to have my name on this score.

We plan to fly to New York on the 26 of
June, and have reserved the usual rooms at the Pierre.
We expect to stay there until mid-August, then go to
Europe if the French revolution is over. There will be
an interesting concert in Cambridge, Mass. August 5,
playing some of the preliminary instrumental versions
of Les Noces, as well as my two new instrumentations of
Wolf's Geistliche Lieder and the Requiem Canticles. Perhaps you might go up, too.

Please let me know if there is anything I
can do to help I Sang Yun. What an appalling story.

If you see Natasha please tell her of our
plans. Many thanks, again, and with love from all of us
to you and Helen.

Igor Stravinsky

P.S.: I really can't judge the recorded performance, nor
can I honestly claim to have heard everything on page 54.

across the range of the instrument the central poetic feature of the composition. Holliger also discussed the oboe concerto repertory, such as it is, with Carter, who became enamored of the Strauss concerto in the process. Holliger showed him how Strauss varied his figuration throughout the piece so that the oboe part is kept fresh-sounding. (I don't hear much of Strauss Oboe Concerto in Carter's, but the Violin Concerto may owe something to its example.)

The Oboe Concerto is scored for a chamber orchestra of oboe solo and four winds, strings and two percussion, divided into two groups. The concertino consists of oboe, violas and percussion 1 (including timpani). The ripieno consists of flute (doubling alto flute and piccolo), clarinet (doubling bass clarinet), horn and trombone, violins, cellos and basses, and percussion 2. The harmonic division of the two groups derives from the twelve-note all-interval chord [8 7 11 2 3 6 4 5 1 10 9] which is heard in the opening measures. The concertino uses the major second, minor third, tritone, perfect fifth, minor sixth and major seventh, the ripieno uses minor second, major third, perfect fourth, major sixth and minor seventh (Chart 44). The structural polyrhythm is 63:80. The ripieno plays rhythms based on 2, 4 or 8 divisions of the beat, while the concertino plays mostly triplet rhythms. As in the Piano Concerto, the concertino serves both as an amplification of the soloist and as a bridge between the solo instrument and the orchestra.

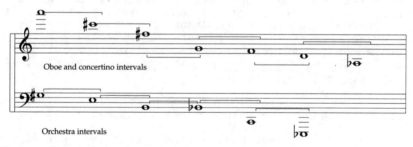

Chart 44 Oboe Concerto: harmonic scheme

The contrast in abstract materials is less obvious than the strong clash of dark and light characters announced at the opening of the piece: the ripieno plays an anxious dirge in its low register while the oboe solo descends calmly from a high A. For a dramatic model Carter here returns to his favorite concerto prototype, the slow movement of Beethoven's Fourth Piano Concerto. The Oboe takes on the role of Orpheus which

Liszt attributed to Beethoven's piano solo. Over the course of the work the soloist attempts to calm and comfort the orchestra. The music progresses from its funereal opening to a jubilant dance through a series of connected sections. Bars 1–91 play off the oboe's lyricism against the orchestra's agitation. In bars 92–186 the oboe plays a long plaintive line against sustained harmonies in the strings. Towards the end of this section the violent mood of the orchestral strings resurfaces, and the oboe silences the outbreak with seven blasts of its lowest note B flat, beginning at bar 186. These stern tones mark the turning point of the piece. The strings now begin to lighten their mood, but at 208 the trombone emerges from the orchestra as an antagonist to the oboe. A second tranquillo section charms the trombone into submission and at 245 the orchestra finally takes on a celebratory tone. At 331 the oboe even sounds like it is urging (or teasing) the orchestra to dance (Ex. 61). The increasingly riotous music is interrupted by a cadenza for the oboe which takes the form of a duet of sustained high melody and low staccato notes, the basic contrast of the entire work. After a final orchestral outburst, the oboe retraces the course of its opening melody, now ascending upward to the calm realms from which it first appeared. It is the most serene of all of Carter's endings.

Oboe Concerto
© 1988 Hendon Music Inc.

Ex. 61 Teasing the orchestra

Violin Concerto

Dedicated to Herbert Blomstedt and Ole Böhn. Commissioned jointly by The San Francisco Symphony through the generosity of Mrs. Ralph I. Dorfman and by Ole Böhn. Completed in Waccabuc 26 February 1990. Première 2 May 1990 by Ole Böhn and the San Francisco Symphony conducted by Herbert Blomstedt.

Carter has described the occasion for his Violin Concerto in an extended program note:

> The first time I met and heard Ole Böhn was at a festival of my music given in Bath, England in 1976, when he gave the first European performance of my Duo for Violin and Piano with Noel Lee. I was very impressed by his remarkable musicianship and his ability to master a score that is very demanding technically and make musical sense out of its many unusual features. In fact he did more, presenting an impassioned, beautiful and very engrossing performance that captivated the audience (as well as myself) in all of the ways I had hoped for in writing the piece, yet it was his own deeply felt, personal interpretation.
>
> After Bath, Ole performed the Duo in various places receiving glowing reviews. During those years he came almost every summer to visit me in America, always urging me to write a concerto for him. I kept putting him off because I was very occupied with many commissions and with teaching, and because I could not resolve in my own mind just what kind of a violin concerto I wanted to write. Such a work poses, to me, many acoustical and expressive problems, ones that worried me a great deal when I listen to many contemporary concerti, such as, how to make the violin not only clearly audible and not be drowned by the orchestra but also to have its expressive role more vivid than that of the orchestra; how to use the highly routinized Paganini-like techniques that show off the soloist so well in a way that modified them so that they fitted into my musical style and became part of it, knowing very well that Ole would be able to master anything practical that I wrote.
>
> So after much thinking I finally accepted his persistent requests in 1989 and combined his commission with one from the San Francisco Symphony. By 1990 I had written out a violin part. Ole came and we went over it in detail. Fortunately nothing was unplayable and he immediately showed his deep understanding of the

music. The score was finished some time later and the première took place on May 2, 1990 with the San Francisco Symphony, Herbert Blomstedt, conducting.

Since that time, Ole performed the work in America in a festival at Ojai, California; in New York; Manchester, New Hampshire; and Cleveland; and in Europe in Saarbrücken, Paris, Brussels, Lyon, Moscow, Amsterdam, the Hague and London where he made the wonderful recording with the augmented London Sinfonietta, conducted by Oliver Knussen who took great pains to follow the indications in the score, allowing Ole's wonderful playing to be clearly heard. For Ole presents the work with great conviction and enthusiasm as is evidenced on the recording and his experience with its many performances allows him to make its technical problems seem to flow with facility for he understands the expressive intentions of the entire work very profoundly.

Reading between the lines of Carter's note, we can detect the underlying anxiety that Carter brought to the genre of the violin concerto, a sense that its traditions were antagonistic to his own style. He studied many of the great concertos, as well as the Paganini Caprices and Ysaÿe Sonatas in preparing to write the piece. The listening list he sent me includes some lesser known works by Piston, Sessions, Hindemith and Maderna, omits the Sibelius Concerto and questions the relevance of both the Beethoven and Tchaikovsky – already we can see that Carter is viewing the tradition from his own angle. He told me that he considered the Mendelssohn Concerto the most technically perfect, but was particularly fond of the rarely performed Schumann concerto even though it was badly scored. Two other favorites are the first concertos by Prokofiev and Szymanowski; the opening of the latter work is strikingly similar to Carter's. For the violin, Carter prefers lyrical concertos to the heroic ones, and he seemed to feel that even the finest examples of the form suffered from a certain vulgarity of emotion. In 1988 he and I listened to a rehearsal of the Berg Concerto at the Cincinnati College/Conservatory of Music. I remarked how impressed I was with Berg's way of connecting diverse materials; Carter replied, 'Yes, but it's so sentimental.' It was a typical way that Carter has of arguing with other music in order to clarify the issues of his own.

Beyond the generic problems posed by the form, the Violin Concerto was written at a difficult time in Carter's life. It was the last large work completed in Waccabuc, in the house where he had composed most of his music since the 1950s. The upkeep of the large, wooded property had become a burden, and the Carters moved to a retirement community in Southbury, Connecticut. Carter's health was also becoming worrisome. In the sketches of the Concerto he notes tests for a heart condition (they turned out normal) and a long, near-fatal bout of pneumonia. He had also lost much of his hearing, which only increased his anxieties about orchestral balance in the concerto.

These dislocations and encumbrances of old age may have made the model of Strauss' Oboe Concerto particularly relevant; at any rate Carter had heard many performances of the Strauss since Heinz Holliger often played it along with Carter's Oboe Concerto. The Violin Concerto follows the three-movement plan of the Strauss, and employs a full orchestra with a restraint that gives it the sound, most of the time, of a chamber ensemble. The style of the concerto might be termed ironic classicism. Never before had Carter written for the orchestra with such a light touch; nor had he ever based entire movements on a single dramatic idea, as he does in the first two movements of the Violin Concerto. The texture and drama of the concerto are remarkably lucid, yet its poetic content is typically Carterian in its enactment of states of alienation. Unlike the Piano and Oboe Concertos, Carter did not give the violin its own orchestra. Throughout the work it stands alone in its materials and moods.

Even the lucidity of the score is deceptive. The sketches indicate that the work went through a process of erasure. Originally Carter considered having a concertino for solo woodwind instruments. The three-level rhythmic plan of the piece suggests a division between solo, concertino and orchestra – but the concertino and its rhythms were absorbed back into the orchestra, leaving the soloist to stand alone. Carter told me that he decided to drop the concertino because he wanted to do something different from his other concertos, but, more importantly, when he arrived at the idea for the slow movement the stark contrast of orchestra and solo became the poetic crux of the entire work. The slow movement evolved as well, becoming ever sparser in the process. The sketches show that the original line was more ornate, and that Carter later erased many of its notes to produce the striking effect of a 'person speaking in single words' as Carter has described the movement.

Technically, the Concerto is built on a three-way harmonic and rhythmic stratification (Chart 45). This division proceeds rigorously throughout the work, so that the three movements differ in mood but not in materials. Carter links the movements with just a few notes on the open strings of

$\quad$ = 52.5

24'

violin	3/28 = 5.625	135	27
orch	4/45 = 4.666	112	28
mixture	5/63 = 4.16667	100	20

hexachord	Violin		Orchestra
H 5	7 3 10 1 8	6	5 9 2 11 4
H 13	3 10 8 7 1	6	9 2 4 5 11
H 20	3 1 10 8 7	6	9 11 2 4 5

Violin triads and interval spacing:

3 – 11 = 1 + 3
3 – 9 = 1 + 7
3 – 11 = 1 + 8
3 – 4 = 1 + 10
3 – 10 = 3 + 7
3 – 12 = 3 + 10
3 – 6 = 7 + 8
3 – 8 = 8 + 10

Chart 45 Violin Concerto: stratification

the violin, as if it were tuning, a gesture whose economy is emblematic of the style of the piece as a whole. The most extravagant device of the work is the opening. The soloist emerges almost imperceptibly from an orchestral tremor (appropriate for San Francisco); by bar 15 it stands by itself. This unprecedented entrance reminds me of lines from Blake: 'My mother cried / My father wept / Into the dangerous / world I leapt.' Within just a few seconds Carter presents the essential dramatic opposition of the piece. The solo violin is a stranger in a strange land. In the first movement most of the orchestral material consists of sparse aftershocks, flurried, rapid notes, short hints of an expressive line that fleetingly connect to the soloist. The entire orchestra only sounds together once, at bar 170. Against these fragmented bursts the violin plays long lyrical phrases in flexible rhythms that gradually move from slow to rapid motion. The entire movement reflects this contrast of materials, a heightened version of the traditional polarity between melody and accompaniment that places an enormous expressive burden on the soloist.

The second movement restates the opposition of orchestra and violin in an even more absolute form. The dualism of the movement is given by its double characterization: tranquillo for the orchestra, angusciato, exitando for the violin. Carter has described it as 'a dramatic recitative by the violin against slowly rising and falling waves of sound in the orchestra.' The orchestral effect may remind listeners of the swelling brass of the first Sea Interlude from *Peter Grimes* – Carter has likened the situation to that of a lone swimmer at sea – but it also recalls the opening of Carter's Duo ('like a man climbing a glacier') or the texture of 'O Breath' where a woman sings in isolation next to the sleeping body of her lover. As in the first movement, Carter maintains a classical unity of affect, relentlessly restating the opposition of soloist and orchestra through subtle variation rather than finding a way out. The violinist begins its line high on the G string – the sound of high anxiety and plays short intense phrases reminiscent of the 'beklemmt' passage from the Cavatina of Beethoven's op. 130. For much of the movement these utterances are broken off, only towards the end does the violinist retrieve something of the lyrical poise of the first movement. The orchestral ocean remains implacably indifferent.

So far Carter has been, so to speak, telling a romantic story through classical means. There is a notable precedent for this paradox in the violin concerto literature – the Mendelssohn Concerto; and in the third movement Carter invokes a comparison – paradoxically. In sketching the movement, he actually copied out a description of Mendelssohn's Finale, in French:

traits de virtuosité
thème: vl
orch.
thème à orchestre avec vl. accomp
cadence

This description fits Carter's scherzando finale as well, though most of the ways he realizes it are far from Mendelssohnian. While the earlier movements had been unthematic, Carter rather surprisingly introduces two clear motives for the solo violin, which suggest the first and second subjects of the Mendelssohn (Ex. 62). The first subject seems to imitate the small intervals of Mendelssohn's elfin theme. The orchestra is also scored with a Mendelssohnian lightness, and the first part of the movement could be termed 'fairy music.' At 464, the tempo slows and the orchestra becomes heavier – but this is a transition to the second subject. The violin now plays more broadly, while the orchestra remains light, counterpointing the warm line of the violin with short giocoso outbursts and pulse phrases that move around the orchestra. The violin returns to its quicker motion at 536, playing with increasing brilliance until it finds its way back to the initial motive at 595. After an orchestral climax the violin continues

Ex. 62 Mendelssohnian theme

its first theme as if it were fading out, but then a huge orchestral chord seems to demand a cadenza. The cadenza that follows could not be more unusual. Although marked 'very dramatically,' it is just three bars long, and consists mainly of double and triple stops on the three lower strings. Just when it sounds like the soloist has begun a cadenza, it is over. The violin goes back into the rapid tempo of the movement and in just five beats rapidly moves upward, disappearing into a string chord as mysteriously as it first appeared.

The cadenza is perhaps the test of how one listens to the concerto. If you hear it as a manneristic shock-effect, the concerto will appear as an ironic exposé of classical norms. The more I listen to the concerto, though, the more I find that its ultimate paradox is a lack of paradox. It presents the three categories of classical poetry – lyric, tragic, comic – succinctly, elegantly and objectively. The concerto achieves a classical poise completely within a musical idiom that Carter developed (and would continue to use) for an anti-classical music of discontinuity and disruption. Strauss's Oboe Concerto sounds, perhaps deceptively, as if it could have been written in an earlier century. Carter's Violin Concerto has no technical connection with the classical period and only the most superficial of resemblances to older music places itself and the listener beyond musical history. Its three-bar cadenza in which the violinist finally stops the music with its weightiest sounds, holding the music briefly in its grip and then releasing its powers, strips the traditional climactic solo down to its essence. This is classicism without any sentimentality.

Clarinet Concerto

Composed in 1996. Commissioned by the Ensemble InterContemporain with support from the Department of Music and Dance of the French Ministry of Culture. Dedicated 'pour Alain Damiens et l'Ensemble InterContemporain.' Première, Paris, 10 January 1997.

The Clarinet Concerto resembles the Fifth Quartet in its formal layout and simplified 'latest' style. It is scored for a chamber orchestra of seventeen players plus the solo clarinet. The orchestra is divided into five family groups to be seated in a semi-circle from left to right: five strings, harp and piano, three percussionists, four brass, four woodwinds. (Percussion 2 joins the piano and harp when it plays marimba.) The clarinet soloist has the option of moving near to each group when they serve as accompaniment. The set-up and floating soloist are a homage to Pierre Boulez's composition 'Domaines.'

The concerto is played without a break but consists of seven sections with linking interludes. Each of the first six sections features one instrumental group, as follows:

1. Scherzando: piano, harp, marimba
2. Deciso: percussion
3. Tranquillo: muted brass
4. Presto (as fast as possible): woodwinds
5. Largo: strings
6. Giocoso: brass
7. Agitato: tutti

The groups of instruments that are not featured in the movements nevertheless make sporadic appearances, usually articulating slow pulses. All the groups play during the interludes. The 'Agitato' movement emerges at bar 388 from the interlude that begins at 359, and may be said to bring together all the strands in the music. It is the only section of the piece where the orchestra may be heard in conflict with the solo as is Carter's usual practice; as in the Fifth Quartet, Carter purges his music of much of its anxiety. Before this last section the concerto is a showcase for the soloist in a variety of different moods. The two slow movements with their extraordinarily simple material and severe restriction in range and poignant expression are perhaps most indicative of Carter's late manner.

Notes

1 Rosen gives a detailed account of the première in *The Musical Languages of Elliott Carter.*
2 CEL, p. 70.
3 CEL, p. 260.
4 Performers should consult Carter's revised Performance Suggestions in the 1994 edition of the score.
5 CEL, p. 271.
6 CEL, p. 246.
7 FW, p. 104.
8 Composer's note in score.
9 CEL, p. 260.
10 Ibid.
11 Igor Stravinsky and Robert Craft, *Dialogues and a Diary* (New York; Doubleday, 1963), pp. 47–9. Since Stravinsky raises the issue of notation, it might be noted that Carter follows the notational conventions of Renée Longy-Miquelle's *Principles of Music Theory.*
12 CEL, p. 36.
13 *Time*, 13 January 1967, p. 44.
14 FW, p. 110.
15 Charles Rosen, *The Classical Style* (New York, Norton, 1972), p. 196.
16 *Newsweek*, 16 January 1967, p. 94.

10 Symphonic Works

Symphony No. 1

Carter completed the Symphony No. 1, dedicated to his wife, Helen, in December 1942 while they were living in Santa Fe, New Mexico. It was premièred by Howard Hanson and The Eastman-Rochester Symphony Orchestra on 27 April 1944.[1] Although it also received an airing from the New York Philharmonic under Mitropoulos (with Varèse present), it was never publicly performed by them or by any other major American orchestra, until Sarah Caldwell's performance with the Boston Symphony in 1976. Despite its neglect, Symphony No. 1 now seems Carter's most whole-hearted response to the ideal of populism; in its unpretentious, idyllic mood it anticipates Copland's *Appalachian Spring*, written two years later. (The published score, however, does not correspond to the original; Carter, who received suggestions about the work from Copland, Hanson, Reiner and Varèse, revised the work substantially in 1954. Its original opening, for instance, was less evocative than the published version.) The Symphony is scored for a small orchestra; it is a pastoral symphony, free of the bombast associated with the 'Great American Symphony' style of the Harris, Schuman and Copland 'Thirds.'

The first movement of Symphony No. 1 was written last, and is closest in structure to Carter's later music. Instead of sonata form, there are a linked series of free variations on two themes. The music unfolds as a series of short episodes of growing intensity. The ultimate goal of the work's motion comes at fig. 403, but the climax at that point dissolves precisely where the listener anticipates a structural downbeat and a new extension of the musical material begins. (Carter first used this climactic gesture in *Heart Not So Heavy As Mine*.)

The novel formal concept of this movement produces many moments of poetic freshness, from the mysterious opening to the evocative flute duet at 234, the warbling background to the trumpet solo at 285, the cinematic dissolve at 320, or the subtle mixture of muted trumpets, plucked and sustained strings, and high woodwinds at 484. Considering the small forces – double winds, timpani and strings – the movement shows a remarkable range of instrumental colors. Carter has said that the music was intended to evoke the land and seascapes of Cape Cod where he and Helen were married; the evanescent orchestral colors and hints of sea-chanteys in the melodic lines accomplish this goal.

The rhythmic design of the movement supports its formal innovations. Although the rhythms appear simple (Carter says he is amused when he sees 'all those quarter notes'), its structural premises are new. There are two basic pulses: a dotted half-note value that establishes the gentle triple motion of the opening, and a half-note pulse that appears at fig. 181. The cross accents inherent in this 3:2 relationship produce the rhythmic development of the score, either by superimposition of pulses or by cross-cutting from one pulse system to the other. The metrical simplicity of the work is deceptive. Instead of indicating a regular pattern of accentuation, the 3/4 bars are themselves pulse units that are accented in irregular groupings, as arrows in the score point out. (Howard Hanson recommended to Carter a renotation in compound rhythms of 6/4 and 9/4 in order to make this rhythmic design clearer.) The tempo is fluid; the dotted half-note pulse gradually accelerates from MM 56 to 80. The half-note pulse similarly accelerates from MM 84 to 120. The relationship between the tempi stays fixed – but the tempi themselves change. The basic arch of speed is recapitulated in microcosm in the closing clarinet solo, whose rubato articulation encapsulates the tempo development of the entire movement.

As in many of Carter's works of this period, there is a harmonic opposition between B and B flat. These pitches are not tonal centres but shifting centers of gravity (or what Stravinsky called polarity) whose enharmonic and directional implications are constantly reinterpreted. Tonally the work moves from B flat minor to E major; but the true structural progression is from the low B flat of the opening chord to the top B of the close (Chart 46). There is a similar opposition between the sonorities of two basic chords, the first presented at the very beginning, and the second at fig. 27 – a juxtaposition which again outlines a B flat/B polarity. The transformation of these two basic sonorities and the interplay of the two

Chart 46 Symphony No. 1: first movement, harmonic scheme

tonal poles colors all the episodes of the movement, which achieves its epiphanic form at the climactic harmonic change at fig. 401.

The second movement is a study in *la grande ligne* which for Nadia Boulanger was the essence of music. It sets forth a developing, hymnlike melody; the opening phrase is twenty-seven bars long. Unlike the first movement, there is little contrasting material. The basic motif of the long melody, however, gradually breaks away to become a cantus firmus underpinning to the main melodic line, first as an ostinato under the long, lyrical trumpet solo, then as the foundation for freer polyphonic elaboration. These two elements – really facets of the same material – unite climactically at fig. 712, the apex of the movement's expressive arch.

The third movement was the first part of the Symphony to be composed. It stems from the original 1936 version of *Pocahontas*, and is simpler in materials and structure than the two movements that were written five years later. The last movement originally contained a chorale-like recapitulation of the other movements. At Copland's suggestion Carter cut this passage (which occurred after fig. 1184).

The third movement pursues the conventions of American populism, replete with square-dance fiddles and a jazz-inflected solo on the E flat clarinet. It begins, however, with a theme that suggests the last movement of Mozart's D minor Piano Concerto in melodic shape and rhythmic irregularity, though its major-minor harmony and arpeggiated accompaniment in the clarinets belong to the world of pop music (Ex. 63).

Symphony No. 1
© 1961 Associated Music Publishers, Inc. Used by permission

Ex. 63 Finale opening

Throughout the movement, pop materials color classical situations, as with the 5/4 ostinato cross-rhythms at fig. 836, the solo trombone at 853 with its squeaky unison response in violins and oboes, the blues-tinted build-up to the return of the main theme at 927, the folky flute and clarinet duo over a sustained fifth in basses and cellos at 987. The cleverest collision of pop and classical styles comes in the central fugue with its heterophonic accents in the trombone (a device that appeared later in Stravinsky's Symphony in Three Movements). The Benny Goodman-style clarinet solo at the end, with a final shrieking lick at the top of the clarinet register (at fig. 1238) caps the high spirits of the movement, but also recalls the wistful clarinet cadenza of the symphony's opening.

Holiday Overture

Carter wrote the *Holiday Overture* in the summer of 1944 to celebrate the liberation of Paris. The Carters were living in Saltaire, Fire Island; Aaron Copland was a house guest. Copland, who was composing *Appalachian Spring* at the time, helped the Overture to win the Independent Music Publishers' Contest in 1945. The prize was supposed to include a performance by Koussevitsky and the Boston Symphony, but Koussevitsky (who was on the jury that awarded the prize) never programmed the piece, and Carter snuck the parts away from the orchestra's library so that they could be duplicated for performance elsewhere. The première took place in 1946 in Frankfurt, Germany; the Frankfurt Symphony had been reestablished by the American Occupation Army and was anxious to establish de-Nazified credentials by playing American music. While Copland told Carter that the overture was 'another complicated Carter composition,' Carter's friends expressed doubts in the other direction. Richard Franko Goldman wrote:

> The contrapuntal complexities are handled with an appearance of casual expertness; the orchestral writing is extremely brilliant. But the piece needs, for a smashing success in our concert halls, an admixture of witlessness and vulgarity which its composer will never, even with the best intentions, acquire.[2]

The *Holiday Overture* seems at first to be a continuation of the festive mood of the Symphony's last movement, but it evolves from diatonic, minstrel-show Americana to dissonant explosions. The simple opening gives little indications of the dense contrapuntal design combining as many as five superimposed lines in prolation canon. If the opening suggests Piston, the ending recalls Ives at his most violent.

The harmonic idiom of the *Holiday Overture* is close to that of *Musicians Wrestle Everywhere*. Like that madrigal, the overture employs pandiatonic harmonies and builds elaborate cross-rhythms out of simple syncopations. These cross rhythms defy the regular bar-lines, giving rise to a freely cross-accented polyphony that unfolds in several layers. A slow element in the rhythmic texture appears in the muted trumpets at fig. 7, forming a background to the fast syncopation in the strings. At fig. 11 the strings superimpose a four-part sustained chorale (a continuation of the slow trumpet music) on rapid music in the woodwinds. The string chorale is irregular in rhythm. It does not create a stable rhythmic framework for the syncopated woodwinds, but functions as an independent stratum. The texture continues to snowball. At fig. 19 three levels of speed are superimposed – two of them internally contrapuntal. The brasses sound the chorale; the strings play an espressivo melody in canon that moves in the initial rhythmic units of syncopated quarters and eighths; the woodwinds add a leggiero, freely imitative texture in eighths and sixteenths. After considerable fugal development, the tuba enters with the slowest material yet – a long augmentation of the chorale theme – underneath the continuing contrapuntal activity in the rest of the orchestra. The tuba line gradually moves upwards through the brasses in a sustained forty-bar phrase. In the middle of this phrase the rest of the orchestra begins a recapitulation of the opening material. The dramatic clash between the two formal and rhythmic layers (a device Carter would use again in the opening movement of the first String Quartet) indicates how far the music has evolved from its naïve-sounding beginning. This textural and structural collision gives rise to dense, chordal fireworks, appropriate for the work's occasion, colored by flutter-tongued clusters in the horns. At fig. 30 the chorale theme is superimposed on itself in four different speeds, based on values of quarter notes, triplet quarters, dotted eighths and half-notes. At fig. 31 five speeds are superimposed in dense stretto, their cross-accents arranged to create a downward arpeggio of increasing note values sweeping from top to bottom of the orchestra and slowing the motion of the music to a tense halt; a jaunty stretto brings the work to a celebratory close.

Variations for Orchestra

The Variations were commissioned by the Louisville Orchestra. Carter tailored the score to conditions in Louisville, particularly the orchestra's small string sections. The opposition of strings, brass and woodwinds heard in much of the work was a means of balancing a full wind section against about half the normal body of strings; the solo string writing in several of the variations was a similar solution to this problem. The rhythmic language of the score, with few of the complex polyrhythms of the First Quartet, at first appears as a compromise, but in fact the ritarding and accelerating variations of the work were the most innovative rhythmic structures Carter had used so far and the most difficult to execute.

The Variations were composed during the first of Carter's stays at the American Academy in Rome during 1953–54, and completed in 1955 in Dorset, Vermont. The première was given by the Louisville Orchestra conducted by Robert Whitney in Columbia Auditorium, Louisville, Kentucky, on 21 April 1956. Despite the excellence of the Louisville recording, performances were rare for many years, though it later became a favorite of Sir Georg Solti.

The last movement of the First Quartet had explored the possibilities of a fluid and dynamic approach to variation form. Instead of the usual division of theme and clearly differentiated variations, the elements of the piece were brought into constant interaction. In the Quartet, however, Carter had used only one means of variation, acceleration. In the Variations for Orchestra he wanted to use as many different kinds of variation as possible, both traditional and new; he studied Vincent D'Indy's chapter on variation in the *Course in Musical Composition*, which outlines all the traditional types in detail, and closely analysed his favorite example of the form, Bach's *Goldberg Variations*. He also studied Schoenberg's Variations, and lectured on them at the Dartington Summer School in 1957; but his work is a reaction against Schoenberg's. Where the Viennese master had followed the formal conception of Brahms, Carter sought a new, formal approach:

> I have tried to give musical expression to experiences anyone living today must have when confronted with so many remarkable examples of unexpected types of changes and relationships of character, uncovered in the human sphere by psychologists and novelists, in the life cycle of insects and certain marine animals by biologists, indeed in every domain of art and science.[3]

Schoenberg's variations, with their invocation of the name BACH are a monument to new-found serial order; Carter's are a celebration of motion and change.

There are three main elements: a theme and two ritornelli. The theme is a seventy-four-note melody, which is treated, loosely speaking, as a series (Chart 47). The theme is unified by several recurring cells – a rising minor third, a cadential falling major third, the diminished seventh chord, and the four-note chord (0, 2, 3, 6). In the course of the work, segments of the

Chart 47 Variations for Orchestra: structure of theme

Chart 48 Variations for Orchestra: variants of theme

theme are transposed, inverted, played backwards (Chart 48, see page 281). These procedures, however, are treated freely. The Variations are not twelve-note music, though the theme contains two twelve-note sequences and Ritornello B is a twelve-note series; the contrapuntal techniques used by Carter derive more from Renaissance and medieval practice than from the Second Viennese School. Other techniques, such as intervallic expansion and contraction that are neither traditional nor serial, are also used as modes of transforming the theme – as will be seen below.

The ritornelli are subject to variation, but of a more restricted kind. Ritornello A, heard descending in small intervals during the Theme, accelerates throughout the piece (Chart 49). Ritornello B, a twelve-note melody stated in two different guises during the introduction, is slower

Chart 49 Variations for Orchestra: Ritornello A

Chart 50 Variations for Orchestra: Ritornello B (twelve-note)

with every recurrence (Chart 50). The criss-crossed trajectories of the ritornelli outline the large formal shape of the work, which moves from extreme opposition to neutralization to renewed contrast.

Introduction   Three chords – one in the woodwinds, one in the strings (based on Ritornello B), the third in the brass (sounding the main four-note harmony of the theme) – announce the three-layered scheme of the music. A cadential chord in the harp punctuates the opening gesture – the harp is to serve throughout as a connecting element between the instrumental choirs. Immediately winds, brass and strings launch simultaneous elaborations of their material in contrasting speeds and textures. The three layers pursue contrasted types of variation. The strings at bar 26 state Ritornello B; at bar 31 the ritornello is transformed, appearing in inversion and in a new rhythmic shape. The brass elaborate fragments of the theme in a developmental manner; their material is the beginning of Variation 1, and continues throughout the Introduction and Theme, gradually evolving into the jig rhythm of the first variation. The woodwinds meanwhile sound a continuous slow-moving line that is the preparation for Ritornello A. Statement, mutation, development and anticipation all appear simultaneously, immediately establishing a nonlinear, multilayered conception of variation.

Theme The woodwind line of the Introduction is taken up by two solo violins. Their tranquil music gradually descends through the Theme, changing color as it moves downwards through the orchestra. This layer of music presents Ritornello A at its slowest speed. Against it, the theme proper unfolds in clearly articulated phrases. A third element, also moving through the orchestra's families, continues the brass music of the Introduction – the sextuplet sixteenths of the Theme move at the same speed as the sixteenths associated with this stratum in the Introduction. Again, three kinds of variation are superimposed. The tranquil music of Ritornello A is gradually transformed in tessitura, while its speed and melodic shape remains constant. By contrast, the rapid sextuplet music changes by abrupt leaps in orchestration, texture and rhythmic shape; at bar 76 its rhythm is suddenly changed from a pattern of rapid even notes to the trochaic pattern of the jig. Against these contrasted types of transmutation the theme is the most stable element, though it too varies in its phrase-shapes and orchestral coloring.

Variation 1 Vivace leggero A developmental variation which continues the rapid material heard from the beginning of the work – the new sixteenths equal the old sextuplet sixteenths. The texture is light, the rhythm dancelike, and at first the variational technique seems to recall that of the *Goldberg Variations*, i.e. a constant rhythmic figuration elaborates the thematic skeleton. However, the leggero music is interrupted by aggressive statements of Ritornello B and by slow, quiet fragments of the theme in horn, strings and harp. These interruptions neutralize the jig material – it seems to evaporate in the course of the variation. Meanwhile at bar 106 Ritornello B appears, moving slowly upwards from the depths of the orchestra in plucked pulses. This sinister gesture belongs to Variation 2, which thus begins in the middle of the first variation.

Variation 2 Pesante   All the values of the first variation are suddenly inverted. The music had been light and fast; now it is heavy and slow. The texture is a parody of the traditional chorale variation. The theme is stated as a cantus firmus. Sounded against it are imitations at different speeds, which compress or expand the intervals of the theme. These mutations themselves give rise to dense imitative elaborations. Twice the contrapuntal clouds part to reveal Ritornello A, which gradually increases in speed in the course of the variation, and fragments of Variation 1 in solo strings, lightly flowing at an ebbing pace.

Variation 3   The first two variations confront each other, tensely. Dense espressivo music and light dance-like material alternate. The heavy texture of Variation 2 congeals into an eight-note chord – related to the opening string chord – whose doubling at a two-octave interval produces a luminous yet mysterious sonority. Against this chord the violins play an expressive mutation of Ritornello B – but after ten bars a sudden accelerando sweeps these massive gestures away, and developmental fragments of the theme appear in the woodwinds in a forlana variant of the first variation's jig rhythm. But the rapid music also fails to establish itself and fades back into a varied restatement of the opening chord. The two contrasted elements seem unable to proceed; instead they cancel each other out. After a second acceleration the rhythm of the first variation fuses with the dynamics of the second in a loud dramatic stretto punctuated by Ritornello B.

Variation 4   A continuous ritardando; the speed halves every four bars. The chamber orchestra scoring and slowing rhythm take up ideas heard at the end of Variation 2. The texture is a free double canon over an ostinato. A solo viola reiterates a four-bar phrase with small alterations, slowing to half its speed and then returning to its initial tempo every four bars. Against this more or less fixed pattern, solo violin and cello play a flowing line, imitated at first in inversion, which gradually slows in tempo across the entire variation. Its rhythmic values are augmented from sixteenths at MM 800 to the entire duration of the four-bar units of the ritardando pattern. A third element unfolds as a four-part canon in the woodwinds. The rhythmic values of this layer actually increase in speed; the woodwinds seem to attempt to accelerate but are pulled backwards by the slowing pulse. A fourth element appears in the background; the strings have plucked chords spaced further and further apart to form an irregular, spasmodic slowing pattern. (This material will continue through Variation 5.) All four elements are themselves variations of a basic type of rhythmic transformation – deceleration. As they slow down, however, their contrasts disappear. The winding down of rhythmic motion is the final phase of the neutralizing process that has marked each successive section since the beginning of the work.

Variation 5   The ritardando brings all the materials to a still point. The theme appears in purely harmonic form, without rhythmic shape, and moves mysteriously through the orchestra in changing colors. This variation combines both the calm and constrained aspects of stillness that Carter had explored in the *Klangfarben* studies in the *Eight Etudes*. Smoothly elided shifts of color contrast with jagged outbreaks in the brass. At the center of the variation is a harp cadenza that is cut off by the slapstick.

Variation 6   The music is notated as a constant acceleration; the tempo triples every six bars. As in Variation 4, the changing pulse is articulated by a canon. The subject, stated by the clarinet, is the retrograde inversion of the opening of the theme. Successive entrances begin slower and become faster; the slowest statement begins in the cellos at bar 331. Although there is not the double canonic structure of Variation 4, a countersubject that first appears at bar 296 again seems to counteract the accelerating pattern, trying to introduce slower values that then get swept up by the quickening pace. Only the harp, which superimposes Ritornello A over the entire variation, seems to stand outside the accelerating tide.

Variation 7   The return to life in the previous variation leads to a new differentiation of the materials. Three strands of music are cross-cut, never overlapping. The opposition of flutes, brass and strings recalls Ives's *The Unanswered Question*. Each level presents a different kind of harmony. The strings play a rugged line in octave doublings; the woodwinds stress melodic and harmonic intervals; the brass intone rich chords. The contrasted densities of each part lead to different patterns of development. The strings gradually expand across musical space, first by way of Ritornello A at bar 388, later through agitated, accelerating motion. The woodwinds expand from single notes to five-note chords, then contract back to intervals, within an unchanging dolce mood. The brass, slow and tranquil at first, gradually crescendo as their harmonies thicken, leading to a remarkable ten-note chord, telescoping the last notes of the theme at bar 404 (Ex. 64).

Variations for Orchestra
© 1957 Associated Music Publishers, Inc. Used by permission

Ex. 64 Brass climax of Variation 7

Variation 8   The flute line of Variation 7 continues in slow motion, moving from flute to solo violin to clarinet. It is superimposed on jazzy giocoso music played very lightly by the rest of the orchestra, with much percussion coloring. Both ritornelli appear: Ritornello B at bar 422, now slowed to 90, Ritornello A at 435, speeded up to 180. As Ritornello A moves downwards, the scherzando music fades away, leaving the flute music, which grows denser and continues uninterrupted into the next variation.

Variation 9   The three strands of Variation 7 are here superimposed, turning Variation 8 into a daydream-like interlude. The three strata move at different speeds: the strings mostly in sixteenths, the brass in dotted quarters, the woodwinds in quarter and half note triplets. The contrasting characters of the three groups are set in relief by a sharp staccato line in an unrelenting steady pulse that enters in the trumpet at bar 455. The trumpet line, though not intervallically based on the ritornelli, relates to the statements of both ritornelli in the previous variation. These light, jazzy pulses are the sound of Time itself, ticking away menacingly behind three levels of swirling clouds. All four elements build to a great climax which suddenly vanishes at the outset of the Finale.

Finale A rapid phantasmagoria, with fragments of all the previous variations and new transformations swimming around in an unstable musical soup. There are four contrasting sections plus an extended coda; all are played continuously and fade in and out of one another.

Section I Allegro molto Thematic fragments moving at different speeds are projected on rapid triplet motion in the woodwinds. The fragments stem from the three strands in Variation 9 and the scherzando material of Variation 8. Ritornello A cuts downwards through the orchestra at bar 500 against slowly rising chords in the strings.

Section II L'istesso tempo The flute continues the dotted eighth pulse of the last section through two tempo modulations. Underneath, the flute, violas and celli begin an intense Andante espressivo, a free fugato derived from Ritornello B which appears at bar 534. At the climax of this phrase it is suddenly cut off by Ritornello A in plucked and tremolo strings, which are silenced in turn by a single chord on the harp, a gesture recalling the very beginning of the Introduction.

Section III Ancora piu mosso The woodwinds relaunch their triplet chatter, against expressive counterpoint of the strings, which continue the contrasting speeds of Section 1, leading directly to:

Section IV Tempo 1, which reinstates the opening speed and texture, now with growing density and excitement. The spiraling development is capped by a climactic statement of the theme's opening motif, which serves as transition to the coda. (Many listeners have compared this climax to that of Debussy's *Jeux*.) A palpable effect of irresolution is produced by the sharp dissonance on the last note of the motto (Ex. 65) exactly where we expect a resolution – instead, new motion is begun.

Ex. 65 Climactic statement of theme

Coda Meno mosso   The tripartite scheme is presented in its most heroic, rhetorical form. Trombones sound a noble variant of the theme's first half, while muted violins in unison state the second half of the theme in a long-lined tranquil melody. Below both lines the timpani expounds a cadenza. The texture is more complex than its first rousing impression may convey; when properly balanced, the contrast of simultaneous gestures so different in mood and sonority creates an effect that is both resolved and tense. At the climax of the brass phrase, the trombones dive down to a sustained pedal B flat, resonated in flutter-tongued horn and trilled winds. As this sound tremor fades, Ritornello B is heard rising softly in basses and tuba, and then upwards to high string harmonics at its slowest rate of MM 32. Against it, at bar 633 Ritornello A rushes downwards from piccolo to the low D on the harp at its fastest rate, 540. The pitches of Ritornello A are exactly those heard moving so slowly across the Theme. The criss-cross pattern of the two ritornelli in space, which dramatizes their cross-trajectories in time, sums up the grand design of the work, completing its 'large, unified musical action.'

Concerto for Orchestra

Commissioned by the New York Philharmonic Symphony Society to celebrate its 125th anniversary, the Concerto was composed at the American Academy in Rome where Carter was composer in residence. The Adagio movement was written at Villa Serbelloni, Bellagio, where Carter was invited for a month by the Rockefeller Foundation. He remembers his stay there for its violent thunder which may have influenced the dramatic timpani writing of the Adagio. The Concerto was first performed at Philharmonic Hall on 5 February 1970. The dedication, omitted by printer's error from the published score, is to its first executants, the New York Philharmonic and its musical director Leonard Bernstein.

Although the orchestral concerto is a popular twentieth-century genre, it stems from two older and opposed traditions. Hindemith's Concerto for Orchestra and Stravinsky's *Dumbarton Oaks* were revivals of the baroque concerto grosso. The orchestral concerti of Bartók and Lutosławski by contrast extend the nineteenth-century symphonic tradition; their combination of orchestral virtuosity and national sentiment looks back to Tchaikovsky's Fourth Symphony. Carter drew upon both traditions. His Concerto is a virtuoso symphonic work in which almost every player at some time becomes a soloist. Instead of the small concertino of the concerto grosso, the orchestra is divided into four groups from which changing ensembles of soloists are drawn. Each string section, for instance, is given a cadenza for seven soloists in the course of the work.

Looking for a form that would dramatize his orchestral conception, Carter came upon the poem *Vents* of St. John Perse. This long, Whitmanesque prose-poem describes winds blowing over the American plains destroying old, dried-up forms and sweeping in the new – a vision particularly relevant to the America of the late sixties, when Bob Dylan's 'Blowing in the Wind' was a counterculture anthem. Many of the poem's images – winds, the rustling of dry straw, clouds of flying insects – inspired the evocative sonic textures of the Concerto. With the text in mind, the listener may find in the Concerto something of an affirmative national work like the Bartók Concerto; it is perhaps Carter's most American vision, evoking an entire continent and a vast heterogeneous society in a state of turmoil. Carter hoped that the four orchestral groups might be seated around the audience so that the music could sweep across the concert hall like winds on the Great Plains. Less literal-minded listeners may prefer to hear the work as an impressionist wind study, Carter's aerial response to Debussy's *La Mer*. For those who prefer their music 'absolute,' the Concerto can be heard as a four-tiered kaleidoscopic collage of shimmering textures and pulsating rhythms, all in a state of continuous flux.

Although scored for a normal orchestra with triple winds but with eight percussionists, the concerto divides the ensemble into four groups, by tessitura:

A violins, flutes, clarinets, metallic percussion (Mov. II)
B violas, oboes, trumpets, horns, snare drums (Mov. IV)
C cellos, bassoons, piano, marimba, harp, wooden percussion (Mov. I)
D basses, trombones, tuba, timpani (Mov. III)

The division into groups is not absolute. Certain instruments, particularly oboes and horns, appear in more than one group, though usually in the background, and the strings occasionally cross boundaries to produce a fuller sonority. The division by tessitura rather than by instrumental families is a Debussyan orchestral conception:

The woodwinds should be dispersed: the bassoons with the cellos, the oboes and clarinets with the violins so that their entries should not produce a package effect.[4]

Like Debussy, Carter sought to achieve an orchestral sonority not based on the string choir. In the Concerto the percussion forms the core of the orchestra's sound; it plays almost continuously throughout and the orchestral fabric constantly emerges from percussive sound, as at the very beginning of the work, where the string harmonics appear imperceptibly out of swelled rolls on triangle and suspended cymbals. Anyone listening to a percussion sectional rehearsal for the concerto would hear how the entire sonority and shape of the music is present in the interplay of metal, skin and wooden percussive timbres.

The grouping of instruments by range rather than by color allows for constant *Klangfarbenmelodie* and mosaic counterpoint within each of the four ensembles. Phrases and chords pass rapidly between instruments from strings to winds to percussion and back, producing a flickering surface. The imbrication of piano, harp, marimba and wooden percussion at bars 15–22 is a typical component of the orchestral tapestry. The fiendish piano writing in the Concerto was Carter's homage to the virtuosity of the Philharmonic's pianist, Paul Jacobs. The rhythmic complexity of the piano part not only exploited Jacobs's particular mastery of polyrhythm, but also allows the conductor – who may be less comfortable with metrical intricacies – to follow the pianist through many of the work's more difficult tempo modulations, as at bar 401 (Ex. 66). (The verbal indications for tempo change were suggested to Carter by Bernstein and greatly facilitate the performance of the Concerto.)

The music of each orchestral group is differentiated in harmony, rhythmic character and expression. Because Carter wanted to use the orchestra in a full manner – as opposed, he has said, to the spare orchestration of late Stravinsky – he needed to devise a rich harmonic vocabulary for the work.

The awkwardness in non-tonal music of octave doubling, the source of most orchestral texture in the past, meant that the harmony would have to be based on many-voiced chords, capable of giving a full sonority without octave duplication. At the opening of the Concerto a twelve-note chord is heard in a swelling orchestral tutti; each instrumental group plays a three-note component of this chord which is the Concerto's primal sound. Starting from the contrasted intervals of these three-note chords, Carter divided all the three-, four- and five-note chords among the four groups (Chart 51).

The harmonic resources of the Concerto – all intervals, three-, four-

Concerto for Orchestra
© 1972 Associated Music Publishers, Inc. Used by permission

Ex. 66 Metric modulation in the piano

and five-note chords and many seven-note chords – are vast; their strict partitioning on the basis of intervallic sound makes them coherent. The expanded possibilities for harmony opened up by the use of the thirty-eight five-note chords (and their seven-note complements) can be put into perspective if we recall that in tonal harmony only two such chords, the major and minor dominant ninths, are officially sanctioned. The listener wanting to explore Carter's harmonic vocabulary might begin with a passage like bar 146 (Ex. 67). Here, five solo violins play in rhythmic unison at a rate of MM 630. Each vertical sonority is a five-note chord associated with Group A; the harmony astonishingly changes with every

Concerto for Orchestra
© 1972 Associated Music Publishers, Inc. Used by permission

Ex. 67 Five-note chords

Chart 51 Concerto for Orchestra: reproduction of Carter's handwritten chart

bar 146, beat 1: five-note chords

5-30   4   30   34   23   9   23

bar 342: three-note chords

3-5   3   8   5   5   3   5   8   8   5

Chart 52 Concerto for Orchestra: harmonic scheme

septuplet thirty-second note, giving the music a vibrant color and a sense of motion that a slower, less inflected rate of harmonic change could not achieve (Chart 52). The music is not everywhere so dense or rapid in its harmonic motion (though frequently it is even more so); a more leisurely exposition of chordal harmonies can be heard in the clarinets at bars 342–4, where the three-note chords of group A drift by (Ex. 68). Throughout the work such streams of chords are the basis of the music's counterpoint and color; they unite contrapuntally independent lines of solo instruments into clear harmonic units which are then set against the contrasted harmonies of the other orchestral groups. At climactic moments all the harmonies merge back into the primal chord of the opening, as at bar 141. Occasionally the texture clears to reveal the basic intervals of each group as at bar 231, when a perfect fifth in the oboes suddenly appears in isolation and is then absorbed back into the orchestral cloud. The constant fluctuation of the music from intervallic to chordal to saturated harmonies parallels and supports the rapid motion of instrumental color between winds, strings and percussion.

Concerto for Orchestra
© 1972 Associated Music Publishers, Inc. Used by permission

Ex. 68 Three-note chords

Carter has related the character of each group's music to certain passages from *Vents*:[5]

> C) 'For a whole century was rustling in the dry sound of its straw, amid strange desinences at the tips of husks of pods, at the tips of trembling things . . . ' (Mov. I)

The tenor-register ensemble, which dominates the first quarter of the work, plays moderately fast, expressive, rubato-style music in phrases that always slow down in speed, beginning faster and ending slower each time. These fading rhetorical gestures perhaps also suggest 'the attrition and drought in the hearts of men.'

> A) 'New lands, out there, in their very lofty perfume of humus and foliage . . .
> Those flights of insects going off in clouds to lose themselves at sea, like fragments of sacred texts . . . ' (Mov. 11)

The soprano-register ensemble plays flowing, pulsed music first heard at a rapid speed, and dominates the second quarter of the piece, marked Presto volando, but gradually slows throughout the work.

> D) 'For man is in question, and his reintegration.
> Will no one in the world raise his voice? Testimony for man.
> Let the Poet speak, and let him guide the judgment!' (Mov. III)

The bass-register group, coming to the fore during the third quarter of the piece, plays slow, expressive music in phrases that accelerate, beginning slower and ending faster each time.

> B) 'And again man casts his shadow on the causeway of men.
> And the smoke of man is on the roofs, the movement of men on the road,
> And the season of man like a new theme on our lips . . .' (Mov. IV)

The alto-register group plays swelling, pulsed music that gradually accelerates throughout the work and dominates the last quarter of the music.

Carter's interpretation of the poetic text can be seen in his assignment of instruments for the poetic ideas. The cellos of group C are given 'romantic' gestures built out of major and minor sixths, but each such gesture is transformed by the dry, rattling sonorities of the piano, marimba and guiro – we can hear the meaning fade from these phrases as the cello cantilena rasps and crackles in the percussion. The prophetic utterances of Perse's poet are assigned to groups of basses and the solo tuba, giving the heightened rhetoric a note of grotesque irony – Carter has said that he was not interested in the overblown, Whitmanesque gestures of some parts of the poem. A similar orchestral irony marks the relation of A and B. Whereas the violins and high woodwinds are given strikingly colored volando material at first, in the course of the piece their fresh sonority fades away and the even more novel sounds of viola, brass and snare drums take their place; it is a rare orchestral work where the violas triumph over the violins.

The four orchestral groups are divided according to the basic characters of musical time often found in Carter's music. A and B are pulsed materials; C and D are rubato. A and C ritard; B and D accelerate. Furthermore the rhythmic character of each group is also its mode of transformation. All four types of music are transfigured in the course of the music, so that their interaction is always changing. In the First Quartet, Carter had let the wind blow through the music of the Variations; in the Concerto for Orchestra, four winds transform each other.

The formal design of the Concerto is perhaps Carter's most complex structure; it combines several of his habitual shapes. The work can be heard as a continuous four-movement sequence Allegro, Presto volando, Maestoso, Allegro agitato, in which each movement features one of the orchestral groups, in the order C, A, D, B. However, all four groups are juxtaposed and superimposed throughout the music, so that the Concerto can also be heard as a cross-cut collage. Because the fragmented statements of each group's material are never literal repetitions, but are always transformations, the Concerto can also be heard as a variational design. The intersecting tempo transformations of A and B, moreover, create an inverted arch pattern, so that there is a dramatic low point near the centre of the work (bars 350–3) where the differences in tempo between A and B are neutralized. These simultaneous designs stem from a large polyrhythmic formal conception, which is an expansion of the superimposed waves of the Double Concerto's coda. The main entrances of each instrumental group occur at regular intervals. The absolute tempi of these structural pulses are in the ratio 10:9:8:7 (Chart 53). The four groups fade in and out of the music, each at a regular speed; Carter likes to derive the appearance of randomness from the certainty of natural laws. The structural pulses nearly coincide at the four climactic turning points (bars 141, 284, 488,

Chart 53 Concerto for Orchestra: structural polyrhythm

550) where the large movements begin. Each of these intersections recalls the twelve-note harmony and stormy texture of the opening, though they never repeat the opening literally. The last such explosion (at bars 550–8) is closest in sound to the opening; the emergence of the solo piano out of the ratchet trill at bar 560 recalls bar 16 where C first bursts out of the primal chaos. The Coda following bar 561 reverses the pattern of the introduction, so that the work ends with a transformation of the opening's unpitched percussion into cadential chimes.

The large four-movement pattern and the criss-cross tempo design of A and B clarify and give direction to a highly fragmented variational structure. The Concerto is a rapidly paced series of fragmented episodes, each one a variation of the material of the four groups. The contrapuntal combination of materials, the sequence of juxtaposition and the character of the materials themselves are all subject to change, so that while the vivid imagery of the music remains constant, its manifestations are always new. The four-movement design helps to place one orchestral group in the foreground, to emphasize the most identifiable aspects of its character. The expressive gestures of C heard clearly at the opening become increasingly abstract and textural as the work progresses; the tidal waves of B which eventually sweep the entire orchestra away in a general accelerando, only emerge slowly in the earlier parts of the Concerto. Although there is little exchange of material the nature of juxtaposition becomes more dramatic as the music unfolds. Where C and A seem to be casually interrupted during their movements, the prophetic rumblings of D give rise to a more antagonistic interaction of materials, while the fresh energies of B emerging out of the darkness at bar 419 seem to absorb all the other music in ever more rapid waves of sound; the music of the last quarter of the Concerto is perhaps the most exhilarating Carter has ever written.

A Symphony of Three Orchestras

Begun in June 1976 and completed on 31 December of that year, A Symphony was commissioned by the New York Philharmonic under a grant to six orchestras (Boston, Chicago, Cleveland, Los Angeles, New York and Philadelphia) from the National Endowment for the Arts in honor of the United States Bicentennial. The score is dedicated to Pierre Boulez and the New York Philharmonic, who gave A Symphony its première at Avery Fisher Hall, 17 February 1977.

Ever since discovering Hart Crane's poem *The Bridge* while he was at Harvard, Carter had planned to set it as a large choral cantata. Although Crane entered his music in *Pocahontas*, whose scenario was derived from *The Bridge*, and in *Voyage*, the projected cantata languished, chiefly, Carter has said, because of the absence of large professional choruses in America willing or able to perform Carter's music. Finally he decided to transform the choral setting into a symphonic work whose sounds, textures and forms would evoke Crane's life and work in purely abstract terms. Neither a traditional symphony nor a tone poem, *A Symphony of Three Orchestras* might best be termed a 'portrait of Hart Crane' to be set beside *pli selon phi*, Boulez's 'portrait' of Mallarmé; the two works are at least as different as the two poets they portray.

Hart Crane lived out the conflicting values of the modernism of the American twenties; he leapt to his death in the Gulf of Mexico in 1932. Like Eliot and Pound, he wrote of a world which (as Carter has said) 'for all its fascinating modernism, would eventually prove a paralysing wasteland, depriving him of his poetic gift, even destroying him completely.' Unlike Eliot or Pound, Crane did not escape to Europe. His fate was more distinctly and tragically American – as was his poetry, which is at once nihilistic and monumental, slangy and Miltonic. Though occasionally pretentious, awkward or reckless in syntax, his poems often achieve the epic vision of modern America Crane self-consciously strove for. Crane's visionary strengths and tragic failings are emblematic of the New York avant-garde of the 1920s, the milieu in which Carter first decided to become a composer. Crane, moreover, as a *poète maudit*, symbolizes in extreme form the perilous position of the American artist. For those unfamiliar with Crane's story, Robert Lowell's 'Words for Hart Crane' can illustrate what his life and work mean to Carter:

When the Pulitzers showered on some dope
or screw who flushed our dry mouths out with soap
few people would consider why I took
to stalking sailors, and scattered Uncle Sam's
phoney gold-plated laurels to the birds.
Because I knew my Whitman like a book
Stranger in America, tell my country: I,
Catullus redivivus, once the rage
of the Village and Paris, used to play my role
of homosexual, wolfing the stray lambs
who hungered by the Place de la Concorde.
My profit was a pocket with a hole.
Who asks for me, the Shelley of my age,
must lay his heart out for my bed and board.[6]

Crane's poetry compresses past, present and future in a fragmented cinematic montage:

I think of cinemas, panoramic sleights
With multitudes bent toward some flashing scene.[7]

The Brooklyn Bridge in Crane's poem is both mythical and real, spanning
a river and a continent, linking the Indian past with the mechanical
future. To suggest the dense, flickering imagery of Crane's poems Carter
conceived a work for three orchestras of contrasting sonorities whose
music would unfold simultaneously. As in the Concerto for Orchestra,
much of the music's sound-imagery was suggested by the text. The opening, which John Russell has called the definitive portrait of New York in
sound, evokes:

How many dawns, chill from his rippling rest
The seagull's wings shall dip and pivot him,
Shedding white rings of tumult, building high
Over the chained bay waters Liberty –

Then, with inviolate curve, forsake our eyes
As apparitional as sails that cross
Some page of figures to be filed away;
– Till elevators drop us from our day . . .[8]

The transition from natural to mechanical motion in these lines is a general theme of *The Bridge*, and inspired the form of *A Symphony*. The music, like the poem, describes a continuous descent:

> Lead-perforated fuselage, escutcheoned wings
> Lift agonized quittance, tilting from the invisible brink
> Now eagle bright, now
> > quarry-hid, twist
> > > -ing, sink with
> Enormous repercussive list
> > -ings down
> Giddily spiraled
> > gauntlets, upturned, unlooping
> in guerrilla sleights, trapped in combustion gyr-
> Ing, dance the curdled depth
> > down whizzing
> Zodiacs, dashed
> > (now nearing fast the Cape!)
> > > down gravitation's
> > > > vortex into crashed
> . . . dispersion . . . into mashed and shapeless debris . . .[9]

A related theme is that of fallen men, like Rip Van Winkle, whom Carter says may be heard in the Scherzando movement of Orchestra III:

> And Rip forgot the office hours,
> > and he forgot the pay:
> Van Winkle sweeps a tenement
> > way down on Avenue A[10]

Crane's Rip Van Winkle is not comic; he is human debris, like the hoboes who appear later in the poem:

> Behind
> My father's cannery works I used to see
> Rail-squatters ranged in nomad raillery,
> The ancient men – wifeless or runaway
> Hobo-trekkers that forever search
> An empire wilderness of freight and rails.[11]

The world's fall from natural beauty to mechanical terror and the fall of men are themes that appear more autobiographically in Crane's other poems. Carter has said that the bell-like movement in Orchestra II was inspired by 'The Broken Tower':

> The bell-rope that gathers God at dawn
> Dispatches me as though I dropped down the knell
> Of a spent day . . .
> The bells, I say the bells break down their tower;
> And swing I know not where. Their tongues engrave
> Membrane through marrow, my long-scattered score
> Of broken intervals . . . And I, their sexton slave! . . . [12]

The connections between the falling bells, symbolizing the disappearance of faith, and Crane's own death are even more explicit in 'The Return':

> The sea raised up a campanile . . . The wind I heard
> Of brine partaking, whirling spout in shower
> Of column kiss – that breakers spouted, sheared
> Back into bosom – me – her, into natal power . . . [13]

Crane made his poems inseparable from his life and death; *A Symphony* evokes the poems and the man in a continuous descent whose inviolate curve, like the poet's life, is suddenly broken:

> The forked crash of split thunder parts
> Our hearing momentwise . . .

The music evokes life and death, lyrical motion and paralysis in a span built from fragments of shattered images, 'one arc synoptic of all tides below.'

Carter divides the standard symphony orchestra (triple winds, five horns, five percussionists) into three contrasting groups:

Orchestra I: brass, timpani, strings

Orchestra II: three clarinets, vibraphone, chimes, xylophone, marimba, long drum, low tom-tom, piano, four violins, six cellos, two basses

Orchestra III: woodwinds (without clarinets), horns, metal percussion, strings (no cellos)

Orchestra II seated at the center is a concertante group, each of whose movements is dominated by solo instruments. The outer orchestras play textural music.

Each orchestra has four movements – the work's only trace of traditional

ORCHESTRA I: BRASS, TIMPANI, STRINGS.

Movement	Bars	Interval	Chord	Speed	Character-colour
1	38-46 237-259	m6	*(notation)*	MM 12	sostenuto
2	55-89 207-226	A4	*(notation)*	60	molto espr.
3	105-121 157-192	M2	*(notation)*	420	flowing
4	127-142 273-309	m2 m9	*(notation)*	120 140	angry

ORCHESTRA II: 3 CLARINETS, VIBRAPHONE, CHIMES, XYLOPHONE, MARIMBA, PIANO, 4 VIOLINS, 6 CELLI, 2 BASSES.

Movement	Bars	Interval	Chord	Speed	Character-colour
1	50-67 131-164	P5	*(notation)*	45	bell-like
2	82-112 250-264	m7	*(notation)*	240	grazioso (clarinets)
3	178-199 298-318	A4	*(notation)*	80	cantabile, espr. (celli)
4	215-242 268-285	m3	*(notation)*	accel. to 540	accelerating (piano)

ORCHESTRA III: FLUTES, OBOES, BASSOONS, HORNS, VIOLINS, VIOLAS, BASSES, NON-PITCHED PERCUSSION.

Movement	Bars	Interval	Chord	Speed	Character-colour
1	40-61 291-314	M7	*(notation)*	360	giocoso
2	75-100 185-221	M3	*(notation)*	24	sostenuto
3	108-136 233-245	P4	*(notation)*	180	flutter-tongue tremolandi
4	150-171 254-280	M6	*(notation)*	105	espr. cantabile

Introduction bars 1-39; Coda, bars 318-394

Chart 54 *A Symphony of Three Orchestras*: twelve movements

symphonic form – which are split and cross-cut. The twelve movements are distinct in harmony, timbre, expressive character and tempo (Chart 54).

The harmonic motion of the work is controlled by the interplay of the dominant intervals and triad of each movement with a recurrent forty-five note 'tonic' chord, made up of four versions of an all-interval twelve-note chord three of whose notes are the same (Chart 55).

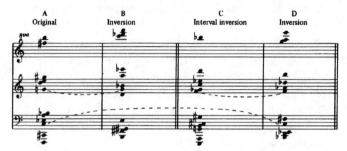

Chart 55 Four versions of all-interval chord (5, 10, 4, 2, 7, 9, 1, 6, 3, 11, 8) = 45-note 'tonic chord'

Each interval of the twelve movements has four fixed positions in the forty-five-note chord, which focus harmonic motion within them (Chart 56).

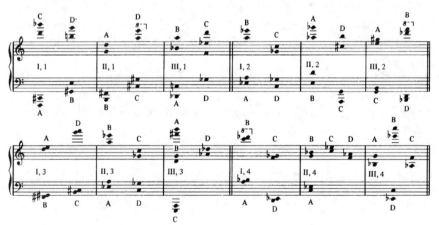

A, B, C, D designate the four all-interval chords.
Roman numerals indicate each of the three orchestras.
Arabic numeral indicates movement number.

Chart 56 Location of each interval of the twelve movements in the four fixed all-interval chords

The word 'Symphony' here denotes the bringing together of sounds. The work falls into three distinct parts: an Introduction in which the highest notes of the tonic chord in suspended strings and screeching woodwinds frame a soaring trumpet solo (written for Gerard Schwarz who was then the NYPO's principal trumpet); the main body of the work, a three-leveled collage of the twelve movements; and a coda in which all the material is reduced to chordal sounds beginning with explosive thunder-chords sounding the central notes of the tonic. The coda proceeds through a series of factory-noise ostinati, unprecedented in Carter's music, to a concluding piano solo, diving downwards to the lowest notes of the tonic chord which reverberate and rumble in the final notes of the tuba and double basses. The introduction and coda are the extremes of the double downfalls of the work, from high to low, from lyrical to mechanical. The main body of the music is a kaleidoscopic *mélange* of characters, which gradually transforms the opening trumpet flight into the piano's clattering descent.

A Symphony of Three Orchestras is Carter's most complex exploration of collage. There are more movements and strata than in the Third Quartet; the motion of the music is also much faster. Listeners do not have time to analyse the constituent elements of the texture, but must let the rapid currents of the music carry them along. The apparent chaos of textures follows a regular and elegant pattern, however. The music sweeps across the orchestra in swelling waves, beginning with one orchestra alone, mounting to two, cresting to three, then subsiding. Each 'trough' is a

Orchestra I	*Orchestra II*	*Orchestra III*
1-augmented triads	5-bells	11-scherzando
8-espressivo	10-clarinets (grazioso)	6-major & minor triads
3-flowing	7-cellos	9-leggero
4-angry	2-piano (accel.)	12-cantabile

```
I    1          8  8  8  8  8        3  3  3       4  4  4          3  3  3
II         5  5  5       10 10 10 10 10          5  5  5  5  5
III  11 11 11 11      6  6  6       9  9  9  9  9          12 12 12

I    3  3          8  8  8      1  1  1  1  1          4  4  4  4  4
II   7  7  7          2  2  2  2  2      10 10 10    2  2  2          7  7  7
III     6  6  6  6  6      9  9  9      12 12 12 12 12          11 11 11
```

Chart 57 Structural scheme

unique isolated occurrence of one of the twelve movements. Chart 57 outlines the form of the middle section of the work, from bar 40 to 318, identifying the movements by the number of their dominant triad. Each vertical unit in the chart lasts about fifteen seconds. It would have been impossible to use every combination of movements as the Third Quartet had done. The montage of movements was selected for variety; the most active materials of each orchestra are reserved for the final intersection, bars 301–9. Because of the great speed of textural change, the interest of the music lies not so much in the interplay of materials as in the constant transformation of the entire tapestry as movements are added and subtracted. Each exposure of a single movement appears as the end of one transmutational progression and the beginning of the next. Repeated hearings reveal ever-receding echoes of the trumpet's opening flight – in the flowing movement of Orchestra I (see bars 169–76), in the grazioso music for the clarinets beginning at 82, and in the shimmering leggero movement of Orchestra III; there are also constantly encroaching intimations of mortality.

The thunder-chords which blot out the last traces of expressive music in Orchestra II are the climactic 'sounding-together' of the symphony. As the last phrases of the solo violins disappear the silence between thunder claps becomes awesome, terrifying. (Carter recalls that as a young boy he was once nearly struck by lightning.) The coda that follows is a transformed world. A few fragments of the earlier music, 'mashed and shapeless debris,' remain: the violas of Orchestra III, the cellos of Orchestra II, and the trumpets of Orchestra I give intense but fading restatements of their lyrical material. But these are dispersed by frighteningly extended, mechanical ostinati, built of scattered intervals, each repeated at a different frequency (bars 348–52). With a grotesque halo of xylophone and marimba parodying the screeching gulls of the opening bars, the piano, the transformed persona of the opening trumpet, leaps downward, *con bravura.*

Penthode

For Five Groups of Six Instruments. Dedicated to Pierre Boulez and l'Ensemble InterContemporain. Composed during 1984 and 1985, completed, 9 June 1985. Première, at the Proms, London, 26 July 1985. Recorded by L'Ensemble Inter-Contemporain conducted by Pierre Boulez.

Pierre Boulez has championed the works of two American composers: the unlikely pair of Elliott Carter and Frank Zappa. Boulez has influenced Carter both as a composer and conductor. Carter always cites his discovery of *Le marteau sans maître* as a moment which expanded his sense of what he could ask of players. Boulez's support for his music from the seventies on finally freed Carter of his unpleasant wrangling for performances by American orchestras and their maestros, none of whom had shown sympathy for his music, and many of whom – in particular Leonard Bernstein and his disciples – were vehemently antagonistic. The first contemporary American piece Boulez conducted was Carter's Concerto for Orchestra, with the Cleveland Orchestra in 1971; he commissioned *A Symphony of Three Orchestras* for the New York Philharmonic and conducted the Double Concerto at Juilliard while he was musical director of the Philharmonic. He commissioned *Penthode* for an American tour by his Ensemble InterContemporain, on which they also performed Boulez's *Répons*. The size of the ensemble was determined by the requirements of the tour and changed as the tour budget was nailed down; Carter had begun the work as a quintet of sextets. Carter has shown his appreciation for Boulez's encouragement through the two *esprit rude/esprit doux* compositions written for Boulez's sixtieth and seventieth birthdays. *Penthode* is written *con amore* from beginning to end.

Whatever its debt to Boulez, Carter has traced the inspiration of *Penthode* to performances of North Indian Dhrupad music by the Dagar brothers that he heard in Berlin in 1964 (performances that may have also inspired Stockhausen's *Stimmung*.) *Penthode* doesn't sound Indian, but Carter borrowed two structural ideas from the Dagar brothers, the unfolding of a single melodic line by two voices and the gradual introduction of an accelerating rhythmic pulse. The first section of a Dhrupad composition is a slow, meditative section, called *alap*; in the next section, *madhya*, a slow pulse is introduced, and in the third, *drut*, the pulse becomes faster. After this the drum enters for the final section or *dhrupad*. The three-part form of *Penthode* follows a similar pattern, though it conflates the last two sections. It achieves the rhythmic transition from near-stasis to frenzied motion that is a fundamental principle of Indian music in general and Dhrupad in particular. The clear three-part design of the work, however, also has western precedents, in particular the ABA da capo aria. The first third of *Penthode* unfolds a melodic line; the third section brings it back (not literally) now accompanied, as in the final section of *Triple Duo*, with an accelerating pulse line. The aria-like structure is confirmed (perhaps parodied) by a climactic quasi-cadenza at bar 435, where the melodic line ascends rapidly from the lowest note on a contrabass clarinet to the highest one on a piccolo (Ex. 69). *Penthode* is rich enough in substance to contain multiple, contradictory paradigms. The melodic thread which holds it together is both Indian and Parisian, a homage to Nadia Boulanger and her principle of a *grande ligne*. The music has the formal coherence of a symphony, but also a feeling of a Joycean stream of consciousness. The voice that wanders throughout, beginning, as if in mid-sentence, recalls the great monologues that conclude *Ulysses* and *Finnegans Wake*.

Penthode
© 1985 Hendon Music Inc.

Ex. 69 Cadenza

Like *Triple Duo*, *Penthode* balances the principles of diversity and unity, improvisation and structural rigor. Each quartet is an unusual combination drawn from four quintets: woodwinds, brass, strings, three percussion, piano and harp:

Group 1: Trumpet 1, Trombone, Harp, Violin 1.
Group 2: Flute, Horn, Percussion 1 (mainly wood) Contrabass
Group 3: Oboe, Tuba, Violin 2, Cello

Group 4: Clarinet, Bass Clarinet, Trumpet 2, Percussion 2 (mainly metal)

Group 5: Bassoon, Piano, Percussion 3 (mainly skins)

Carter divides up the groups harmonically, based on a distribution of three-note chords, and rhythmically, based on a structural polyrhythm (Chart 58).

Speeds calculated on the basis of $\downarrow$ = **84**

Group I 3/55 MM 4.5818. Three-note chords: 1, 8, 11.
Group II 3/64 MM 3.9375 Three-note chords: 4, 9.
Group III 5/98 MM 4.2857 Three-note chords: 5, 7.
Group IV 5/104 MM 4.03846 Three-note chords: 3, 10.
Group V 4/85 MM 3.95294 Three-note chords: 2, 6, 12.

Chart 58 Penthode: stratification of speeds and three-note chords

Given the density of counterpoint that Carter could draw from the double duo of the Third Quartet, the problem of writing a piece for five quartets was how to achieve clarity rather than chaos and still give each quartet its own voice. Carter solved this problem through the elegant three-part design of the work and the importance of the shared melodic line in the outer thirds of the work. By contrast, the middle of the work, from 178 to 287 presents a double contrast of the five quartets and the four quintets in rapidly cross-cut episodes. The final third of the piece doubles the texture of the first part by adding a line of pulses, which also move around the orchestra and accelerate.

Expressively, *Penthode* stands out from Carter's oeuvre for its lack of anxiety. It begins in a mood of lyrical calm. The unfolding melodic line has the abstract quality of a cantus firmus, only occasionally hinting at greater turbulence. Behind the melodic line a series of chords appear which expose the triadic identity of each group as well as their rhythmic pulse, but these also have an abstract non-rhetorical quality. At the end of the exposition the chords converge, raising a question whose answer is the new texture of the central part of the piece. The double contrast of quintets and quartets also intensifies the rhythmic contrast. The music seems to jump from the accelerator to the brakes, with sudden spurts of activity, mixing with sustained chords. Only with the last third of the piece does Carter release its full energies. The melodic line returns, but is much more ornate, and in addition to the new line of accelerating pulses, there is also a new level of contrapuntal filigree. This section is similar in texture to the finale of the *Triple Duo*, but the two pieces arrive at the state of euphoric fantasy through very different paths. *Triple Duo* set up a course of convergence, a motion from diversity to unity. *Penthode* feels more like a huge whirlpool. The music begins at its outermost edges, barely registering its motion, then gradually gets pulled into its powerful spin.

Three Occasions

Between 1986 and 1988 Carter composed three relatively short orchestral works. Although written for different occasions, they may be performed together as a suite. Carter writes that both *Remembrance* and *Anniversary* 'should be dedicated to Oliver Knussen, without whom they would not have taken the orchestral shape they now have.' Knussen conducted the première of *Remembrance*, and then, sensing that a third orchestral piece would round out a satisfying short symphony, urged Carter to compose the work that became *Anniversary*. The *Three Occasions* together form a sixteen-minute long symphonic suite equal in length, and emotional depth to the two orchestral sets of Ives.

A Celebration of Some 100 × 150 Notes

Commissioned by the Houston Symphony Orchestra to celebrate the 150th anniversary of the founding of the state of Texas. Completed 28 December 1986 in New York. Première by the Houston Symphony Orchestra conducted by Sergiu Commissiona 10 April 1987.

The Houston Symphony marked the 150th anniversary of the Lone Star State by commissioning three-minute fanfares. Carter's *Celebration* is both three minutes and 150 bars long. (The tempo is MM 150, the meter is 3/4 except for six bars each of 4/4 and 2/4, so there are exactly 450 beats.) The 100 notes per bar implied by the title is a conservative estimate. If it weren't for the precedents of Debussy and Stravinsky Carter might have called it 'Fireworks' – but the true prototype for *Celebration* is Ives's *The Fourth of July*. Heard impressionistically, the music suggests a patriotic festival heard through a din of explosive bursts, but on a metaphoric level it celebrates the glittering evanescence of music itself.

Celebration is built out of eleven fanfares, one for each musical interval (Chart 59). The fanfares occur in little fragments in the beginning of the piece, coming together with an Ivesian exuberance at bar 115. Carter ties these together with the harmony of a twelve-note chord which occurs at

Chart 59 *A Celebration*: fanfares

the very beginning and then sporadically, but comes to the fore in the terrifying *tutti* at the very center (bars 70–100). A structural polyrhythm of 56:45 runs from bar 6 to 146. Although the tempo of MM 150 never changes, and the rhythmic subdivisions are in simple rations of 2:3:4, the music has all the characteristic rhythmic tension of Carter's earlier music.

Carter's fluid use of the orchestra, and his humorous approach to the commission appears in the very opening. A low flute tremolo spreads throughout the orchestra, leading to a massive twelve-tone chord which then dissolves down to the sound least expected in a fanfare: an extended celesta solo. This sweep across the entire dynamic spectrum occurs within twenty rapidly paced bars and establishes the breathless sequence of explosions that fill the short piece.

Remembrance

'*In memory of a great patron and believer in music of our time, Paul Fromm.' Commissioned by The Fromm Music Foundation for The Tanglewood Music Center in Memory of Paul Fromm. Première 10 August 1988 by the Tanglewood Festival Orchestra, Oliver Knussen, conductor.*

Paul Fromm was an important benefactor of contemporary music in America. His Foundation sponsored the week of Contemporary Music at Tanglewood for many years, as well as commissioning and recording works by many composers. For Carter, Fromm's support had a particular significance. Fromm provided money for an extended amount of rehearsal time for the première of the Double Concerto. Carter has told me that this was the first time that American works were given the preparation time found in Darmstadt and other European festivals. He felt that for the first time he was completely free to pursue his rhythmic ideas for a large ensemble.

Remembrance is a eulogy for solo trombone and orchestra, but just as *Celebration* was a 'fantasy' around fanfares, *Remembrance* is a meditation around a eulogy. There are three elements: the trombone solo, a wide-ranging line, made up largely of short, isolated phrases; a series of twelve-note chords that sound like a slowly tolling bell; and fragmented bits of 'music.' If the Ivesian subtext of *Celebration* was *The Fourth of July*, here it is *The Unanswered Question*. Each element seems to exist in its own time world (a structural polyrhythm of 28:27 isolates the trombone from the orchestra), and each one reaches its own moment of epiphany. The trombone solo takes up a 'trope' that Carter had used in the opening of the Duo and would explore further in the Violin Concerto, the pathos of a broken utterance. Many of its phrases consist of a single note, surrounded by many beats of silence. Just once does it summon up a complete sentence: at bar 28–35. This full statement is amplified and extended by the entire brass section. The tolling chord is actually a changing chord; Carter uses all thirty similarly structured chords in the piece (Chart 60). The chord is also scored differently on every appearance, although its sonority is always centered on the strings. At the end of the piece the violins approach the chord through an expressive rising melody which connects the 'bell' element to the trombone's melodic line. The fragmented musical

Chart 60 Remembrance chords

reminiscences occur mainly in the woodwinds; their liveliness serves as a foil to the solemn tone of the eulogy. Most of the reminiscences are of 'imagined' works, but at bar 39 the piano quotes the Double Concerto – the beginning of the double cadenza at the end of the slow movement.

Anniversary

'For Helen.' 'A gift to my wife celebrating our 50th wedding anniversary.'

> Only our love hath no decay
> This, no tomorrow hath, nor yesterday,
> Running it never runs from us away
> But truly keepes his first, last, everlasting day.

John Donne

Completed 25 May 1989. Première 5 October 1989, Royal Festival Hall, London, by the BBC Symphony, Oliver Knussen conductor.

Anniversary was written for Oliver Knussen who, after performing both *A Celebration* and *Remembrance*, urged Carter to complete an orchestral triptych. If the first two pieces were vignettes raised to a higher power, *Anniversary* seems more abstract. It unfolds energetically as a two-part counterpoint, with each line moving around the orchestra. Half-way through, a third element is added. The three lines are labeled x, y, and z in the score to help performers understand the way their parts fit into the larger scheme. The dedication, however, suggests a less abstract basis for the structure. *Anniversary* is Carter's tongue-in-cheek *Sinfonia Domestica*. The contrapuntal lines represent husband and wife – the listener can decide which is which – and half-way through they are joined by a child who, as Carter told me, has the last word. It's probably futile to look for the domestic realism of Strauss's score here; *Anniversary* is a study of temporal relativity, of the multiple movement from yesterday to tomorrow. Whereas Strauss expanded a domestic incident into a symphony, Carter compresses fifty years of partnership into six minutes; years, events and emotions seem to flash by.

Carter's sketches reveal that the piece evolved quickly from the specific event of an anniversary to an abstract presentation of what Carter calls 'the drift of time, thinning and thickening.' The sketches show that Carter first looked for motives based on the letters of Helen and Elliott (as he had done with Boulez's name), then he wrote out some rhythmic motives based on their names; but there are no traces of these devices, except, perhaps for the sustained E and C at the conclusion. At first, also, he considered dividing the three elements between the three instrumental families of the orchestra, but the sketches show that he drafted almost the entire score on two staves first. The clear contrapuntal design of the piece allowed an unconstricted use of the orchestra; the lines move through the orchestra to create a series of dovetailed duets (and later trios that change in both color and character. The sketches also reveal that Carter was always conscious that *Anniversary* would be played with the other two pieces, and therefore had to contrast with them. He noted to himself that he would avoid the trills of *Celebration* and also the continuous density of *Remembrance*.

The three contrapuntal lines are differentiated by their melodic intervals. Line x, which begins briskly in the oboe in bar 6 uses intervals 1, 3, 7, 8 and 10. Line y, starting out ploddingly in bar 3, uses intervals 2, 4, 5, 9 and 11. Line z, which appears in bar 99, emphasizes intervals 1 and 6. All three lines move through various emotions, passionate, mysterious, humorous – though line x seems to have the best sense of humor – see the clarinet in bars 170–179 (Ex. 70). Surrounding the contrapuntal lines are two elements which denote the passage of time: rustling sixteenth notes, and ticking pulses. Both of these elements appear sporadically throughout the work. The pulse speeds change, while the rate of the sixteenths stays fixed. All the elements collide rhythmically at a climactic chord in bar 204. In the coda that follows the contrapuntal lines and the pulses fuse, and the sixteenth note figures freeze into chords. Then the tuba has the last word, picking up the thread of line z with a question to be answered at some future time.

'Anniversary' from Three Occasions for Orchestra
© Hendon Music Inc.

Ex. 70 Clarinet whimsy

Symphonia: Sum Fluxae Pretiam Spei

I Partita – *Sum sidus scilicet aequoris/Naturae jucus aureus/Naturae vag fabula/Naturae breve somnium*

       I am the star of the sea, as it were, the golden wit of nature, the rambling tale of nature, the brief dream of nature

II Adagio tenebroso – *Sum caecae speculum Deae*

       I am the glass of the blind goddess

III Allegro scorrevole – *Sum venti ingenium breve/Flos sum, scilicet, aeris.*

       I am the brief nature of the wind. To be sure, I am the flower of the air.

According to Carter, the project of a large orchestral triptych was instigated by Oliver Knussen. From the beginning Carter knew that he was writing a three movement work, but the movements were commissioned and premièred by three different orchestras. The three pieces were first performed in 1994, 1995 and 1997; the première of the complete *Symphonia* took place on 25 April 1998 in Manchester. Like the *Three Occasions*, therefore, Partita, Adagio tenebroso and Allegro scorrevole can be played either separately or together. Almost inadvertently Carter had arrived at a symphonic form different from the intertwined movements of the Concerto for Orchestra and *A Symphony of Three Orchestras*. The three-movement structure of the Violin Concerto, composed between the two orchestral triptychs, shows that he was already moving in the direction of this new formal ideal. Instead of interweaving the contrasting structures of the music, he now erected discrete structures which, when brought together, reflect or complement each other. By their independence the three symphonic movements defy narrative, yet brought together they become a great summation of the composer's poetic world.

As if to ironize the monumental aspects of the project, Carter decided to base it on a Latin poem by the English metaphysical poet Richard Crashaw entitled 'Bulla,' or bubble. Crashaw's bubble is an emblem of poetry itself:

To be sure, I am the flower of air,
the star of the sea, as it were.
the golden wit of nature,
the pride of trifles and grief,
sweet and learned aimlessness,

the golden daughter of treachery,
the mother of the quick smile
I am the prize of flowing hope
   (trans. Phyllis Bowman)

Carter considered using the last Latin line 'sum fluxae pretiam spei' as the title for Partita, but he finally appended it to the title *Symphonia*.

The 'bubble' theme is emblematic not programmatic. Crashaw's poem does not play the role here that Carter had given the narrative structures of Lucretius, Perse or Crane. In the seventeenth century the bubble often appeared in pictures as a child's plaything emblematic of life's brevity. In Crashaw's poem, however, the bubble seems to be an emblem of art; the bubble is a transient mirror of human existence. In the lines Carter cites, Crashaw's bubble, the flower of the air, takes a view of art very similar to Calvino's idea of 'thoughtful lightness' and also reminiscent of late Stevens:

And yet nothing has been changed except what is
Unreal, as if nothing had been changed at all.

At the end of Bulla the bubble similarly celebrates its unreality:

I am charming, wanton, inconstant,
beautiful, gleaming and noble,
ornate, somewhat blooming, and fresh,
distinguished by snows, roses,
waves, fires, air,
painted, bejewelled, and golden,
O I am, of course, O nothing.

Carter decided on the character of his three movements from the inception, though the only explicit cross reference is between bars 19–33 of Partita and 8–25 of Adagio tenebroso. The three works are similar in their materials but strikingly contrasted in effect. Partita is explosive; Adagio tenebroso, darkly meditative; Allegro scorrevole, effervescent. Carter deliberately wrote a symphony without a 'finale.' Allegro scorrevole does not resolve the life-against-death contrast of the two earlier movements; moving ever upward in register, it celebrates its own gaudy lightness, like the golden bird in Stevens's last poem, whose 'fire-fangled feathers dangle down.'

PARTITA

Commissioned by the Chicago Symphony Orchestra. Completed 12 June 1993. First Performance, Chicago, 17 February 1994.

Carter's sketches contain a list of possible titles for the piece that became Partita: Windy City, Hocket, Figurations, Episodes, Diaphonic, Passing Measures, Intermittences (fr.) Mercurial, Constellations, Allegro spezzato. Chicago, of course, is the 'windy city,' but Carter had already written a 'wind' symphony; the final work, however, mirrors the energy of Chicago and the virtuosity of its great orchestra. The final choice of title, however, had European connotations. Partita is a word used to designate a baroque suite, but it also is the Italian word for a soccer game. Carter's Partita, far from being the autumnal work we might expect from an eighty-four year old composer, has the explosive energy of a World Cup match.

If Carter wanted to demonstrate that he still had all his creative energy, he may also have wanted to give the younger generation a lesson in the pleasures of modernism; the music is angular, brash, chaotic, unpredictable, violent and exhilarating; Carter compared its rapidly changing landscape to the view of the world from a jet plane. There are no themes and no 'form.' The only formal pattern that the listener may notice is a gradual movement in register. The music begins with a shrill chord that contains the highest and lowest notes possible; it ends with thick brass chords right in the middle of the orchestral range. This narrowing wedge-shaped motion is not carried out continuously, however. The music is also interrupted by a series of woodwind solos, for the English horn (bars 120–147), piccolo and flute (192–207), E flat clarinet (271–293) and bass clarinet (515–536). These solos do not give the music a concertante quality so much as they give a relief from the protean tutti writing that dominates the movement. Partita is an encyclopedia of the resources of a modern virtuoso orchestra. Late in his life Carter finally arrived at a truly orchestral style; his earlier orchestral pieces always seemed to aspire to the condition of chamber music. Here Carter no longer disassembles the orchestra; instead he exploits the connections between instrumental groups through constantly varied doublings. The orchestral writing is also more idiomatic in its demands than the earlier works; Carter now knows how to meet the orchestra on its own ground, as it were. There are far fewer tempo and meter changes and less divisi writing in the strings; yet the sound is vibrant.

The improvisatory surface of Partita might be compared to the events of a soccer game; every match is unpredictable, but the rules remain the same. The rules behind the music are rhythmic and harmonic. The rhythms have their source in a structural polyrhythm, which, according to the sketches, sounds every thirty-fifth sixteenth note against every thirty-fourth triplet eighth at a basic tempo of MM 105 to the quarter. The two systems are heard in the trombones and harp respectively in bars 19–35 as counterpoints to a slow expressive melody in the flutes and strings. Harmonically, the music is built on an all-interval 'Link' chord: [1 3 4 E 7 9 T 6 2 5 8]. The first six pitches of this chord form the all-triad hexachord 6–35; the remainder form the hexachord 6–36. Carter's sketches show that he used four versions of this chord which correspond in serial terms to the retrograde, inversion and retrograde inversion, though Carter uses them vertically, not as melodic series. The structure of the 'Link' chords, however, suggests a relationship between melodic statements, such as the wind solos, that are based on 6–35 and the chords that surround them.

ADAGIO TENEBROSO

Commissioned by the BBC for the one hundredth season of the Promenade Concerts. Dedicated to the Proms and to Amira and Alexander Goehr. Première, London, 13 September 1995, Andrew Davis, conductor.

Carter has written great slow movements, but nothing before like Adagio tenebroso. Listeners have been at a loss to explain its impact; I have heard comparisons to both Bruckner and Morton Feldman. Carter does not belong to any church and has never written religious music, but this movement implies both a solemn ritual and anguished meditation. 'Tenebroso' means dark; Carter has said that here the 'bubble' floats over the dark side of human experience. But the title also suggests the Tenebrae service when *Lamentations* is chanted and candles are gradually extinguished. Twenty minutes long, and without clear formal divisions, the movement, with its terrifying climax, seems to encompass all the suffering of the twentieth century. Its desolate, pain-filled landscape may stem from an early memory: 'Shortly after the war, at the beginning of the twenties, my father took me on a tour of the still horrifying battlefields of Metz, Reims and Verdun – deserted, chalky, ruined fields where only a few scraggly weeds would grow among rust barbed wire, and still strewn terribly with human vestiges.'[14]

The Adagio may be thought of as a chorale prelude reconceived in terms of Carter's rhythmic and harmonic language. Although the entire movement is written in an unchanging tempo and 4/4 meter, the actual rhythmic structure is based on a polyrhythm of every thirty-eighth triplet eighth against every thirty-third sixteenth. The two systems coincide on the downbeat of bar 28 and on the final chord on the third beat of bar 341. The slow regular pulses from these two rhythms are hidden in the texture but are stated explicitly more often than is Carter's usual practice; the relentless movement of the pulses gives the Adagio the feeling of a processional. The harmonic material of the movement derives from 'Link'

Ex. 71 Appearances of theme

chords: a good example appears at bars 44–45, using the intervals (from bottom to top) 2 5 8 6 1 3 4 E 7 9 T. At the center of this chord are the pitches (from bottom to top) A sharp, B, D, F sharp, F, C intervals: 1 3 4 E 7) which state the all-triad hexachord 6–35. The all-triad interval serves as the basis of most of the melodic material. The chorale 'melody' appears in two forms: at the opening (bars 2–25) it is stated in small intervals in the muted brass, violas and flutes beginning with a minor third from A to C, similar statements appear in the brass at 160–171 and, gradually fading away, 201–224. An expressive, large interval 'chorale melody' is launched in the first violins in bar 45 with the rising interval of a major sixth form C to A. A series of melodic phrases emphasize this melodic motif in a way that is unusual in Carter's music. The rising C to A sixth appears in bars 45, 49, 52, 55, 59, 62, 76–7, 78, then disappears until bars 148–9 (Ex. 71). The motif does not return after that; in the quiet passage immediately after the climax, however, there are a series of short phrases which seem to be looking for the motif without success. The motif is, in effect, a failed theme. Carter reiterates it at the opening of the movement to call attention to its absence later on. It may (or may not) be significant that the rising major sixth from C to A forms the opening interval of the Heiliger Dankgesang from Beethoven's op. 132. The Adagio's broken chain of expressive phrases seem to reject the possibility of Beethoven's prayer of thanks; Carter's music, instead, demands that the listener confront the horror which appears in its full extent in the protracted cry of pain in bars 273–284.

ALLEGRO SCORREVOLE

Commissioned by the Cleveland Orchestra. Première Cleveland 22 May 1997, Christopher von Dohnányi, conductor. Dedicated to the Cleveland Orchestra and Oliver Knussen.

Allegro scorrevole was originally commissioned by Zubin Mehta and the New York Philharmonic for the 150th anniversary of the orchestra. On 12 January 1996, Carter received a letter from Deborah Borda, executive Director of the NYPO, stating that the NYPO 'was unable to proceed with the commission.' According to the composer, the NYPO and its music director Kurt Masur had attached new requirements to the commission: Maestro Masur refused to make a commitment to perform the work until he had examined the score; the NYPO retained exclusive rights to a first recording. In tandem these conditions could have prevented a recording; Maestro Masur has never conducted any of Carter's music. The

Philharmonic denied that they intended to refuse the work, but Carter, who had written two major works for the NYPO, was insulted by the gesture of disrespect by the current musical director. In the *New York Times* on 29 June 1997, Paul Griffiths wrote, 'Reasonably enough, as a composer with an international reputation at the highest level and a man with half a century of published orchestral music behind him, Mr. Carter felt any uncertainty on the part of a commissioning institution to be unwarranted and undignified . . .'

From the inception of *Symphonia*, Carter had decided to end it with a 'Queen Mab scherzo.' Instead of a 'finale' his magnum opus would conclude with the shimmering, scurrying motion that Carter had first introduced in to his music in the Piano Sonata. Carter has said that nineteenth-century music often moves to the rhythm of an army marching across the land; his music moved at the speed of jet travel. Although the high tessitura and delicate orchestration of Allegro scorrevole is a tribute to Berlioz's marvelous portrait of Queen Mab, it is more dialectical in its form. The light, fast motion is opposed by a more traditional lyricism which is finally overcome. The upward motion of the piece suggests an early favorite of Carter's, Scriabin's 'Vers la flamme.'

Carter has described Allegro scorrevole as follows:

> [it] consists primarily of a continuous flow of soft, rapid passages that move over the entire range of the sound spectrum, and here and there form into thematic material. Against this is a lyrical idea also developed throughout, sometimes slowing down to hesitantly separated notes and at other times tightly joined together to form intensely expressive lines.

The two main elements in the piece are clearly contrasted. The filigree moves around the orchestra in a buzz of small intervals. The lyrical idea appears only in the strings and moves in large intervals. As in the Oboe Concerto, Carter is building a structure out of the contrast of light and heavy ideas. The lyrical idea here seems to continue the mood of the Adagio tenebroso, while the scorrevole figures feel like an ever-rising current of fresh air. The presence or absence of the lyrical idea divides the movement into three large sections, 1–74, 75–145, 146–214 plus a coda; or ABA¹C. In the opening A section the lyrical idea interrupts the flow of the scorrevole and seems to pull the tempo back. In B a series of delicate solos based on the small-interval scorrevole material take over the melodic function from the lyrical idea: flute 75–85; oboe, 88–97; solo violin

125–145. In A′ the two elements are superimposed, rather than alternating as they had in A, so that the lyrical idea now seems buoyed up by the rapid tempo of the scorrevole. The lyrical idea culminates in a climactic phrase beginning at 180, which reaches a high D at 199. From then on it is transformed from a string melody to dense brass chords which converge with the scorrevole material at the movement's high point, bar 215. In the coda the scorrevole moves ever upward; the movement ends with the highest G sharp on the piccolo, a prize of flowing hope (Ex. 72).

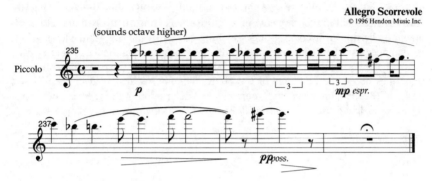

Ex. 72 Ending

Notes

1 A reviewer, Bernard Rogers, wrote that 'Carter can write a tune, but he can also surround it with an esoteric tonal haze.' *Modern Music* XXI, 4 (May–June 1944), p. 248.
2 RFG, p. 68.
3 WEC, pp. 308–9.
4 Quoted in Stefan Jarocinski, *Debussy: Impressionism and Symbolism* (London, Eulenburg, 1976), p. 139.
5 St. John Perse, *Vents* ('Winds'), trans. Hugh Chisolm (New York; Pantheon Books, Bollingen Series No. 34, 1953).
6 Robert Lowell, *Life Studies* (New York, Farrar, Straus and Cudahy, 1959).
7 *The Complete Poems of Hart Crane* (New York, Liveright, 1958), p. 3.
8 Ibid.
9 Ibid., pp. 38–9.
10 Ibid., p. 13.
11 Ibid., p. 17.
12 Ibid., p. 139.
13 Ibid., p. 163.
14 FW, p. 49.

APPENDIX A: *Carter's Listing of Three- to Six-Note Chords; 'Link' Chords*

Computations of all possible chords in the chromatic scale have been made by Haba, Slonimsky, Schillinger, and more recently by Allen Forte, who introduced the term 'pitch-class set' and the use of set theory into this field of speculation. Carter began to make his own list of chords around the time of the Piano Concerto. His method was intuitive and pragmatic, related to the compositional needs at hand. His ordering differs from Forte's, but they agree on basic definitions and on the number of chords. Although Carter's numbering is in no way superior to Forte's, his habitual use of his own numbering in discussing and sketching his music makes a knowledge of his system necessary for a detailed understanding of the music. In the list of chords given below the order number appears first, and the numbers inside the parentheses indicate semitones above the first note of the chord. The chords are given in their closest position. (Readers interested in a more detailed description of the premises of this list should see Allen Forte, *The Structure of Atonal Music* (New Haven, 1973) pp. 1–21.)

Three-note chords

1 (0 4 8)	7 (0 1 6)
2 (0 3 6)	8 (0 2 6)
3 (0 2 4)	9 (0 1 5)
4 (0 1 2)	10 (0 2 5)
5 (0 2 7)	11 (0 1 4)
6 (0 3 7)	12 (0 1 3)

Four-note chords

1 (0 1 2 3)	16 (0 2 4 8)
2 (0 1 6 7)	17 (0 1 2 4)
3 (0 2 3 5)	18 (0 1 4 6) all-interval
4 (0 2 5 7)	19 (0 1 5 7)
5 (0 3 6 9)	20 (0 1 2 5)
6 (0 1 2 7)	21 (0 1 4 7)
7 (0 1 3 6)	22 (0 1 2 6)
8 (0 1 4 5)	23 (0 1 3 7) all-interval
9 (0 1 3 4)	24 (0 3 4 8)
10 (0 1 5 6)	25 (0 2 3 7)
11 (0 2 4 6)	26 (0 1 3 5)
12 (0 2 6 8)	27 (0 2 4 7)
13 (0 3 4 7)	28 (0 2 3 6)
14 (0 3 5 8)	29 (0 2 5 8)
15 (0 1 5 8)	

Five-note chords

1 (0 1 2 3 4)	11 (0 1 2 3 5)	21 (0 1 4 5 8)	31 (0 1 3 6 7)
2 (0 2 3 4 6)	12 (0 1 2 3 6)	22 (0 1 3 5 7)	32 (0 1 3 6 8)
3 (0 3 4 5 8)	13 (0 1 2 3 7)	23 (0 1 3 5 8)	33 (0 1 3 6 9)
4 (0 1 2 6 8)	14 (0 1 2 4 5)	24 (0 2 3 5 8)	34 (0 1 3 7 8)
5 (0 1 3 5 6)	15 (0 1 2 4 6)	25 (0 2 3 5 7)	35 (0 1 4 5 7)
6 (0 2 4 6 8)	16 (0 1 2 4 7)	26 (0 2 4 5 8)	36 (0 2 3 6 8)
7 (0 2 4 7 9)	17 (0 1 2 4 8)	27 (0 1 2 5 6)	37 (0 1 4 6 8)
8 (0 1 4 7 8)	18 (0 2 3 4 7)	28 (0 1 2 5 7)	38 (0 1 4 7 9)
9 (0 2 4 6 9)	19 (0 1 3 4 6)	29 (0 1 2 5 8)	
10 (0 1 3 4 8)	20 (0 1 3 4 7)	30 (0 1 2 6 7)	

Six-note chords

1 (0 2 4 6 8 10)	14 (0 2 3 5 6 9)	27 (0 2 3 5 6 8)	40 (0 1 2 4 6 9)
2 (0 1 4 5 8 9)	15 (0 1 3 6 7 9)	28 (0 2 3 4 6 9)	41 (0 2 3 4 5 8)
3 (0 1 3 4 5 8)	16 (0 1 2 3 6 7)	29 (0 1 3 4 6 7)	42 (0 1 3 4 5 7)
4 (0 1 2 3 4 5)	17 (0 1 2 5 7 8)	30 (0 1 2 3 6 9)	43 (0 1 3 5 6 8)
5 (0 2 3 4 5 7)	18 (0 2 3 5 7 9)	31 (0 1 4 6 7 9)	44 (0 1 2 4 7 9)
6 (0 2 4 5 7 9)	19 (0 1 2 3 4 6)	32 (0 1 3 6 8 9)	45 (0 1 2 3 6 8)
7 (0 1 2 6 7 8)	20 (0 1 2 3 5 7)	33 (0 1 2 5 6 7)	46 (0 1 2 4 6 7)
8 (0 1 4 5 7 9)	21 (0 1 3 5 6 9)	34 (0 1 2 3 7 8)	47 (0 1 2 4 5 7)
9 (0 1 3 5 7 9)	22 (0 1 3 4 7 9)	35 (0 1 2 4 7 8) all-triad	48 (0 1 2 3 5 8)
10 (0 1 2 4 6 8)	23 (0 1 2 3 4 8)	36 (0 1 2 5 6 8)	49 (0 1 2 3 5 6)
11 (0 1 4 5 6 8)	24 (0 1 2 4 5 6)	37 (0 1 3 4 7 8)	50 (0 1 2 3 4 7)
12 (0 2 3 4 6 8)	25 (0 1 2 5 7 9)	38 (0 1 2 5 6 9)	
13 (0 1 2 4 5 8)	26 (0 1 3 5 7 8)	39 (0 1 3 4 6 8)	

"Link" chords: all-interval 12-note sets containing statements of 6–35 (all-triad hexachord)

Numbers signify intervals in half-steps; A = 10, B = 11.

214376598BA – 43765	14B6A783529 – 78352	4769B251A38 – 9B251
214976538BA – 49765	176852B34A9 – 52B34	18A352B7964 – 352B7
274316B985A – 4316B	134B78526A9 – 134B7	416352B7A98 – 352B7
274916B385A – 4916B	134B79A6258 – 134B7	4618A352B79 – 352B7
4BA85692317 – A8569	2586134B79A – 134B7	361A872495B – 361A8
179236B8A54 – 236B8	2B86794513A – 79451	2654A1783B9 – A1783
47B9685123A – 85123	1A63B874259 – 74259	269A1783B45 – A1783
5B316724A98 – 16724	3B87425961A – 74259	2965387B41A – 65387
125634A97B8 – 25634	259164738BA – 91647	2B465387A19 – 65387
5B376124A98 – 76124	2B91647385A – 91647	4B2683A5179 – B2683
25189AB7463 – 25189	19742538B6A – 97425	4B8623A5179 – B8623
3625189AB74 – 25189	197425A6B83 – 97425	43826BA5179 – 3826B
2587B43169A – B4316	1A974253B68 – 97425	2654B3871A9 – B3871
18734B5296A – 34B52	26B451A7389 – 451A7	269B3871A45 – B3871

329B71A4568 – 29B71
5429B71A368 – 29B71
142965837BA – 29658
4B29658A317 – 29658
26359817A4B – 59817
26B459817A3 – 59817
2B783A51469 – 2B783
187B259436A – B2594
1852B43769A – B4376
35681A7942B – 1A794
14B379A6528 – 79A65
179A65234B8 – 79A65
145638B729A – 8B729
368B729451A – 8B729
38B7295416A – 8B729
38B729A6145 – 8B729
415368B729A – 8B729
1852B79463A – B7946
2653B718A49 – B718A
137B982456A – 7B982
1456A729B83 – 729B8
1456A982B73 – 982B7
5217B9A4368 – 17B9A
14598B63A72 – 8B63A
18B63A79452 – 8B63A
3A17B924568 – A17B9
54A17B92368 – A17B9
179245A8B63 – A8B63
179A8B63254 – A8B63
1974A8B6352 – A8B63
2143B86597A – B8659
2743B86591A – B8659
4AB86592317 – B8659
21A8B956347 – 1A8B9
267431A8B95 – 1A8B9
347621A8B95 – 1A8B9

134B7 – 134B78526A9
134B7 – 134B79A6258
134B7 – 2586134B79A
152B9 – 83A152B9674
15497 – A31549768B2
16724 – 5B316724A98
1783B – 54A1783B962
1783B – 9A1783B4562
17892 – 863A1789245

17B92 – 8654A17B923
17B9A – 5217B9A4368
1A794 – 35681A7942B
1A8B9 – 21A8B956347
1A8B9 – 267431A8B95
1A8B9 – 347621A8B95
1A8B9 – 3521A8B9674
1A8B9 – 46731A8B925
1A8B9 – 5267341A8B9
236B8 – 179236B8A54
25189 – 25189AB7463
3521A8B9674 – 1A8B9
46731A8B925 – 1A8B9
5267341A8B9 – 1A8B9
43A9B865217 – 9B865
25691A8B473 – 91A8B
591A8B26347 – 91A8B
25189 – 3625189AB74
25387 – 925387A6B41
25634 – 125634A97B8
25B43 – A6925B43781
289B7 – A654289B731
29658 – 1429658378A
29658 – 4B29658A317
29B71 – 329B71A4568
29B71 – 5429B71A368
2B783 – 2B783A51469
32158 – A3215869B74
3268B – 9715A3268B4
34B52 – 18734B5296A
352B7 – 18A352B7964
352B7 – 416352B7A98
352B7 – 4618A352B79
361A8 – 361A872495B
36B8A – 2536B8A4791
36B8A – 36B8A542971
36B8A – 45236B8A971
3826B – 43826BA5179
18A497B3562 – A497B
2618A497B35 – A497B
23689B7A145 – 689B7
134B79A6258 – B79A6

3862B – 9715A3862B4
3871A – 54B3871A962
3871A – 9B3871A4562

387B2 – 96415A387B2
42167 – 89A421673B5
42761 – 89A427613B5
4316B – 274316B985A
43652 – 8B79A436521
43765 – 214376598BA
43B25 – 9A43B258671
451A7 – 26B451A7389
4916B – 274916B385A
4952B – A634952B781
49765 – 214976538BA
497A1 – B2497A18653
52479 – 38B6A524791
52479 – 86B352479A1
52479 – A6B83524791
52B34 – 176852B34A9
56734 – AB895673412
56794 – AB835679412
568B9 – 712568B9A34
56A97 – 8256A973B41
56A97 – 8B43256A971
59817 – 26359817A4B
59817 – 26B459817A3
6134B – A96134B7852
6497B – A36497B2581
65387 – 2965387B41A
65387 – 2B465387A19
6734B – A96734B2581
689B7 – 23689B7A145
6A978 – 8526A97B431
71895 – 3A718954B62
71895 – B4A71895362
729B8 – 1456A729B83
74259 – 1A63B874259
74259 – 3B87425961A
74619 – A58374619B2
74619 – AB837461952
76124 – 5B376124A98
78352 – 14B6A783529
78356 – 91A783564B2
78356 – A14B7835692
79451 – 2B86794513A
79A65 – 14B379A6528
79A65 – 179A65234B8
7A154 – 9837A154B62
7B253 – 4697B253A81

7B253 – 89A7B253614	927B8 – A927B863514	A497B – 18A497B3562
7B253 – 97B253A8164	95247 – 952478B36A1	A497B – 2618A497B35
7B289 – 37B289A6541	95247 – A16952478B3	A817B – 94A817B3562
7B431 – 8526A97B431	9568B – 71329568BA4	A8569 – 4BA85692317
7B431 – 9A62587B431	9568B – A19568B3472	A8B63 – 179245A8B63
7B431 – A97B4316852	9568B – A79568B3412	A8B63 – 179A8B63254
7B982 – 137B982456A	9658A – 71329658AB4	A8B63 – 1974A8B6352
7B986 – 541A7B98632	97425 – 19742538B6A	A9B71 – 8634A9B7125
85123 – 47B9685123A	97425 – 197425A6B83	B2594 – 187B259436A
85692 – 713A85692B4	97425 – 1A974253B68	B2683 – 4B2683A5179
85692 – AB738569241	98152 – 3647BA98152	B3871 – 2654B3871A9
8A163 – B594278A163	98152 – 47BA9815263	B3871 – 269B3871A45
8B632 – 45A8B632971	982B7 – 1456A982B73	B4316 – 2587B43169A
8B63A – 14598B63A72	9B251 – 4769B251A38	B4376 – 1852B43769A
8B63A – 18B63A79452	9B71A – 86329B71A45	B6134 – A589B613472
8B729 – 145638B729A	9B71A – 865429B71A3	B6194 – A583B619472
8B729 – 368B729451A	9B865 – 43A9B865217	B6283 – 9715AB62834
8B729 – 38B7295416A	9B8A1 – 4769B8A1253	B718A – 2653B718A49
8B729 – 38B729A6145	9B8A1 – 529B8A13764	B7946 – 1852B79463A
8B729 – 415368B729A	9B8A1 – 59B8A126743	B794A – 2653B794A81
8B927 – 38B927A6541	9B8A1 – 59B8A134762	B794A – 53B794A8162
91647 – 259164738BA	9B8A1 – 743659B8A12	B79A6 – 134B79A6258
91647 – 2B91647385A	9B8A1 – 9B8A1437625	B8623 – 4B8623A5179
91A8B – 25691A8B473	A1783 – 2654A1783B9	B8659 – 2143B86597A
91A8B – 591A8B26347	A1783 – 269A1783B45	B8659 – 2743B86591A
927B8 – 5416A927883	A17B9 – 3A17B924568	B8659 – 4AB86592317
927B8 – A154927B863	A17B9 – 54A17B92368	B8A19 – 374B8A19652
927B8 – A6145927B83	A36B8 – 25497A36B81	B8A19 – 74362B8A195
927B8 – A927B836541	A36B8 – 27A36B89541	

APPENDIX B: *Carter's Note on* Voyage

A Commentary on the Poem by the Composer

To help the singer (and possibly the listener) in forming an interpretation of the text of this song (the third in a series of six 'Voyages' by Hart Crane), it would perhaps be pertinent to describe something of what it has meant to the composer.

As with most poetry, this poem can be read in several ways. I venture neither to deal with them exhaustively nor least of all to construct a definitive interpretation. In the music I have tried to reflect its poetic meaning and lyrical beauty. Without going into the psychological and emotional implications which every line challenges, I would like to give a short account of its meaning (for me) on the most matter-of-fact level.

There are three protagonists: the Sea which is the medium through which everything in the poem moves and changes and to which every idea is referred, Love (to whom the poem is addressed) and the Poet.

The argument (stripped of symbols and conditions) runs something like this: since Love is never far from his thoughts and represents the most desirable of conditions (first section, lines 1–8) the Poet entreats Love to allow him to go safely through an ordeal which will bring him under Love's power (second section, lines 1–8).

The Sea is thought of under several aspects. In the first section, the relation of sea to sky suggests the unifying, harmonizing power of love; while in the second, the sea forms an obstacle to be voyaged through to reach Love. At the end of each part, the transforming power of the sea (with the peril of loss of identity) looms up as a danger which, by implication, is like that of love. This transforming power is exemplified in the ordering of images and ideas in the poem itself, which uses many metaphors and moves rapidly from one level of meaning to another.

Love, in the same manner, is in one place an actual person and in another seems transformed into the principle or power under whose spell the Poet wishes to come. In the following line-by-line analysis, I assume (for purposes of simplicity) that the poem is addressed to the power, Love, although it can just as well be explained in terms of a particular person. In this respect the poem has a double meaning.

The Poet first envisions the Sea as bearing a relationship infinite in time, in space as well as in proximity to all things. It is like the mother of all; like a great blood stream uniting all in a common bond (line 1).

Considered from this point of view, which was suggested by the close relationship of sea and sky that the light of day reveals, the sea is comparable to love (lines 2–4).

Coming down to the particular scene or experience that may have suggested the poem, the Poet then describes his beloved and himself swimming in the sea. He follows no path far removed from his beloved, and, maintaining the level of meaning taken for the first four lines, this would naturally imply that his thoughts are constantly with Love (lines 5–7).

The section closes with a hint of the dangers lurking in the sea pictured as grasping at both swimmers with hand-like waves that could transform them into relics by disintegrating their bodies (lines 7–8). In another poem, Crane wrote: 'The dice of drowned men's bones', which suggests the meaning implied here.

In the second section (which is one long sentence: 'And so, . . . Permit me voyage, love, into your hands . . .'), the Poet turns to consider the ordeal he must undergo in order to come under the spell of Love. Using other elements of the swimming scene, the ordeal is represented metaphorically as a voyage into the depths, a rise to the surface and a swim over the waves to reach the floating body of his beloved. The different depths of the sea suggest a turbulent architectural façade before which he rises, with gates at the bottom, pillars and pediments above them, and on top a roof of waves reflecting glittering lights and stars (lines 9–14).

Then once again the Poet becomes aware of the danger involved in the voyage. Death at sea is not bloody but a disintegration into relics scattered over the bottom from one end of the world to the other. It is like the transformation of a poet's experience that suffers disintegration and reorganization into word-relics made into a poem by the subtle poetic art (lines 14–15).

In the final line the Poet asks permission of Love to be allowed to complete his ordeal or voyage safely and to come under its power, wishing to surrender himself wholly to it.

I have purposely avoided an attempt to explain the ordeal described metaphorically in the poem, for that would involve a much lengthier discussion than there is room for here. Certainly the tragic career of Hart Crane himself throws one kind of light on the matter. In fact, viewed autobiographically, this particular work can be considered as a prophecy of his own personal voyage through life, which met its end when he wilfully extinguished himself in the hands of the sea.

Elliott Carter
(1945)

Chronological Catalogue of Works

1928 *My love is in a light attire*; for voice and piano. Unpublished.

1931 Incidental music for Sophocles' *Philoctetes*; for baritone, tenor, men's chorus and chamber orchestra. 1st perf. Harvard Classical Club, 15 March 1933. Unpublished.

1936 Incidental music for Plautus' *Mostellaria*; for baritone, tenor, men's chorus and chamber orchestra. 1st perf. Harvard Classical Club, 15 April 1936. Unpublished.
Tarantella (finale to Mostellaria); for men's chorus (TTBB) and piano 4-hands or orchestra. 1st perf. Harvard Glee Club, G. Wallace Woodworth, cond., 29 April 1937. Pub. AMP (piano version).

1937 *Let's Be Gay*; for women's chorus (SSAA) and 2 pianos. 1st perf. Wells College Glee Club, Nicholas Nabokov, cond., Spring 1938. Revised version (1997) published by B&H.
Harvest Home; for chorus (SATB) a cappella. 1st perf. Lehman Engel Madrigal Singers, New York, Spring 1938. Revised version (1997) published by B&H.
To Music; for mixed chorus (SSAATTBB) a cappella. 1st perf. Lehman Engel Madrigal Singers, New York, Spring 1938. Pub. Peer.

1938 *Prelude, Fanfare and Polka*; for small orchestra. Unpublished.
Tell Me Where Is Fancy Bred; for alto voice and guitar. Recorded by Orson Welles and the Mercury Theater as incidental music for The Merchant of Venice. Pub. AMP (1972) guitar part ed. Stanley Silverman.
Heart Not So Heavy As Mine; for chorus (SATB) a cappella. 1st perf. Temple Emanu-El Choir, Lazare Saminsky, cond., New York, 31 March 1939. Pub. AMP (originally Arrow Music Press).

1939 *Pocahontas*; Ballet Legend in one act for orchestra. 1st perf. Ballet Caravan, Fritz Kitzinger, cond., New York, 24 May 1939. Pub. AMP.
Suite from Pocahontas. Pub. Edwin Kalmus; revised version (1961) AMP.
Canonic Suite (Musical Studies); (a) for Quartet of alto saxophones. Pub. BMI, 1945; revised version (1984) AMP; (b) revised for four clarinets (1956). Pub. AMP; Andante espressivo, a fourth study, unpublished.
Elegy (Adagio); (a) for cello and piano. Unpublished; (b) for string quartet (rev. 1946) 1st perf. Lanier Quartet, Eliot, Maine, 21 August 1946. Pub. Peer; (c) for string orchestra (rev. 1952). 1st perf. David Boekman, cond., New York, 1 March 1953. Pub. Peer; (d) for viola and piano (rev. 1961). 1st perf. George Humphrey, viola; Alice Canady, piano, Cambridge, Mass. 16 April 1963. Pub. Peer.

1940 *Pastoral*; for viola or English horn or clarinet and piano. 1st perf. Ralph Hersh, viola; Elliott Carter, piano, New York, 1942. Joseph Marx, English horn, 12 November 1944. Pub. New Music 18 No. 3 (April 1945); Presser.

1941 *The Defense of Corinth*; for speaker, men's chorus and piano 4-hands. 1st perf. Harvard Glee Club, G. Wallace Woodworth, cond. 12 March 1942. Pub. Presser.

1942 *Symphony No. 1*; for orchestra. 1st perf. Eastman-Rochester Symphony Orchestra, Howard Hanson, cond., 27 April 1944. Pub. AMP (revised 1954 version).
Three Poems by Robert Frost; for voice and piano; i. 'Dust of Snow'; ii. 'The Rose Family'; iii. 'The Line Gang'. Pub. AMP.

1943 *Warble for Lilac Time*; for soprano or tenor and piano, or soprano and small orchestra. 1st perf. Helen Boatwright, Yaddo orchestra; Frederick Fennell, cond., Saratoga Springs, NY, 14 September 1946. Pub. Peer.
Voyage; for medium voice and piano; orch. version 1975. 1st perf. Helen Boatwright, soprano; Helmut Baerwald, piano, New York, 16 March 1947. Pub. AMP (originally Valley Music Press).

1944 *The Difference*; for soprano, baritone and piano. Unpublished.
Holiday Overture; for orchestra. 1st perf. Frankfurt Symphony Orchestra, Hans Blumer, cond., 1946. Pub. Arrow Press; rev. (1961) AMP.
The Harmony of Morning; for women's chorus (SSAA) and chamber orchestra. 1st perf. Temple Emanu-El Choir, Lazare Saminsky, cond., New York, 25 February 1945. Pub. AMP.

1945 *Musicians Wrestle Everywhere*; for chorus (SSATB) with optional string accompaniment. 1st perf. Randolph Singers, David Randolph, cond., New York, 12 February 1946. Pub. Presser (originally Mercury).

1946 *Piano Sonata*. 1st perf. Webster Aiken, New York, 16 February 1947 (broadcast); James Sykes, New York, 5 March 1947. Pub. Presser (Originally Mercury).

1947 *The Minotaur*; Ballet in one act and two scenes for orchestra. 1st perf. Ballet Society, Leon Barzin, cond., New York, 26 March 1947. Pub. AMP.
Suite from The Minotaur. Pub. AMP (1956).
Emblems; for men's chorus (TTBB) and piano solo. 1st perf. Harvard Glee Club, G. Wallace Woodworth, cond. (Part II only), New York, 3 April 1951; Colgate College Singers (first complete concert performance) European tour, summer 1952. Pub. Presser (originally Mercury).

1948 *Woodwind Quintet*. 1st perf. Martin Oberstein, flute, David Abosch, oboe, Louis Paul, clarinet, Pinson Bobo, horn, Mark Popkin, bassoon, New York, 27 February 1949. Pub. AMP.
Sonata for Violoncello and Piano. 1st perf. Bernard Greenhouse, cello, Anthony Makas, piano, New York, 27 February 1950. Pub. AMP (originally Society for the Publication of Amercian Music).

1949 *Eight Etudes and a Fantasy*; for flute, oboe, clarinet and bassoon. 1st perf. New York Woodwind Quintet: Murray Panitz, flute, Jerome Roth, oboe, David Glazer, cello, Bernard Garfield, bassoon, New York, 28 October 1952. Pub. AMP.

1950 Timpani Pieces: i. Recitative and Improvisation. Pub. AMP (1960); ii. Saëta, Moto Perpetuo, Canaries, March. Pub. AMP with above and Adagio and Canto of 1966 (q.v.) as *Eight Pieces for Four Timpani*; all revised in 1966 with the assistance of Jan Williams.

1951   *String Quartet No. 1.* 1st perf. Walden Quartet, Homer Schmitt, Bernard Goodman, John Garvey, Robert Swenson, New York, 26 February 1953. Pub. AMP.

1952   *Sonata for Flute, Oboe, Cello and Harpsichord.* 1st perf. Harpsichord Quartet, Sylvia Marlowe, harpsichord, Claude Monteux, flute, Henry Shulman, oboe, Bernard Greenhouse, cello, New York, 19 November 1953. Pub. AMP.

1953–55 *Variations for Orchestra.* 1st perf. Louisville Orchestra, Robert Whitney, cond., Louisville, Kentucky, 21 April 1956. Pub. AMP.

1959   *String Quartet No. 2.* 1st perf. Juilliard Quartet: Robert Mann, Isidore Cohen, Raphael Hillyer, Claus Adam; New York, 25 March 1960. Pub. AMP.

1961   *Double Concerto for Harpsichord and Piano with two chamber orchestras.* 1st perf. Ralph Kirkpatrick, harpsichord, Charles Rosen, piano, Gustav Meier, cond., New York, 6 September 1961. Pub. AMP.

1965   *Piano Concerto.* 1st perf. Jacob Lateiner, piano, Boston Symphony Orchestra, Erich Leinsdorf, cond., Boston, 6 January 1967. Pub. AMP.

1966   *Adagio* and *Canto* for Timpani. Pub. in *Eight Pieces for Four Timpani*, AMP

1969   *Concerto for Orchestra.* 1st perf. New York Philharmonic Orchestra, Leonard Bernstein, cond., New York, 5 February 1970. Pub. AMP.

1971   *String Quartet No. 3.* 1st perf. Juilliard Quartet: Robert Mann, Earl Carlyss, Samuel Rhodes and Claus Adam, New York, 23 January 1973. Pub. AMP.
       Canon for 3; in memoriam Igor Stravinsky for equal instrumental voices. 1st perf. Joel Timm, oboe, Alan Blustein, clarinet, James Stubb, trumpet, New York, 23 January 1972. Pub. AMP, also in Tempo No. 98.

1974   *Duo for Violin and Piano.* 1st perf. Paul Zukovsky, violin, Gilbert Kalish, piano, New York, 5 March 1975. Pub. AMP.
       Brass Quintet. 1st perf. American Brass Quintet: Robert Bidlecombe, Edward Birdwell, Louis Ranger, Raymond Mase and Herbert Rankin, BBC broadcast, 20 October 1974. Pub. AMP.
       A Fantasy on Purcell's 'Fantasia on One Note'; for brass quintet. 1st perf. American Brass Quintet, New York, January 1975. Pub. AMP.

1975   *A Mirror on Which to Dwell*; six poems of Elizabeth Bishop for soprano and chamber orchestra. 1st perf. Susan Davenny Wyner and Speculum Musicae, Richard Fitz, cond., New York, 24 February 1976. Pub. AMP.

1976   *A Symphony of Three Orchestras.* 1st perf. New York Philharmonic Orchestra, Pierre Boulez, cond., New York, 17 February 1977. Pub. AMP.

1978   *Birthday Fanfare*; for Sir William Glock's 70th, for 3 trumpets, vibraphone and glockenspiel. 1st perf. London, 3 May 1978. Unpublished.

Syringa; for mezz-soprano, baritone and chamber orchestra. 1st perf. Jan DeGaetani, Thomas Paul, Speculum Musicae, Harvey Sollberger, cond., New York, 10 December 1978. Pub. AMP.

1980 *Night Fantasies*; for piano. 1st perf. Ursula Oppens, Bath Festival, 2 June 1980.

[NB: All remaining works published by Boosey & Hawkes]

1981 *In Sleep, In Thunder*; six poems of Robert Lowell for tenor and chamber orchestra; 1st perf. Martyn Hill, London Sinfonietta, Oliver Knussen, cond., London, 27 October 1982.

1982 *Triple Duo*; for Flute, Clarinet, Violin, Cello, Piano and Percussion; 1st perf. The Fires of London, New York, 23 April 1983.

1983 *Changes*; for solo guitar; 1st perf. David Starobin, New York, 11 December 1983.

1984 *Riconoscenza per Goffredo Petrassi*; for solo violin. 1st perf. Pontino, Italy, 15 June 1984.
esprit rude/ esprit doux; for flute and clarinet; 1st perf. Südwestfunk, Baden-Baden, members of the Ensemble Intercontemporain: Lawrence Bauregard, flute, Alain Damiens, clarinet, 31 March 1985.
Canon for 4, Homage to William [Glock]; for flute, clarinet, violin and cello. 1st perf. Bath Festival, 8 June 1984.

1985 *Penthode*; for five instrumental quintets; 1st perf. Ensemble InterContemporain, Pierre Boulez, cond., London, 26 July 1985.
String Quartet No. 4. 1st perf. Composer's Quartet, Miami, 17 September 1986.

1986 *A Celebration of Some 100 × 150 Notes* (Three Occasions). 1st perf. Houston Symphony Orchestra, Sergiu Commissiona, cond., Houston 10 April 1987.

1987 *Oboe Concerto*. 1st perf. Heinz Holliger, oboe, Zurich Collegium Musicum, John Carewe, cond., Zurich, 17 June 1988.

1988 *Enchanted Preludes*; for flute and cello. 1st perf. Patricia Spencer, flute, Andre Emelianoff, cello, New York, 16 May 1988.
Remembrance (Three Occasions). 1st perf. Tanglewood Festival Orchestra, Oliver Knussen, cond., Tanglewood, 10 August 1988.
Birthday Flourish; for five trumpets or brass quintet. 1st performance of trumpet version by members of the San Francisco Symphony, Herbert Blomstedt, cond., 26 November 1988; 1st performance of brass quintet version by members of the Cincinnati Symphony, Jesus Lopez-Cobos, cond., Cincinnati, 20 January 1989.

1989 *Anniversary* (Three Occasions). 1st perf. BBC Symphony, Oliver Knussen, cond., London, 5 October 1989.

1990 *Violin Concerto*. 1st perf. Ole Böhn, violin, San Francisco Symphony, Herbert Blomstedt, cond., San Francisco, 2 May 1990.
Con Leggerezza Pensosa; for clarinet, violin and cello. 1st perf. Ciro Scarponi, clarinet, Jorge Risi, violin, Luigi Lanzillotta, cello, Latina, Italy, 29 September 1990.

1991 *Scrivo in vento*; flute solo. 1st perf. Robert Aitken, Avignon, 20 July 1991.
Quintet for Piano and Winds (oboe, clarinet, bassoon, horn) 1st perf. Heinz Holliger, oboe, Elmar Schmid, clarinet, Klaus Thunemann, bassoon, Radovan Vlatkovic, horn, Andras Schiff, piano, Cologne, 13 September 1992.

1992 *Trilogy*, for oboe and harp. i. Bariolage: 1st perf. Ursula Holliger, harp, Geneva, March 1992. ii. Inner Song: 1st perf., Heinz Holleger, Witten, Germany, April 1992. iii. Immer Neu: 1st perf. Ursula and Heinz Holliger, Pontino 30 June 1992.

1993 *Partita* (*Symphonia: Sum Fluxae Pretiam Spei*); 1st perf. Chicago Symphony, Daniel Barenboim, cond., Chicago, 17 February 1994.
Gra; for clarinet solo. 1st perf. Roland Dury, Pontino, 4 June 1993.

1994 *90+*; piano solo. 1st perf. Giuseppe Scotese, Pontino, 11 June 1994.
Fragment; for string quartet. 1st perf. Kronos Quartet, New York, 13 October 1994.
Of Challenge and of Love, Five Poems of John Hollander; soprano and piano. 1st perf. Lucy Shelton, soprano, John Constable, piano, Aldeburgh, 19 June 1995.

1995 *Adagio tenebroso* (*Symphonia: Sum Fluxae Pretiam Spei*) 1st perf. BBC symphony, Andrew Davis, cond., London, 13 September 1995.
esprit rude/ esprit doux II; for flute, clarinet and marimba. 1st perf. by members of the Chicago Symphony, Chicago, 31 March 1995.
Figment; for cello solo 1st perf. Thomas Demenga, New York, 8 May 1995.
String Quartet No. 5. 1st perf. Arditti Quartet, Antwerp, 19 September 1995.

1996 *Clarinet Concerto* 1st perf. Alain Damiens, clarinet, Ensemble InterContemporain, Pierre Boulez, cond., Paris, 10 January 1997.
A 6 Letter Letter; English horn solo. 1st perf. Heinz Holliger, Basel, 27 April 1996.

1997 *Allegro scorrevole* (*Symphonia: Sum Fluxae Pretiam Spei*) 1st perf. Cleveland Orchestra, Christoph von Dohnanyi, cond., Cleveland, 22 May 1997.
Shard; solo guitar. 1st perf. David Starobin, Humlebaek, Denmark, 11 June 1997.
Luimen; for trumpet, trombone, harp, vibraphone, mandoline and guitar. 1st perf, Nieuw Ensemble, Amsterdam, 31 March 1998.
Quintet for Piano and String Quartet. 1st perf. Ursula Oppens and the Arditti Quartet Washington D.C., 18 November 1998.
Symphonia: Sum Fluxae Pretiam Spei. 1st complete performance, BBC Symphony, Oliver Knussen, cond., Manchester, 25 April 1998.

1998 *What's Next?* Opera to a libretto by Paul Griffiths.

Selected Bibliography
compiled by John F. Link

Bibliographies and Discographies

Doering, William T. *Elliott Carter: A Bio-Bibliography.* Bio-bibliographies in Music, no. 51. Westpark, CT: Greenwood, 1993.
Elliott Carter; Sketches and Scores in Manuscript. New York: The New York Public Library and Readex Books, 1973.
Link, John F. *Elliott Carter: A Guide to Research.* New York and London: Garland, forthcoming, 1999.
Weber, Jerome. F. *Carter and Schuman.* Discography Series vol. 19. Utica, NY: J. F. Weber, 1978.
Whipple, Harold. 'An Elliott Carter Discography.' *Perspectives of New Music* 20 (1981–82): 169–181.

Writings by and Interviews with Elliott Carter

Collections

Carter (in Italian). Edited by Enzo Restagno. Torino: E.D.T. (Edizioni di Torino), 1989.
Collected Essays and Lectures, 1937–1995. Edited by Jonathan W. Bernard. Rochester, NY: University of Rochester Press, 1997.
Schiff, David, *Elliott Carter* (in Italian). Translated by F. Pontani Wagner and R. Pozzi. Napoli: Edizioni Scientifiche Italiane, 1990.
The Writings of Elliott Carter. Edited by Else Stone and Kurt Stone. Bloomington and London: Indiana University Press, 1977.

Other Sources

'Abseits des Mainstreams: Ein Gespräch mit dem amerikanischen Komponisten Elliott Carter.' Interview by Heinz Holliger, translated by Sigfried Schibli, *Neue Zeitschrift für Musik* 152, no. 3 (March 1991): 4–9.
    French translation (Elliott Carter: écrire par couches superposées), trans. Daniel Haefliger, *Dissonanz • Disonance* 31 (February 1992): 10–13. Also printed as 'Entretien avec Elliott Carter' in *Entretiens avec Elliott Carter,* 101–109. Geneva: Contrechamps Editions, 1992.
Autobiographical Sketch. In *The 25th Anniversary Report of the Harvard Class of 1930,* 165–169. Cambridge, MA: Harvard University Press, 1955.
Autobiographical Sketch. In *The 50th Anniversary Report of the Harvard Class of 1930,* 836-838. Cambridge, MA: Harvard University Press, 1980.
'La Base rhythmique de la musique américaine.' Translated by Jacques Demierre. *Contrechamps* 6 (April 1986): 105–111.
'Ben Weber and Virgil Thomson Questioned by Eight Composers.' *Possibilities* 1 (Winter 1947): 18–24.

'Composers by the Alphabet.' *Modern Music* 19, no. 1 (November–December 1941): 70–71.

'Concerto for Orchestra.' In Edward Downes, *The New York Philharmonic Guide to the Symphony*, 246–248. New York: Walker & Co., 1976.

'Conversation with Elliott Carter.' Interview by Benjamin Boretz. *Contemporary Music Newsletter* 2, no. 8 (November–December 1968), 1–4. Reprinted in revised form in *Perspectives of New Music* 8, no. 2 (Spring–Summer 1970): 1–22.

'Creators on Creating: Elliott Carter.' Interview by Leighton Kerner. *Saturday Review*, December 1980, 38–42.

'Elliott Carter.' Interview by Cole Gagne and Tracy Caras. In *Soundpieces: Interviews with American Composers*, 87–99. Metuchen NJ: Scarecrow Press, 1982.

'Elliott Carter.' Interview by Ruth Dreier. *Musical America* 108, no. 5 (November 1988): 6–10.

'Elliott Carter' (in Italian). Interview by Marvin A. Wolfthal. *Musica* 3, no. 14 (1979): 232–233.

'Elliott Carter' (in Italian). Interview by Raffaele Pozzi. *Piano Time* 24 (March 1985): 31–33. English translation (Elliott Carter: Talking to Raffaele Pozzi), trans. Louise Forster, *Tempo* 167 (December 1988): 14–17.

'Elliott Carter.' Interview by Richard Dufallo. In *Trackings*, 269–285. Oxford and New York: Oxford University Press, 1989.

'Elliott Carter: "A la manière de Rameau".' Interview by André Gauthier. *Les nouvelles littéraires* 55, no. 2569 (27 January–3 February 1977): 13.

'Elliott Carter: The Communication of Time.' Interview by Robert Hurwitz. *Changes* 78 (November 1972): 10–11.

Elliott Carter: In Conversation with Enzo Restagno for Settembre Musica 1989. Interview by Enzo Restagno. Translated by Katherine Silberblatt Wolfthal. I.S.A.M. Monographs, no. 32. Brooklyn, NY: Institute for Studies in American Music, 1989.

'Elliott Carter in Interview.' Interview by Sue Knussen. *Tempo* 197 (July 1996): 2–5.

'Elliott Carter Speaks About His Own Work and Directions of New Music.' Interview by David Sanders. *The World at Boston University*, special supplement 4, no. 23 (March 14, 1984): A–D.

'Elliott Carter: sulla musica moderna.' *Musica/Realtà* 5, no. 15 (December, 1984): 24–27.

'Elliott Carter's Imagery Drawn from Modern Life.' Interview by Robert Johnston. *Music Magazine* 8, no. 5 (November–December 1985): 12–14, 33.

'Entretien avec Elliott Carter.' Interview by Heinz Holliger. In *Entretiens avec Elliott Carter*, 101–109. Geneva: Contrechamps Editions, 1992.

'Expressionismus und amerikanische Musik.' Translated by Felix Meyer. In *Amerikanische Musik seit Charles Ives*, 275–287. Laaber: Laaber Verlag, 1987.

Flawed Words and Stubborn Sounds. Interview by Allen Edwards. New York: Norton, 1971.

    French translation of excerpts (Une Conversation avec Elliott Carter), trans. Suzanne Rollier, in *Entretiens avec Elliott Carter*, 9–85. Geneva: Contrechamps Editions, 1992.

Foreword to *Selected Essays and Reviews 1948–1968*, by Richard Franko Goldman, edited by Dorothy Klotzman, vii–ix. Brooklyn, NY: Institute for Studies in American Music, 1980.

'Fragment.' Musical Supplement in *Tempo* 192 (April 1995): 1–7.

'France Amérique Ltd.' In *Paris–New York*, 7–11. Paris: Centre national d'art et de culture Georges Pompidou/Musée national d'art moderne, 1977.

'Für Pierre zum Sechzigsten.' In *Pierre Boulez: Eine Festschrift zum 60. Geburtstag am 26. März 1985*, translated by Josef Häusler, 14–15. Vienna: Universal Edition, 1985.

'Gentility and Apocalypse; Elliott Carter.' Interview by Andrew Ford. In *Composer to Composer: Conversations about Contemporary Music*, 2–9. St. Leonards, Australia: Allen & Unwin, 1993. London: Quartet, 1993.

'IGNM-Jury vor neuen Problemen.' Translated by Gertrud Marbach. *Melos* 27, no.6 (June 1960): 165–166.

'In Memoriam: Paul Fromm.' In *A Life for New Music: Selected Papers of Paul Fromm*, edited by David Gable and Cristoph Wolff, 8–9. Cambridge, MA: Department of Music, Harvard University, 1988.

'An Interview with Elliott Carter.' Interview by Charles Rosen. In *The Musical Languages of Elliott Carter*, 33–43. Washington: Library of Congress, 1984.
     French translation (Entretien avec Elliott Carter), trans. Carlo Russi, *Contrechamps* 6 (April 1986): 112–122. Revised version in *Entretiens avec Elliott Carter*, 87–109. Geneva: Contrechamps Editions, 1992.

'An Interview with Elliott Carter.' Interview by Jonathan W. Bernard. *Perspectives of New Music* 28, no. 2 (Summer 1990): 180–214.

Introduction to *Mademoiselle: Conversations with Nadia Boulanger*, by Bruno Monsaingeon, 12–13. Manchester: Carcanet Press, 1985.

'Letter to the Editor.' *Journal of Music Theory* 7, no. 2 (Winter 1963): 270–273.

'Letter to the Editor.' *Musical America* 84, no. 7 (September 1964): 4.

'Mozart's Human Touch.' *Musical Times* 132 (November 1991): 549.

'Music of the Twentieth Century.' In *Encyclopaedia Britannica*, vol. 16, 16–18. Chicago: Encyclopaedia Britannica, 1953.

'La Musique américaine: une plante dépaysée.' Translated by Thierry Beauvert. *Le monde de la musique* 117 (December 1988): 92.

'La Musique aux États-Unis.' *Synthèses* 9, no. 96 (May 1954): 206–211.

'La Musique et l'écran du temps' (Music and the Time Screen). Translated by Stéphane Goldet. *Entre temps* 4 (June 1987): 55–67.

'La Musique sérielle aujourd'hui.' *Preuves* 177 (November 1965): 32–33.

'The New Compositions: the Trend is to the Clear and Intelligible.' *Saturday Review* 27, no. 4 (22 January 1944): 32–33.

Notes for sound recording of Elliott Carter, *Night Fantasies* and *Piano Sonata*, Nonesuch 79047–1.

'One Touch of Venus' (in German). In *Über Kurt Weill*, translated by Josef Heinzelmann, edited by David Drew, 137–138. Frankfurt am Main: Suhrkamp Verlag, 1975.

'Orchestra, Audience, Musical Problems: As Seen by Elliott Carter.' Interview by George Gelles. *The Boston Sunday Globe*, September 12, 1965, sec. A, p. 39.

'Un paso adelante' (A Further Step). *Buenos Aires Musical* 14 numero speciale (December 1959): 63–67.

Program Note to *String Quartet No. 1*. 1994 edition. New York: Associated Music
Publishers, 1994.

'Reel Vs Real' *Newsletter of the American Symphony League* 11, no. 5–6 (July 1960); 8–10.

'Riflessioni su *Tre per sette*.' In *Petrassi*, edited by Enzo Restagno, 310–312. Torino:
E.D.T. (Edizioni di Torino), 1986.

'Roger Sessions, 1896–1985.' *Proceedings of the American Academy of Arts and Letters
and the National Institute of Arts and Letters*, second series, no. 36 (1985): 57–62.

'Roger Sessions Admired.' *Perspectives of New Music* 23, no. 2 (Spring–Summer 1985):
120–122.

'Stefan Wolpe 1902–1972.' *Proceedings of the American Academy of Arts and Letters and
the National Institute of Arts and Letters*, second series, no. 23 (1973): 115–117.

'Le Temps restitué.' Interview by Patrick Szersnovicz. *Le Monde de la musique* 117
(December 1988): 90–94.

'To the Editor.' *Music Library Association Notes* 41, no. 1 (1984): 195.

'Le Tournant des années cinquante.' In *Acanthes, An XV: Composer, enseigner, jouer la
musique d'aujourd'hui*, edited by Cécile Gilly and Claude Samuel, 136–143. Paris: Van
De Velde, 1991.

'Tribute to Paul Jacobs.' Eulogy given on 27 September, 1983, during funeral services
for Paul Jacobs, reprinted in the program book from 'A Concert In Memory of Paul
Jacobs,' 24 February, 1984, Symphony Space, New York, NY.

'Variations for Orchestra.' In Edward Downes, *The New York Philharmonic Guide to
the Symphony*, 250–25 1. New York: Walker & Co., 1976.

'What is American Music?' *Österreichische Musikzeitschrift* 31, no. 10 (October 1976)
special English issue: 4–6. Simultaneously published in German
translation (Was ist amerikanische Musik?) in the regular German version of the
same issue: 468–470.

'What's New in Music.' *Saturday Review*, 20 January 1945, 13–14, 34.

Carter, Elliott and Goffredo Petrassi, 'Goffredo Petrassi, Elliott Carter: cronaca di
un'amicizia.' Interview with Roman Vlad. Edited by Raffaele Pozzi. *Piano Time* 30
(September 1985): 32–37.

Carter, Elliott, et al. 'Discussion.' In *The New Worlds of Edgard Varèse: A Symposium*,
edited by Sherman Van Solkema, 75–90. I.S.A.M. Monographs, no. 11. Brooklyn,
NY: Institute for Studies in American Music, Brooklyn College, 1979.

Writings About Elliott Carter and his Music by Other Authors

Below, Robert, 'Elliott Carter's Piano Sonata: an Important Contribution to Piano
Literature.' *Music Review* 34, nos. 3–4 (August–November 1973): 282–293.

Bernard, Jonathan W., 'Spatial Sets in Recent Music of Elliott Carter.' *Music Analysis* 2,
no. 1 (1983): 5–34.

– 'The Evolution of Elliott Carter's Rhythmic Practice.' *Perspectives of New Music* 26,
no. 2 (1988): 164–203.

– 'Problems of Pitch Structure in Elliott Carter's First and Second String Quartets.'
Journal of Music Theory 37, no. 2 (Fall 1993): 231–266.

– 'Elliott Carter and the Modern Meaning of Time.' *Musical Quarterly* 79, no. 4
(Winter 1995): 644–682.

– 'Poem as Non-Verbal Text: Elliott Carter's Concerto for Orchestra and Saint-John

Perse's *Winds*.' In *Analytical Strategies and Musical Interpretation*, edited by Craig Ayrey and Mark Everist. Cambridge: Cambridge University Press, 1996.

Black, Robert, 'Boulez's Third Piano Sonata: Surface and Sensibility.' *Perspectives of New Music* 20 (1981–82): 182–198. (Second section on Carter's and John Ashbery's *Syringa*.)

Boykan, Martin, 'Elliott Carter and the Postwar Composers.' *Perspectives of New Music* 2, no. 2 (Spring–Summer, 1964): 125–128. Reprinted in *Perspectives on American Composers*, ed. Benjamin Boretz and Edward T. Cone, 213–6 (New York: Norton, 1971).

Brandt, William E., 'The Music of Elliott Carter: Simultaneity and Complexity.' *Music Educators Journal* 60, no. 9 (May 1974): 24–32. Reprinted as 'The Music of Elliott Carter', in *Breaking the Sound Barrier: A Critical Anthology of the New Music*, ed. Gregory Battcock, 221–234. (New York: E. P. Dutton, 1981.)

Bye, Antony, 'A Note on Elliott Carter's Violin Concerto.' *Musical Times* 132, no. 1776 (1991): 75–76.

– 'Carter's "Classic" Modernism.' *Tempo* 189 (June 1994): 2–5.

Capuzzo, Guy. 'Letter to the Editor.' *Tempo* 204 (April 1998): 53.

'Catálogo cronológico clasificado de la obra del compositor estadounidense Elliott Carter.' *Boletin interamericano de música* 17 (May 1960): 23–27.

Cogan, Robert, 'Elliott Carter: *Eight Etudes and a Fantasy*, Etude III.' In *New Images of Musical Sound*, 66–72. Cambridge, MA, and London: Harvard University Press, 1984.

Cogan, Robert and Pozzi Escot, *Sonic Design: The Nature of Sound and Music*, 59–71, 204–207, 284–289. Englewood Cliffs, NJ: Prentice-Hall, 1976.

Danuser, Hermann, 'Plädoyer für die Amerikanische Moderne.' In *Die Musik der fünfziger Jahre*, 21–38. Mainz: Schott, 1985.

– 'Spätwerk als Lyrik: Über Elliott Carters Gesänge nach Dichtungen von Elizabeth Bishop, John Ashbery und Robert Lowell.' In *Bericht über das internationale Symposion 'Charles Ives und die amerikanische Musiktradition bis zur Gegenwart,' Köln, 1988*, edited by Klaus Wolfgang Niemöller, 195–222. Regensburg: Gustav Bosse Verlag, 1990.

Darbellay, Etienne. 'Continuité, coherence et formes de temps: A propos des *Night Fantasies* d'Elliott Carter.' *Il saggiatore musicale: Rivista semestrale di musicologia* 2, no. 2 (1995): 297-327.

DeLio, Thomas, 'Spatial Design in Elliott Carter's *Canon for Three*.' *Winds Quarterly* 1 (Fall 1980): 9–15. Also in *Indiana Theory Review* 4, no. 1 (Fall 1980): 1–12.

DeLone, Richard P., 'Timbre and Texture in Twentieth-Century Music.' In *Aspects of Twentieth-Century Music*, edited by Gary E. Wittlich, 66–207. Englewood Cliffs, NJ: Prentice Hall, 1975.

Derby, Richard, 'Carter's *Duo for Violin and Piano*.' *Perspectives of New Music* 20 (1981–82), 149–168.

Derrien, Jean-Pierre, 'Elliott Carter aujourd'hui.' *Entre temps* 4 (June 1987): 51–53.

Durieux, Frédéric, '*A Mirror on Which to Dwell*: Domaines d'une écriture.' *Entre temps* 4 (June 1987), 55–67.

Garrison, Leonard L. 'Elliott Carter's *Scrivo in vento*.' *The Flutist Quarterly* 19, no. 4 (Summer 1994): 86–92, and 20, no. 1 (Fall 1994): 75–80.

Gass, G. 'Elliott Carter's Second String Quartet: Aspects of Time and Rhythm.' *Indiana Theory Review* 4, no. 3 (1981): 12–23.

Glock, William, 'A Note on Elliott Carter.' *The Score* 12 (June 1955): 47–52.

– *Notes in Advance: An Autobiography*. Oxford and New York: Oxford University Press, 1991.

Godfrey, Daniel, 'A Unique Vision of Musical Time: Carter's *String Quartet No. 3*.' *Sonus* 8, no. 1 (Fall 1987): 40–59.

Goldet, Stéphane. *Quatuors du 20ᵉ siècle*, 96–104. Paris: Coédition IRCAM/Papiers (1986).

– 'Distant Music' (in French). *Entre temps* 4 (June 1987): 69–75.

Goldman, Richard Franko, 'Current Chronicle.' *Musical Quarterly* 37, no. 1 (January 1951): 83–89. Reprinted in Richard Franko Goldman, *Selected Essays and Reviews 1948–1968*, ed. Dorothy Klotzman, 69–74. (Brooklyn, NY: Institute for Studies in American Music, 1980.)

– 'The Music of Elliott Carter.' *Musical Quarterly* 43, no. 2 (April 1957): 151–170. Reprinted in Goldman, *op. cit.*, 33–47.

– 'Current Chronicle.' *Musical Quarterly* 46, no. 3 (July 1960): 361–367. Reprinted in Goldman, *op. cit.*, 119–125.

– 'Current Chronicle.' *Musical Quarterly* 48, no. 1 (January 1962): 93–99. Reprinted in Goldman, *op. cit.*, 135–141.

Gratzer, Wolfgang, 'Wahlverwandter des Expressionismus: Über Elliott Carters Traditionsverständnis.' In *Studien zur Wertungsforschung* 27 (1994): *Die Neue Musik in Amerika: Über Traditionslosigkeit und Traditionslastigkeit*, edited by Otto Kolleritsch, 113–132. Vienna: Universal Edition, 1994.

Griffiths, Paul, 'Variation 2: Cage or Carter.' In *The String Quartet: A History*, 194–209. London: Thames and Hudson, 1983.

Groth, Renate, 'Über die Konzerte Elliott Carters.' In *Amerikanische Musik seit Charles Ives*, 177–190. Laaber: Laaber Verlag, 1987.

Harvey, David I. H., *The Later Music of Elliott Carter: A Study in Music Theory and Analysis*. New York and London: Garland, 1989.

Henderson, Robert, 'Elliott Carter.' *Music and Musicians* 14, no. 5 (1966): 20–23.

Hudson, Richard. *Stolen Time: The History of Tempo Rubato*. Oxford and New York: Clarendon Press (Oxford University Press), 1994.

Jacobs, Paul, Notes for sound recording of Elliott Carter, *Night Fantasies* and Piano Sonata, Nonesuch 79047–1.

– 'Paul Jacobs Talks about Carter and Messiaen.' Interview with Will Crutchfield. *Keynote*, December 1983, 19–24.

Kerman, Joseph, 'American Music: The Columbia Series.' *Hudson Review* 11 (Autumn 1958): 420–430.

Kliewer, Vernon L., 'Melody: Linear Aspects of Twentieth-Century Music.' In *Aspects of Twentieth-Century Music*, edited by Gary E. Wittlich, 270–321. Englewood Cliffs, NJ: Prentice Hall, 1975.

Koegler, Horst, 'Begegnungen mit Elliott Carter.' *Melos* 26 (January 1959): 256–258.

Koivisto, Tiina, 'Aspects of Motion in Elliott Carter's Second String Quartet.' *Intégral* 10 (1996).

Kostelanetz, Richard, 'The Astounding Success of Elliott Carter.' *High Fidelity* 18, no. 5 (May 1968): 41–45. Revised version reprinted as 'Elliott Carter: Effort and

Excellence,' in Richard Kostelanetz *Master Minds: Portraits of Contemporary American Artists and Intellectuals*, 289–303. Toronto: The Macmillan Company, 1969.

Kozinn, Allan, 'Elliott Carter's *Changes.' Guitar Review* 57 (September 1984): 1–4.

Kramer, Lawrence,' " Syringa": John Ashbery and Elliott Carter.' In *Beyond Amazement: New Essays on John Ashbery*, edited by David Lehman, 255–271. Ithaca and London: Cornell University Press, 1980.

– 'Song as Insight – John Ashbery, Elliott Carter, and Orpheus.' In *Music and Poetry: The Nineteenth Century and After*, 203–221. Berkeley and Los Angeles: University of California Press, 1984.

Larrick, Geary H., '*Eight Pieces for Four Timpani.' Percussionist* 12, no. 1 (Fall 1974): 12–15.

– 'Elliott Carter and His Timpani Pieces.' *NACWPI Journal* (National Association of College Wind and Percussion Instructors) 36, no. 2 (Winter 1987–88): 22–25.

Lederman, Minna, *The Life and Death of a Small Magazine (Modern Music, 1924–1946)*, 43–46. I.S.A.M. Monographs, no. 18. Brooklyn, NY: Institute for Studies in American Music, 1983.

Lewin, David, *Generalized Musical Intervals and Transformations*, 60–81. New Haven and London: Yale University Press, 1987.

Link, John F., 'Note sulla Sonata e le Night Fantasies di Carter.' Translated by Antonietta Cerocchi Pozzi. In *Da Beethoven a Boulez: Il pianoforte in ventidue saggi*, 229–236. Milano: Longanesi, 1994.

– 'The Composition of Elliott Carter's *Night Fantasies.' Sonus* 14, no. 2 (Spring, 1994): 67–89.

Lochhead, Judy, 'Temporal Structure in Recent Music.' *Journal of Musicological Research* 6, nos. 1–2 (January 1986): 49–93. Reprinted in *Understanding the Musical Experience*, 121–166. New York: Gordon and Breach, 1989.

– 'On the "Framing" Music of Elliott Carter's First String Quartet.' In *Musical Transformation and Musical Intuition: Essays in Honor of David Lewin*, edited by Raphael Atlas and Michael Cherlin, 179–198. Roxbury MA: Ovenbird Press, 1994.

Mead, Andrew, 'Pitch Structure in Elliott Carter's *String Quartet No. 3.' Perspectives of New Music* 22, no. 1 (1983): 31–60.

French translation (Le 3e quatuor a cordes: Structure des hauteurs), trans. Hubert Guery, *Entre temps* 4 (June 1987): 55–67.

– 'To the Editor.' *Music Library Association Notes* 42, no. 1 (1985): 187.

– 'The Role of Octave Equivalence in Elliott Carter's Recent Music: A Birthday Celebration.' *Sonus* 14, no. 2 (Spring 1994): 13–37.

– 'Twelve-Tone Composition and the Music of Elliott Carter.' In *Concert Music, Rock, and Jazz Since 1945: Essays and Analytic Studies*, edited by Elizabeth West Marvin and Richard Hermann, 67–102. Rochester, NY: University of Rochester Press, 1995.

Melis, Andrea, 'Elliott Carter e l'ordine sensibile.' *Musica/Realtà* 15, no. 45 (December 1994): 49–65.

Mellers, Wilfrid, 'The Pioneer's Energy and the Artist's Order: Elliott Carter.' In *Music in a New Found Land*, 102–121. London: Barrie and Rockliff, 1964.

Meyer, Felix. 'Klassizistische Tendenzen in der amerikanischen Musik der zwanziger bis vierziger Jahre.' In *Die klassizistische Moderne in der Musik des 20. Jahrhunderts*, edited by Hermann Danuser, 187–200. Publications of the Paul Sacher Foundation, vol. 5. Winterthur: Amadeus, 1997.

Mili, Isabelle Dominique, 'Elliott Carter: la lucidité de la critique sociale et de la conception musicale.' *Dissonanz • Disonance* 31 (February 1992): 4–9.

Moe, Orin, 'The Music of Elliott Carter.' *College Music Symposium* 22, no. 1 (1982): 7–31.

Moevs, R., 'String Quartets no. 2–3.' *The Musical Quarterly* 61, no. 1 (January 1975): 157–168.

Northcott, Bayan, 'Elliott Carter: Continuity and Coherence.' *Music and Musicians* 20, no. 12 (August 1972): 28–39.

– 'Carter in Perspective.' *Musical Times* 119, no. 1630 (1978): 1039–1041.

– 'Carter the Progressive.' In *Elliott Carter, A 70th Birthday Tribute*, 4–11. London: G. Schirmer, 1978.

– 'Elliott Carter at 80.' *Musical Times* 129, no. 1750 (December 1988): 644–647.

Piencikowski, Robert, 'Fonction relative du timbre dans la musique contemporaine: Messiaen, Carter, Boulez, Stockhausen.' (The Relative Function of Timbre in Contemporary Music) *Analyse musicale* 3 (April 1986): 51–53.

Pollack, Howard, *Harvard Composers: Walter Piston and His Students, from Elliott Carter to Frederic Rzewski*. Metuchen, NJ and London: The Scarecrow Press, 1992.

Price, Harry E., Cornelia Yarbrough, and Michael Kinney, 'Eminences of American Composers: University Faculty Attitudes and Symphony Orchestra Programming.' *Council for Research in Music Education Bulletin, USA* 106 (Fall 1990): 37–48.

Rockwell, John, *All American Music: Composition in the Late Twentieth Century*. New York: Alfred A. Knopf, 1983.

Roeder, John, 'Voice Leading As Transformation.' In *Musical Transformation and Musical Intuition: Essays in Honor of David Lewin*, edited by Raphael Atlas and Michael Cherlin, 41–58. Roxbury MA: Ovenbird Press, 1994.

Rorem, Ned, 'Messiaen and Carter on their Birthdays.' *Tempo* 127 (December 1978): 22–24.

Rosen, Charles, 'One Easy Piece.' *The New York Review of Books* 20, no. 2 (February 22, 1973): 25–29. Reprinted in *The Musical Languages of Elliott Carter*, 21–31. Washington: Library of Congress, 1984.

French translation of excerpts (Un morceau facile: le *Double Concerto* d'Elliott Carter), translated by Pierre-Etienne Will, *Critique* 36, no. 408 (May 1981): 496–505.

– 'The Musical Languages of Elliott Carter.' In *The Musical Languages of Elliott Carter*, 1–20. Washington: Library of Congress, 1984.

French translation (Les langages musicaux d'Elliott Carter), trans. Thierry Baud, *Contrechamps* 6 (April 1986): 123–139.

Rosenfeld, Paul, 'The Newest American Composers.' *Modern Music* 15, no. 3 (March–April 1938): 153–159.

Rothstein, Edward, 'The Twilight Fantasies of Elliott Carter.' *New Republic*, 26 December 1988, 23–28.

Saez, Richard, 'To Regain Wholeness: the Many and the One in Elliott Carter's Songs.'
  Parnassus 10, no. 2 (Fall–Winter 1982): 289–329.
Salzman, Eric, 'New York Report: The New Virtuosity.' *Perspectives of New Music* 1, no.
  2 (Spring 1963): 174–188.
Schiff, David, 'Carter in the Seventies.' *Tempo* 130 (September 1979): 2–10.
– 'Carter For Winds.' *Winds Quarterly* 1 (Fall 1980): 2–6.
– '"In Sleep, In Thunder": Elliott Carter's Portrait of Robert Lowell.' *Tempo* 142
  (September 1982): 2–9.
– 'Musical Time in Elliott Carter's *Night Fantasies*.' Booklet published for the
  Arnold Schoenberg Institute's Elliott Carter Festival, Spring (11–14 April) 1983,
  4–22.
– 'Elliott Carter, America's Much-Honored Composer is Still Creating Challenging
  Music at Age 75.' *Ovation* 4, no. 11 (December 1983): 12–15, 50–52.
– 'Elliott Carter's Harvest Home.' *Tempo* 167 (December 1988): 2–13.
– 'Carter's New Classicism.' *College Music Symposium* 29 (1989): 115–122.
Schiffer, Brigitte, 'New York: Elliott Carter.' *Music and Musicians* 27, no. 8 (April 1979):
  61–62.
Schmidt, Dörte, 'Das "bemerkenswerte" Interesse an Alois Hába: Anmerkung zu
  Elliott Carters "Harmony Book".' (The 'remarkable' interest in Alois Hába: An
  Observation on Elliott Carter's 'Harmony Book') *Mitteilungen der Paul Sacher Stiftung*
  6 (March 1993): 38–42.
– 'Emanzipation des musikalischen Diskurses. Die Skizzen zu Elliott Carters zweitem
  Streichquartett un seine theoretischen Arbeiten in den späten 50er Jahren.'
  In *Jahrbuch des Staatlichen Instituts fur Musikforschung Preußischer Kulturbesitz*,
  edited by Günther Wagner, 209–248. Stuttgart: J. B. Metzler, 1995.
– ' "The practical problems of the composer": Der schwierige Weg vom Auftrag zur
  Urauffuhrung von Elliott Carters zweitem Streichquartett.' *Die Musikforschung* 48,
  no. 4 (October–December 1995): 400–403.
Schreiner, Martin, 'Expansion as Design in the *Fantasia* of Elliott Carter's *String Quartet
  No. 1*.' *Sonus* 12, no. 2 (1992): 11–26.
Schwartz, Lloyd, 'Elliott Carter and the Conflict of Chaos and Order.' *Harvard Magazine*,
  November–December 1983, 57–62.
Shreffler, Anne, ' "Give the Music Room": Elliott Carter's "View of the Capitol from the
  Library of Congress" aus *A Mirror on Which to Dwell*' (in German). In *Quellenstudien
  II*, edited by Felix Meyer, 255–283. Winterthur: Amadeus Verlag, 1993.
– 'Elliott Carter and His America.' *Sonus* 14, no. 2 (Spring 1994): 38–66.
Skulsky, Abraham, 'Elliott Carter.' *Bulletin of American Composers Alliance* 3, no. 2
  (Summer, 1953): 2–16.
– 'The High Cost of Creativity.' *HiFi Review* 2, no. 5 (May 1959): 31–36.
Steinberg, Michael, 'Elliott Carter's Second String Quartet.' *The Score* 27 (July 1960):
  22–26.
    Elaborated German translation (Elliott Carter's 2. Streichquartett), *Melos* 28, no.
  2 (February 1961): 35–37.
– 'Elliott Carter: An American Original at Seventy.' *Keynote*, December, 1978, 8–14.
– 'Celebrating the Music of Elliott Carter.' *Symphony Magazine*, January–February
  1989, 24–27, 98–99.

Stewart, Robert, 'Serial Aspects of Elliott Carter's *Variations for Orchestra.' Music Review* 34, no. 1 (1973): 62–65.

Stone, Kurt, 'Current Chronicle.' *Musical Quarterly* 55, no. 4 (October 1969): 559–572.

Thomas, Gavin, 'Crashing Through the Picturesque.' *Musical Times* 136, no. 1828 (June, 1995): 285–288.

Tingley, G. P., 'Metric Modulation and Elliott Carter's First String Quartet.' *Indiana Theory Review* 4, no. 3 (1981): 3–11.

Trimble, Lester, 'Elliott Carter.' *Stereo Review* 29, no. 6 (1972): 64–72.

Various authors, *Elliott Carter: A 70th Birthday Tribute.* London: G. Schirmer, 1978.

Vlad, Roman, 'Recensioni: Musica.' *La Rassegna Musicale* 24, no. 4 (October–December 1954): 369–371.

Warburton, Thomas, 'A Literary Approach to Carter's *Night Fantasies.' Music Review* 51, no. 3 (August 1990): 208–220.

Whittall, Arnold, 'Elliott Carter.' In *First American Music Conference, Keele University, England, April 18–21, 1975*, 82–98. Keele University, 1975.

– 'Summer's Long Shadows.' *The Musical Times* (April 1997): 14–22.

Winold, Allen, 'Rhythm in Twentieth-Century Music.' In *Aspects of Twentieth-Century Music*, edited by Gary E. Wittlich, 208–269. Englewood Cliffs, NJ: Prentice Hall, 1975.

Wolfthal, Marvin Allen, 'Elliott Carter (le opere dal 1946 al 1971).' *Musica/Realtà* 4, no. 11 (August 1983): 107–122.

Wuorinen, Charles, 'The Outlook for Young Composers.' *Perspectives of New Music* 1, no. 2 (Spring–Summer 1963): 54–61.

Films and Video recordings

Elliott Carter. A film by Chris Hegedus and D. A. Pennebaker. Produced by Programs in the Arts of SUNY and Pennebaker Inc. Center of Creative and Performing Arts at the State University of New York at Buffalo, 1980. ca. 45 minutes.

Elliott Carter: Partita. Video recording. Chicago Symphony Orchestra, Daniel Barenboim, conductor. Recorded in performance, Cologne, Germany, 1994. ca. 20 minutes.

Speculum Musicae. Video recording. Bath Festival Series, Program no. LMA R138D. Produced by Jonathan Fulford. Directed by Peter Maniura. St. George's, Brandon Hill, Bristol, England. British Broadcasting Corporation, 1988. ca. 77 minutes.

Time is Music: Elliott Carter and John Cage. Film. Produced by Henk Pauwels. Directed by Frank Scheffer. Sine Flim/Video, June 1988. ca. 57 minutes.

Discography
compiled by John F. Link

Across the Yard: La Ignota
see *In Sleep, In Thunder*

Adagio
see *Eight Pieces for Four Timpani*

Adagio tenebroso
see *Symphonia – Sum Fluxae Pretiam Spei*

Allegro scorrevole
see *Symphonia – Sum Fluxae Pretiam Spei*

Am Klavier (At the Piano)
see *Of Challenge and of Love*

Anaphora
see *A Mirror on Which to Dwell*

Anniversary
see *Three Occasions for Orchestra*

Argument
see *A Mirror on Which to Dwell*

Brass Quintet
Columbia Odyssey Y 34137 (stereo LP) (1976); The American Brass Quintet: Raymond
Mase (tpt), Louis Ranger (tpt), Edward Birdwell (hn), Herbert Rankin (t tb), Robert
Biddlecome (b tb); with *Eight Pieces for Four Timpani; A Fantasy About Purcell's
Fantasia Upon One Note*
Collins Classics 12292 (CD) (1991); The Wallace Collection, John Wallace, Simon
Wright (director)

Canaries
see *Eight Pieces for Four Timpani*

Canon for Four
GM Recordings GM2020CD (CD) (1990); *Perle/Carter*; Da Capo Chamber Players:
Patricia Spencer (fl), Laura Flax (b cl), Joel Lester (vn), André Emelianoff (vc); with
Enchanted Preludes; Pastorale; Esprit rude/Esprit doux
New Albion NA019 CD (CD) (1990); California EAR Unit: Dorothy Stone (fl), James
Rohrig (b cl), Robin Lorentz (vn), Erika Duke (vc); with *Enchanted Preludes; Esprit
rude/Esprit doux*

Canon for 3
Desto DC-7133 (stereo LP) (1973); *New Music for Trumpet, Played by Gerard Schwarz*; Two
performances: 1. Gerard Schwarz (tpt), Louis Ranger (tpt), Stanley Rosenzweig (tpt);

2. Gerard Schwarz (flugelhorn), Louis Ranger (cornet), Stanley Rosenzweig (tpt)
Reissued as: **Phoenix PHCD 115** (CD) (1997)
Crystal S 361 (stereo LP) (1976); *Music for Trumpet*; Thomas Stevens (tpt), Mario Guarneri (tpt), Roy Poper (tpt)
Capriccio 10 439 (CD) (1992); *Music for Trumpet*; Thomas Stevens (tpt), Wolfgang Bauer (tpt), Markus Mester (tpt)

Canonic Suite
Vanguard Classics 99163 (CD) (1998); *Blow!*; Aurelia Saxophone Quartet: Johan van der Linden (sop sax), André Arends (alto sax), Arno Bornkamp (tenor sax), Willem van Merwijk (bari sax)

Canto
see *Eight Pieces for Four Timpani*

Careless Night
see *In Sleep, In Thunder*

A Celebration of Some 100 × 150 Notes
see *Three Occasions for Orchestra*

Changes
Bridge BDG 2004 (stereo LP) (1984); *New Music with Guitar, Volume 2*; David Starobin (gui)
Reissued as: **Bridge BCD 9009** (CD) (1988); *New Music with Guitar: Selected Works from Volumes 1, 2, & 3*
Bridge BCD 9044 (CD) (1994); *Elliott Carter: Eight Compositions (1943–1993)*; The Group for Contemporary Music: David Starobin (gui); with *Gra*; *Enchanted Preludes*; *Duo for Violin and Piano*; *Scrivo in Vento*; *Con Leggerezza Pensosa*; *Riconoscenza per Goffredo Petrassi*; *Sonata for Violoncello and Piano*

Con Leggerezza Pensosa
Bridge BCD 9044 (CD) (1994); *Elliott Carter: Eight Compositions (1943–1993)*; The Group for Contemporary Music: Charles Neidich (cl), Rolf Schulte (vn), Fred Sherry (vc); with *Gra*; *Enchanted Preludes*; *Duo for Violin and Piano*; *Scrivo in Vento*; *Changes*; *Riconoscenza per Goffredo Petrassi*; *Sonata for Violoncello and Piano*

Concerto for Orchestra
Columbia M 30112 (stereo LP) (1970); New York Philharmonic, Leonard Bernstein (cond)
Reissued as: **CRI SD 469** (stereo LP) (1982); with *Syringa*
Also reissued as: **Sony Classical SMK 60203**
Virgin Classics VC 7 91503–2 (CD) (1992); London Sinfonietta, Oliver Knussen (cond); with *Three Occasions for Orchestra*; *Violin Concerto*
Arte Nova Classics 74321 2773 2 (CD) (1995); SWF Symphony Orchestra, Michael Gielen (cond); with *Piano Concerto*; *Three Occasions for Orchestra*

The Defense of Corinth
Harvard Glee Club F-HGC 64 (1964); Thomas G. Gutheil (narrator), Harvard Glee Club, Elliot Forbes (cond)

Vox SVBX 5353 (stereo LP) (1977); America Sings (1920–1950); Jan Opalach (narrator), Edward Green and Mark Suttonsmith (pno), Columbia University Men's Glee Club, Gregg Smith (cond); with *Musicians Wrestle Everywhere*

Reissued as: **CRI CD 648** (CD) (1993); with *Warble for Lilac-time; Voyage; Three Poems of Robert Frost; Tarantella; Emblems; The Harmony of Morning; Heart Not So Heavy As Mine; Musicians Wrestle Everywhere; To Music*

Dies Irae
see *In Sleep, In Thunder*

Dolphin
see *In Sleep, In Thunder*

Double Concerto for Harpsichord and Piano with Two Chamber Orchestras

Epic LC 3830 (mono LP) (1962); **Epic BC 1157** (stereo LP) (1962); Ralph Kirkpatrick (hps), Charles Rosen (pno), English Chamber Orchestra, Gustav Meier (cond)

Also issued as: **EMI ALP 2052** (mono LP) (1962); **EMI ASD 601** (stereo LP) (1962); with *Piano Sonata*

Columbia MS 7191 (stereo LP) (1968); Paul Jacobs (hps), Charles Rosen (pno), English Chamber Orchestra, Frederik Prausnitz (cond); with *Variations for Orchestra*

Nonesuch H-71314 (stereo LP) (1975); Paul Jacobs (hps), Gilbert Kalish (pno), The Contemporary Chamber Ensemble, Arthur Weisberg (cond); with *Duo for Violin and Piano*

Reissued as: **Elektra Nonesuch 79183–2** (CD) (1992); with *Sonata for Flute, Oboe, Cello, and Harpsichord; Sonata for Violoncello and Piano*

Duo for Violin and Piano

Nonesuch H-71314 (stereo LP) (1975); Paul Zukofsky (vn), Gilbert Kalish (pno); with *Double Concerto*

Sony Classical S2K 47229 (2 CD) (1991); Robert Mann (vn), Christopher Oldfather (pno); with *String Quartet No. 1; String Quartet No. 2; String Quartet No. 3; String Quartet No. 4*

Bridge BCD 9044 (CD) (1994); *Elliott Carter: Eight Compositions (1943–1993)*; The Group for Contemporary Music: Rolf Schulte (vn), Martin Goldray (pno); with *Gra; Enchanted Preludes; Scrivo in Vento; Changes; Con Leggerezza Pensosa; Riconoscenza per Goffredo Petrassi; Sonata for Violoncello and Piano*

Victoria VCD 19094 (CD) (1996); *Contemporary Music from America*; Ole Böhn (vn), Noël Lee (pno); with *Riconoscenza per Goffredo Petrassi*

Auvidis Montaigne MO 782091 (CD) (1998) Irvine Arditti (vn), Ursula Oppens (pno); with *String Quartet No. 5; Sonata for Violoncello and Piano; 90+; Fragment; Figment*

Dust of Snow
see *Three Poems of Robert Frost*

Eight Etudes and A Fantasy

CRI 118 (mono LP) (1958); **CRI SD 118** (stereo LP) (1958); Members of New York Woodwind Quintet: Murray Panitz (fl), Jerome Roth (ob), David Glazer (cl), Bernard Garfield (bn)

Concert-Disc CM 1229 (mono LP) (1963); **Concert-Disc CS 229** (stereo LP) (1963);
   Members of New York Woodwind Quintet: Samuel Baron (fl), Ronald Roseman or
   Jerome Roth (ob), David Glazer (cl), Arthur Weisberg (bn)
Reissued as: **Boston Skyline BSD 137** (CD) (1996); *The Best of the New York Woodwind
   Quintet v. 1*
Candide CE 31016 (stereo LP) (1969); Members of Dorian Woodwind Quintet: Karl
   Kraber (fl), Charles Kuskin (ob), William Lewis (cl), Jane Taylor (bn); with *Woodwind
   Quintet*
Reissued as: **Musical Heritage Society MHS 4876** (stereo LP) (1983); *Chamber Music*;
   with *String Quartet No. 3*
Eight Etudes only: **Classics Record Library SQM 80–5731** (stereo LP) (1975); The
   Chamber Music Society of Lincoln Center: Paula Robison (fl), Leonard Arner (ob),
   Gervase de Peyer (cl), Loren Glickman (bn)
Complete work reissued as: **Musical Heritage Society MHS 824704X (MHS 4704, MHS
   4705)** (stereo LP) (1983); *Three Centuries of Chamber Music*
River City Studios 44711 (stereo LP) (1985); *20th Century Chamber Music*; La Sonore
   Wind Quintet
Stradivarius STR 33304 (CD) (1991); *Musica per Quartetto e Quintetto a Fiati*; Quintetto
   Arnold; with *Woodwind Quintet*
Cambria CD 1091 (CD) (1993); *Another View*; Sierra Wind Quintet: Richard L. Soule
   (fl), Stephen Caplan (ob), Felix Viscuglia (cl), Kristin Wolfe (bn)
KOCH Schwann 3–1153–2 (CD) (1993); *The Aulos Wind Quintet Plays Music by American
   Composers v. 1*; Aulos Woodwind Quintet: Peter Rijks (fl), Diethelm Jonas (ob), Karl-
   Theo Adler (cl), Dietmar Ullrich (hn), Ralph Sabow (bn); with *Woodwind Quintet*
cpo 999 453–2 (CD) (1998); Ensemble Contrasts; with *Woodwind Quintet*; *Sonata for
   Flute, Oboe, Cello, and Harpsichord*; *Esprit rude/Esprit doux*; *Enchanted Preludes*

Eight Pieces for Four Timpani

1. Saëta   2. Moto Perpetuo   3. Adagio   4. Recitative
5. Improvisation   6. Canto   7. Canaries   8. March
Columbia Odyssey Y 34137 (stereo LP) (1976); Morris Lang (timp); with *Brass Quintet*;
   A Fantasy About Purcell's Fantasia Upon One Note
4, 2, 1, and 5 only: **Erato STU 71106** (stereo LP) (1978); *Percussion v. 2*; Sylvio Gualda
   (timp)
4, 6, 1, and 8 only: **BIS LP-256** (stereo LP) (1984); *Neue Musik für Schlagzeug*; Gert
   Mortenson (timp)
Reissued as: **BIS CD-52** (CD) (1995); *The Contemporary American 'C'*

Elegy [version for string quartet]

New England Conservatory NEC-115 (quadrophonic LP) (1977); *The Composer's String
   Quartet Plays Literature of American Contemporary Composers*; The Composer's
   String Quartet: Matthew Raimondi (vn I), Anahid Ajemian (vn II), Jean Dane (va),
   Michael Rudiakov (vc)
Etcetera KTC 1066 (CD) (1988); *Elliott Carter: The Works for String Quartet Vol. II:
   Quartets 2 & 3, Elegy*; The Arditti String Quartet: Irvine Arditti (vn I), David
   Alberman (vn II), Levine Andrade (va), Rohan De Saram (vc); with *String Quartet
   No. 2*; *String Quartet No. 3*

Auvidis Montaigne MO 782010 (CD) (1994); The Arditti String Quartet: Irvine Arditti
(vn I), David Alberman (vn II), Garth Knox (va), Rohan De Saram (vc)
Also issued as: **Auvidis Montaigne MO 782070** (CD) (1994); *1974 Arditti Quartet 1994*
Musikszene Schweitz MGB (CD) 6144 (CD) (1996); Amati Quartett

Elegy [version for viola and piano]
ECM 1316 (ECM 827 744) (ECM New Series 25043) (stereo LP; CD) (1986); *Elegies*;
Kim Kashkashian (va), Robert Levin (pno)
Crystal Records CD 636 (CD) (1991); Paul Cortese (va), Jon Klibonoff (pno)
Albany TROY 141–2 (CD) (1994); Lawrence Wheeler (va), Ruth Tomfohrde (pno)

Elegy [version for string orchestra]
Nonesuch D 79002 (stereo LP; CD) (1980); *American Music for Strings*; Los Angeles
Chamber Orchestra, Gerard Schwarz (cond)
Albany TROY 194 (CD) (1996); Metamorphosen Chamber Orchestra, Scott Yoo (cond)

Emblems
GSS Recordings GSS 103 (stereo LP) (1984); Men's choruses of the Gregg Smith
Singers and The Long Island Symphonic Choral Association, Paul Suits (pno),
Gregg Smith (cond); with *Tarantella*; *The Harmony of Morning*; *Heart Not So Heavy
As Mine*; *Musicians Wrestle Everywhere*; *To Music*; *The Defense of Corinth*
Reissued as: **CRI CD 648** (CD) (1993); with the addition of *Warble for Lilac-time*; *Voyage*;
Three Poems of Robert Frost
Koch 3–7178–2HI (CD) (1994); John Oliver Chorale, John Oliver (music director); with
The Harmony of Morning; *Heart Not So Heavy As Mine*; *Musicians Wrestle Everywhere*

Enchanted Preludes
New Albion NA019 CD (CD) (1989); California EAR Unit: Dorothy Stone (fl), Erika
Duke (vc); with *Canon for Four*; *Esprit rude/Esprit doux*
GM Recordings GM2020CD (CD) (1990); *Perle/Carter*; Da Capo Chamber Players:
Patricia Spencer (fl), André Emelianoff (vc); with *Canon for Four*; *Pastorale*; *Esprit
rude/Esprit doux*
ECM New Series 1391 (CD) (1990); Philippe Racine (fl), Thomas Demenga (vc); with
Esprit rude/Esprit doux; *Riconoscenza per Goffredo Petrassi*; *Triple Duo*
Reissued as: **ECM New Series 839 617–2** (CD); **ECM New Series 21391** (CD) (1994)
Bridge BCD 9044 (CD) (1994); *Elliott Carter: Eight Compositions (1943–1993)*; The
Group for Contemporary Music: Harvey Sollberger (fl), Fred Sherry (vc); with *Gra*;
Duo for Violin and Piano; *Scrivo in Vento*; *Changes*; *Con Leggerezza Pensosa*;
Riconoscenza per Goffredo Petrassi; *Sonata for Violoncello and Piano*
cpo 999 453–2 (CD) (1998); Ensemble Contrasts; with *Woodwind Quintet*; *Eight
Etudes and a Fantasy*; *Sonata for Flute, Oboe, Cello, and Harpsichord*; *Esprit rude/Esprit
doux*

End of a Chapter
see *Of Challenge and of Love*

Esprit rude/Esprit doux
New Albion NA019 CD (CD) (1989); California EAR Unit: Dorothy Stone (fl), Theresa
Tunnicliff (cl); with *Enchanted Preludes*; *Canon for Four*

Erato ECD 75553 (Erato 2292–45364–2) (CD) (1990); Ensemble InterContemporain: Sophie Cherrier (fl), André Trouttet (cl); with *Oboe Concerto*; *A Mirror on Which to Dwell*; *Penthode*

GM Recordings GM2020CD (CD) (1990); *Perle/Carter*; Da Capo Chamber Players: Patricia Spencer (fl), Laura Flax (cl); with *Enchanted Preludes*; *Canon for Four*; *Pastorale*

ECM New Series 1391 (CD) (1990); Philippe Racine (fl), Ernesto Molinari (cl); with *Enchanted Preludes*; *Riconoscenza per Goffredo Petrassi*; *Triple Duo*
Reissued as: **ECM New Series 839 617–2** (CD); **ECM New Series 21391** (CD) (1994)

Centaur CRC 2274 (CD) (1996); Earplay: Janet Kutulas (fl), Peter Josheff (cl)

cpo 999 453–2 (CD) (1998); Ensemble Contrasts; with *Woodwind Quintet*; *Eight Etudes and a Fantasy*; *Sonata for Flute, Oboe, Cello, and Harpsichord*; *Enchanted Preludes*

A Fantasy About Purcell's Fantasia Upon One Note

Columbia Odyssey Y 34137 (stereo LP) (1976); The American Brass Quintet: Raymond Mase (tpt), Louis Ranger (tpt), Edward Birdwell (hn), Herbert Rankin (t tb), Robert Biddlecome (b tb); with *Brass Quintet*; *Eight Pieces for Four Timpani*

Capriccio 10361 (CD) (1992); Frankfurt Radio Orchestra Brass Ensemble, Lutz Köhler (cond)

Hyperion CDA66517 (CD) (1992); *From the Steeples and the Mountains*; London Gabrieli Brass Ensemble, Christopher Larkin (cond)

Figment

Auvidis Montaigne MO 782091 (CD) (1998); Rohan de Saram (vc); with *String Quartet No. 5*; *Sonata for Violoncello and Piano*; *90+*; *Fragment*; *Duo for Violin and Piano*

Fragment

Auvidis Montaigne MO 782091 (CD) (1998); Arditti Quartet; with *String Quartet No. 5*; *Sonata for Violoncello and Piano*; *90+*; *Figment*; *Duo for Violin and Piano*

Gra

Bridge BCD 9044 (CD) (1994); *Elliott Carter: Eight Compositions (1943–1993)*; The Group for Contemporary Music: Charles Neidich (cl); with *Enchanted Preludes*; *Duo for Violin and Piano*; *Scrivo in Vento*; *Changes*; *Con Leggerezza Pensosa*; *Riconoscenza per Goffredo Petrassi*; *Sonata for Violoncello and Piano*

The Harmony of Morning

Vox Box SVBX 5354 (stereo LP) (1979); *America Sings: American Choral Music*; Gregg Smith Singers, Orpheus Ensemble, Peabody Conservatory Chorus and Texas Boys' Choir, Gregg Smith (cond)

Reissued as: **GSS Recordings GSS 103** (stereo LP) (1984); Women of the Gregg Smith Singers, Gregg Smith (cond); with *Tarantella*; *Emblems*; *Heart Not So Heavy As Mine*; *Musicians Wrestle Everywhere*; *To Music*; *The Defense of Corinth*

Also reissued as: **CRI CD 648** (CD) (1993); with the addition of *Warble for Lilac-time*; *Voyage*; *Three Poems of Robert Frost*

Koch 3–7178–2H1 (CD) (1994); John Oliver Chorale, John Oliver (music director); with *Emblems*; *Heart Not So Heavy As Mine*; *Musicians Wrestle Everywhere*

Harriet
see *In Sleep, In Thunder*

Harvest Home
Koch International Classics (CD) (forthcoming, 1998); John Oliver Chorale; with *Let's Be Gay*, and other works

Heart Not So Heavy As Mine
Society for the Preservation of the American Musical Heritage MIA 116 (stereo LP) (1961); *Choral Music in 20th-Century America*; Hamline A Cappella Choir, Robert Holliday (cond)

Nonesuch H-1115 (mono LP) (1966); **Nonesuch H-71115** (stereo LP) (1966); *The Dove Descending*; Canby Singers, Edward Tatnall Canby (cond); with *Musicians Wrestle Everywhere*

GSS Recordings GSS 103 (stereo LP) (1984); The Gregg Smith Singers, Gregg Smith (cond); with *Tarantella*; *Emblems*; *The Harmony of Morning*; *Musicians Wrestle Everywhere*; *To Music*; *The Defense of Corinth*

Reissued as: **CRI CD 648** (CD) (1993); with the addition of *Warble for Lilac-time*; *Voyage*; *Three Poems of Robert Frost*

Koch 3-7178-2H1 (CD) (1994); John Oliver Chorale, John Oliver (music director); with *Emblems*; *The Harmony of Morning*; *Musicians Wrestle Everywhere*

AmCam Recordings ACR 10307 (CD) (1995); *Darest Thou, O Soul: Twentieth Century American Choral Music*; Alexandria Choral Society, Kerry Krebill (artistic director)

High on Our Tower
see *Of Challenge and of Love*

Holiday Overture
CRI SD 475 (stereo LP) (1982); *Elliott Carter: The Early Music*; American Composers Orchestra, Paul Dunkel (cond); with *Symphony No. 1*; *Pocahontas* [suite from the ballet]

Reissued as: **CRI CD 610** (CD) (1991); with *Pocahontas* [suite from the ballet]; *Syringa*

Improvisation
see *Eight Pieces for Four Timpani*

In Genesis
see *In Sleep, In Thunder*

Inner Song
see *Trilogy*

In Sleep, in Thunder
1. Dolphin   2. Across the Yard: La Ignota   3. Harriet
4. Dies Irae   5. Careless Night   6. In Genesis

Nonesuch 79110-1 (stereo LP) (1985); **Wergo 6278-2** (stereo LP) (1985); Martyn Hill (ten), London Sinfonietta, Oliver Knussen (cond); with *Triple Duo*

Reissued as: **Wergo WER 286-278** (CD) (1995)

Bridge BCD 9014 (CD) (1989); Jon Garrison (ten), Speculum Musicae, Robert Black (cond); with *Three Poems of Robert Frost*; *Syringa*; *A Mirror on Which to Dwell*

Insomnia
see *A Mirror on Which to Dwell*

Let's Be Gay
Koch International Classics (CD) (forthcoming, 1998); John Oliver Chorale; with
Harvest Home, and other works

The Line Gang
see *Three Poems of Robert Frost*

March
see *Eight Pieces for Four Timpani*

The Minotaur
Elektra Nonesuch 79248–2 (CD) (1990); New York Chamber Symphony, Gerard
Schwarz (cond); with 'Dust of Snow,' and 'The Rose Family' from *Three Poems of
Robert Frost*; *Piano Sonata*

The Minotaur [suite from the ballet]
Mercury MG50103 (mono LP) (1956); Eastman-Rochester Symphony Orchestra,
Howard Hanson (cond)
Reissued as: **Mercury Golden Imports SRI 75111** (mono LP, electronically altered to
simulate stereo) (1978)

A Mirror on Which to Dwell
1. Anaphora   2. Argument   3. Sandpiper   4. Insomnia
5. View of the Capitol from the Library of Congress   6. O Breath
2 and 3 only: *Le Temps Musical 3*; Radio France/IRCAM (4 stereo cassettes) (1980);
Deborah Cook (sop), Ensemble InterContemporain, Pierre Boulez (cond)
Columbia M 35171 (stereo LP) (1980); Susan Davenny Wyner (sop), Speculum
Musicae, Richard Fitz (cond); with *A Symphony of Three Orchestras*
Bridge BCD 9014 (CD) (1989); Christine Schadeberg (sop), Speculum Musicae,
Donald Palma (cond); with *Three Poems of Robert Frost*; *Syringa*; *In Sleep, in
Thunder*
Erato ECD 75553 (Erato 2292–45364–2) (CD) (1990); Phyllis Bryn-Julson (sop),
Ensemble InterContemporain, Pierre Boulez (cond); with *Oboe Concerto*; *Esprit rude/
Esprit doux*; *Penthode*

Moto Perpetuo
see *Eight Pieces for Four Timpani*

Musicians Wrestle Everywhere
Nonesuch H-1115 (mono LP) (1966); **Nonesuch H-71115** (stereo LP) (1966); *The Dove
Descending*; Canby Singers, Edward Tatnall Canby (cond); with *Heart Not So Heavy
As Mine*
Vox SVBX 5353 (stereo LP) (1977); *America Sings (1920–1950)*; Gregg Smith Singers,
Gregg Smith (cond); with *The Defense of Corinth*
GSS Recordings GSS 103 (stereo LP) (1984); The Gregg Smith Singers, Gregg Smith
(cond); with *Tarantella*; *Emblems*; *The Harmony of Morning*; *Heart Not So Heavy As
Mine*; *To Music*; *The Defense of Corinth*

Reissued as: **Deutsche Grammophon 2530 912** (stereo LP) (1978); *American Choral Music of the 20th Century*; Tanglewood Festival Chorus, John Oliver (cond)

Also reissued as: **CRI CD 648** (CD) (1993); with the addition of *Warble for Lilac-time*; *Voyage*; *Three Poems of Robert Frost*

Koch 3–7178–2H1 (CD) (1994); John Oliver Chorale, John Oliver (music director); with *Emblems*; *The Harmony of Morning*; *Heart Not So Heavy As Mine*

Night Fantasies

Nonesuch 79047 (stereo LP) (1983); Paul Jacobs (pno); with *Piano Sonata*

Etcetera ETC 1008 (stereo LP) (1983); **Etcetera KTC 1008** (CD) (1988); Charles Rosen (pno); with *Piano Sonata*

Reissued as: **Bridge 9090** (CD) (1997); *The Complete Music for Piano*; with *Piano Sonata*; *90+*

Bridge BCD 9001 (CD) (1986); Aleck Karis (pno)

Music & Arts CD-604 (CD) (1989); Ursula Oppens (pno)

Reissued as: **Music & Arts MUA 862** (2 CD) (1995)

Neuma 450–76 (CD) (1991); Stephen Drury (pno)

Pianovox PIA 501–2 (CD) (1998); Florence Millet (pno); with *90+*

90+

Bridge 9090 (CD) (1997); *The Complete Music for Piano*; Charles Rosen (pno); with *Night Fantasies*; *Piano Sonata*

Auvidis Montaigne MO 782091 (CD) (1998); Ursula Oppens (pno); with *String Quartet No. 5*; *Sonata for Violoncello and Piano*; *Figment*; *Fragment*; *Duo for Violin and Piano*

Pianovox PIA 501–2 (CD) (1998); Florence Millet (pno); with *Night Fantasies*

O Breath
see *A Mirror on Which to Dwell*

Oboe Concerto

Erato ECD 75553 (Erato 2292–45364–2) (CD) (1990); Heinz Holliger (ob), Ensemble InterContemporain, Pierre Boulez (cond); with *Penthode*; *Esprit rude/Esprit doux*; *A Mirror on Which to Dwell*

Col Legno AU 31800 (4 CD) (ca. 1995); *40 Jahre Donaueschinger Musiktage 1950–1990*; Heinz Holliger (ob), South West German Radio Orchestra, Michael Gielen (cond)

Editiones Roche 72118 (CD) (1996) (private release); Heinz Holliger (ob), Ensemble InterContemporain, Pierre Boulez (cond); with *A Six Letter Letter*

Of Challenge and of Love
1. High on Our Tower   2. Under the Dome
3. Am Klavier (At the Piano)   4. Quatrains from Harp Lake
5. End of a Chapter

Koch International Classics 3–7425–2-H1 (CD) (1997); Lucy Shelton (sop), John Constable (pno); with *Three Poems of Robert Frost*; *Warble for Lilac-Time*; *Voyage*

Partita
see *Symphonia: Sum Fluxae Pretium Spei*

Pastorale [version for clarinet and piano]

Orion ORS 77275 (stereo LP) (1977); *Pastorale*; John Russo (cl), Lydia Walton Ignacio (pno)

Reissued as: **CRS Master Recordings CD 9255** (CD) (1992); *Contemporary/Classic Masters*

Grenadilla GS 1018 (stereo LP) (1978); *Pastorale*; Else Ludewig-Verdehr (cl), David Liptak (pno)

Golden Crest Records RE 7075 (stereo LP) (1982); *Music for Clarinet*; Keith Wilson (cl), Donald Currier (pno)

GM Recordings GM2020CD (CD) (1990); *Perle/Carter*; Da Capo Chamber Players: Laura Flax (cl), Sarah Rothenberg (pno); with *Enchanted Preludes*; *Canon for Four*; *Esprit rude/Esprit doux*

Pastorale [version for english horn and piano]

Crystal CD 328 (CD) (1996); Carolyn Hove (eh), Gloria Cheng (pno)

Penthode

Erato ECD 75553 (Erato 2292–45364–2) (CD) (1990); Ensemble InterContemporain, Pierre Boulez (cond); with *A Mirror on Which to Dwell*; *Oboe Concerto*; *Esprit rude/ Esprit doux*

Piano Concerto

RCA Victor LM 3001 (RCA RB 6756) (mono LP) (1968); **RCA Victor LSC 3001 (RCA SB 6756)** (stereo LP) (1968); Jacob Lateiner (pno), Boston Symphony Orchestra, Erich Leinsdorf (cond)

New World Records NW 347 (stereo LP; CD) (1986); Ursula Oppens (pno), Cincinnati Symphony Orchestra, Michael Gielen (cond); with *Variations for Orchestra*

Arte Nova Classics 74321 2773 2 (CD) (1995); Ursula Oppens (pno), SWF Symphony Orchestra, Michael Gielen (cond); with *Three Occasions for Orchestra*; *Concerto for Orchestra*

Piano Sonata

American Recording Society ARS-25 (mono LP) (1952); Beveridge Webster (pno); with *Sonata for Violoncello and Piano*

Reissued as: **Desto D 419** (mono LP) (1965); **Desto DST 6419** (mono LP, electronically altered to simulate stereo) (1965)

Epic LC 3850 (mono LP) (1962); **Epic BC 1250** (stereo LP) (1962); Charles Rosen (pno); with *Pocahontas* [Suite from the Ballet]

Also issued as: **EMI ALP 2052** (mono LP) (1962); **EMI ASD 601** (stereo LP) (1962); with *Double Concerto*

Dover HCR 5265 (mono LP) (1966); **Dover HCR-ST 7265** (stereo LP) (1966); *Modern American Piano Music*; Beveridge Webster (pno)

Valois MB 755 (stereo LP) (1967); Noël Lee (pno)

Orion ORS 79342 (stereo LP) (1979); Evelinde Trenker (pno)

Nonesuch 79047 (stereo LP) (1983); Paul Jacobs (pno); with *Night Fantasies*

Reissued as: **Elektra Nonesuch 79248–2** (CD) (1990); with 'Dust of Snow' and 'The Rose Family' from *Three Poems of Robert Frost*; *Piano Sonata*

Etcetera ETC 1008 (stereo LP) (1983); **Etcetera KTC 1008** (CD) (1988); Charles Rosen (pno); with *Night Fantasies*

Reissued as: **Bridge 9090** (CD) (1997); *The Complete Music for Piano*; with *Night Fantasies*; *90+*

Factory FACD 256 (CD) (1989); R. Hind (pno)

Virgin Classics VC 7 91163–2 (CD) (1991); *American Piano Sonatas Vol. One*; Peter Lawson (pno)

Continuum CCD 1028/9 (2 CD) (1991); *Transatlantic Piano*; John McCabe (pno)

Chant du monde LDC 278 1067 (CD) (1991); *Musique Américaine pour Piano*; Noël Lee (pno)

Program Promotions 1992 PP-2 (CD) (1992); Michael Kieran Harvey (pno)

Melodiya MEL CD 10 00529 (CD) (1997); Veda Zuponcic (pno)

Pocahontas [Suite from the Ballet]

Epic LC 3850 (mono LP) (1962); **Epic BC 1250** (stereo LP) (1962); Zürich Radio Orchestra, Jacques Monod (cond); with *Piano Sonata*

CRI SD 475 (stereo LP) (1982); American Composers Orchestra, Paul Dunkel (cond); with *Symphony No. 1*; *Holiday Overture*

Reissued as: **CRI CD 610** (CD) (1991); with *Holiday Overture*; *Syringa*

Quatrains from Harp Lake
see *Of Challenge and of Love*

Quintet for Piano and Winds

Philips 445 095–2 (CD) (1997); *Inner Song*; KölnMusik: Elmar Schmid (cl), Heinz Holliger (ob), Klaus Thunemann (bn), Radovan Vlatković (hn), András Schiff (pno); with *Trilogy*

Recitative
see *Eight Pieces for Four Timpani*

Remembrance
see *Three Occasions for Orchestra*

Riconoscenza per Goffredo Petrassi

New World Records NW 333 (stereo LP) (1986); **New World Records 80333–2** (CD) (1997); *Hidden Sparks*; Maryvonne Le Dizes-Richard (vn)

ECM New Series 1391 (CD) (1990); Hansheinz Schneeberger (vn); with *Esprit rude/ Esprit doux*; *Enchanted Preludes*; *Triple Duo*

Reissued as: **ECM New Series 839 617–2** (CD); **ECM New Series 21391** (CD) (1994)

Neuma 45081 (CD) (1993); *New Music Series Vol. 3*; Carol Lieberman (vn)

Bridge BCD 9044 (CD) (1994); *Elliott Carter: Eight Compositions (1943–1993)*; The Group for Contemporary Music: Rolf Schulte (vn); with *Gra*; *Enchanted Preludes*; *Duo for Violin and Piano*; *Scrivo in Vento*; *Changes*; *Con Leggerezza Pensosa*; *Sonata for Violoncello and Piano*

Auvidis Montaigne MO 789003 (CD) (1995); *Solo Violin*; Irvine Arditti (vn)

CRI CD 706 (CD) (1996); *Songs of Solitude*; Curtis Macomber (vn)

Victoria VCD 19094 (CD) (1996); *Contemporary Music from America*; Ole Böhn (vn); with *Duo for Violin and Piano*

The Rose Family
see *Three Poems of Robert Frost*

Saëta
see *Eight Pieces for Four Timpani*

Sandpiper
see *A Mirror on Which to Dwell*

Scrivo in Vento
La Flute traversière 9304–6 (CD) (1993); Kathleen Chastain (fl)
Bridge BCD 9044 (CD) (1994); *Elliott Carter: Eight Compositions (1943–1993)*; The Group for Contemporary Music: Harvey Sollberger (fl); with *Gra*; *Enchanted Preludes*; *Duo for Violin and Piano*; *Changes*; *Con Leggerezza Pensosa*; *Riconoscenza per Goffredo Petrassi*; *Sonata for Violoncello and Piano*
Neuma 45088 (CD) (1994); *The Now And Present Flute*; Patricia Spencer (fl)

Shard
Bridge (CD) (forthcoming, 1998); David Starobin (gui)

A Six Letter Letter to Paul Sacher for His 90th Birthday
Editiones Roche 72118 (CD) (1996) (private release); Heinz Holliger (eh); with spoken introduction by Heinz Holliger; *Oboe Concerto*

Sonata for Flute, Oboe, Cello, and Harpsichord
Columbia ML 5576 (mono LP) (1960); **Columbia MS 6176** (stereo LP) (1960); Anabel Brieff (fl), Josef Marx (ob), Lorin Bernsohn (vc), Robert Conant (hps)
Decca DL 10108 (mono LP) (1965); **Decca DL 710108** (stereo LP) (1965); Samuel Baron (fl), Ronald Roseman (ob), Alexander Kouguell (vc), Sylvia Marlowe (hps)
Reissued as: **Serenus SRS 12056** (stereo LP) (1974); *Sylvia Marlowe Plays Harpsichord Music of the 20th Century*
Nonesuch H-71234 (stereo LP) (1969); Harvey Sollberger (fl), Charles Kuskin (ob), Fred Sherry (vc), Paul Jacobs (hps); with *Sonata for Violoncello and Piano*
Reissued as: **Elektra Nonesuch 79183–2** (CD) (1992); with *Sonata for Violoncello and Piano*; *Double Concerto*
Deutsche Grammophon 2530 104 (stereo LP) (1971); *American Chamber Music*; Boston Symphony Chamber Players: Doriot Anthony Dwyer (fl), Ralph Gomberg (ob), Jules Eskin (vc), Robert Levin (hps)
New England Conservatory NEC-109 (stereo LP) (1975); *Contemporary American Music*; New England Conservatory of Music Chamber Players: Jolie Troob (fl), Cheryl Priebe (ob), Gloria Johns (vc), Christopher Kies (hps), John Heiss (cond)
Cedille CDR 90000 011 (CD) (1992); *20th Century Baroque*; Rembrandt Chamber Players: Sandra Morgan (fl), Robert Morgan (ob), Barbara Haffner (vc), David Schrader (hps)
cpo 999 453–2 (CD) (1998); Ensemble Contrasts; with *Woodwind Quintet*; *Eight Etudes and a Fantasy*; *Esprit rude/Esprit doux*; *Enchanted Preludes*

Sonata for Violoncello and Piano
American Recording Society ARS-25 (mono LP) (1952); Bernard Greenhouse (vc), Anthony Makas (pno); with *Piano Sonata*

Reissued as: **Desto D 419** (mono LP) (1965); **Desto DST 6419** (mono LP, electronically altered to simulate stereo) (1965)

Nonesuch H-71234 (stereo LP) (1969); Joel Krosnick (vc), Paul Jacobs (pno); with *Sonata for Flute, Oboe, Cello, and Harpsichord*

Reissued as: **Elektra Nonesuch 79183–2** (CD) (1992); with *Sonata for Flute, Oboe, Cello, and Harpsichord; Double Concerto*

Golden Crest RE 7081 (stereo LP) (1979); *The Art of Michael Rudiakov;* Michael Rudiakov (vc), Ursula Oppens (pno)

Finlandia FACD 362 (CD) (1988); *Contemporary Music for Cello and Piano;* Anssi Karttunen (vc), Tuija Hakkila (pno)

Musikproduktion Dabringhaus und Grimm MD+G L 3397 (CD) (1992); *Cellosonaten von 1948;* Tilmann Wick (vc), Heasook Rhee (pno)

Boston Records BR1006 (CD) (1994); Anthony Ross (vc), Evelyne Brancart (pno)

Bridge BCD 9044 (CD) (1994); *Elliott Carter: Eight Compositions (1943–1993);* The Group for Contemporary Music: Fred Sherry (vc), Charles Wuorinen (pno); with *Gra; Enchanted Preludes; Duo for Violin and Piano; Scrivo in Vento; Changes; Con Leggerezza Pensosa; Riconoscenza per Goffredo Petrassi*

Tall Poppies TP032 (CD) (1995); *Prokofiev & Carter;* David Pereira (vc), Lisa Moore (pno)

Arabesque ARA 6682 (CD) (1996); Joel Krosnick (vc); Gilbert Kalish (pno)

Centaur CRC 2267 (CD) (1996); Rhonda Rider (vc); Lois Shapiro (pno)

Auvidis Montaigne MO 782091 (CD) (forthcoming, 1998); Rohan de Saram (vc), Ursula Oppens (pno); with *String Quartet No. 5; 90+; Figment; Fragment; Duo for Violin and Piano*

String Quartet No. 1

Columbia ML 5104 (LP) (1956); Walden Quartet of the University of Illinois: Homer Schmitt (vn I), Bernard Goodman (vn II), John Garvey (va), Robert Swenson (vc)

Nonesuch H 71249 (stereo LP) (1970); **Elektra Nonesuch 71249–2** (CD); Composers Quartet: Matthew Raimondi (vn I), Anahid Ajemian (vn II), Jean Dupouy (va), Michael Rudiakov (vc); with *String Quartet No. 2*

Etcetera KTC 1065 (CD) (1988); *Elliott Carter: The Works for String Quartet Vol. I: String Quartets 1 + 4;* The Arditti String Quartet: Irvine Arditti (vn I), David Alberman (vn II), Levine Andrade (va), Rohan De Saram (vc); with *String Quartet No. 4*

Sony Classical S2K 47229 (2 CD) (1991); The Juilliard String Quartet: Robert Mann (vn I), Joel Smirnoff (vn II), Samuel Rhodes (va), Joel Krosnick (vc); with *String Quartet No. 2; String Quartet No. 3; String Quartet No. 4; Duo for Violin and Piano*

String Quartet No. 2

RCA Victor LM 2481 (mono LP) (1961); **RCA Victor LSC 2481** (stereo LP) (1961); Juilliard String Quartet: Robert Mann (vn I), Isidore Cohen (vn II), Raphael Hillyer (va), Claus Adam (vc)

Nonesuch H 71249 (stereo LP) (1970); **Elektra Nonesuch 71249–2** (CD); Composers Quartet: Matthew Raimondi (vn I), Anahid Ajemian (vn II), Jean Dupouy (va), Michael Rudiakov (vc); with *String Quartet No. 1*

Columbia M 32738 (stereo LP) (1974); **Columbia MQ 32738** (quadraphonic LP)

(1974); Juilliard Quartet: Robert Mann (vn I), Earl Carlyss (vn II), Raphael Hillyer (va), Claus Adam (vc); with *String Quartet No. 3*

Etcetera KTC 1066 (CD) (1988); *Elliott Carter: The Works for String Quartet Vol. II: Quartets 2 & 3, Elegy*; The Arditti String Quartet: Irvine Arditti (vn I), David Alberman (vn II), Levine Andrade (va), Rohan De Saram (vc); with *String Quartet No. 3; Elegy*

Sony Classical S2K 47229 (2 CD) (1991); The Juilliard String Quartet: Robert Mann (vn I), Joel Smirnoff (vn II), Samuel Rhodes (va), Joel Krosnick (vc); with *String Quartet No. 1; String Quartet No. 3; String Quartet No. 4; Duo for Violin and Piano*

String Quartet No. 3

Columbia M 32738 (stereo LP) (1974); **Columbia MQ 32738** (quadraphonic LP) (1974); Juilliard Quartet: Robert Mann (vn I), Earl Carlyss (vn II), Samuel Rhodes (va), Claus Adam (vc); with *String Quartet No. 2*

Musical Heritage Society MHS 4876 (stereo LP) (1983); Composers Quartet: Matthew Raimondi (vn I), Anahid Ajemian (vn II), Jean Dane (va), Mark Shuman (vc); with *Eight Etudes and a Fantasy*

RCA Red Seal RS 9006 (stereo LP) (1983); Arditti String Quartet

Etcetera KTC 1066 (CD) (1988); *Elliott Carter: The Works for String Quartet Vol. II: Quartets 2 & 3, Elegy*; The Arditti String Quartet: Irvine Arditti (vn I), David Alberman (vn II), Levine Andrade (va), Rohan De Saram (vc); with *String Quartet No. 2; Elegy*

Sony Classical S2K 47229 (2 CD) (1991); The Juilliard String Quartet: Robert Mann (vn I), Joel Smirnoff (vn II), Samuel Rhodes (va), Joel Krosnick (vc); with *String Quartet No. 1; String Quartet No. 2; String Quartet No. 4; Duo for Violin and Piano*

String Quartet No. 4

Etcetera KTC 1065 (CD) (1988); *Elliott Carter: The Works for String Quartet Vol. I: String Quartets 1 + 4*; The Arditti String Quartet: Irvine Arditti (vn I), David Alberman (vn II), Levine Andrade (va), Rohan De Saram (vc); with *String Quartet No. 1*

Music & Arts CD-606 (CD) (1990); The Composers Quartet: Matthew Raimondi (vn I), Anahid Ajemian (vn II), Maureen Gallagher (va), Mark Shuman (vc)

Sony Classical S2K 47229 (2 CD) (1991); The Juilliard String Quartet: Robert Mann (vn I), Joel Smirnoff (vn II), Samuel Rhodes (va), Joel Krosnick (vc); with *String Quartet No. 1; String Quartet No. 2; String Quartet No. 3; Duo for Violin and Piano*

String Quartet No. 5

Auvidis Montaigne MO 782091 (CD) (forthcoming, 1998); Arditti Quartet; with *Sonata for Violoncello and Piano; 90+; Figment; Fragment; Duo for Violin and Piano*

Symphonia: Sum fluxae pretiam spei

1. *Partita*
2. *Adagio tenebroso*
3. *Allegro scorrevole*

1 only: **Teldec 4509–99596–2** (CD) (1995); Chicago Symphony Orchestra, Daniel Barenboim (cond)

Symphony No. 1
The Louisville Orchestra first edition records LOU-611 (mono LP) (1961); The Louisville Orchestra, Robert Whitney (cond)

CRI SD 475 (stereo LP) (1982); *Elliott Carter: The Early Music*; American Composers Orchestra, Paul Dunkel (cond); with *Holiday Overture*; *Pocahontas* [suite from the ballet]

Reissued as: **CRI CD 552** (CD) (1988)

A Symphony of Three Orchestras
Columbia M 35171 (stereo LP) (1980); New York Philharmonic, Pierre Boulez (cond); with *A Mirror on Which to Dwell*

Reissued as: **Sony Classical SMK 68 334** (CD) (1995)

Syringa
CRI SD 469 (stereo LP) (1982); Jan DeGaetani (ms), Thomas Paul (bar), Speculum Musicae, The Group for Contemporary Music, Harvey Sollberger (cond); with *Concerto for Orchestra*

Reissued as: **CRI CD 610** (CD) (1991); with *Holiday Overture*; *Pocahontas* [suite from the ballet]

Bridge BCD 9014 (CD) (1989); Katherine Ciesinski (ms), Jan Opalach (b-bar), Speculum Musicae, William Purvis (cond); with *Three Poems of Robert Frost*; *A Mirror on Which to Dwell*; *In Sleep, in Thunder*

Tarantella
Carillon 118 (mono LP) (1961); *Harvard in Song*; Harvard University Glee Club, Elliot Forbes (cond)

GSS Recordings GSS 103 (stereo LP) (1984); The Gregg Smith Singers, Paul Suits, Jerald Stone (pno); with *Emblems*; *The Harmony of Morning*; *Heart Not So Heavy As Mine*; *Musicians Wrestle Everywhere*; *To Music*; *The Defense of Corinth*

Reissued as: **CRI CD 648** (CD) (1993); with the addition of *Warble for Lilac-time*; *Voyage*; *Three Poems of Robert Frost*

Tell Me Where Is Fancy Bred?
Columbia MC 6 (12 mono 12" 78) (1938); [unidentified] (alto), [unidentified] (gui); From the Orson Welles Mercury Theatre production of William Shakespeare's 'The Merchant of Venice'

Turnabout TV 34727 (stereo LP) (1978); *20th Century Music for Voice and Guitar*; Rosalind Rees (sop), David Starobin (gui)

Reissued as: **Vox Box CDX 5145** (2 CD) (1995); *20th Century Voices in America*

Three Occasions for Orchestra
1. *A Celebration of some 100 × 150 Notes*
2. *Remembrance*
3. *Anniversary*

Virgin Classics VC 7 91503–2 (CD) (1992); London Sinfonietta, Oliver Knussen (cond); with *Concerto for Orchestra*; *Violin Concerto*

Arte Nova Classics 74321 2773 2 (CD) (1995); SWF Symphony Orchestra, Michael Gielen (cond); with *Piano Concerto*; *Concerto for Orchestra*

1 only: **EMI CDM5 66137–2**; City of Birmingham Symphony Orchestra, Simon Rattle (cond)

Three Poems of Robert Frost [version for voice and piano]
1. Dust of Snow   2. The Rose Family   3. The Line Gang

1 and 2 only: **Hargail HN 708** (mono 10″ 78) (1947); *American Songs*; William Hess (ten), Robert Fizdale (pno)

Unicorn RHS 353 (stereo LP) (1978); **Unicorn UN1–72017** (stereo LP) (1978); *An American Anthology*; Meriel Dickinson (ms), Peter Dickinson (pno); with *Voyage*

1 and 2 only: **Elektra Nonesuch 79178–2** (CD) (1988); *Songs of America: On Home, Love, Nature, and Death*; Jan DeGaetani (ms), Gilbert Kalish (pno)

Reissued as: **Elektra Nonesuch 79248–2** (CD) (1990); with *The Minotaur*; *Piano Sonata*

1. and 2. only: **Albany TROY 081** (CD) (1993); *Paul Sperry Sings an American Sampler from Billings to Bolcom*; Paul Sperry (ten), Irma Vallecillo (pno)

Music & Arts CD900 (CD) (1995); *Three Modern American Song Cycles*; Phyllis Bryn-Julson (sop), Mark Markham (pno); with *Voyage*; *Warble For Lilac-time*

Koch International Classics 3–7425–2-H1 (CD) (1997); Lucy Shelton (sop), John Constable (pno); with *Warble for Lilac-time*; *Voyage*; *Of Challenge And Of Love*

Three Poems of Robert Frost [version for voice and chamber orchestra]
1. Dust of Snow   2. The Rose Family   3. The Line Gang

Bridge BCD 9014 (CD) (1989); Patrick Mason (bar), Speculum Musicae, David Starobin (cond); with *A Mirror on Which to Dwell*; *Syringa*; *In Sleep, In Thunder*

CRI CD 648 (CD) (1993); Rosalind Rees (sop), Adirondack Chamber Orchestra, Gregg Smith (cond); with *Warble for Lilac-time*; *Voyage*; *Tarantella*; *Emblems*; *The Harmony of Morning*; *Heart Not So Heavy As Mine*; *Musicians Wrestle Everywhere*; *To Music*; *The Defense of Corinth*

To Music
New World NW 219 (stereo LP) (1977); *Americana*; University of Michigan Chamber Choir, Thomas Hilbish (cond)

Reissued as: **New World 80219** (CD) (1996)

GSS Recordings GSS 103 (stereo LP) (1984); Rosalind Rees (sop), The Gregg Smith Singers, Gregg Smith (cond); with *Tarantella*; *Emblems*; *The Harmony of Morning*; *Heart Not So Heavy As Mine*; *Musicians Wrestle Everywhere*; *The Defense of Corinth*

Reissued as: **CRI CD 648** (CD) (1993); with the addition of *Warble for Lilac-time*; *Voyage*; *Three Poems of Robert Frost*

Trilogy
1. *Bariolage*
2. *Inner Song*
3. *Immer neu*

2 only: **Auvidis Montaigne MO 782048** (CD) (1996); Ensemble recherche: Peter Veale (ob)

Philips 445 095–2 (CD) (1997); *Inner Song*; Heinz Holliger (ob), Ursula Holliger (hp); with *Quintet for Piano and Winds*

Triple Duo
Nonesuch 79110 (stereo LP; CD) (1985); **Wergo 6278–2** (stereo LP) (1985); The Fires of London; with *In Sleep, In Thunder*
Reissued as: **Wergo WER 286–278** (CD) (1995)
ECM New Series 1391 (CD) (1990); Philippe Racine (fl), Ernesto Molinari (cl), Paul Cleemann (pno), Gerhard Huber (perc), Hansheinz Schneeberger (vn), Thomas Demenga (vc); with *Esprit rude/Esprit doux*; *Enchanted Preludes*; *Riconoscenza per Goffredo Petrassi*
Reissued as: **ECM New Series 839 617–2** (CD); **ECM New Series 21391** (CD) (1994)
GM Recordings GM 2047CD (CD) (1997); The New York New Music Ensemble: Jayn Rosenfeld (fl), Jean Kopperud (cl), James Winn (pno), Daniel Druckman (perc), Linda Quan (vn), Chris Finckel (vc), Robert Black (cond)

Under the Dome
see *Of Challenge and of Love*

Variations for Orchestra
LOU-58–3 (mono LP) (1958); The Louisville Orchestra, Robert Whitney (cond)
Columbia MS 7191 (stereo LP) (1968); The New Philharmonia Orchestra, Frederik Prausnitz (cond); with *Double Concerto*
New World Records NW 347–2 (NW 80347) (CD) (1986); Cincinnati Symphony Orchestra, Michael Gielen (cond); with *Piano Concerto*
Deutsche Grammophon 431 698–2 (CD) (1994); Chicago Symphony Orchestra, James Levine (cond)

View of the Capitol from the Library of Congress
see *A Mirror on Which to Dwell*

Violin Concerto
Virgin Classics VC 7 91503–2 (CD) (1992); Ole Böhn (vn), London Sinfonietta, Oliver Knussen (cond); with *Three Occasions for Orchestra*; *Concerto for Orchestra*

Voyage
Unicorn RHS 353 (stereo LP) (1978); **Unicorn UN1–72017** (stereo LP) (1978); *An American Anthology*; Meriel Dickinson (ms), Peter Dickinson (pno); with *Three Poems of Robert Frost*
CRI CD 648 (CD) (1993); Rosalind Rees (sop), Adirondack Chamber Orchestra, Gregg Smith (cond); with *Warble for Lilac-time*; *Three Poems of Robert Frost*; *Tarantella*; *Emblems*; *The Harmony of Morning*; *Heart Not So Heavy As Mine*; *Musicians Wrestle Everywhere*; *To Music*; *The Defense of Corinth*
Albany TROY 118 (CD) (1994); *Permit Me Voyage*; Mary Ann Hart (mezzo), Dennis Helmrich (pno)
Music & Arts CD900 (CD) (1995); *Three Modern American Song Cycles*; Phyllis Bryn-Julson (sop), Mark Markham (pno); with *Three Poems of Robert Frost*; *Warble For Lilac-time*
Koch International Classics 3–7425–2-H1 (CD) (1997); Lucy Shelton (sop), John Constable (pno); with *Three Poems of Robert Frost*; *Warble for Lilac-Time*; *Of Challenge And Of Love*

Warble for Lilac-Time
CRI CD 648 (CD) (1993); Rosalind Rees (sop), Adirondack Chamber Orchestra, Gregg Smith (cond); with *Voyage*; *Three Poems of Robert Frost*; *Tarantella*; *Emblems*; *The Harmony of Morning*; *Heart Not So Heavy As Mine*; *Musicians Wrestle Everywhere*; *To Music*; *The Defense of Corinth*

Music & Arts CD900 (CD) (1995); *Three Modern American Song Cycles*; Phyllis Bryn-Julson (sop), Mark Markham (pno); with *Three Poems of Robert Frost*; *Voyage*

International Classics 3–7425–2-H1 (CD) (1997); Lucy Shelton (sop), John Constable (pno); with *Three Poems of Robert Frost*; *Voyage*; *Of Challenge And Of Love*

Woodwind Quintet
Classic Editions CE 2003 (1953) (mono LP); *An American Woodwind Symposium*; New Art Wind Quintet: Andrew Lolya (fl), Melvin Kaplan (ob), Irving Neidich (cl), Tina di Dario (bn), Elizabeth Bobo (hn)

RCA Victor LM 6167 (mono LP) (1966); **RCA Victor LSC 6167** (stereo LP) (1966); Boston Symphony Chamber Players: Doriot Anthony Dwyer (fl), Ralph Gombert (ob), Gino Cioffi (cl), Sherman Walt (bn), James Stagliano (hn)

Candide CE 31016 (stereo LP) (1969); Dorian Wind Quintet: Karl Kraber (fl), Charles Kuskin (ob), William Lewis (cl), Jane Taylor (bn), Barry Benjamin (hn)

Vox SVBX 5307 (stereo LP) (1977); *The Avant Garde Woodwind Quintet in the U.S.A.*

KM Records KM 15131 (stereo LP) (1980s); Travis Chamber Players (U.S. Air Force Band of Golden Gate)

Melbourne Records SMLP 4040 (stereo LP) (1980); *The York Winds Play Music*; Douglas Stewart (fl), Lawrence Cherney (ob), Paul Grice (cl), Harcus Hennigar (hn), Gerald Robinson (bn)

Musical Heritage Society 4782 (stereo LP) (1983); *20th Century Works for Wind Ensemble*; Soni Ventorum Wind Quintet

Premiere PRCD 1006 (CD) (1990); *American Winds, volume one*; Boehm Quintette: Sheryl Henze (fl), Phyllis Lanini (ob), Steven Hartman (cl), Joseph Anderer (hn), Robert Wagner (bn)

Stradivarius STR 33304 (CD) (1991); *Musica per Quartetto e Quintetto a Fiati*; Quintetto Arnold; with *Eight Etudes and a Fantasy*

KOCH Schwann 3–1153–2 (CD) (1993); *The Aulos Wind Quintet Plays Music By American Composers v. 1*; Aulos Woodwind Quintet: Peter Rijks (fl), Diethelm Jonas (ob), Karl-Theo Adler (cl), Dietmar Ullrich (hn), Ralph Sabow (bn); with *Eight Etudes and a Fantasy*

Summit DCD 149 (CD) (1993); Lieurance Woodwind Quintet

Crystal CD 752 (CD) (1993); Westwood Woodwind Quintet: John Barcellona (fl), Peter Christ (ob), David Atkins (cl), Joseph Meyer (hn), David Muller (bn)

cpo 999 453–2 (CD) (1998); Ensemble Contrasts; with *Eight Etudes and a Fantasy*; *Sonata for Flute, Oboe, Cello, and Harpsichord*; *Esprit rude/Esprit doux*; *Enchanted Preludes*

List of Charts

Index of Works

General Index